Praise for *Reactive Programming with RxJava*

"This book is a deep dive into the concepts and uses of RxJava in particular, and reactive programming in general, by authors who have countless hours of experience implementing and using RxJava in the real world. If you want to go reactive, there is no better way than to buy this book."

—*Erik Meijer, President and Founder, Applied Duality, Inc.*

"RxJava is an invaluable tool for managing the highly stateful, concurrent, and asynchronous implementations that a modern Android application requires. [This book] serves as both an incremental learning tool and a reference for a library, which can otherwise be quite daunting to fully understand."

—*Jake Wharton, Software Engineer, Square, Inc.*

"Tomasz and Ben have a great talent for explaining complicated matters in an uncomplicated manner. That's what makes this book a real pleasure to read and a must-have for every JVM developer who wants to grasp reactive programming and RxJava. The authors touch on many topics like concurrency, functional programming, design patterns, and reactive programming; yet the result doesn't overwhelm readers but rather guides them, gradually introducing more and more advanced concepts and techniques."

—*Szymon Homa, Senior Software Developer*

Reactive Programming
with RxJava
Creating Asynchronous, Event-Based Applications

Tomasz Nurkiewicz and Ben Christensen

Beijing · Boston · Farnham · Sebastopol · Tokyo

Reactive Programming with RxJava

by Tomasz Nurkiewicz and Ben Christensen

Printed in the United States of America.

Published by O'Reilly Media, Inc., 1005 Gravenstein Highway North, Sebastopol, CA 95472.

O'Reilly books may be purchased for educational, business, or sales promotional use. Online editions are also available for most titles (*http://safaribooksonline.com*). For more information, contact our corporate/institutional sales department: 800-998-9938 or *corporate@oreilly.com*.

Editors: Nan Barber and Brian Foster	**Indexer:** Judy McConville
Production Editor: Melanie Yarbrough	**Interior Designer:** David Futato
Copyeditor: Octal Publishing, Inc.	**Cover Designer:** Karen Montgomery
Proofreader: Christina Edwards	**Illustrator:** Rebecca Demarest

October 2016:   First Edition

Revision History for the First Edition

2016-10-04:   First Release

See *http://oreilly.com/catalog/errata.csp?isbn=9781491931653* for release details.

The O'Reilly logo is a registered trademark of O'Reilly Media, Inc. *Reactive Programming with RxJava*, the cover image, and related trade dress are trademarks of O'Reilly Media, Inc.

978-1-491-93165-3

[LSI]

I dedicate this book to Paulina Ścieżka, the most honest and direct person I ever met.
For trust and guidance far beyond just writing a book.
For changing my life more than she ever imagined.
—Tomasz Nurkiewicz

Table of Contents

Foreword

On October 28, 2005, the then newly appointed chief architect of Microsoft, Ray Ozzie, emailed a now infamous memo to his staff with the subject "The Internet Services Disruption". In this memo, Ray Ozzie outlines basically how the world looks today where enterprises like Microsoft, Google, Facebook, Amazon, and Netflix use the Web as the main delivery channel for their services.

From a developer perspective, Ozzie made a rather remarkable statement for an executive of a large corporation:

> Complexity kills. It sucks the life out of developers, it makes products difficult to plan, build and test, it introduces security challenges, and it causes end-user and administrator frustration.

First of all, we have to take into account that in 2005, the big IT enterprises were deeply in love with mind-blowingly complicated technologies like SOAP, WS-*, and XML. This was a time where the word "microservice" was not yet invented, and there was no simple technology on the horizon to help developers manage the complexity of asynchronously composing complex services from smaller ones, and dealing with concerns such as failure, latency, security, and efficiency.

For my Cloud Programmability Team at Microsoft, Ozzie's memo was a rude wakeup call to focus on inventing a simple programming model for building large scale asynchronous and data-intensive Internet service architectures. After many false starts it finally dawned on us that by dualizing the Iterable/Iterator interface for synchronous collections, we could obtain a pair of interfaces to represent asynchronous event streams, with all the familiar sequence operators such as map, filter, scan, zip, groupBy, etc. for transforming and combining asynchronous data streams, and thus Rx was born somewhere in the summer of 2007. During the implementation process we realized that we needed to manage concurrency and time, and for that we extended the idea of Java's executors with virtual time and cooperative re-scheduling.

After an intense two year hackathon where we explored numerous design choices, we first shipped Rx.NET on November 18, 2009. Soon thereafter we ported Rx to Microsoft.Phone.Reactive for Windows Phone 7 and started to implement Rx in various other languages such as JavaScript, and C++, and dabbled with experimental versions in Ruby and Objective-C.

The first Rx user inside Microsoft was Jafar Husain, and he brought the technology with him when he joined Netflix in 2011. Jafar evangelized Rx within the company, and eventually re-architected the Netflix UI's client-side stack to fully embrace asynchronous stream processing. Also, most fortunately for all of us, he managed to pass on his enthusiasm to Ben Christensen who was working on Netflix's middle tier API and since Netflix uses Java on the middle tier, Ben started to work on RxJava in 2012 and moved the codebase to Github in early 2013 for continued open source development. Another early adopter of Rx at Microsoft was Paul Betts and when he moved to Github, he managed to convince his colleagues at Github such as Justin Spahr-Summers to implement and release ReactiveCocoa for Objective-C in the spring of 2012.

As Rx became more popular in the industry, we convinced Microsoft Open Tech to open-source Rx .NET in the fall of 2012. Soon thereafter, I left Microsoft to start Applied Duality and focus 100% of my time on making Rx the standard cross-language and cross-platform API for asynchronous real-time data stream processing.

Fast forward to 2016 and the popularity and use of Rx has skyrocketed. All traffic through the Netflix API relies upon RxJava, as does the Hystrix fault-tolerance library that bulkheads all internal service traffic, and via related reactive libraries RxNetty and Mantis, Netflix is now creating a completely reactive network stack for connecting all internal services across machine and process boundaries. RxJava is also extremely successful in the Android space with companies like SoundCloud, Square, NYT, Seatgeek all using RxJava for their Android apps and contributing to the RxAndroid extension library. noSQL vendors such as Couchbase and Splunk also offer Rx-based bindings to their data access layer. Other Java libraries that have adopted RxJava amongst others include Camel Rx, Square Retrofit, and Vert.x. In the JavaScript community, RxJS is widely used and powers popular frameworks such as Angular 2. The community maintains a website (*http://reactivex.io*) where you can find information about Rx implementations in many languages, as well as fantastic Marble Diagram artwork and explanations by David Gross (@CallHimMoorlock).

Since its inception, Rx has evolved with the needs and the input from the developer community. The original implementation of Rx in .NET focussed squarely on transforming asynchronous event streams, and used asynchronous enumerable for scenarios that needed back pressure. Since Java does not have language support for async await, the community extended the Observer and Observable types with the concept of reactive pull and introduced the Producer interface. Thanks to many open source contributors, the implementation of RxJava is also extremely sophisticated and highly optimized.

Even though the details of RxJava are slightly different that that of other Rx implementations, it is still built specially for all you developers that need to survive in the brave new world of distributed real-time data processing and focus on essential complexity without accidental complexity that suck the life out of you. This book is a deep and thorough dive into the concepts and uses of RxJava in particular and Rx in general by two authors that have countless hours of experience in implementing and using RxJava in the real world. If you want to go "reactive" there is no better way than to buy this book.

— Erik Meijer, President and Founder,
Applied Duality, Inc.

Introduction

Who Should Read This Book

Reactive Programming with RxJava targets intermediate and advanced Java programmers. You should be fairly comfortable with Java; however, prior knowledge of reactive programming is not required. Many concepts in this book relate to functional programming, but you do not need to be familiar with it either. There are two distinct groups of programmers that can benefit from this book:

- Craftsmen who seek improved performance on the server or more maintainable code on mobile devices. If you fall into this category, you will find ideas and solutions to real problems as well as practical advice. In this case, RxJava is just another tool that this book will help to master.
- Curious developers who've heard about reactive programming or RxJava in particular and want to get a fair understanding of it. If this is you, and if you are not planning to take advantage of RxJava in production code, you will significantly broaden your horizons.

Additionally, if you are a hands-on software architect, this book will likely help you. RxJava influences the overall architecture of entire systems, so it is worth knowing. But even if you are just beginning your adventure with programming, try to go through the first few chapters, which explain the basics. Underlying concepts like transformations and composition are quite universal and not related to reactive programming.

Note from Ben Christensen

In 2012, I was working on a new architecture for the Netflix API. Along the way it became clear that we needed to embrace concurrency and asynchronous network requests to achieve our goals. During the process of exploring approaches, I ran into Jafar Husain (*https://github.com/jhusain*) who tried to sell me on an approach he learned while at Microsoft called "Rx." At that time, I was pretty comfortable with concurrency but still thought about it imperatively, and very much in a Java-centric manner, as Java has been my predominant breadwinner, and thus where I have spent the most time.

So, as Jafar tried selling me on the approach, it was difficult to grasp the concepts due to their functional programming style, and I pushed back on it. Months of arguments and discussions followed as the overall system architecture continued maturing, during which Jafar and I continued our many whiteboard sessions until I grasped the theoretical principles and subsequently the elegance and power of what Reactive Extensions could offer.

We decided to embrace the Rx programming model in the Netflix API and ultimately created the Java implementation of Reactive Extensions called RxJava, following the naming convention started by Microsoft with Rx.Net and RxJS.

In the roughly three years that I worked on RxJava, most of it done in the open on GitHub, I had the privilege to work with a growing community and 120-plus contributors to turn RxJava into a mature product used in many production systems both server and client side. It has succeeded enough to get more than 15,000 stars on GitHub, making it one of the top 200 projects (*http://bit.ly/2bRAewk*), and third highest of projects using Java (*http://bit.ly/2bRAhYY*).

George Campbell (*https://github.com/abersnaze*), Aaron Tull (*https://github.com/stealthcode*), and Matt Jacobs (*https://github.com/mattrjacobs*) at Netflix were essential in maturing RxJava from early builds to what it became, including the addition of lift, Subscriber, backpressure, and JVM-polyglot support. Dávid Karnok (*https://github.com/akarnokd*) became involved in the project and has now surpassed me in commits and lines of code. He has been a significant factor in the project's success and has now taken over as the project lead.

I have to thank Erik Meijer who created Rx while he was at Microsoft. Since he left that company, I had the opportunity to collaborate with him at Netflix on RxJava, and now I'm lucky enough to be working directly with him at Facebook. I consider it a real honor to be able to spend so many hours at a whiteboard with him discussing and learning. It makes a real difference having a mentor like Erik to level-up one's thinking.

Along the way I also got to speak at many conferences about RxJava and reactive programming, and through that process met many people who have helped me learn far more about code and architecture than I would have ever done on my own.

Netflix was phenomenal in supporting my time and efforts on the project as well as providing support for technical documentation that I could have never written by myself. Open source of this maturity and scope does not succeed without being able to do it during your "day job" and with the involvement of many people with different skillsets.

The first chapter is my attempt at introducing why reactive programming is a useful programming approach, and how RxJava in particular provides a concrete implementation of those principles.

The rest of this book is written by Tomasz, who has done an amazing job. I had the opportunity to review and provide suggestions, but this is his book, and he will teach the details from Chapter 2 onward.

Note from Tomasz Nurkiewicz

I first came across RxJava around 2013 while working for a financial institution. We were dealing with large streams of market data processed in real-time. By then, the data pipeline consisted of Kafka delivering messages, Akka processing trades, Clojure transforming data, and a custom-built language for propagating changes throughout the system. RxJava was a very compelling choice because it had a uniform API that worked very well for different sources of data.

Over time, I tried reactive programming in more scenarios for which scalability and throughput were essential. Implementing systems in a reactive fashion is definitely more demanding. But the benefits are far more important, including better hardware utilization and thus energy savings. To fully appreciate the advantages of this programming model, developers must have relatively easy-to-use tooling. We believe that Reactive Extensions are in the sweet spot between abstraction, complexity, and performance.

This book covers RxJava 1.1.6, unless stated otherwise. Even though RxJava supports Java 6 and later, almost all of the examples use lambda syntax from Java 8. Some examples in the chapter in which we discuss Android (Chapter 8) show how to deal with verbose syntax prior to lambda expressions. That being said, we do not always use the shortest possible syntax (like method references) to improve readability where it makes sense.

Navigating This Book

The book was structured such that you will derive the most from it by reading it from cover to cover. If you can not afford that much time, however, feel free to cherry pick only the parts that are most interesting. If there is a concept that was introduced earlier, you will most likely find a back reference to it. Following is an overview of each chapter:

- Chapter 1 very briefly goes through the inception of RxJava, basic concepts, and ideas (*Ben*).

- Chapter 2 explains how RxJava can appear in your application and how to interact with it. This chapter is very basic, but understanding concepts like hot versus cold sources is tremendously important (*Tomasz*).

- Chapter 3 is a whirlwind tour of the many operators provided by RxJava. We will introduce you to the expressive and powerful functions that are a foundation of this library (*Tomasz*).

- Chapter 4 is more practical, showing how to embed RxJava in various places across your codebase. It also touches on concurrency (*Tomasz*).

- Chapter 5 is advanced, explaining how to implement reactive applications from top to bottom (*Tomasz*).

- Chapter 6 explains an important problem of flow control and backpressure mechanisms in RxJava that support it (*Tomasz*).

- Chapter 7 shows techniques of unit testing, maintaining, and troubleshooting Rx-based applications (*Tomasz*).

- Chapter 8 shows a few selected applications of RxJava, especially in distributed systems (*Tomasz*).

- Chapter 9 highlights future plans for RxJava 2.x (*Ben*).

Online Resources

All marble diagrams throughout this book are taken from official RxJava documentation (*https://github.com/ReactiveX/RxJava/wiki*) published under Apache License Version 2.0.

Conventions Used in This Book

The following typographical conventions are used in this book:

Italic
: Indicates new terms, URLs, email addresses, filenames, and file extensions.

`Constant width`
: Used for program listings, as well as within paragraphs to refer to program elements such as variable or function names, databases, data types, environment variables, statements, and keywords.

`Constant width bold`
: Shows commands or other text that should be typed literally by the user.

Constant width italic

Shows text that should be replaced with user-supplied values or by values determined by context.

This icon signifies a tip, suggestion, or general note.

This icon signifies a general note.

This icon indicates a warning or caution.

Safari® Books Online

Safari Books Online is an on-demand digital library that delivers expert content in both book and video form from the world's leading authors in technology and business.

Technology professionals, software developers, web designers, and business and creative professionals use Safari Books Online as their primary resource for research, problem solving, learning, and certification training.

Safari Books Online offers a range of plans and pricing for enterprise, government, education, and individuals.

Members have access to thousands of books, training videos, and prepublication manuscripts in one fully searchable database from publishers like O'Reilly Media, Prentice Hall Professional, Addison-Wesley Professional, Microsoft Press, Sams, Que, Peachpit Press, Focal Press, Cisco Press, John Wiley & Sons, Syngress, Morgan Kaufmann, IBM Redbooks, Packt, Adobe Press, FT Press, Apress, Manning, New Riders, McGraw-Hill, Jones & Bartlett, Course Technology, and hundreds more. For more information about Safari Books Online, please visit us online.

How to Contact Us

Please address comments and questions concerning this book to the publisher:

O'Reilly Media, Inc.
1005 Gravenstein Highway North
Sebastopol, CA 95472
800-998-9938 (in the United States or Canada)
707-829-0515 (international or local)
707-829-0104 (fax)

We have a web page for this book, where we list errata, examples, and any additional information. You can access this page at *http://bit.ly/reactive-prog-with-rxjava*.

To comment or ask technical questions about this book, send email to *bookquestions@oreilly.com*.

For more information about our books, courses, conferences, and news, see our website at *http://www.oreilly.com*.

Find us on Facebook: *http://facebook.com/oreilly*

Follow us on Twitter: *http://twitter.com/oreillymedia*

Watch us on YouTube: *http://www.youtube.com/oreillymedia*

Acknowledgments

From Ben

This book wouldn't exist without Tomasz, who wrote most of it, and Nan Barber, our editor who was incredibly helpful and patient in getting us to the end. Thank you Tomasz for responding to my message on Twitter (*http://bit.ly/2dqLBtD*) looking for an author and making this book a reality!

I also am very appreciative of the support Netflix Open Source (*https://netflix.github.io*) and Daniel Jacobson (*https://twitter.com/daniel_jacobson*) provided to me personally, and the project generally over the years. They were great sponsors of the project and the immense amount of time I put into the community. Thank you!

And thank you Erik for creating Rx, teaching me so much, and taking the time to write the foreword to this book.

From Tomasz

First and foremost, I would like to thank my parents who gave me my first computer almost 20 years ago (486DX2 with 8 MB of RAM: you never forget that). This is how my journey with programming began. Several people contributed to the making of this book. Beginning with Ben who agreed to write the first and last chapters as well as review my content.

Speaking of reviewers, Venkat Subramaniam put a lot of effort into structuring this book in a meaningful and consistent way. He often suggested a different order of sentences, paragraphs, and chapters, or even removing entire pages of irrelevant content. Our other reviewer was the extremely knowledgable and experienced Dávid Karnok. Being the project lead of RxJava, he spotted dozens of bugs, race conditions, inconsistencies, and other problems. Both reviewers provided hundreds of comments that significantly improved the quality of this book. In the very early stages of this book, many of my colleagues read the manuscript and gave very valuable feedback, as well. I would like to thank: Dariusz Baciński, Szymon Homa, Piotr Pietrzak, Jakub Pilimon, Adam Wojszczyk, Marcin Zajączkowski, and Maciej Ziarko.

CHAPTER 1
Reactive Programming with RxJava

Ben Christensen

RxJava is a specific implementation of reactive programming for Java and Android that is influenced by functional programming. It favors function composition, avoidance of global state and side effects, and thinking in streams to compose asynchronous and event-based programs. It begins with the observer pattern of producer/consumer callbacks and extends it with dozens of operators that allow composing, transforming, scheduling, throttling, error handling, and lifecycle management.

RxJava is a mature open source library (*https://github.com/ReactiveX/RxJava*) that has found broad adoption both on the server and on Android mobile devices. Along with the library, an active community (*http://reactivex.io/tutorials.html*) of developers has built up around RxJava and reactive programming to contribute to the project, speak, write, and help one another.

This chapter will provide an overview of RxJava—what it is and how it works—and the rest of this book will take you through all of the details of how to use and apply it in your applications. You can begin reading this book with no prior experience with reactive programming, but we will start at the beginning and take you through the concepts and practices of RxJava so that you can apply its strengths to your use cases.

Reactive Programming and RxJava

Reactive programming is a general programming term that is focused on reacting to changes, such as data values or events. It can and often is done imperatively. A callback is an approach to reactive programming done imperatively. A spreadsheet is a great example of reactive programming: cells dependent on other cells automatically "react" when those other cells change.

Functional Reactive Programming?

Despite the influence of functional programming on Reactive Extensions (Rx generally, and RxJava specifically), it is *not* Functional Reactive Programming (FRP). FRP is a very specific type of reactive programming (*http://stackoverflow.com/a/1030631*) that involves continuous time, whereas RxJava only deals with discrete events over time. I myself fell into this naming trap in the early days of RxJava and advertised it as "functional reactive" until I learned that the natural combination of those two words was already taken by something else defined years earlier. As a result, there isn't a well-accepted generic term that covers RxJava more specifically than "reactive programming." FRP is still commonly misused to represent RxJava and similar solutions, and the debate occasionally continues on the Internet as to whether the meaning should be broadened (as it has become used informally over the past several years) or remain strictly focused on continuous time implementations.

With that confusion addressed, we can focus on the fact that RxJava is indeed influenced by functional programming and purposefully adopts a programming model different than imperative programming. In this chapter, when I refer to "reactive," I am referring to the reactive + functional style that RxJava uses. As a counterpoint, when I refer to "imperative," I am not saying that reactive programming cannot be implemented imperatively; I am addressing the use of imperative programming as opposed to the functional style employed by RxJava. When I'm specifically comparing imperative and functional approaches, I will use "reactive-functional" and "reactive-imperative" to be precise.

On today's computers everything ends up being imperative at some point as it hits the operating system and hardware. The computer must be told explicitly what needs to be done and how to do it. Humans do not think like CPUs and related systems, so we add abstractions. Reactive-functional programming is an abstraction, just like our higher-level imperative programming idioms are abstractions for the underlying binary and assembly instructions. The fact that everything ends up imperative is important to remember and understand because it helps us with the mental model of what reactive-functional programming is addressing and how it ultimately executes—there is no magic.

Reactive-functional programming therefore is an approach to programming—an abstraction on top of imperative systems—that allows us to program asynchronous and event-driven use cases without having to think like the computer itself and imperatively define the complex interactions of state, particularly across thread and network boundaries. Not having to think like the computer is a useful trait when it comes to asynchrony and event-driven systems, because concurrency and parallelism are involved, and these are very challenging characteristics to use correctly and efficiently. Within the Java community, the books *Java Concurrency in Practice* by Brian Goetz and *Concurrent Programming in Java* by Doug Lea (Addison-Wesley), and forums such as "Mechanical Sympathy" (*http://bit.ly/2d0hmeX*) are representative of the depth, breadth, and complexity of mastering concurrency. My interactions with experts from these books, forums, and communities since I started using RxJava has convinced me even more than before of how difficult it really is to write high-performance, efficient, scalable, and correct concurrent software. And we haven't even brought in distributed systems, which take concurrency and parallelism to another level.

So, the short answer to what reactive-functional programming is solving is concurrency and parallelism. More colloquially, it is solving callback hell, which results from addressing reactive and asynchronous use cases in an imperative way. Reactive programming such as that implemented by RxJava is influenced by functional programming and uses a declarative approach to avoiding the typical pitfalls of reactive-imperative code.

When You Need Reactive Programming

Reactive programming is useful in scenarios such as the following:

- Processing user events such as mouse movement and clicks, keyboard typing, GPS signals changing over time as users move with their device, device gyroscope signals, touch events, and so on.

- Responding to and processing any and all latency-bound IO events from disk or network, given that IO is inherently asynchronous (a request is made, time passes, a response might or might not be received, which then triggers further work).

- Handling events or data pushed at an application by a producer it cannot control (system events from a server, the aforementioned user events, signals from hardware, events triggered by the analog world from sensors, and so on).

Now, if the code in question is handling only one event stream, reactive-imperative programming with a callback is going to be fine, and bringing in reactive-functional programming is not going to give you much benefit. You can have hundreds of different event streams, and if they are all completely independent of one another, imperative programming is not likely to be a problem. In such straightforward use cases, imperative approaches are going to be the most efficient because they eliminate the abstraction layer of reactive programming and stay closer to that for which current operating systems, languages, and compilers are optimized.

If your program is like most though, you need to combine events (or asynchronous responses from functions or network calls), have conditional logic interacting between them, and must handle failure scenarios and resource cleanup on any and all of them. This is where the reactive-imperative approach begins to dramatically increase in complexity and reactive-functional programming begins to shine. A non-scientific view I have come to accept is that reactive-functional programming has an initially higher learning curve and barrier to entry but that the ceiling for complexity is far lower than with reactive-imperative programming.

Hence this is where the tagline for Reactive Extensions (Rx) (*https://github.com/Reacti veX/RxJava*) in general and RxJava specifically comes from, "a library for composing asynchronous and event-based programs." RxJava is a concrete implementation of reactive programming principles influenced by functional and data-flow programming. There are different approaches to being "reactive," and RxJava is but one of them. Let's dig into how it works.

How RxJava Works

Central to RxJava is the Observable type that represents a stream of data or events. It is intended for push (reactive) but can also be used for pull (interactive). It is lazy rather than eager. It can be used asynchronously or synchronously. It can represent 0, 1, many, or infinite values or events over time.

That's a lot of buzzwords and details, so let's unpack it. You'll get the full details in "Anatomy of rx.Observable" on page 27.

Push versus Pull

The entire point of RxJava being reactive is to support push, so the Observable and related Observer type signatures support events being pushed at it. This in turn generally is accompanied by asynchrony, which is discussed in the next section. But the Observable type also supports an asynchronous feedback channel (also sometimes referred to as async-pull or reactive-pull), as an approach to flow control or backpressure in async systems. A later section in this chapter will address flow control and how this mechanism fits in.

To support receiving events via push, an Observable/Observer pair connect via subscription. The Observable represents the stream of data and can be subscribed to by an Observer (which you'll learn more about in "Capturing All Notifications by Using Observer<T>" on page 32):

```
interface Observable<T> {
    Subscription subscribe(Observer s)
}
```

Upon subscription, the Observer can have three types of events pushed to it:

- Data via the onNext() function

- Errors (exceptions or throwables) via the onError() function

- Stream completion via the onCompleted() function

```
interface Observer<T> {
    void onNext(T t)
    void onError(Throwable t)
    void onCompleted()
}
```

The onNext() method might never be called or might be called once, many, or infinite times. The onError() and onCompleted() are terminal events, meaning that only one of them can be called and only once. When a terminal event is called, the Observable stream is finished and no further events can be sent over it. Terminal events might never occur if the stream is infinite and does not fail.

As will be shown in "Flow Control" on page 211 and "Backpressure" on page 226, there is an additional type of signature to permit interactive pull:

```
interface Producer {
    void request(long n)
}
```

This is used with a more advanced Observer called Subscriber (with more details given in "Controlling Listeners by Using Subscription and Subscriber<T>" on page 32):

```
interface Subscriber<T> implements Observer<T>, Subscription {
    void onNext(T t)
    void onError(Throwable t)
    void onCompleted()
    ...
    void unsubscribe()
    void setProducer(Producer p)
}
```

The unsubcribe function as part of the Subscription interface is used to allow a subscriber to unsubscribe from an Observable stream. The setProducer function and Producer types are used to form a bidirectional communication channel between the producer and consumer used for flow control.

Async versus Sync

Generally, an Observable is going to be asynchronous, but it doesn't need to be. An Observable can be synchronous, and in fact defaults to being synchronous. RxJava never adds concurrency unless it is asked to do so. A synchronous Observable would be subscribed to, emit all data using the subscriber's thread, and complete (if finite).

An `Observable` backed by blocking network I/O would synchronously block the subscribing thread and then emit via `onNext()` when the blocking network I/O returned.

For example, the following is completely synchronous:

```
Observable.create(s -> {
    s.onNext("Hello World!");
    s.onCompleted();
}).subscribe(hello -> System.out.println(hello));
```

You will learn more about `Observable.create` in "Mastering Observable.create()" on page 35 and `Observable.subscribe` in "Subscribing to Notifications from Observable" on page 30.

Now, as you are probably thinking, this is generally not the desired behavior of a reactive system, and you are right. It is bad form to use an `Observable` with synchronous blocking I/O (if blocking I/O needs to be used, it needs to be made asynchronous with threads). However, sometimes it is appropriate to synchronously fetch data from an in-memory cache and return it immediately. The "Hello World" case shown in the previous example does not need concurrency, and in fact will be far slower if asynchronous scheduling is added to it. Thus, the actual criteria that is generally important is whether the `Observable` event production is blocking or nonblocking, not whether it is synchronous or asynchronous. The "Hello World" example is nonblocking because it never blocks a thread, thus it is correct (though superfluous) use of an `Observable`.

The RxJava `Observable` is purposefully agnostic with regard to async versus sync, and whether concurrency exists or where it comes from. This is by design and allows the implementation of the `Observable` to decide what is best. Why might this be useful?

First of all, concurrency can come from multiple places, not just threadpools. If the data source is already async because it is on an event loop, RxJava should not add more scheduling overhead or force a particular scheduling implementation. Concurrency can come from threadpools, event loops, actors, and so on. It can be added, or it can originate from the data source. RxJava is agnostic with respect to where the asynchrony originates.

Second, there are two good reasons to use synchronous behavior, which we'll look at in the following subsections.

In-memory data

If data exists in a local in-memory cache (with constant microsecond/nanosecond lookup times), it does not make sense to pay the scheduling cost to make it asynchronous. The `Observable` can just fetch the data synchronously and emit it on the subscribing thread, as shown here:

```
Observable.create(s -> {
    s.onNext(cache.get(SOME_KEY));
    s.onCompleted();
}).subscribe(value -> System.out.println(value));
```

This scheduling choice is powerful when the data might or might not be in memory. If it is in memory, emit it synchronously; if it's not, perform the network call asynchronously and return the data when it arrives. This choice can reside conditionally within the Observable:

```
// pseudo-code
Observable.create(s -> {
    T fromCache = getFromCache(SOME_KEY);
    if(fromCache != null) {
        // emit synchronously
        s.onNext(fromCache);
        s.onCompleted();
    } else {
        // fetch asynchronously
        getDataAsynchronously(SOME_KEY)
            .onResponse(v -> {
                putInCache(SOME_KEY, v);
                s.onNext(v);
                s.onCompleted();
            })
            .onFailure(exception -> {
                s.onError(exception);
            });
    }
}).subscribe(s -> System.out.println(s));
```

Synchronous computation (such as operators)

The more common reason for remaining synchronous is stream composition and transformation via operators. RxJava mostly uses the large API of operators used to manipulate, combine, and transform data, such as map(), filter(), take(), flat Map(), and groupBy(). Most of these operators are synchronous, meaning that they perform their computation synchronously inside the onNext() as the events pass by.

These operators are synchronous for performance reasons. Take this as an example:

```
Observable<Integer> o = Observable.create(s -> {
    s.onNext(1);
    s.onNext(2);
    s.onNext(3);
    s.onCompleted();
});

o.map(i -> "Number " + i)
  .subscribe(s -> System.out.println(s));
```

If the `map` operator defaulted to being asynchronous, each number (1, 2, 3) would be scheduled onto a thread where the string concatenation would be performed ("Number " + i). This is very inefficient and generally has nondeterministic latency due to scheduling, context switching, and so on.

The important thing to understand here is that most `Observable` function pipelines are synchronous (unless a specific operator needs to be async, such as `timeout` or `observeOn`), whereas the `Observable` itself can be async. These topics receive more in-depth treatment in "Declarative Concurrency with observeOn()" on page 159 and "Timing Out When Events Do Not Occur" on page 251.

The following example demonstrates this mixture of sync and async:

```
Observable.create(s -> {
    ... async subscription and data emission ...
})
.doOnNext(i -> System.out.println(Thread.currentThread()))
.filter(i -> i % 2 == 0)
.map(i -> "Value " + i + " processed on " + Thread.currentThread())
.subscribe(s -> System.out.println("SOME VALUE =>" + s));
System.out.println("Will print BEFORE values are emitted")
```

In this example, the `Observable` is async (it emits on a thread different from that of the subscriber), so `subscribe` is nonblocking, and the `println` at the end will output before events are propagated and "SOME VALUE ⇒" output is shown.

However, the `filter()` and `map()` functions are synchronously executed on the calling thread that emits the events. This is generally the behavior we want: an asynchronous pipeline (the `Observable` and composed operators) with efficient synchronous computation of the events.

Thus, the `Observable` type itself supports both sync and async concrete implementations, and this is by design.

Concurrency and Parallelism

Individual `Observable` streams permit neither concurrency nor parallelism. Instead, they are achieved via composition of async `Observables`.

Parallelism is simultaneous execution of tasks, typically on different CPUs or machines. Concurrency, on the other hand, is the composition or interleaving of multiple tasks. If a single CPU has multiple tasks (such as threads) on it, they are executing concurrently but not in parallel by "time slicing." Each thread gets a portion of CPU time before yielding to another thread, even if a thread has not yet finished.

Parallel execution is concurrent by definition, but concurrency is not necessarily parallelism. In practice, this means being multithreaded is concurrency, but parallelism only occurs if those threads are being scheduled and executed on different CPUs at the exact same time. Thus, generically we speak about concurrency and being concurrent, but parallelism is a specific form of concurrency.

The contract of an RxJava Observable is that events (onNext(), onCompleted(), onError()) can never be emitted concurrently. In other words, a single Observable stream must always be serialized and thread-safe. Each event can be emitted from a different thread, as long as the emissions are not concurrent. This means no interleaving or simultaneous execution of onNext(). If onNext() is still being executed on one thread, another thread cannot begin invoking it again (interleaving).

Here's an example of what's okay:

```
Observable.create(s -> {
  new Thread(() -> {
    s.onNext("one");
    s.onNext("two");
    s.onNext("three");
    s.onNext("four");
    s.onCompleted();
  }).start();
});
```

This code emits data sequentially, so it complies with the contract. (Note, however, that it is generally advised to not start a thread like that inside an Observable. Use schedulers, instead, as discussed in "Multithreading in RxJava" on page 140.)

Here's an example of code that is illegal:

```
// DO NOT DO THIS
Observable.create(s -> {
  // Thread A
  new Thread(() -> {
    s.onNext("one");
    s.onNext("two");
  }).start();

  // Thread B
  new Thread(() -> {
    s.onNext("three");
    s.onNext("four");
  }).start();

  // ignoring need to emit s.onCompleted() due to race of threads
});
// DO NOT DO THIS
```

This code is illegal because it has two threads that can both invoke onNext() concurrently. This breaks the contract. (Also, it would need to safely wait for both threads to complete to call onComplete, and as mentioned earlier, it is generally a bad idea to manually start threads like this.)

So, how do you take advantage of concurrency and/or parallelism with RxJava? Composition.

A single Observable stream is always serialized, but each Observable stream can operate independently of one another, and thus concurrently and/or in parallel. This is why merge and flatMap end up being so commonly used in RxJava—to compose asynchronous streams together concurrently. (You can learn more about the details of merge and flatMap in "Wrapping Up Using flatMap()" on page 67 and "Treating Several Observables as One Using merge()" on page 78.)

Here is a contrived example showing the mechanics of two asynchronous Observables running on separate threads and merged together:

```
Observable<String> a = Observable.create(s -> {
  new Thread(() -> {
    s.onNext("one");
    s.onNext("two");
    s.onCompleted();
  }).start();
});

Observable<String> b = Observable.create(s -> {
  new Thread(() -> {
    s.onNext("three");
    s.onNext("four");
    s.onCompleted();
  }).start();
});

// this subscribes to a and b concurrently,
// and merges into a third sequential stream
Observable<String> c = Observable.merge(a, b);
```

Observable c will receive items from both a and b, and due to their asynchrony, three things occur:

- "one" will appear before "two"
- "three" will appear before "four"
- The order between one/two and three/four is unspecified

So why not just allow onNext() to be invoked concurrently?

Primarily because onNext() is meant for us humans to use, and concurrency is difficult. If onNext() could be invoked concurrently, it would mean that every Observer would need to code defensively for concurrent invocation, even when not expected or wanted.

A second reason is because some operations just aren't possible with concurrent emission; for example, scan and reduce, which are common and important behaviors. Operators such as scan and reduce require sequential event propagation so that state can be accumulated on streams of events that are not both associative and commutative. Allowing concurrent Observable streams (with concurrent onNext()) would limit the types of events that can be processed and require thread-safe data structures.

The Java 8 Stream type supports concurrent emission. This is why java.util.stream.Stream requires reduce functions to be associative (*http://bit.ly/2cJJrVG*), because they must support concurrent invocation on parallel streams. The documentation of the java.util.stream package (*http://bit.ly/2cJHVmG*) about parallelism, ordering (related to commutativity), reduction operations, and associativity further illustrates the complexity of the same Stream type permitting both sequential and concurrent emission.

A third reason is that performance is affected by synchronization overhead because all observers and operators would need to be thread-safe, even if most of the time data arrives sequentially. Despite the JVM often being good at eliminating synchronization overhead, it is not always possible (particularly with nonblocking algorithms using atomics) so this ends up being a performance tax not needed on sequential streams.

Additionally, it is often slower to do generic fine-grained parallelism. Parallelism typically needs to be done coarsely, such as in batches of work, to make up for the overhead of switching threads, scheduling work, and recombining. It is far more efficient to synchronously execute on a single thread and take advantage of the many memory and CPU optimizations for sequential computation. On a List or array, it is quite easy to have reasonable defaults for batched parallelism, because all the items are known upfront and can be split into batches (though even then it is often faster to just process the full list on a single CPU unless the list is very large, or the compute per item is significant). A stream, however, does not know the work ahead of time, it just receives data via onNext() and therefore cannot automatically chunk the work.

In fact, prior to RxJava v1, a .parallel(Function f) operator was added to try to behave like java.util.stream.Stream.parallel() because that was considered a nice convenience. It was done in a way to not break the RxJava contract by splitting a single Observable into many Observables that each executed in parallel, and then merging them back together. However, it ended up being removed (*http://bit.ly/2cJIDQF*) from the library prior to v1 because it was very confusing and almost always resulted in worse performance. Adding computational parallelism to a stream of events almost always needs to be reasoned about and tested. Perhaps a ParallelOb servable could make sense, for which the operators are restricted to a subset that assume associativity, but in the years of RxJava being used, it has never ended up being worth the effort, because composition with `merge` and `flatMap` are effective building blocks to address the use cases.

Chapter 3 will teach how to use operators to compose `Observables` to benefit from concurrency and parallelism.

Lazy versus Eager

The `Observable` type is *lazy*, meaning it does nothing until it is subscribed to. This differs from an *eager* type such as a `Future`, which when created represents active work. Lazyiness allows composing `Observables` together without data loss due to race conditions without caching. In a `Future`, this isn't a concern, because the single value can be cached, so if the value is delivered before composition, the value will be fetched. With an unbounded stream, an unbounded buffer would be required to provide this same guarantee. Thus, the `Observable` is lazy and will not start until subscribed to so that all composition can be done before data starts flowing.

In practice, this means two things:

Subscription, not construction starts work

Due to the laziness of an `Observable`, creating one does not actually cause any work to happen (ignoring the "work" of allocating the `Observable` object itself). All it does is define what work should be done when it is eventually subscribed to. Consider an `Observable` defined like this:

```
Observable<T> someData = Observable.create(s -> {
    getDataFromServerWithCallback(args, data -> {
        s.onNext(data);
        s.onCompleted();
    });
})
```

The `someData` reference now exists, but `getDataFromServerWithCallback` is not yet being executed. All that has happened is that the `Observable` wrapper has been declared around a unit of work to be performed, the function that lives inside the `Observable`.

Subscribing to the `Observable` causes the work to be done:

```
someData.subscribe(s -> System.out.println(s));
```

This lazily executes the work represented by the `Observable`.

Observables can be reused

Because the `Observable` is lazy, it also means a particular instance can be invoked more than once. Continuing with the previous example this means we can do the following:

```
someData.subscribe(s -> System.out.println("Subscriber 1: " + s));
someData.subscribe(s -> System.out.println("Subscriber 2: " + s));
```

Now there will be two separate subscriptions, each calling `getDataFromServer WithCallback` and emitting events.

This laziness differs from async types such as `Future` where the `Future` is created to represent work already started. A `Future` cannot be reused (subscribed to multiple times to trigger work). If a reference to a `Future` exists, it means work is already happening. You can see in the preceding sample code exactly where the eagerness is; the `getDataFromServerWithCallback` method is eager because it immediately executes when invoked. Wrapping an `Observable` around `getData FromServerWithCallback` allows it to be used lazily.

This laziness is powerful when doing composition. For example:

```
someData
    .onErrorResumeNext(lazyFallback)
    .subscribe(s -> System.out.println(s));
```

In this case, `lazyFallback` `Observable` represents work that *can* be done, but will only be done if something subscribes to it, and that we only want subscribed to if `someData` fails. Of course, eager types can be made lazy by using function calls (such as `getDataAsFutureA()`).

Eagerness and laziness each have their strengths and weaknesses, but RxJava `Observable` is lazy. Therefore, if you have an `Observable` it won't do anything until you subscribe to it.

This topic is discussed in greater detail in "Embracing Laziness" on page 121.

Duality

An Rx `Observable` is the async "dual" of an `Iterable`. By "dual," we mean the `Observable` provides all the functionality of an `Iterable` except in the reverse flow of data: it is push instead of pull. The table that follows shows types that serve both push and pull functionality:

Pull (Iterable)	Push (Observable)
T next()	onNext(T)
throws Exception	onError(Throwable)
returns	onCompleted()

As per the table, instead of data being pulled out via next() by the consumer, it is pushed to onNext(T) by the producer. Successful termination is signaled via the onCompleted() callback rather than blocking the thread until all items have been iterated. In place of exceptions being thrown up the callstack, errors are emitted as events to the onError(Throwable) callback.

The fact that it behaves as a dual effectively means anything you can do synchronously via pull with an Iterable and Iterator can be done asynchronously via push with an Observable and Observer. This means that the same programming model can be applied to both!

For example, as of Java 8 an Iterable can be upgraded to have function composition via the java.util.stream.Stream type to work like this:

```
// Iterable<String> as Stream<String>
// that contains 75 strings
getDataFromLocalMemorySynchronously()
    .skip(10)
    .limit(5)
    .map(s -> s + "_transformed")
    .forEach(System.out::println)
```

This will retrieve 75 strings from getDataFromLocalMemorySynchronously(), get items 11–15 and ignore the rest, transform the strings, and print them out. (Learn more about operators such as take, skip, and limit in "Slicing and Dicing Using skip(), takeWhile(), and Others" on page 94.)

An RxJava Observable is used the same way:

```
// Observable<String>
// that emits 75 strings
getDataFromNetworkAsynchronously()
    .skip(10)
    .take(5)
    .map(s -> s + "_transformed")
    .subscribe(System.out::println)
```

This will receive 5 strings (15 were emitted but the first 10 were dropped), and then unsubscribe (ignoring or stopping the rest of the strings that were to be emitted). It transforms and prints the strings just like the previous Iterable/Stream example.

In other words, the Rx Observable allows programming with async data via push just like Streams around Iterables and Lists using synchronous pull.

Cardinality

The Observable supports asynchronously pushing multiple values. This nicely fits into the lower right of the following table, the async dual of Iterable (or Stream, List, Enumerable, etc.) and multivalued version of a Future:

	One	Many
Synchronous	T getData()	Iterable<T> getData()
Asynchronous	Future<T> getData()	Observable<T> getData()

Note that this section refers to Future generically. It uses Future.onSuccess(call back) syntax to represent its behavior. Different implementations exist, such as Com pletableFuture (*http://bit.ly/2cJK7dY*), ListenableFuture (*http://bit.ly/2d41UMv*), or the Scala Future (*http://bit.ly/12STMkt*). But whatever you do, don't use java.util.Future, which requires blocking to retrieve a value.

So, why might an Observable be valuable instead of just Future? The most obvious reason is that you are dealing with either an event stream or a multivalued response. The less obvious reason is composition of multiple single-valued responses. Let's look at each of these.

Event stream

Event stream is straightforward. Over time the producer pushes events at the consumer, as demonstrated here:

```
// producer
Observable<Event> mouseEvents = ...;

// consumer
mouseEvents.subscribe(e -> doSomethingWithEvent(e));
```

This doesn't work very well with a Future:

```
// producer
Future<Event> mouseEvents = ...;

// consumer
mouseEvents.onSuccess(e -> doSomethingWithEvent(e));
```

The onSuccess callback could have received the "last event," but some questions remain: Does the consumer now need to poll? Will the producer enqueue them? Or will they be lost in between each fetch? The Observable is definitely beneficial here.

In the absence of `Observable`, a callback approach would be better than modeling this with a `Future`.

Multiple values

Multivalued responses are the next use of `Observable`. Basically, anywhere that a `List`, `Iterable`, or `Stream` would be used, `Observable` can be used instead:

```
// producer
Observable<Friend> friends = ...

// consumer
friends.subscribe(friend -> sayHello(friend));
```

Now, this can work with a `Future`, like this:

```
// producer
Future<List<Friend>> friends = ...

// consumer
friends.onSuccess(listOfFriends -> {
    listOfFriends.forEach(friend -> sayHello(friend));
});
```

So why use the `Observable<Friend>` approach?

If the list of data to return is small, it probably doesn't matter for performance and it becomes a subjective choice. If the list is large, though, or the remote data source must fetch different portions of the list from different locations, using the `Observable<Friend>` approach can be a performance or latency benefit.

The most compelling reason is that items can be processed as received rather than waiting for the entire collection to arrive. This is particularly true when different network latencies on the backend can affect each item differently, which is actually fairly common due to long-tail latencies (such as in service-oriented or microservice architectures) and shared data stores. If waiting for the entire collection, the consumer will always experience the maximum latency of the aggregate work done for the collection. If items are returned as an `Observable` stream, the consumer receives them immediately and "time to first item" can be significantly lower than the last and slowest item. To make this work, ordering of the stream must be sacrified so that the items can be emitted in whatever order the server gets them. If order is eventually important to the consumer, a ranking or position can be included in the item data or metadata, and the client can then sort or position the items as needed.

Additionally, it keeps memory usage limited to that needed per item rather than needing to allocate and collect memory for the entire collection.

Composition

A multivalued `Observable` type is also useful when composing single-valued responses, such as from `Futures`.

When merging together multiple `Futures`, they emit another `Future` with a single value, such as this:

```
CompletableFuture<String> f1 = getDataAsFuture(1);
CompletableFuture<String> f2 = getDataAsFuture(2);

CompletableFuture<String> f3 = f1.thenCombine(f2, (x, y) -> {
  return x+y;
});
```

That might be exactly what is wanted, and is actually available in RxJava via `Observable.zip` (which you'll learn more about in "Pairwise Composing Using zip() and zip-With()" on page 79):

```
Observable<String> o1 = getDataAsObservable(1);
Observable<String> o2 = getDataAsObservable(2);

Observable<String> o3 = Observable.zip(o1, o2, (x, y) -> {
  return x+y;
});
```

However, it means waiting until all `Futures` are completed before emitting anything. Oftentimes, it is preferable to emit each returned `Future` value as it completes. In this case, `Observable.merge` (or the related `flatMap`) is preferable. It allows composing the results (even if each is just an `Observable` emitting one value) into a stream of values that are each emitted as soon as they are ready:

```
Observable<String> o1 = getDataAsObservable(1);
Observable<String> o2 = getDataAsObservable(2);

// o3 is now a stream of o1 and o2 that emits each item without waiting
Observable<String> o3 = Observable.merge(o1, o2);
```

Single

Now, despite Rx `Observable` being great at handling multivalued streams, the simplicity of a single-valued representation is very nice for API design and consumption. Additionally, basic request/response behavior is extremely common in applications. For this reason, RxJava provides a `Single` type, which is a lazy equivalent to a `Future`. Think of it as a `Future` with two benefits: first, it is lazy, so it can be subscribed to multiple times and easily composed, and second, it fits the RxJava API, so it can easily interact with an `Observable`.

For example, consider these accessors:

```
public static Single<String> getDataA() {
    return Single.<String> create(o -> {
        o.onSuccess("DataA");
    }).subscribeOn(Schedulers.io());
}

public static Single<String> getDataB() {
    return Single.just("DataB")
            .subscribeOn(Schedulers.io());
}
```

These can then be used and optionally composed like this:

```
// merge a & b into an Observable stream of 2 values
Observable<String> a_merge_b = getDataA().mergeWith(getDataB());
```

Note how two Singles are merged into an Observable. This could result in an emission of [A, B] or [B, A], depending on which completes first.

Going back to the previous example, we can now use Single instead of Observable to represent the data fetches, but merge them into a stream of values:

```
// Observable<String> o1 = getDataAsObservable(1);
// Observable<String> o2 = getDataAsObservable(2);

Single<String> s1 = getDataAsSingle(1);
Single<String> s2 = getDataAsSingle(2);

// o3 is now a stream of s1 and s2 that emits each item without waiting
Observable<String> o3 = Single.merge(s1, s2);
```

Using Single instead of Observable to represent a "stream of one" simplifies consumption because a developer must consider only the following behaviors for the Single type:

- It can respond with an error
- Never respond
- Respond with a success

Compare this with the additional states a consumer must consider with an Observable:

- It can respond with an error
- Never respond
- Respond successfully with no data and terminate
- Respond successfully with a single value and terminate
- Respond successfully with multiple values and terminate

- Respond successfully with one or more values and never terminate (waiting for more data)

By using Single, the mental model is simpler for consuming the API, and only after composition into an Observable happens must a developer consider the additional states. This is often a better place for it to occur because typically the developer controls that code, whereas the data API is often from a third party.

You'll learn more about Single in "Observable versus Single" on page 202.

Completable

In addition to Single, RxJava also has a Completable type that addresses the surprisingly common use case of having no return type, just the need to represent successful or failed completion. Often Observable<Void> or Single<Void> ends up being used. This is awkward, so Completable came to be, as demonstrated here:

```
Completable c = writeToDatabase("data");
```

This use case is common when doing asynchronous writes for which no return value is expected but notification of successful or failed completion is needed. The preceding code with Completable is similar to this:

```
Observable<Void> c = writeToDatabase("data");
```

The Completable itself is an abstraction for two callbacks, completion and failure, like this:

```
static Completable writeToDatabase(Object data) {
  return Completable.create(s -> {
    doAsyncWrite(data,
        // callback for successful completion
        () -> s.onCompleted(),
        // callback for failure with Throwable
        error -> s.onError(error));
  });
}
```

Zero to infinity

Observable can support cardinalities from zero to infinity (which is explored more in "Infinite Streams" on page 38). But for simplicity and clarity, Single is an "Observable of One," and Completable is an "Observable of None."

With these newly introduced types, our table ends up looking like this:

	Zero	One	Many
Synchronous	void doSomething()	T getData()	Iterable<T> getData()
Asynchronous	Completable doSomething()	Single<T> getData()	Observable<T> getData()

Mechanical Sympathy: Blocking versus Nonblocking I/O

Thus far, the argument for the reactive-functional style of programming has primarily been about providing an abstraction over async callbacks to allow more manageable composition. And, it is fairly obvious that performing unrelated network requests concurrently rather than sequentially is beneficial to experienced latency, thus the reason for adopting asynchrony and needing composition.

But is there an efficiency reason for adopting the reactive approach (either imperative or functional) in how we perform I/O? Are there benefits to using nonblocking I/O, or is blocking I/O threads to wait on a single network request okay? Performance testing I was involved in at Netflix demonstrated that there are objective and measurable efficiency benefits to adopting nonblocking I/O and event loops over thread-per-request blocking I/O. This section provides reasons why this is the case as well as the data to help you make your own decision.

The Pursuit of Answers

After using RxJava for a while, I wanted an answer to the question of blocking versus nonblocking I/O (specifically thread-per-request versus event loops), but I found it very difficult to get clear answers. In fact, I found contradicting answers, myths, theories, opinions, and confusion in my research on the topic. Ultimately, I came to the conclusion that in theory, all different approaches (such as fibers, event loops, threads, and CSP) should result in the same performance (throughput and latency) because ultimately all approaches use the same CPU resources. In practice, though, concrete implementations are made of data structures and algorithms and must deal with the realities of hardware and thus be "sympathetic" first to how the hardware functions, and then to the realities of how our operating systems and runtimes are implemented.

I myself did not have the expertise to answer these questions, but I was lucky enough to end up working with Brendan Gregg (*http://www.brendangregg.com*), who definitely has the expertise (*http://amzn.to/2cJMrl5*). Together with Nitesh Kant (*https://twitter.com/niteshkant*), we had the opportunity over several months of work to profile Tomcat and Netty-based applications (*http://bit.ly/2cJMBsG*).

We specifically chose "real world" code like Tomcat and Netty because they directly related to our choices for production systems (we already used Tomcat and were exploring the use of Netty). The two of them differ most significantly in their architecture of thread-per-request versus event loop.

You can find the details of the study on GitHub at Netflix-Skunkworks/WsPerfLab (*http://bit.ly/2cJMBsG*) along with the code used for testing (*http://bit.ly/2cJMs8R*). You can find a summary and presentation narrative on SpeakerDeck in a presentation titled "Applying Reactive Programming with RxJava" (*http://bit.ly/2cJMRIe*).

As referenced in "The Pursuit of Answers", tests (*http://bit.ly/2cJMBsG*) were done to compare performance of blocking and nonblocking I/O with Tomcat and Netty on Linux. Because this type of testing is always controversial and difficult to get right, I'll be very clear that this test is only intended to be relevant for the following:

- Behavior on typical Linux systems being used around 2015/2016
- Java 8 (OpenJDK and Oracle)
- Unmodified Tomcat and Netty as used in typical production environments
- Representative (*http://bit.ly/2cJMAFe*) web service request/response workload involving composition of multiple other web services

Considering that context, we learned the following:

- Netty code is more efficient than Tomcat code, allowing it to consume less CPU per request.
- The Netty event-loop architecture reduces thread migrations under load, which improves CPU cache warmth and memory locality, which improves CPU Instructions-per-Cycle (IPC), which lowers CPU cycle consumption per request.
- Tomcat code has higher latencies under load due to its thread pool architecture, which involves thread pool locks (and lock contention) and thread migrations to service load.

The following graph best illustrates the difference between the architectures:

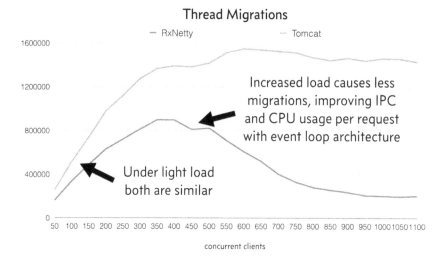

Note how the lines diverge as load increases. These are the thread migrations. The most interesting thing I learned was that the Netty application actually becomes more efficient as it is put under load and the threads become "hot" and stick to a CPU core. Tomcat, on the other hand, has a separate thread per request and thus cannot gain this benefit and retains higher thread migrations due to each thread needing to be scheduled for every request.

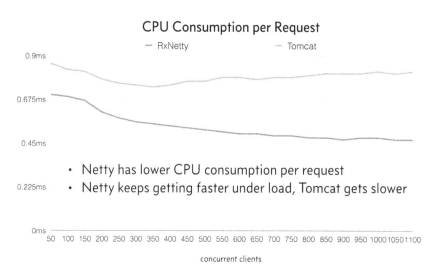

CPU Instructions per Cycle

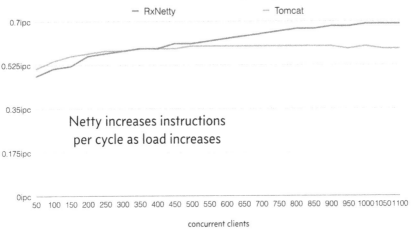

Netty increases instructions
per cycle as load increases

Netty CPU consumption remains mostly flat through increasing load and actually becomes slightly more efficient as the load is maxed out, as opposed to Tomcat, which becomes less efficient.

The resulting impact on latency and throughput is seen in the following graph:

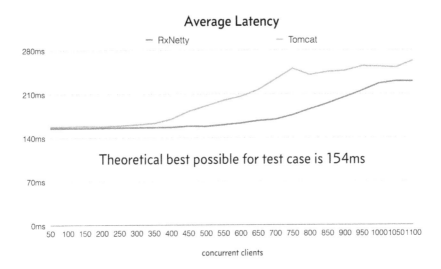

Theoretical best possible for test case is 154ms

Despite averages not being very valuable (as opposed to percentiles), this graph shows how both have similar latency with little load, but diverge significantly as load increases. Netty is able to better utilize the machine until higher load with less impact on latency:

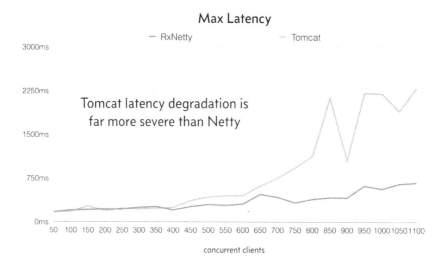

This graph of maximum latency was chosen to show how the outliers affect users and system resources. Netty handles load far more gracefully and avoids the worst-case outliers.

The following image shows throughput:

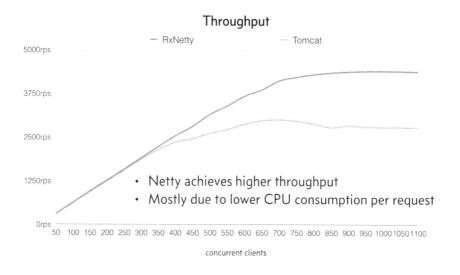

Two strong benefits come out of these findings. First, better latency and throughput means both better user experience and lower infrastructure cost. Second, though, the event-loop architecture is more resilient under load. Instead of falling apart when the load is increased, the machine can be pushed to its limit and handles it gracefully. This is a very compelling argument for large-scale production systems that need to handle unexpected spikes of traffic and remain responsive (*http://www.reactivemani festo.org*).

I also found the event-loop architecture easier to operate. It does not[1] require tuning to get optimal performance, whereas the thread-per-request architecture often needs tweaking of thread pool sizes (and subsequently garbage collection) depending on workload.

This is not intended to be an exhaustive study of the topic, but I found this experiment and resulting data as compelling evidence for pursuing the "reactive" architecture in the form of nonblocking IO and event loops. In other words, with hardware, the Linux kernel, and JVM circa 2015/2016, nonblocking I/O via event loops does have benefits.

Using Netty with RxJava will be further explored later in "Nonblocking HTTP Server with Netty and RxNetty" on page 169.

Reactive Abstraction

Ultimately RxJava types and operators are just an abstraction over imperative callbacks. However, this abstraction completely changes the coding style and provides very powerful tools for doing async and nonblocking programming. It takes effort to learn and requires a shift of thinking to be comfortable with function composition and thinking in streams, but when you've achieved this it is a very effective tool alongside our typical object-oriented and imperative programming styles.

The rest of this book takes you through the many details of how RxJava works and how to use it. Chapter 2 explains where `Observables` come from and how you can consume them. Chapter 3 will guide you through several dozen declarative and powerful transformations.

---

1 Beyond perhaps debating when the number of event loops is sized at 1x, 1.5x, or 2x the number of cores. I have not found strong differences between these values, though, and generally default to 1x.

Reactive Extensions

Tomasz Nurkiewicz

This chapter will guide you through the core concepts related to Reactive Extensions and RxJava. You will become very comfortable with `Observable<T>`, `Observer<T>`, and `Subscriber<T>` and a few helpful utility methods called *operators*. `Observable` is *the* core API RxJava, so make sure you understand how it works and what it represents. Throughout this chapter, you will learn what `Observable` really is and how to create it and interact with it. The knowledge you gain is essential to idiomatically provide and consume reactive APIs based on RxJava. RxJava was designed to ease the pain of asynchronous and event-driven programming, but you must understand some core principles and semantics in order to take advantage of that. When you grasp how `Observable` collaborates with client code, you will feel a lot of power under your fingertips. After reading this chapter, you will be capable of creating simple streams of data, ready to be combined and composed in very interesting ways.

Anatomy of rx.Observable

`rx.Observable<T>` represent a flowing sequence of values. It is *the* abstraction that you will use all of the time. Because these values often appear over a wide time range, we tend to think about an `Observable` as a stream of events. If you look around you will find many examples of streams:

- User interface events
- Bytes transferred over the network
- New orders in online shopping
- Posts on social-media websites

If you want to compare `Observable<T>` with something more familiar, `Iterable<T>` is probably the closest abstraction. Just like `Iterator<T>` created from `Iterable<T>`, `Observable<T>` can have zero to an infinite number of values of type T. `Iterator` is very effective at generating infinite sequences; for example, all natural numbers, as demonstrated here:

```
class NaturalNumbersIterator implements Iterator<BigInteger> {

    private BigInteger current = BigInteger.ZERO;

    public boolean hasNext() {
        return true;
    }

    @Override
    public BigInteger next() {
        current = current.add(BigInteger.ONE);
        return current;
    }
}
```

Another similarity is the fact that `Iterator` itself can signal its client that it has no more items to produce (more on that later). However, the similarities end here. `Observable` is inherently push-based, which means that it decides when to produce values. `Iterator`, on the other hand, sits idle until someone actually asks for `next()` item. Traditionally, such behavior was not possible with `Observable`—at some point in time client code can *subscribe* to an `Observable` and will be notified when `Observable` feels it should emit a value. It can happen anytime between immediately and never. Much later in the book, we will examine "Backpressure" on page 226; this is a mechanism that gives `Subscribers` a way to control `Observable`'s pace under some circumstances.

Also, `Observable` can produce an arbitrary number of events. Obviously, this sounds much like the classic observer pattern, also known as publish-subscribe (if you'd like to learn more about that, read *Design Patterns: Elements of Reusable Object-Oriented Software* by Erich Gamma and Richard Helm [Addison-Wesley]) However, just like `Iterator` does not need to be backed by the underlying collection (see `NaturalNumbersIterator`), `Observable` does not necessarily need to represent a stream of events. It's time to see some examples of `Observables`:

`Observable<Tweet> tweets`

   `tweets` is probably the most obvious example of stream of events. We immediately understand that status updates on any social-media website are being created all the time and can certainly be represented as a stream of events. Also, unlike `Iterator`, we can not pull data manually when it is useful for us. `Observable` must push data as it comes.

`Observable<Double> temperature`

> `temperature` Observable is quite similar; it generates the temperature value of some device and pushes it to subscribers. Both `tweets` and `temperature` Observables are examples of infinite streams of future events.

`Observable<Customer> customers`

> What `Observable<Customer>` represents depends on the context. Most likely it returns a list of customers, probably from a database query. It can be zero, a few, or even thousands of entries, possibly lazy loaded. Or, this `Observable` can represent a stream of a `Customer`'s log in to your system. The client programming model does not change, no matter how `Observable<Customer>` is implemented.

`Observable<HttpResponse> response`

> `Observable<HttpResponse>`, on the other hand, most likely yields just one event (value) until it terminates. This value will appear some time in the future and will be pushed to the client code. To read that response we must subscribe.

`Observable<Void> completionCallback`

> Finally, there is odd-looking `Observable<Void>`. Technically speaking `Observable` can emit zero items and terminate. In that case, we do not care about the actual type of values pushed by an `Observable` because they will never appear anyway.

Indeed, `Observable<T>` can actually produce three types of events:

- Values of type `T`, as declared by `Observable`
- Completion event
- Error event

The specification of reactive extensions clearly states that every `Observable` can emit an arbitrary number of values optionally followed by completion or error (but not both). Strictly speaking *Rx Design Guidelines* define this rule as follows:[1] `OnNext*` `(OnCompleted | OnError)?`—where `OnNext` represents a new event. Interestingly, every possible combination of this regular expression-like rule is valid and useful:

`OnNext OnCompleted`

> `Observable` emits one value and terminates gracefully. This can be used when `Observable` represents a request to an external system and we expect a single response.

---

1 *http://go.microsoft.com/fwlink/?LinkID=205219*

OnNext+ OnCompleted

Observable emits multiple events before it terminates. This can represent reading a list from a database and receiving each record as a single value. Another example can be tracking progress of some long-running process that eventually finishes.

OnNext+

Infinite list of events, like comments on a social-media website or status updates of some component (e.g., mouse movements and ping requests). This stream is infinite and must be consumed on the fly.

OnCompleted *or* OnError *only*

Such an Observable signals only normal or abnormal termination. OnError additionally wraps a Throwable that caused the stream to terminate. Errors are signaled via event rather than using standard throw statement.

OnNext+ OnError

A stream might successfully emit one or more events but eventually fail. Typically, this means that a stream was supposed to be infinite but failed in the meantime due to fatal error. Think about a sequence of network packets that deliver events for hours but at some point becomes interrupted due to connectivity loss.

OnError notification is quite interesting. Because of the asynchronous nature of Observables, simply throwing exceptions makes little sense. Instead, we must transfer errors to whoever is interested, possibly across threads and over some period of time. OnError is a special type of event that encapsulates exceptions in a functional way. You can read more about exceptions in "Error Handling" on page 243.

Additionally, you can implement an Observable to never emit any event at all, including completion or error. Such an Observable is useful for testing purposes—for example, to exercise timeouts.

Subscribing to Notifications from Observable

An instance of Observable does not emit any events until someone is actually interested in receiving them. To begin watching an Observable, you use the subscribe() family of methods:

```
Observable<Tweet> tweets = //...

tweets.subscribe((Tweet tweet) ->
    System.out.println(tweet));
```

The preceding code snippet subscribes to tweets Observable by registering a callback. This callback will be invoked every time the tweets stream decides to push an event downstream. The RxJava contract makes sure that your callback will not be invoked from more than one thread at a time, even though events can be emitted from many threads. There are multiple overloaded versions of subscribe() that are more specific. We already mentioned that idiomatically Observable does not throw exceptions. Instead, exceptions are just another type of notification (event) that Observable can propagate. Therefore, you do not use the try-catch block around subscribe() to catch exceptions produced along the way. Instead, you provide a separate callback:

```
tweets.subscribe(
        (Tweet tweet) -> { System.out.println(tweet); },
        (Throwable t) -> { t.printStackTrace(); }
);
```

The second argument to subscribe() is optional. It notifies about exceptions that can potentially occur while producing items. It is guaranteed that no other Tweet will appear after the exception. You almost always want to subscribe for exceptions as well, not only legitimate items, even if you do not expect them. Exceptions are first-class citizens in Observable. Thrown exceptions can propagate quickly, causing lots of side effects like inconsistent data structures or failed transactions. This is generally a good idea, but often exceptions are not fatal. Thus, resilient systems should anticipate and have a systematic way of handling exceptions. That is why Observable models them explicitly.

The third optional callback allows us to listen for stream completion:

```
tweets.subscribe(
        (Tweet tweet) -> { System.out.println(tweet); },
        (Throwable t) -> { t.printStackTrace(); },
        () -> {this.noMore();}
);
```

Remember that RxJava is not opinionated with regard to how many items are produced, when, and when to stop. As a stream can be infinite or it can complete immediately upon subscription, it is up to the Subscriber whether it wants to receive completion notification. If you know at the outset that a stream is infinite, obviously it makes no sense. On the other hand, in some cases the completion of a stream might be the event for which we are actually waiting. As an example, think about Observable<Progress> that keeps track of long-running processes. The client might or might not be interested in tracking progress, but it definitely wants to know when the process finishes.

As a side note, often you can use Java 8 method references instead of lambdas to improve readability, as illustrated here:

```
tweets.subscribe(
    System.out::println,
    Throwable::printStackTrace,
    this::noMore);
```

Capturing All Notifications by Using Observer<T>

It turns out that providing all three arguments to subscribe() is quite useful, thus it would be helpful to have a simple wrapper holding all three callbacks. This is what Observer<T> was designed for. Observer<T> is a container for all three callbacks, receiving all possible notifications from Observable<T>. Here is how you can register an Observer<T>:

```java
Observer<Tweet> observer = new Observer<Tweet>() {
    @Override
    public void onNext(Tweet tweet) {
        System.out.println(tweet);
    }

    @Override
    public void onError(Throwable e) {
        e.printStackTrace();
    }

    @Override
    public void onCompleted() {
        noMore();
    }
};

//...

tweets.subscribe(observer);
```

As a matter of fact Observer<T> is the core abstraction for listening in RxJava. Yet if you want even greater control, Subscriber (Observers abstract implementation) is even more powerful.

Controlling Listeners by Using Subscription and Subscriber<T>

A single Observable can naturally have numerous subscribers. Just like in a publisher-subscriber pattern, a single publisher can dispatch events to multiple consumers. In RxJava, Observable<T> is just a typed data structure that can exist very briefly or for many days, as long as a server application runs. The same story applies for subscribers. You can subscribe to an Observable, consume a handful of events, and discard all the others. Or quite the opposite: drain events as long as Observable is alive, possibly for hours or days.

Imagine an Observer that knows in advance how many items it wants to receive or when to stop receiving them. For example, we subscribed for stock price changes, but when the price falls below $1, we no longer want to listen. Obviously, just as Observer has the ability to subscribe, it also should be capable of unsubscribing whenever it finds it suitable. There are two means to support that: Subscription and Subscriber. Let's talk about the former. We did not yet explore what subscribe() actually returns:

```
Subscription subscription =
        tweets.subscribe(System.out::println);

//...

subscription.unsubscribe();
```

Subscription is a handle that allows client code to cancel a subscription by using the unsubscribe() method. Additionally, you can query the status of a subscription by using isUnsubscribed(). It is important to unsubscribe from Observable<T> as soon as you no longer want to receive more events; this avoids memory leaks and unnecessary load on the system. Sometimes, we subscribe to an Observable and fully consume it, never really unsubscribing, even if that stream is infinite. However, there are cases in which subscribers come and go while the Observable keeps producing events forever.

There is a second way to request unsubscribe, this time from within the listener. We know that we can use Subscription to control subscription outside of the Observer or callback. Subscriber<T>, on the other hand, implements both Observer<T> and Subscription. Thus, it can be used both to consume notifications (events, completions, or errors) and control subscription. The code example that follows subscribes to all events, but the subscriber itself decides to give up receiving notifications under certain criteria. Normally, this can be done by using the built-in takeUntil() operator, but for the time being we can unsubscribe manually:

```
Subscriber<Tweet> subscriber = new Subscriber<Tweet>() {
    @Override
    public void onNext(Tweet tweet) {
        if (tweet.getText().contains("Java")) {
            unsubscribe();
        }
    }

    @Override
    public void onCompleted() {}

    @Override
    public void onError(Throwable e) {
        e.printStackTrace();
    }
};
tweets.subscribe(subscriber);
```

When Subscriber decides it no longer wants to receive more items, it can unsubscribe itself. As an exercise, you can implement a Subscriber that receives only the first n events and then gives up. The `Subscriber` class is more powerful than that, but for the time being just remember it is capable of unsubscribing itself from `Observable`.

Creating Observables

We began by subscribing to an `Observable` in order to receive events pushed downstream. This is not a coincidence. Most of the time while working with RxJava you will be interacting with existing `Observables`, typically combining, filtering, and wrapping them with one another. However, unless you work with an external API that already exposes `Observables`, you first must learn where `Observables` come from and how you can create a stream and handle subscriptions. First, there are several factory methods that create fixed constant `Observables`. These are useful if you want to use RxJava consistently across an entire codebase or when values to be emitted are cheap to produce and known in advance:

`Observable.just(value)`

Creates an `Observable` instance that emits exactly one `value` to all future subscribers and completes afterward. Overloaded versions of the `just()` operator can take anything from two to nine values to be emitted.

`Observable.from(values)`

Similar to `just()` but accepts `Iterable<T>` or `T[]`, thus creating `Observable<T>` with as many values emitted as elements in `values` collection. Another overloaded version accepts a `Future<T>`, emitting an event when the underlying `Future` completes.

`Observable.range(from, n)`

Produces n integer numbers starting from `from`. For example, `range(5, 3)` will emit 5, 6, and 7 and then complete normally. Each subscriber will receive the same set of numbers.

`Observable.empty()`

Completes immediately after subscription, without emitting any values.

`Observable.never()`

Such `Observable` never emits any notifications, neither values nor completion or error. This stream is useful for testing purposes.

`Observable.error()`

Emits an `onError()` notification immediately to every subscriber. No other values are emitted and according to contract `onCompleted()` cannot occur as well.

Mastering Observable.create()

Dummy `empty()`, `never()`, and `error()` factories don't seem terribly useful; however, they are quite handy when composing with genuine `Observables`. Interestingly, even though RxJava is all about asynchronous processing of streams of events, the afore-mentioned factory methods by default operate on the client thread. Have a look at the following code sample:

```
private static void log(Object msg) {
    System.out.println(
            Thread.currentThread().getName() +
            ": " + msg);
}

//...

log("Before");
Observable
    .range(5, 3)
    .subscribe(i -> {
        log(i);
    });
log("After");
```

What we are interested in is the thread that executed each log statement:

```
main: Before
main: 5
main: 6
main: 7
main: After
```

The order of `print` statements is also relevant. It is not a surprise that `Before` and `After` messages are printed by the `main` client thread. However, notice that subscription also happened in the client thread and `subscribe()` actually blocked the client thread until all events were received. Unless required by some operator RxJava does not implicitly run your code in any thread pool. To better understand this behavior, let's study the low-level operator used for manufacturing `Observables`: `create()`:

```
Observable<Integer> ints = Observable
    .create(new Observable.OnSubscribe<Integer>() {
        @Override
        public void call(Subscriber<? super Integer> subscriber) {
            log("Create");
            subscriber.onNext(5);
            subscriber.onNext(6);
            subscriber.onNext(7);
            subscriber.onCompleted();
            log("Completed");
        }
    });
```

```
log("Starting");
ints.subscribe(i -> log("Element: " + i));
log("Exit");
```

The preceding code sample is intentionally verbose. Here is the output, including the thread name that executed each particular line:

```
main: Starting
main: Create
main: Element: 5
main: Element: 6
main: Element: 7
main: Completed
main: Exit
```

To understand how `Observable.create()` works and how RxJava deals with concurrency, we will analyze the execution step by step. First, we create `ints` Observable by supplying an implementation of the `OnSubscribe` callback interface to `create()` (later, we almost always replace it with a simple lambda expression). At this point, nothing happened yet apart from creating an instance of `Observable`; therefore, the first line of output we see is `main: Starting`. `Observable` defers emission of events by default, meaning it will not begin to emit any items until you actually subscribe, so the lambda expression given to `create()` is not executed yet. Later, we do subscribe, `ints.subscribe(...)`, forcing `Observable` to begin emitting items. This is true for streams known as *cold*. *Hot* streams, on the other hand, emit events even if no one subscribed. This important distinction will be explained soon in "Hot and Cold Observables" on page 43.

> The lambda expression receiving emitted items (`i -> log("Ele ment: " + i`) is wrapped with `Subscriber<Integer>` internally. This subscriber is nearly directly passed as an argument to a function you specified when calling `create()`. So every time you subscribe to an `Observable`, a new `Subscriber` instance is created and passed to your `create()` method. Calling `onNext()` or other methods of `Subscriber` inside `create()` indirectly invokes your own `Subscriber`.

`Observable.create()` is so versatile that in fact you can mimic all of the previously discovered factory methods on top of it. For example, `Observable.just(x)`, emits a single value x and immediately completes afterward, might look like this:

```
static <T> Observable<T> just(T x) {
    return Observable.create(subscriber -> {
        subscriber.onNext(x);
        subscriber.onCompleted();
    }
```

```
    );
}
```

As an exercise, try to implement `never()`, `empty()`, or even `range()` by using only `create()`.

Managing multiple subscribers

Emitting does not begin until we actually subscribe. But every time `subscribe()` is called, our subscription handler inside `create()` is invoked. This is neither an advantage nor a disadvantage, it is just something you must keep in mind. In some cases, the fact that every subscriber gets its own unique handler invocation works great. For example, `Observable.just(42)` should emit 42 to every subscriber, not just the first one. On the other hand, if you put a database query or heavyweight computation inside `create()`, it might be beneficial to share a single invocation among all subscribers.

To ensure that you truly understand how subscription works, consider the following code sample that subscribes to the same `Observable` twice:

```
Observable<Integer> ints =
        Observable.create(subscriber -> {
                    log("Create");
                    subscriber.onNext(42);
                    subscriber.onCompleted();
                }
        );
log("Starting");
ints.subscribe(i -> log("Element A: " + i));
ints.subscribe(i -> log("Element B: " + i));
log("Exit");
```

What kind of output do you expect? Remember that every time you subscribe to an `Observable` created via the `create()` factory method, the lambda expression passed as an argument to `create()` is executed independently by default within the thread that initiated the subscription:

```
main: Starting
main: Create
main: Element A: 42
main: Create
main: Element B: 42
main: Exit
```

If you would like to avoid calling `create()` for each subscriber and simply reuse events that were already computed, there exists a handy `cache()` operator:

```
Observable<Integer> ints =
    Observable.<Integer>create(subscriber -> {
                //...
```

```
            }
        )
        .cache();
```

`cache()` is the first operator that you learn. Operators wrap existing `Observables`, enhancing them, typically by intercepting subscription. What `cache()` does is stand between `subscribe()` and our custom `Observable`. When the first subscriber appears, `cache()` delegates subscription to the underlying `Observable` and forwards all notifications (events, completions, or errors) downstream. However, at the same time, it keeps a copy of all notifications internally. When a subsequent subscriber wants to receive pushed notifications, `cache()` no longer delegates to the underlying `Observable` but instead feeds cached values. With caching, the output for two `Sub scribers` is quite different:

```
main: Starting
main: Create
main: Element A: 42
main: Element B: 42
main: Exit
```

Of course, you must keep in mind that `cache()` plus infinite stream is the recipe for a disaster, also known as `OutOfMemoryError`. But this will be covered in "Memory Consumption and Leaks" on page 315, much later.

Infinite Streams

Infinite data structures are an important concept. Computer memory is finite so having an infinite list or stream sounds impossible. But RxJava allows you to produce and consume events on the fly. That traditional queue can be treated as an infinite source of values, despite not keeping all of them in memory at the same time. That being said how would you implement such an infinite stream by using `create()`? For example, let's build an `Observable` that produces all natural numbers:

```
//BROKEN! Don't do this
Observable<BigInteger> naturalNumbers = Observable.create(
        subscriber -> {
            BigInteger i = ZERO;
            while (true) {  //don't do this!
                subscriber.onNext(i);
                i = i.add(ONE);
            }
        });
naturalNumbers.subscribe(x -> log(x));
```

The presence of `while(true)` should trigger an alarm bell in any codebase. It seems OK at first, but you should quickly realize that this implementation is broken. But not because it is infinite—as a matter of fact infinite `Observables` are perfectly OK and quite useful. Of course, as long as they are implemented properly. The moment you hit subscribe(), the lambda expression inside create() is invoked in the context of your thread. And because this lambda never ends, subscribe() blocks infinitely as well. But, you might ask, "But shouldn't subscription be asynchronous rather than running subscription handler in the client thread?" This is a valid question, so let's spend some time introducing explicit concurrency:

```
Observable<BigInteger> naturalNumbers = Observable.create(
    subscriber -> {
        Runnable r = () -> {
            BigInteger i = ZERO;
            while (!subscriber.isUnsubscribed()) {
                subscriber.onNext(i);
                i = i.add(ONE);
            }
        };
        new Thread(r).start();
    });
```

Rather than have a blocking loop running directly in the client thread, we spawn a custom thread and emit events directly from there. Luckily subscribe() no longer blocks client thread, because all it does underneath is spawn a thread. All invocations of the x -> log(x) callback are executed from within our custom thread in the background. Now imagine we are not interested in all the natural numbers (there are too many of them after all), but just the first few. We know already how to stop receiving notifications from Observable—by unsubscribing:

```
Subscription subscription = naturalNumbers.subscribe(x -> log(x));
//after some time...
subscription.unsubscribe();
```

If you pay attention to details, you probably noticed the suspicious-looking while(true) loop was replaced with the following:

```
while (!subscriber.isUnsubscribed()) {
```

For every iteration we make, we need to ensure that someone is actually listening. When a subscriber decides to stop listening, the subscriber.isUnsubscribed() condition tells us about it so we can safely complete the stream and exit Runnable, effectively stopping the thread. Obviously, each subscriber has its own thread and loop, so when one subscriber decides to unsubscribe, others keep receiving their independent stream of events. Although creating your own thread is not a good design decision, and RxJava has much better declarative tools for handling concurrency, the preceding code sample shows how you can properly handle subscription events.

It is advised to check the isUnsubscribed() flag as often as possible to avoid sending events after a subscriber no longer wants to receive new events. Moreover, when producing events is costly, there is no point in eagerly sending them when no one wants them anyway. Even though there is nothing inherently wrong with spawning your own threads within create(), it is error prone and scales poorly. In "Multithreading in RxJava" on page 140, we explore declarative concurrency and custom schedulers that allow you to write concurrent code without really interacting with threads yourself.

Handling unsubscription immediately before trying to send an event is fine as long as events are pushed relatively often. But imagine a situation in which events appear very rarely. Observable can only determine that a subscriber unsubscribed when it attempts to push some event to it. Take the following useful factory method as an example: delayed(x) creates an Observable that emits value x after sleeping for 10 seconds. It is similar to Observable.just(), but with extra delay. We know already that extra thread needs to be used, even though it is not the best usage pattern:

```
static <T> Observable<T> delayed(T x) {
    return Observable.create(
        subscriber -> {
            Runnable r = () -> {
                sleep(10, SECONDS);
                if (!subscriber.isUnsubscribed()) {
                    subscriber.onNext(x);
                    subscriber.onCompleted();
                }
            };
            new Thread(r).start();
        });
}

static void sleep(int timeout, TimeUnit unit) {
    try {
        unit.sleep(timeout);
    } catch (InterruptedException ignored) {
        //intentionally ignored
    }
}
```

The naive implementation spawns a new thread and goes to sleep for 10 seconds. A more robust implementation should at least use java.util.concurrent.ScheduledExecutorService, but this is for educational purposes only. After 10 seconds we ensure that someone is still listening, and if that is the case, we emit a single item and complete. But what if the subscriber decides to unsubscribe one second after subscribing, long before the event is supposed to be emitted? Well, nothing really. The background thread sleeps for the remaining nine seconds just to realize the subscriber is long gone. This is what bothers us; holding the resource for an extra nine seconds seems wasteful. Imagine this was an expensive connection to some data feed for which we pay for every second of usage but where events occur very rarely. Waiting several seconds or even minutes just to realize that there is no longer anyone subscribed and we should terminate the connection sounds suboptimal to say the least.

Luckily, with a subscriber instance we can be notified as soon as it unsubscribes, cleaning up resources as soon as possible, not when the next message appears:

```
static <T> Observable<T> delayed(T x) {
    return Observable.create(
        subscriber -> {
            Runnable r = () -> {/* ... */};
            final Thread thread = new Thread(r);
            thread.start();
            subscriber.add(Subscriptions.create(thread::interrupt));
        });
}
```

The last line is crucial, but everything else remained the same. The background thread is already running—or, to be precise, sleeping for 10 seconds. But just after spawning a thread, we ask the subscriber to let us know by invoking a callback if it unsubscribes and is registered via `Subscriber.add()`. This callback has basically a single purpose: to interrupt a thread. What calling `Thread.interrupt()` does is throw an `InterruptedException` inside `sleep()`, prematurely interrupting our 10-second pause. `sleep()` exits gracefully after swallowing the exception. However, at this point `subscriber.isUnsubscribed()` returns `false` and no event is emitted. The thread stops immediately and no resources are wasted. You can use the same pattern to perform any cleanup. However, if your stream produces a steady, frequent flow of events, you can probably live without explicit callback.

There is another reason why you should not use explicit threads inside `create()`. The *Rx Design Guidelines* in section 4.2. *Assume observer instances are called in a serialized fashion* require that subscribers never receive notifications concurrently. It is easy to violate this requirement when explicit threads are involved. This behavior is similar to actors, for example, in the Akka toolkit (*http://akka.io*), in which each actor can process one message at a time. Such an assumption allows writing `Observer`s as if they were synchronized, always accessed by at most one thread. This holds true despite events that can come from multiple threads. Custom implementations of `Observable` must ensure that this contract is met. With that in mind, look at the following code that nonidiomatically tries to parallelize loading of multiple chunks of `Data`:

```
Observable<Data> loadAll(Collection<Integer> ids) {
    return Observable.create(subscriber -> {
        ExecutorService pool = Executors.newFixedThreadPool(10);
        AtomicInteger countDown = new AtomicInteger(ids.size());
        //DANGER, violates Rx contract. Don't do this!
        ids.forEach(id -> pool.submit(() -> {
            final Data data = load(id);
            subscriber.onNext(data);
            if (countDown.decrementAndGet() == 0) {
                pool.shutdownNow();
                subscriber.onCompleted();
```

```
            }
        }));
    });
}
```

This code, apart from accidentally being quite complex, violates some Rx principles. Namely it allows calling the `subscriber`'s `onNext()` method from multiple threads concurrently. Second, you can avoid the complexity by simply applying idiomatic RxJava operators, such as `merge()` and `flatMap()`, but we will get there in "Treating Several Observables as One Using merge()" on page 78. The good news is that even if someone poorly implemented the `Observable`, we can easily fix it by applying the `serialize()` operator, such as `loadAll(...).serialize()`. This operator ensures that events are serialized and sequenced. It also enforces that no more events are sent after completion or error.

The last aspect of creating `Observables` that we have not yet covered is error propagation. We've learned so far that `Observer<T>` can receive values of type `T`, optionally followed by either completion or error. But how do you push errors downstream to all subscribers? It is a good practice to wrap entire expressions within `create()` in a try-catch block. `Throwables` should be propagated downstream rather than logged or rethrown, as demonstrated here:

```
Observable<Data> rxLoad(int id) {
    return Observable.create(subscriber -> {
        try {
            subscriber.onNext(load(id));
            subscriber.onCompleted();
        } catch (Exception e) {
            subscriber.onError(e);
        }
    });
}
```

This extra try-catch block is necessary to propagate the possible `Exception` thrown from, for example, `load(id)`. Otherwise, RxJava will do its best to at least print the exception to standard output, but to build resilient streams, exceptions need to be treated as first-class citizens, not just as extra features in the language that no one truly understands.

The pattern of completing an `Observable` with one value and wrapping with the try-catch statement is so prevalent that the built-in `fromCallable()` operator was introduced:

```
Observable<Data> rxLoad(int id) {
    return Observable.fromCallable(() ->
        load(id));
}
```

It is semantically equivalent but much shorter and has some other benefits over `cre ate()` that you will discover later.

Timing: timer() and interval()

We've devoted quite a few pages to studying `Observables` that create threads on their own, which is not the best pattern in RxJava. In later chapters, we will explore schedulers, but first let's discover two very useful operators that use threads underneath: `timer()` and `interval()`. The former simply creates an `Observable` that emits a `long` value of zero after a specified delay and then completes:

```
Observable
        .timer(1, TimeUnit.SECONDS)
        .subscribe((Long zero) -> log(zero));
```

As silly as it sounds, `timer()` is extremely useful. It is basically an asynchronous equivalent of `Thread.sleep()`. Rather than blocking the current thread, we create an `Observable` and `subscribe()` to it. It will become significantly more important after we learn how to compose simple `Observables` into more complex computations. The fixed value of `0` (in variable `zero`) is just a convention without any specific meaning. However, it makes more sense when `interval()` is introduced. `interval()` generates a sequence of `long` numbers, beginning with zero, with a fixed delay between each one of them:

```
Observable
        .interval(1_000_000 / 60, MICROSECONDS)
        .subscribe((Long i) -> log(i));
```

`Observable.interval()` produces a sequence of consecutive `long` numbers, beginning with `0`. However, unlike `range()`, `interval()` places a fixed delay before every event, including the first one. In our example, this delay is about 16666 μs, which roughly corresponds to 60 Hz, which is the frame rate often used in various animations. This is not a coincidence: `interval()` is sometimes used to control animations or processes that need to run with certain frequency. `interval()` is somewhat similar to `scheduleAtFixedRate()` from `ScheduledExecutorService`. You can probably imagine multiple usage scenarios of `interval()`, like periodic polling for data, refreshing user interfaces, or modeling elapsing time in simulation.

Hot and Cold Observables

After you get an instance of `Observable`, it is important to understand whether the stream is *hot* or *cold*. The API and semantics remain the same, but the way you use `Observable` will depend on the type. A cold `Observable` is entirely lazy and never begins to emit events until someone is actually interested. If there are no observers, `Observable` is just a static data structure. This also implies that every subscriber receives its own copy of the stream because events are produced lazily but also not likely cached in any way. Cold Observables typically come from Observable.cre ate(), which idiomatically should not start any logic but instead postpone it until someone actually listens. A cold Observable is thus somewhat dependent on Sub scriber. Examples of cold Observables, apart from create(), include Observa ble.just(), from(), and range(). Subscribing to a cold Observable often involves a side effect happening inside create(). For example, the database is queried or a con‐ nection is opened.

Hot Observables are different. After you get a hold of such an Observable it might already be emitting events no matter how many Subscribers they have. Observable pushes events downstream, even if no one listens and events are possibly missed. Whereas typically you have full control over cold Observables, hot Observables are independent from consumers. When a Subscriber appears, a hot Observable behaves like a wire tap,[2] transparently publishing events flowing through it. The pres‐ ence or absence of Subscriber does not alter the behavior of Observable; it is entirely decoupled and independent.

Surprisingly, Observable.interval() is not hot. You might think it simply produces timer ticks with some interval, irrespective of the environment, but in reality the timer events are produced only when someone subscribes and each subscriber receives independent stream. This is a definition of a cold Observable.

Hot Observables typically occur when we have absolutely no control over the source of events. Examples of such Observables include mouse movements, keyboard inputs, or button clicks. So far, we haven't even mentioned the user interface, but it turns out that RxJava fits perfectly when implementing user interfaces. This library is especially appreciated in the Android community, where it helps in transforming from nested callbacks to flat composition of streams. We will explore how you can use RxJava on mobile devices running Android in "Android Development with RxJava" on page 277.

The importance of hot versus cold distinction becomes essential when we rely on delivery of events. No matter when you subscribe to a cold Observable—immediately or after hours—you always receive a complete and consistent set of events. On the other hand, if the Observable is hot, you can never be sure you received all events from the beginning. Later in this chapter, we will learn some techniques on how to ensure that every subscriber received all events. One such technique already sneaked into this chapter: the cache() operator (see "Managing multiple subscribers" on page 37). Technically, it can buffer all events from a hot Observable and allow subsequent

---

2 Hohpe, G. and Woolf, B., *Enterprise Integration Patterns: Designing, Building, and Deploying Messaging Solu‐ tions*, Addison-Wesley Professional.

subscribers to receive the same sequence of events. However, because it consumes theoretically an unlimited amount of memory, be careful with caching hot Observables.

Another interesting distinction that comes to mind between hot and cold sources is time dependency. A cold Observable produces values on demand and possibly multiple times so the exact instant when an item was created is irrelevant. Conversely, hot Observables represent events as they come, typically from some external source. This means that the instant when a given value was generated is very significant because it places the event on the timescale.

Use Case: From Callback API to Observable Stream

The majority of Java APIs like JDBC, java.io, servlets[3] as well as proprietary solutions are blocking. This means that the client thread must wait for whatever the result or side effect is. However, there are use cases that are inherently asynchronous; for example, pushing events from some external source. You can technically build a block-streaming API in the following manner:

```
while(true) {
    Event event = blockWaitingForNewEvent();
    doSomethingWith(event);
}
```

Luckily, when a domain is so inherently asynchronous, you will most likely find some sort of callback-based API, so prevalent, for example, in JavaScript. These APIs will accept some form of callback, typically an interface with a bunch of methods that you can implement to notify you about various events. The most striking example of such an API is almost every graphical user interface library out there: for example, Swing. When various listeners like onClick() or onKeyUp() are used, callbacks are certainly inevitable. If you've worked in such environments, the term *callback hell* is definitely familiar to you. Callbacks have a tendency to nest in one another, so coordinating multiple callbacks is virtually impossible. Here is an example of a callback nested four times:

```
button.setOnClickListener(view -> {
    MyApi.asyncRequest(response -> {
        Thread thread = new Thread(() -> {
            int year = datePicker.getYear();
            runOnUiThread(() -> {
                button.setEnabled(false);
                button.setText("" + year);
            });
        });
    });
```

---

3 At least until version 3.0.

```
        thread.setDaemon(true);
        thread.start();
    });
});
```

The simplest requirements, like reacting when two callbacks are invoked shortly after each other, becomes a nightmare, and is additionally hindered by multithreading. In this section, we will refactor a callback-based API into RxJava with all the benefits such as controlling threads, lifecycle, and cleanup.

One of my favorite examples of streams are status updates from Twitter (*http://www.twitter.com*), known as *tweets*. There are several thousand user updates per second. Many accompanied by geolocalization, language, and other metadata. For the purpose of this exercise, we will use the open source Twitter4J (*http://twitter4j.org*) library that can push a subset of new tweets using a callback-based API. This chapter is not intended to explain how Twitter4J works or to provide robust examples. Twitter4J was chosen as a good example of an API using callbacks with an interesting domain. The simplest working example of reading tweets in real-time might look like this:

```
import twitter4j.Status;
import twitter4j.StatusDeletionNotice;
import twitter4j.StatusListener;
import twitter4j.TwitterStream;
import twitter4j.TwitterStreamFactory;

TwitterStream twitterStream = new TwitterStreamFactory().getInstance();
twitterStream.addListener(new twitter4j.StatusListener() {
    @Override
    public void onStatus(Status status) {
        log.info("Status: {}", status);
    }

    @Override
    public void onException(Exception ex) {
        log.error("Error callback", ex);
    }

    //other callbacks
});
twitterStream.sample();
TimeUnit.SECONDS.sleep(10);
twitterStream.shutdown();
```

Calling `twitterStream.sample()` starts a background thread that logs in to Twitter and awaits new messages. Every time a tweet appears, the `onStatus` callback is executed. Execution can jump between threads, therefore we can no longer rely on throwing exceptions. Instead the `onException()` notification is used. After sleeping for 10 seconds, we shutdown() the stream, cleaning up all underlying resources like HTTP connections or threads.

Overall, it does not look that bad, the problem is that this program is not doing anything. In real life, you would probably process each Status message (*tweet*) somehow. For example, save it to a database or feed a machine-learning algorithm. You can technically put that logic inside the callback, but this couples the infrastructural call with the business logic. Simple delegation to a separate class is better, but unfortunately not reusable. What we really want is clean separation between the technical domain (consuming data from an HTTP connection) and the business domain (interpreting input data). So we build a second layer of callbacks:

```
void consume(
            Consumer<Status> onStatus,
            Consumer<Exception> onException) {
    TwitterStream twitterStream = new TwitterStreamFactory().getInstance();
    twitterStream.addListener(new StatusListener() {
        @Override
        public void onStatus(Status status) {
            onStatus.accept(status);
        }

        @Override
        public void onException(Exception ex) {
            onException.accept(ex);
        }

        //other callbacks
    });
    twitterStream.sample();
}
```

By adding this one extra level of abstraction we can now reuse the consume() method in various ways. Imagine that instead of logging you have persistence, analytics, or fraud detection:

```
consume(
        status -> log.info("Status: {}", status),
        ex      -> log.error("Error callback", ex)
);
```

But we just shifted the problem up in the hierarchy. What if we want to count the number of tweets per second? Or consume just the first five? And what if we would like to have multiple listeners? In these situations, each of these situations opens a new HTTP connection. Last but not least, this API does not allow unsubscribing when we are done, risking resource leak. We hope you realize that we are heading toward an Rx-powered API. Rather than passing callbacks down to the place where they can be executed, we can return an Observable<Status> and let everyone subscribe whenever they want. However, keep in mind that the following implementation still opens a new network connection for each Subscriber:

```
Observable<Status> observe() {
    return Observable.create(subscriber -> {
        TwitterStream twitterStream =
            new TwitterStreamFactory().getInstance();
        twitterStream.addListener(new StatusListener() {
            @Override
            public void onStatus(Status status) {
                subscriber.onNext(status);
            }

            @Override
            public void onException(Exception ex) {
                subscriber.onError(ex);
            }

            //other callbacks
        });
        subscriber.add(Subscriptions.create(twitterStream::shutdown));
    });
}
```

At this point, we can simply call observe(), which only creates an Observable and does not contact the external server. We learned that unless someone actually subscribes, the contents of create() are not executed. The subscription is very similar:

```
observe().subscribe(
    status -> log.info("Status: {}", status),
    ex -> log.error("Error callback", ex)
);
```

The big difference here, compared to consume(...), is that we are not forced to pass callbacks as arguments to observe(). Instead, we can return Observable<Status>, pass it around, store it somewhere, and use it whenever and wherever we feel like it is needed. We can also compose this Observable with other Observables, which is what Chapter 3 covers. One important aspect that we have not covered is resource cleanup. When someone unsubscribes, we should shut down TwitterStream to avoid resource leak. We already know two techniques for that; let's use the simpler one first:

```
@Override
public void onStatus(Status status) {
    if (subscriber.isUnsubscribed()) {
        twitterStream.shutdown();
    } else {
        subscriber.onNext(status);
    }
}

@Override
```

```
    public void onException(Exception ex) {
        if (subscriber.isUnsubscribed()) {
            twitterStream.shutdown();
        } else {
            subscriber.onError(ex);
        }
    }
}
```

When someone subscribes only to receive a small fraction of the stream, our `Observa
ble` will make sure to clean up the resources. We know a second technique to imple-
ment clean-up that does not require waiting for an upstream event. The moment a
subscriber unsubscribes, we call `shutdown()` immediately, rather than waiting for the
next tweet to come just to trigger clean-up behavior (last line):

```
twitterStream.addListener(new StatusListener() {
    //callbacks...
});
twitterStream.sample();

subscriber.add(Subscriptions.create(twitterStream::shutdown));
```

Interestingly, this `Observable` blurs the difference between hot and cold streams. On
one hand, it represents external events that appear without our control (hot behavior). On the other hand, events will not begin flowing (no underlying HTTP connection) to our system until we actually `subscribe()`. One more side effect that we
forgot about is still creeping in: every new `subscribe()` will start a new background
thread and new connection to an external system. The same instance of `Observa
ble<Status>` should be reusable across many subscribers, and because `Observable` is
lazy, you should technically be able to call `observe()` once upon startup and keep it
in some singleton. But the current implementation simply opens a new connection,
effectively fetching the same data multiple times from the network, for each `Sub
scriber`. We certainly want to register multiple `Subscribers` of that stream, but there
is no reason why every `Subscriber` is supposed to fetch the same data independently.
What we really want is a *pub-sub* behavior wherein one publisher (external system)
delivers data to multiple `Subscribers`. In theory, the `cache()` operator can do that,
but we don't want to buffer old events forever. We will now explore some solutions to
this problem.

Manually Managing Subscribers

Manually keeping track of all subscribers and shutting down the connection to the
external system only when all subscribers leave is a Sisyphean task that we will implement anyway, just to appreciate idiomatic solutions later on. The idea is to keep track
of all subscribers in some sort of `Set<Subscriber<Status>>` and start/shut down the
external system connection when it becomes empty/nonempty:

```
//DON'T DO THIS, very brittle and error prone
class LazyTwitterObservable {

  private final Set<Subscriber<? super Status>> subscribers =
    new CopyOnWriteArraySet<>();

  private final TwitterStream twitterStream;

  public LazyTwitterObservable() {
    this.twitterStream = new TwitterStreamFactory().getInstance();
    this.twitterStream.addListener(new StatusListener() {
      @Override
      public void onStatus(Status status) {
        subscribers.forEach(s -> s.onNext(status));
      }

      @Override
      public void onException(Exception ex) {
        subscribers.forEach(s -> s.onError(ex));
      }

      //other callbacks
    });
  }

  private final Observable<Status> observable = Observable.create(
      subscriber -> {
        register(subscriber);
        subscriber.add(Subscriptions.create(() ->
            this.deregister(subscriber)));
      });

  Observable<Status> observe() {
    return observable;
  }

  private synchronized void register(Subscriber<? super Status> subscriber) {
    if (subscribers.isEmpty()) {
      subscribers.add(subscriber);
      twitterStream.sample();
    } else {
      subscribers.add(subscriber);
    }
  }

  private synchronized void deregister(Subscriber<? super Status> subscriber) {
    subscribers.remove(subscriber);
    if (subscribers.isEmpty()) {
      twitterStream.shutdown();
    }
  }
}
```

}

The `subscribers` set thread-safely stores a collection of currently subscribed `Observers`. Every time a new `Subscriber` appears, we add it to a set and connect to the underlying source of events lazily. Conversely, when the last `Subscriber` disappears, we shut down the upstream source. The key here is to always have exactly one connection to the upstream system rather than one connection per subscriber. This works and is quite robust, however, the implementation seems too low-level and error-prone. Access to the `subscribers` set must be `synchronized`, but the collection itself must also support safe iteration. Calling `register()` *must* appear before adding the `deregister()` callback; otherwise, the latter can be called before we register. There must be a better way to implement such a common scenario of multiplexing a single upstream source to multiple `Observers`—luckily, there are at least two such mechanisms. RxJava is all about reducing such dangerous boilerplate and abstracting away concurrency.

rx.subjects.Subject

The `Subject` class is quite interesting because it extends `Observable` and implements `Observer` at the same time. What that means is that you can treat it as `Observable` on the client side (subscribing to upstream events) and as `Observer` on the provider side (pushing events downstream on demand by calling `onNext()` on it). Typically, what you do is keep a reference to `Subject` internally so that you can push events from any source you like but externally expose this `Subject` as `Observable`. Let's reimplement streaming `Status` updates using `Subject`. To further simplify implementation, we connect to the external system eagerly and do not keep track of subscribers. Apart from simplifying our example, this has the benefit of smaller latency when the first `Subscriber` appears. Events are already flowing, we don't need to wait to reconnect to some third-party application:

```
class TwitterSubject {

    private final PublishSubject<Status> subject = PublishSubject.create();

    public TwitterSubject() {
        TwitterStream twitterStream = new TwitterStreamFactory().getInstance();
        twitterStream.addListener(new StatusListener() {
            @Override
            public void onStatus(Status status) {
                subject.onNext(status);
            }

            @Override
            public void onException(Exception ex) {
                subject.onError(ex);
```

```
        }

        //other callbacks
    });
    twitterStream.sample();
}

public Observable<Status> observe() {
    return subject;
}

}
```

PublishSubject is one of the flavors (subclasses) of Subject. We eagerly begin
receiving events from the upstream system and simply push them (by calling sub
ject.onNext(...)) to all Subscribers. Subject keeps track of these events internally
so that we no longer need to. Notice how we simply return subject in observe(),
pretending it is a plain Observable. Now when someone subscribes, the Subscriber
will receive all subsequent events immediately after onNext() is called on the backend
—at least until it unsubscribes. Because Subject manages the lifecycle of Subscribers
internally, we simply call onNext() without worrying about how many subscribers
are listening.

Error Propagation in Subjects

Subjects are useful, but there are many subtleties you must understand. For example, after calling subject.onError(), the Subject
silently drops subsequent onError notifications, effectively swallowing them.

Subject is a useful tool for creating Observable instances when Observable.cre
ate(...) seems too complex to manage. Other types of Subjects include the following:

AsyncSubject
Remembers last emitted value and pushes it to subscribers when onComplete() is
called. As long as AsyncSubject has not completed, events except the last one are
discarded.

BehaviorSubject
Pushes all events emitted after subscription happened, just like PublishSubject.
However, first it emits the most recent event that occurred just before subscription. This allows Subscriber to be immediately notified about the state of the
stream. For example, Subject may represent the current temperature broadcas-
ted every minute. When a client subscribes, he will receive the last seen temperature immediately rather than waiting several seconds for the next event. But the

same `Subscriber` is not interested in historical temperatures, only the last one. If no events have yet been emitted, a special default event is pushed first (if provided).

ReplaySubject
> The most interesting type of `Subject` that caches events pushed through the entire history. If someone subscribes, first he receives a batch of missed (cached) events and only later events in real-time. By default, all events since the creation of this `Subject` are cached. This can be become dangerous if the stream is infinite or very long (see "Memory Consumption and Leaks" on page 315). In that case, there are overloaded versions of `ReplaySubject` that keep only the following:
>
> - Configurable number of events in memory (`createWithSize()`)
> - Configurable time window of most recent events (`createWithTime()`)
> - Or even constraint both size and time (whichever limit is reached first) with `createWithTimeAndSize()`

`Subjects` should be treated with caution: often there are more idiomatic ways of sharing subscriptions and caching events—for example, see "ConnectableObservable". For the time being, prefer relatively low-level `Observable.create()` or even better, consider standard factory methods like `from()` and `just()`.

One more thing to keep in mind is concurrency. By default calling `onNext()` on a `Subject` is directly propagated to all `Observer`'s `onNext()` callback methods. It is not a surprise that these methods share the same name. In a way, calling `onNext()` on `Subject` indirectly invokes `onNext()` on each and every `Subscriber`. But you need to keep in mind that according to *Rx Design Guidelines* all calls to `onNext()` on `Observer` must be serialized (i.e., sequential), thus two threads cannot call `onNext()` at the same time. However, depending on the way you stimulate `Subject`, you can easily break this rule—e.g., calling `Subject.onNext()` from multiple threads from a thread pool. Luckily, if you are worried that this might be the case, simply call `.toSerialized()` on a `Subject`, which is quite similar to calling `Observable.serialize()`. This operator makes sure downstream events occur in the correct order.

ConnectableObservable

`ConnectableObservable` is an interesting way of coordinating multiple `Subscribers` and sharing a single underlying subscription. Remember our first attempt at creating a single, lazy connection to an underlying resource with `LazyTwitterObservable`? We had to manually keep track of all `subscribers` and connect/disconnect as soon as the first subscriber appeared or the last one left. `ConnectableObservable` is a type of

Observable that ensures there exists at most one Subscriber at all times, but in reality there can be many of them sharing the same underlying resource.

There are many applications of ConnectableObservable; for example, making sure all Subscribers receive the same sequence of events regardless of when they subscribed. ConnectableObservable can also force subscription if it generates important side effects, even when no "real" Subscriber has appeared yet. We will quickly discover all of these use cases. Subjects are imperative ways of creating Observables, whereas ConnectableObservable shields the original upstream Observable and guarantees at most one Subscriber reaches it. No matter how many Subscribers connect to ConnectableObservable, it opens just one subscription to the Observable from which it was created.

Single Subscription with publish().refCount()

Let us recap: we have a single handle to the underlying resource; for example, HTTP connection to stream of Twitter status updates. However, an Observable pushing these events will be shared among multiple Subscribers. The naive implementation of this Observable created earlier had no control over this; therefore, each Sub scriber started its own connection. This is quite wasteful:

```
Observable<Status> observable = Observable.create(subscriber -> {
    System.out.println("Establishing connection");
    TwitterStream twitterStream = new TwitterStreamFactory().getInstance();
    //...
    subscriber.add(Subscriptions.create(() -> {
        System.out.println("Disconnecting");
        twitterStream.shutdown();
    }));
    twitterStream.sample();
});
```

When we try to use this Observable, each Subscriber establishes a new connection, like so:

```
Subscription sub1 = observable.subscribe();
System.out.println("Subscribed 1");
Subscription sub2 = observable.subscribe();
System.out.println("Subscribed 2");
sub1.unsubscribe();
System.out.println("Unsubscribed 1");
sub2.unsubscribe();
System.out.println("Unsubscribed 2");
```

Here is the output:

```
Establishing connection
Subscribed 1
Establishing connection
```

```
Subscribed 2
Disconnecting
Unsubscribed 1
Disconnecting
Unsubscribed 2
```

This time, to simplify, we use a parameterless subscribe() method that triggers subscription but drops all events and notifications. After spending almost half of the chapter fighting with this problem and familiarizing ourselves with plenty of RxJava features, we can finally introduce the most scalable and simplest solution: the publish().refCount() pair:

```
lazy = observable.publish().refCount();
//...
System.out.println("Before subscribers");
Subscription sub1 = lazy.subscribe();
System.out.println("Subscribed 1");
Subscription sub2 = lazy.subscribe();
System.out.println("Subscribed 2");
sub1.unsubscribe();
System.out.println("Unsubscribed 1");
sub2.unsubscribe();
System.out.println("Unsubscribed 2");
```

The output is much like what we expect:

```
Before subscribers
Establishing connection
Subscribed 1
Subscribed 2
Unsubscribed 1
Disconnecting
Unsubscribed 2
```

The connection is not established until we actually get the first Subscriber. But, more important, the second Subscriber does not initiate a new connection, it does not even touch the original Observable. The publish().refCount() tandem wrapped the underlying Observable and intercepted all subscriptions. We will explain later why we need two methods and what using publish() alone means. For the time being, we will focus on refCount(). What this operator does is basically count how many active Subscribers we have at the moment, much like reference counting in historic garbage-collection algorithms. When this number goes from zero to one, it subscribes to the upstream Observable. Every number above one is ignored and the same upstream Subscriber is simply shared between all downstream Subscribers. However, when the very last downstream Subscriber unsubscribes, the counter drops from one to zero and refCount() knows it must unsubscribe right away. Thankfully, refCount() does precisely what we implemented manually with Lazy TwitterObservable. You can use the publish().refCount() duet to allow sharing of a single `Subscriber` while remaining lazy. This pair of operators is used very frequently and therefore has an alias named `share()`. Keep in mind that if unsubscription is shortly followed by subscription, `share()` still performs reconnection, as if there were no caching at all.

ConnectableObservable Lifecycle

Another useful use case of the `publish()` operator is forcing subscription in the absence of any `Subscriber`. Imagine that we have our `Observable<Status>`. Before we expose it to our clients we want to store each event in the database, regardless of whether someone is subscribed. A naive approach is not sufficient:

```
Observable<Status> tweets = //...
return tweets
    .doOnNext(this::saveStatus);
```

We are using the `doOnNext()` operator that peeks every item that flows through the stream and performs some action, like `saveStatus()`. However, remember that `Observables` are lazy by design; therefore, as long as no one subscribed, `doOnNext()` is not triggered. What we want is a fake `Observer` that does not really listen to events but forces upstream `Observables` to produce events. There is actually an overloaded version of `subscribe()` that does exactly this:

```
Observable<Status> tweets = //...
tweets
    .doOnNext(this::saveStatus)
    .subscribe();
```

This empty `Subscriber` in the end invokes `Observable.create()` and connects to the upstream source of events. This seems to solve the problem, but we again forgot to protect ourselves from multiple subscribers. If we expose `tweets` outside, the second subscriber will make a second attempt to connect to the external resource—for example, opening a second HTTP connection. The idiomatic solution is to use `pub lish().connect()` duet that creates an artificial `Subscriber` immediately while keeping just one upstream `Subscriber`. This is best explained with an example. And at last we are about to learn how `publish()` alone works:

```
ConnectableObservable<Status> published = tweets.publish();
published.connect();
```

Finally, we see `ConnectableObservable` in its full glory. We can call `Observable.pub lish()` on any `Observable` and get `ConnectableObservable` in return. We can continue using the original upstream `Observable` (`tweets` in the preceding example): `publish()` does not affect it. But we will focus on the returned `ConnectableObserva ble`. Anyone who subscribes to `ConnectableObservable` is placed in a set of `Sub scribers`. As long as `connect()` is not called, these `Subscribers` are put on hold, they never directly subscribe to upstream `Observable`. However, when `connect()` is called, a dedicated mediating `Subscriber` subscribes to upstream `Observable` (tweets), no matter how many downstream subscribers appeared before—even if there were none. But if there were some `Subscribers` of `ConnectableObservable` put on hold, they will all receive the same sequence of notifications.

This mechanism has multiple advantages. Imagine that you have an `Observable` in your application in which multiple `Subscribers` are interested. On startup, several components (e.g., Spring beans or EJBs) subscribe to that `Observable` and begin listening. Without `ConnectableObservable`, it is very likely that hot `Observable` will begin emitting events that will be consumed by the first `Subscriber`, but `Subscribers` started later will miss out on the early events. This can be a problem if you want to be absolutely sure that all `Subscribers` receive a consistent view of the world. All of them will receive events in the same order, unfortunately `Subscriber` appearing late will lose early notifications.

The solution to this problem is to `publish()` such an `Observable` first and make it possible for all of the components in your system to `subscribe()`; for example, during application startup. When you are 100% sure that all `Subscribers` that need to receive the same sequence of events (including initial event) had a chance to `sub scribe()`, connect such `ConnectableObservable` with `connect()`. This will create a single `Subscriber` in upstream `Observable` and begin pushing events to all downstream `Subscribers`. The following example uses Spring framework (*http:// projects.spring.io/spring-framework/*), but as a matter of fact it is framework agnostic:

```
import org.springframework.context.ApplicationListener;
import org.springframework.context.annotation.Bean;
import org.springframework.context.annotation.Configuration;
import org.springframework.context.event.ContextRefreshedEvent;
import rx.Observable;
import rx.observables.ConnectableObservable;

@Configuration
class Config implements ApplicationListener<ContextRefreshedEvent> {

    private final ConnectableObservable<Status> observable =
        Observable.<Status>create(subscriber -> {
            log.info("Starting");
            //...
        }).publish();

    @Bean
    public Observable<Status> observable() {
        return observable;
    }

    @Override
```

```
    public void onApplicationEvent(ContextRefreshedEvent event) {
        log.info("Connecting");
        observable.connect();
    }
}

@Component
class Foo {

    @Autowired
    public Foo(Observable<Status> tweets) {
        tweets.subscribe(status -> {
            log.info(status.getText());
        });
        log.info("Subscribed");
    }
}

@Component
class Bar {

    @Autowired
    public Bar(Observable<Status> tweets) {
        tweets.subscribe(status -> {
            log.info(status.getText());
        });
        log.info("Subscribed");
    }
}
```

Our simple application first eagerly creates an Observable (ConnectableObservable
subclass underneath). Observables are lazy by design, so it is fine to create them even
statically. This Observable is publish()-ed so that all subsequent Subscribers are
put on hold and do not receive any notifications until we do connect(). Later, two
@Components are found that require this Observable. Dependency injection framework provides our ConnectableObservable and allows everyone to subscribe. However, the events, even in case of hot Observable will not arrive until full application
startup. When all of the components are instantiated and wired together, a ContextRe
freshedEvent sent from the framework can be consumed. At this point, we can guarantee that all components had a chance to request a given Observable and
subscribe() to it. When the application is about to start, we call connect(). This
subscribes to the underlying Observable exactly once and forwards the exact same
sequence of events to every component. The trimmed-down logging output might
look as follows (the component names are in square brackets):

```
[Foo   ] Subscribed
[Bar   ] Subscribed
[Config] Connecting
[Config] Starting
```

```
[Foo  ] Msg 1
[Bar  ] Msg 1
[Foo  ] Msg 2
[Bar  ] Msg 2
```

Notice how `Foo` and `Bar` components report that they are subscribed even though they did not yet receive any events. Only after the application fully started, `connect()` subscribed to the underlying `Observable` and began forwarding `Msg 1` and `Msg 2` to all components. Let's look at this in contrast with a plain `Observable` in the same scenario, in which `ConnectableObservable` was not used and we allow every component to subscribe immediately:

```
[Config] Starting
[Foo  ] Subscribed
[Foo  ] Msg 1
[Config] Starting
[Bar  ] Subscribed
[Foo  ] Msg 2
[Bar  ] Msg 2
```

There are two differences for which you need to be aware. First and foremost, when the `Foo` component subscribes, it immediately starts a connection to the underlying resource; it does not wait for application startup. Even worse, the `Bar` component initiates another connection (notice that `Starting` occurs twice). Second, do you see that the `Bar` component started from `Msg 2` and never really got a hold of `Msg 1`, exclusively received by `Foo`? This inconsistency when consuming hot `Observable` might or might not be an issue in some circumstances, but you must be aware of it.

Summary

Creating and subscribing to `Observable` are essential features of RxJava. Especially beginners tend to forget about subscription and are surprised that no events are emitted. Many developers focus on amazing operators provided by this library (see Chapter 3), but failing to understand how these operators perform subscription underneath can cause subtle bugs.

Moreover, the asynchronous nature of RxJava is typically taken for granted, which is not really the case. As a matter of fact, most operators in RxJava do not use any particular thread pool. More precisely this means that by default no concurrency is involved whatsoever and everything happens in client thread. This is another important take away of this chapter. Now, when you understand subscription and concurrency principles, you are ready to begin using RxJava painlessly and effectively.

Chapter 3 browses through the library of built-in operators and how you can combine them. Declarative transformations and composition of streams is what makes RxJava so compelling.

Operators and Transformations

Tomasz Nurkiewicz

The aim of this chapter is to explain fundamentals of RxJava's operators and how you can compose them to build high-level, easy-to-reason data pipelines. One of the reasons why RxJava is so powerful is the rich universe of built-in operators it provides and the possibility of creating custom ones. An operator is a function that takes upstream `Observable<T>` and returns downstream `Observable<R>`, where types `T` and `R` might or might not be the same. Operators allow composing simple transformations into complex processing graphs.

For example, the `Observable.filter()` operator receives items from an upstream `Observable` but forwards only those matching a given predicate. Conversely, `Observable.map()` transforms items it receives as they fly through. This allows extracting, enriching, or wrapping original events. Some operators are much more involved. For example, `Observable.delay()` will pass through events as-is; however, each and every one of them will appear after a fixed delay. Finally, there are operators (like `Observable.buffer()`) that consume several input events before emitting them, possibly batched.

But even when you recognize how wonderful Rx operators are, the true power comes from combining them together. Chaining several operators, forking stream into multiple substreams and then joining them back is idiomatic and you should feel fairly comfortable with it.

Core Operators: Mapping and Filtering

Operators are typically instance methods on `Observable` that somehow alter the behavior of upstream `Observable` as seen by downstream `Observables` or `Subscribers`. This might sound complex, but it is actually quite flexible and not that difficult to grasp. One of the simplest examples of operators is `filter()`, which takes a predicate and either passes events further or discards them:

```
Observable<String> strings = //...
Observable<String> filtered = strings.filter(s -> s.startsWith("#"));
```

It's now time to introduce the so-called *marble diagrams*, the ubiquitous visualizations in RxJava documentation. A marble diagram illustrates how various operators work. Most of the time you will see two horizontal axes representing time flying by from left to right. Shapes on these diagrams (the aforementioned marbles) visualize events. Between the top and bottom axes there is an operator in question that somehow alters the sequence of events coming from the source Observable (upstream) to form the resulting Observable (downstream), as demonstrated in the following graphic:

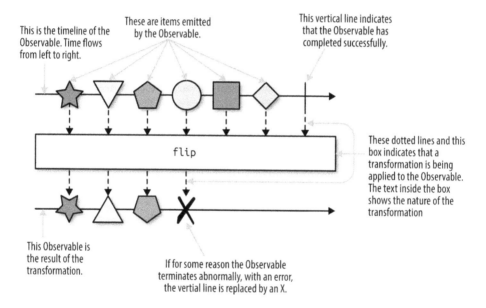

The diagram that follows is a concrete example of a marble diagram representing a `filter()` operator. The `Observable.filter()` returns the exact same events (so the marbles on top and on the bottom are the same), but some events are skipped because they did not satisfy the predicate:

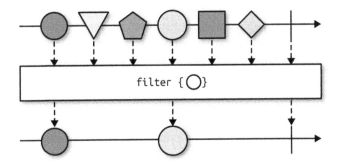

When dealing with certain types of `Observables`, some events might be out of your interest, for example when consuming high volumes of data. It is also a common practice to `filter()` the same `Observable` multiple times, each time with a different predicate. We can apply several filters on original `Observable` and even chain them (`filter(p1).filter(p2).filter(p3)`), effectively implementing logical conjunction (`filter(p1 && p2 && p3)`). Collapsing consecutive operators (which does not only apply to `filter()`) into one has pros and cons. Having more, smaller transformations (like multiple filters) is preferable if you can reuse smaller transformations or compose them in different ways. On the other hand, more operators add overhead[1] and increase the stack depth. Which style you choose depends on your requirements and coding style:

```
Observable<String> strings = someFileSource.lines();
Observable<String> comments = strings.filter(s -> s.startsWith("#"));
Observable<String> instructions = strings.filter(s -> s.startsWith(">"));
Observable<String> empty = strings.filter(String::isBlank);
```

You might ask yourself this question: what happens to the original upstream `strings` source? Having an object-oriented background you might remember methods like `java.util.List.sort()` that rearrange items within a `List` internally and returns nothing. Java's `List<T>` is mutable (for better or worse) so rearranging its contents is acceptable. Similarly, one could imagine a hypothetical `void List.filter()` that takes a predicate and internally removes nonmatching elements. In RxJava, you must forget about mutating data structures internally: modifying variables outside of stream is considered very nonidiomatic and dangerous. Every single operator returns a *new* `Observable`, leaving the original one untouched.

This makes reasoning about the flow of events much simpler. You can fork a stream into multiple independent sources, each having different characteristics. One of the powers of RxJava is that you can reuse a single `Observable` in multiple places without

---

1 There is ongoing research regarding operator fusion that seamlessly collapses several operators into one.

affecting other consumers. If you pass an Observable to some unknown function you can be sure that this Observable will not become corrupted in any way by that function. You cannot say that about mutable java.util.Date, which can be modified by anyone who has a reference to it. That is why the new java.time API is entirely immutable.

1-to-1 Transformations Using map()

Imagine that you have a stream of some events and you must perform certain transformation on each event. This can be decoding from JSON to Java object (or vice versa), enriching, wrapping, extracting from the event, and so on. This is where the invaluable map() operator is useful. It applies a transformation to each and every value from upstream, as shown here:

```java
import rx.functions.Func1;


Observable<Status> tweets = //...
Observable<Date> dates = tweets.map(new Func1<Status, Date>() {
    @Override
    public Date call(Status status) {
        return status.getCreatedAt();
    }
});

Observable<Date> dates =
        tweets.map((Status status) -> status.getCreatedAt());

Observable<Date> dates =
        tweets.map((status) -> status.getCreatedAt());

Observable<Date> dates =
        tweets.map(Status::getCreatedAt);
```

All of the ways in which you can define dates Observable are equivalent, from the most verbose using Func1<T, R> to the most compact Java 8 syntax method reference and type inference. But look carefully! The original Observable named tweets produces events of type Status. Later, we call map() with a function that takes a single event (Status s) and returns a value of type Date. By the way having mutable events (like java.util.Date) is problematic because any operator or Subscriber can unintentionally mutate events consumed by other Subscribers. We can quickly fix this by applying subsequent map():

```java
Observable<Instant> instants = tweets
        .map(Status::getCreatedAt)
        .map((Date d) -> d.toInstant());
```

The marble diagram for map() follows:

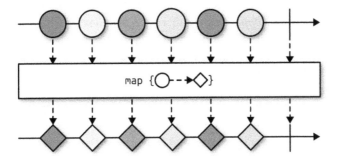

The map() operator takes a function that can change the shape of input event from circle to square. This transformation is applied to each item flowing through it.

Now it is time for a pop quiz to make sure that you understand how Observables work. Look at the following and try to predict what values will be emitted when the following Observable is subscribed to:

```
Observable
        .just(8, 9, 10)
        .filter(i -> i % 3 > 0)
        .map(i -> "#" + i * 10)
        .filter(s -> s.length() < 4);
```

Observables are *lazy*, meaning that they do not begin producing events until someone subscribes. You can create infinite streams that take hours to compute the first value, but until you actually express your desire to be notified about these events, Observable is just a passive and idle data structure for some type T. This even applies to hot Observables—even though the source of events keeps producing them, not a single operator like map() or filter() is evaluated until someone actually shows an interest. Otherwise, running all of these computational steps and throwing away the result would make no sense. Every time you use any operator, including those that we did not explain yet, you basically create a wrapper around original Observable. This wrapper can intercept events flying through it but typically does not subscribe on its own:

```
Observable
        .just(8, 9, 10)
        .doOnNext(i -> System.out.println("A: " + i))
        .filter(i -> i % 3 > 0)
        .doOnNext(i -> System.out.println("B: " + i))
        .map(i -> "#" + i * 10)
        .doOnNext(s -> System.out.println("C: " + s))
        .filter(s -> s.length() < 4)
        .subscribe(s -> System.out.println("D: " + s));
```

Logging or otherwise peeking at messages as they flow through our stream is so useful that there is a special *impure* operator called doOnNext() that allows looking at items going through without touching them. It is impure because it must rely on side effects like logging or accessing global state. doOnNext() simply receives every event that flew from upstream Observable and passes it downstream, it cannot modify it in any way. doOnNext() is like a probe that you can safely inject anywhere in your pipeline of Observables to keep an eye on what is flowing through. This is a straightforward implementation of the Wiretap pattern (*http://bit.ly/2d2vbJT*), as found in *Enterprise Integration Patterns: Designing, Building, and Deploying Messaging Solutions* by Hohpe and Woolf (Addison-Wesley). Technically, doOnNext() can mutate the event. However, having mutable events controlled by Observable is a recipe for a disaster. Soon you will learn how to process events concurrently, fork execution, and so on. Guarding thread safety in each event would become a major problem. As a rule of thumb, all types wrapped with Observable should be immutable for all practical applications.

First we will walk through the execution path that RxJava takes. Every line in the previous code example creates new Observable, in a way wrapping the original one. For example, the first filter() does not remove 9 from Observable.just(8, 9, 10) Instead, it creates a new Observable that, when subscribed to, will eventually emit values 8 and 10. The same principle applies to most of the operators: they do not modify the contents or behavior of an existing Observable, they create new ones. However, saying that filter() or map() *creates* a new Observable is a bit of a shorthand. Most of the operators are lazy until someone actually subscribes. So what happens when Rx sees subscribe() at the very end of the chain? Understanding the internals will help you to realize how streams are processed under the hood. We will be looking at the code bottom-up.

- First, subscribe() informs the upstream Observable that it wants to receive values.

- The upstream Observable (filter(s -> s.length() < 4)) does not have any items by itself, it is just a decorator around another Obervable. So it subscribes to upstream, as well.

- map(i -> "#" + i * 10), just like filter(), is not able to deliver any items on its own. It barely transforms whatever it receives—thus, it must subscribe to upstream just like the others.

- The story continues until we reach just(8, 9, 10). This Observable is the true source of events. As soon as the filter(i -> i % 3 > 0) subscribes to it (as a consequence of our explicit subscribe() down below), it begins pumping the events downstream.

- Now we can observe how events are passed through all of the stages of the pipeline. `filter()` internally receives 8 and passes it downstream (`i % 3 > 0` predicate holds). Later on, `map()` transforms 8 into string `"#80"` and wakes up the `filter()` operator below it.
- The predicate `s.length() < 4` holds, and we can finally pass the transformed value into `System.out`.

Take your time to study how 9 and 10 are discarded to result with the following output, as produced by the version with `doOnNext()`:

```
A: 8
B: 8
C: #80
D: #80
A: 9
A: 10
B: 10
C: #100
```

Wrapping Up Using flatMap()

`flatMap()` is among the most important operators in RxJava. At first sight, it is similar to `map()` but the transformation of each element can return another (nested, inner) `Observable`. Recognizing that `Observable` can represent another asynchronous operation, we quickly discover that `flatMap()` can be used to spawn asynchronous computation for each upstream event (fork execution) and join the results back. Conceptually `flatMap()` takes `Observable<T>` and a function from `T` to `Observable<R>`. `flatMap()` first constructs `Observable<Observable<R>>` replacing all upstream values of type `T` with `Observable<R>` (just like `map()`). However, it does not stop there: it automatically subscribes to these inner `Observable<R>` streams to produce a single stream of type `R`, containing all values from all inner streams, as they come. The marble diagram that follows shows how this works:

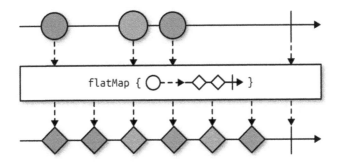

The marble diagram touches on an important aspect of flatMap(). Each upstream event (circle) is turned into an Observable of two diamonds separated by some delay. If two upstream events appear close to each other, flatMap() will automatically apply a transformation and turn them into two streams of diamonds. However, because RxJava concurrently subscribes to both of them and merges them together, events produced from one inner Observable can interleave with events from another. We will explore this behavior later.

flatMap() is the most fundamental operator in RxJava, using it one can easily[2] implement map() or filter():

```
import static rx.Observable.empty;
import static rx.Observable.just;

numbers.map(x -> x * 2);
numbers.filter(x -> x != 10);

//equivalent
numbers.flatMap(x -> just(x * 2));
numbers.flatMap(x -> (x != 10) ? just(x) : empty());
```

But first a more realistic example of flatMap(). Imagine that you receive a stream of photographs of cars entering a highway. For each car, we can run a rather expensive optical character recognition algorithm that returns the registration number from the license plate of the cars. Obviously, the recognition can fail, in which case this algorithm returns nothing. It can also fail with an exception, or for some bizarre reason it can return two license plates for a single car. This can be easily modeled with Observables:

```
Observable<CarPhoto> cars() {
    //...
}

Observable<LicensePlate> recognize(CarPhoto photo) {
    //...
}
```

By using Observable<LicensePlate> as the basis of the data stream you can model to accommodate the following:

- No license plate found on photo (empty stream)
- Fatal internal failure (onError() callback); for example, when a recognition module failed entirely and permanently without recovery options

---

2 However, RxJava has dedicated map() and filter() implementations due to performance reasons

- One or multiple license plates recognized, followed by `onComplete()`

And even better, `recognize()` can steadily produce better results over time—for example, starting from rough estimates or running two algorithms concurrently. This is how you can take advantage of the preceding methods:

```
Observable<CarPhoto> cars = cars();

Observable<Observable<LicensePlate>> plates =
        cars.map(this::recognize);

Observable<LicensePlate> plates2 =
        cars.flatMap(this::recognize);
```

Whatever you return from a function in `map()` is wrapped again inside an `Observable`. This means that if you return `Observable<LicensePlate>`, you would get `Observable<Observable<LicensePlate>>` in return. Not only is `Observable` nested in another `Observable` quite cumbersome to work with, you must first subscribe to each inner `Observable` to get any results. Moreover, you would have to somehow synchronize the inner results back to a single stream, which is very difficult.

`flatMap()` solves these problems by *flattening* the result so that you get a simple stream of `LicensePlates`. Additionally, in "Multithreading in RxJava" on page 140 we will learn how to parallelize work using `flatMap()`. As a rule of thumb, you use `flatMap()` for the following situations:

- The result of transformation in `map()` must be an `Observable`. For example, performing long-running, asynchronous operation on each element of the stream without blocking.
- You need a one-to-many transformation, a single event is expanded into multiple sub-events. For example, a stream of customers is translated into streams of their orders, for which each customer can have an arbitrary number of orders.

Now imagine that you would like to use a method returning an `Iterable` (like `List` or `Set`). For example, if `Customer` has a simple `List<Order> getOrders()`, you are forced to go through several operators to take advantage of it in `Observable` pipeline:

```
Observable<Customer> customers = //...
Observable<Order> orders = customers
        .flatMap(customer ->
            Observable.from(customer.getOrders()));
```

Or, equivalent and equally verbose:

```
Observable<Order> orders = customers
        .map(Customer::getOrders)
        .flatMap(Observable::from);
```

The need to map from a single item to `Iterable` is so popular that an operator, `flat MapIterable()`, was created to perform just such a transformation:

```
Observable<Order> orders = customers
        .flatMapIterable(Customer::getOrders);
```

You must take care when simply wrapping methods in an `Observable`. If `getOr ders()` was not a simple getter but an expensive operation in terms of run time, it is better to implement `getOrders()` to explicitly return `Observable<Order>`.

Another interesting variant of `flatMap()` can react not only to events, but on any notification, namely events, errors, and completion. The simplified signature of this `flatMap()` overload follows. For an `Observable<T>` we must provide the following:

- A function mapping single T → `Observable<R>`
- A function mapping an error notification → `Observable<R>`
- A no-arg function reacting on upstream completion that can return `Observa ble<R>`

Here is what the code looks like:

```
<R> Observable<R> flatMap(
        Func1<T, Observable<R>> onNext,
        Func1<Throwable, Observable<R>> onError,
        Func0<Observable<R>> onCompleted)
```

Imagine that you are creating a service that uploads videos. It takes a `UUID` and returns upload progress with `Observable<Long>`—how many bytes it transferred. We can take advantage of that progress anyway—for example, displaying it in the user interface. But what we are really interested in is completion, when the upload is finally done. Only after a successful upload can we begin rating the video. Naive implementation can simply subscribe to the progress stream, ignoring events and only reacting on completion (last callback):

```
void store(UUID id) {
    upload(id).subscribe(
            bytes -> {}, //ignore
            e -> log.error("Error", e),
            () -> rate(id)
    );
}

Observable<Long> upload(UUID id) {
    //...
}

Observable<Rating> rate(UUID id) {
    //...
}
```

However, notice that the `rate()` method actually returns `Observable<Rating>` that got lost. What we really want is for the `store()` method to return that second `Observable<Rating>`. But we can't simply call `upload()` and `rate()` concurrently, because the latter will fail if the former did not finish yet. The answer is `flatMap()` again in the most complex form:

```
upload(id)
        .flatMap(
                bytes -> Observable.empty(),
                e -> Observable.error(e),
                () -> rate(id)
        );
```

Take a moment to digest the preceding code snippet. We have an `Observable<Long>` as returned by the `upload()` method. For each progress update of type `Long` we return `Observable.empty()`, effectively discarding these events. We are not interested in progress indicator values. Moreover, we are not interested in errors, but contrary to logging them, we pass them through to the subscriber. Notice that the naive approach was simply logging errors, effectively hiding them. The rule of thumb is that if you don't know how to handle an exception, let your supervisor (e.g., the calling method, parent task, or downstream `Observable`) make a decision. Finally, the last lambda expression (`() -> rate(id)`) reacts upon stream completion. At this point, we replace completion notification with another `Observable<Rating>`. So, even if the original `Observable` wanted to terminate, we ignore that and in a way append a different `Observable`. Keep in mind that all three callbacks must return `Observable<R>` of the same type R.

In practice, we do not replace `map()` and `filter()` with `flatMap()` due to the clarity of code and performance. Just to make sure you understand the syntactic part of `flatMap()`, another abstract example translates from a sequence of characters to Morse code:

```
import static rx.Observable.empty;
import static rx.Observable.just;

Observable<Sound> toMorseCode(char ch) {
    switch(ch) {
        case 'a': return just(DI, DAH);
        case 'b': return just(DAH, DI, DI, DI);
        case 'c': return just(DAH, DI, DAH, DI);
        //...
        case 'p': return just(DI, DAH, DAH, DI);
        case 'r': return just(DI, DAH, DI);
        case 's': return just(DI, DI, DI);
        case 't': return just(DAH);
        //...
        default:
            return empty();
```

```
        }
    }

    enum Sound { DI, DAH }

    //...

    just('S', 'p', 'a', 'r', 't', 'a')
        .map(Character::toLowerCase)
        .flatMap(this::toMorseCode)
```

As you can clearly see, every character is replaced by a sequence of DI and DAH sounds (*dots* and *dashes*). When character is unrecognizable, an empty sequence is returned. flatMap() ensures that we get a steady, flat stream of sounds, as opposed to Observable<Observable<Sound>>, which we would get with plain map(). At this point, we touch an important aspect of flatMap(): order of events. This is best explained with an example, which will be much more enjoyable with *delay()* operator.

Postponing Events Using the delay() Operator

delay() basically takes an upstream Observable and shifts all events further in time. So, a construct as simple as:

```
    import java.util.concurrent.TimeUnit;


    just(x, y, z).delay(1, TimeUnit.SECONDS);
```

will not emit x, y and z immediately upon subscription but after given delay.

We already learned about the timer() operator in Chapter 2, and they are very similar. We can replace delay() with timer() and (surprise!) flatMap() like this:

```
    Observable
        .timer(1, TimeUnit.SECONDS)
        .flatMap(i -> Observable.just(x, y, z))
```

I hope this is clear: we generate an artificial event from timer() that we completely ignore. However, using flatMap() we replace that artificial event (zero, in i value) with three immediately emitted values: x, y, and z. This is somewhat equivalent to just(x, y, z).delay(1, SECONDS) in this particular case; however, it is not so in general. delay() is more comprehensive than timer() because it shifts every single event further by a given amount of time, whereas timer() simply "sleeps" and emits a special event after given time. For completeness, let us mention about an overloaded variant of delay() that can compute the amount of delay on a per-event basis rather than globally for every event. The following code snippet delays the emission of every String, depending on how long that String is:

```
import static rx.Observable.timer;
import static java.util.concurrent.TimeUnit.SECONDS;


Observable
    .just("Lorem", "ipsum", "dolor", "sit", "amet",
          "consectetur", "adipiscing", "elit")
    .delay(word -> timer(word.length(), SECONDS))
    .subscribe(System.out::println);

TimeUnit.SECONDS.sleep(15);
```

When running this program, even after subscribing, your application will terminate immediately without displaying any results because emission occurs in the background. In Chapter 4, you will learn about BlockingObservable that makes such simple testing easier. For the time being, though, we just put an arbitrary sleep() in the end. What you will notice then is that the first word to occur is *sit*, followed by *amet* and *elit* one second later. Remember that delay() can be rewritten to timer() plus flatMap()? Can you try that yourself? The solutions follows:

```
Observable
    .just("Lorem", "ipsum", "dolor", "sit", "amet",
          "consectetur", "adipiscing", "elit")
    .flatMap(word ->
        timer(word.length(), SECONDS).map(x -> word))
```

The preceding examples reveals an interesting characteristic of flatMap(): it does not preserve the original order of events. Knowing how delay() work, we can finally tackle this problem.

Order of Events After flatMap()

What flatMap() essentially does is take a *master* sequence (Observable) of values appearing over time (events) and replaces each of the events with an independent subsequence. These subsequences are generally unrelated to one another and to the event that generated them from master sequence. To make it clear, you no longer have a single the master sequence but a set of Observables, each working on its own, coming and going over time. Therefore, flatMap() cannot give *any* guarantee about what order of those subevents will arrive at the downstream operator/subscriber. Take this simple code snippet as an example:

```
just(10L, 1L)
    .flatMap(x ->
        just(x).delay(x, TimeUnit.SECONDS))
    .subscribe(System.out::println);
```

In this example, we delay event 10L by 10 seconds and event 1L (chronologically appearing later in upstream) by 1 second. As a result, we see 1 after a second and 10 nine seconds later—the order of events in upstream and downstream is different!

Even worse, imagine a `flatMap()` transformation producing multiple events (even infinite number of them) over wide range of time:

```
Observable
        .just(DayOfWeek.SUNDAY, DayOfWeek.MONDAY)
        .flatMap(this::loadRecordsFor);
```

The `loadRecordsFor()` method returns different streams depending on the day of the week:

```
Observable<String> loadRecordsFor(DayOfWeek dow) {
    switch(dow) {
        case SUNDAY:
            return Observable
                .interval(90, MILLISECONDS)
                .take(5)
                .map(i -> "Sun-" + i);
        case MONDAY:
            return Observable
                .interval(65, MILLISECONDS)
                .take(5)
                .map(i -> "Mon-" + i);
        //...
    }
}
```

The duplication in `loadRecordsFor()` is intentional to improve readability of the example that already was becoming increasingly complex. Nonetheless, let's study what this `flatMap()` is doing step by step. We have a simple `Observable` that emits days of the week: Sunday immediately followed by Monday. Now, we transform both of these values with a subsequence generated using `interval()`. A quick reminder, `interval()` will generate increasing numbers starting from zero preceded by a fixed delay. In our case, this delay depends on the day of the week: 65 and 90 milliseconds for Saturday and Monday, respectively. Both sequences are limited to the first five items (`take(5)`, see: "Slicing and Dicing Using skip(), takeWhile(), and Others" on page 94). What we ended up with here are two `Observables` counting up at the same time with different frequencies. What kind of output do you expect? The most straightforward answer would be this:

```
Sun-0, Sun-1, Sun-2, Sun-3, Sun-4, Mon-0, Mon-1, Mon-2, Mon-3, Mon-4
```

But, in fact, you have two streams that work independently but their results must somehow *merge* into a single `Observable`. When `flatMap()` encounters Sunday in the upstream, it immediately invokes `loadRecordsFor(Sunday)` and redirects all events emitted by the result of that function (`Observable<String>`) downstream. However, almost exactly at the same time, Monday appears and `flatMap()` calls `loadRecords For(Monday)`. Events from the latter substream are also passed downstream, interleaving with events from first substream. If `flatMap()` was suppose to avoid overlapping it would either need to buffer all subsequent sub-Observables until the first one finishes or subscribe to a second sub-Observable only when the first one completed. Such behavior is actually implemented in concatMap() (see "Preserving Order Using concatMap()" on page 75). But flatMap() instead subscribes to all substreams immediately and merges them together, pushing events downstream whenever any of the inner streams emit anything. All subsequences returned from flatMap() are merged and treated equally; that is, RxJava subscribes to all of them immediately and pushes events downstream evenly:

```
Mon-0, Sun-0, Mon-1, Sun-1, Mon-2, Mon-3, Sun-2, Mon-4, Sun-3, Sun-4
```

If you carefully track all delays, you will notice that this order is in fact correct. For example, even though Sunday was the first event in the upstream Observable, Mon-0 event appeared first because the substream produced by Monday begins emitting faster. This is also the reason why Mon-4 appears before Sun-3 and Sun-4.

Preserving Order Using concatMap()

What if you absolutely need to keep the order of downstream events so that they align perfectly with upstream events? In other words, downstream events resulted from upstream event N must occur before events from N + 1. It turns out there is a handy concatMap() operator that has the exact same syntax as flatMap() but works quite differently:

```
Observable
        .just(DayOfWeek.SUNDAY, DayOfWeek.MONDAY)
        .concatMap(this::loadRecordsFor);
```

This time the output is exactly what we anticipated:

```
Sun-0, Sun-1, Sun-2, Sun-3, Sun-4, Mon-0, Mon-1, Mon-2, Mon-3, Mon-4
```

So what happened under the hood? When the first event (Sunday) appears from upstream, concatMap() subscribes to an Observable returned from loadRecords For() and passes all events emitted from it downstream. When this inner stream completes, concatMap() waits for the next upstream event (Monday) and continues. concatMap() does not introduce any concurrency whatsoever but it preserves the order of upstream events, avoiding overlapping.

flatMap() uses the merge() operator internally that subscribes to all sub-Observables at the same time and does not make any distinction between them (see "Treating Several Observables as One Using merge()" on page 78). That is why downstream events interleave with one another. concatMap(), on the other hand, could technically use the concat() operator (see "Ways of Combining Streams: concat(), merge(), and switchOnNext()" on page 97). concat() subscribes only to the first underlying Observable and continues with the second one when the first one completes.

Controlling the concurrency of flatMap()

Suppose that you have a large list of users wrapped in an Observable. Each User has a loadProfile() method that returns an Observable<Profile> instance fetched using an HTTP request. Our aim is to load the profiles of all users as fast as possible. flatMap() was designed exactly for that: to allow spawning concurrent computation for each upstream value:

```
class User {
    Observable<Profile> loadProfile() {
        //Make HTTP request...
    }
}

class Profile {/* ... */}

//...

List<User> veryLargeList = //...
Observable<Profile> profiles = Observable
        .from(veryLargeList)
        .flatMap(User::loadProfile);
```

At first sight it looks great. Observable<User> is constructed from a fixed List using the from() operator; thus, when subscribed it emits all users pretty much instantaneously. For every new User flatMap() calls, loadProfile() returns Observable<Profile>. Then, flatMap() transparently subscribes to every new Observable<Profile>, redirecting all Profile events downstream. Subscription to inner Observable<Profile> most likely makes a new HTTP connection. Therefore, if we have, say 10,000 Users, we suddenly triggered 10,000 concurrent HTTP connections. If all of them hit the same server, we can expect any of the following:

- Rejected connections
- Long wait time and timeouts
- Crashing the server
- Hitting rate-limit or blacklisting

- Overall latency increase
- Issues on the client, including too many open sockets, threads, excessive memory usage

Increasing concurrency pays off only up to certain point. If you try to run too many operations concurrently, you will most likely end up with a lot of context switches, high memory and CPU utilization, and overall performance degradation. One solution could be to slow down `Observable<User>` somehow so that it does not emit all `Users` at once. However, tuning that delay to achieve optimal concurrency level is troublesome. Instead `flatMap()` has a very simple overloaded version that limits the total number of concurrent subscriptions to inner streams:

```
flatMap(User::loadProfile, 10);
```

The `maxConcurrent` parameter limits the number of ongoing inner `Observables`. In practice when `flatMap()` receives the first 10 `Users` it invokes `loadProfile()` for each of them. However, when the 11th `User` appears from upstream,[3] `flatMap()` will not even call `loadProfile()`. Instead, it will wait for any ongoing inner streams to complete. Therefore, the `maxConcurrent` parameter limits the number of background tasks that are forked from `flatMap()`.

You can probably see that `concatMap(f)` is semantically equivalent to `flatMap(f, 1)` —`flatMap()` with `maxConcurrent` equal to one. We could spend a couple of extra pages discussing the nuances of `flatMap()`, but more exciting operators lie ahead of us.

More Than One Observable

Transforming a single `Observable` is interesting, but what if there are more `Observables` that need to cooperate? If you come from traditional concurrent programing in Java, full of `Threads` and `Executors`, you know how difficult shared mutable state and synchronization is. Fortunately, RxJava works even better in such circumstances. Also the library has a consistent way of handling errors in all operators involving multiple streams. If any of the upstream sources emits an error notification, it will be forwarded downstream and complete the downstream sequence with an error, as well. If more than one upstream `Observable` emits an error, the first one wins and the others are discarded (any `Observable` can emit `onError` only once, see "Anatomy of rx.Observable" on page 27). Finally, if you want to continue processing and emit

---

3 Actually, `flatMap()` will not even *request* more users at this point, a feature that will be explained in "Honoring the Requested Amount of Data" on page 237

errors only when all normal events were produced, many operators have a `*DelayEr ror` variant.

Treating Several Observables as One Using merge()

Do you remember the `Observable<LicensePlate>` `recognize(CarPhoto photo)` method that was asynchronously trying to recognize `LicensePlate` from a `CarPhoto` in "Wrapping Up Using flatMap()" on page 67? We mentioned briefly that such a stream can actually use several algorithms at the same time, some being faster, others being more precise. However, we do not want to expose the details of these algorithms to the outside world, we just want a stream of progressively better results from each algorithm, from fastest to most accurate.

Imagine that we have three algorithms that are already RxJava-enabled, each one nicely encapsulated within `Observable`. Of course, each algorithm alone can produce zero to possibly an infinite number of results:

```
Observable<LicensePlate> fastAlgo(CarPhoto photo) {
    //Fast but poor quality
}

Observable<LicensePlate> preciseAlgo(CarPhoto photo) {
    //Precise but can be expensive
}

Observable<LicensePlate> experimentalAlgo(CarPhoto photo) {
    //Unpredictable, running anyway
}
```

What we would like to do is run these three algorithms side by side (see: "Declarative Subscription with subscribeOn()" on page 150 for more details how RxJava handles concurrency) and receive results as soon as possible. We do not care which algorithm emitted an event, we want to catch all of them and aggregate into a single stream. This is what the `merge()` operator does:

```
Observable<LicensePlate> all = Observable.merge(
        preciseAlgo(photo),
        fastAlgo(photo),
        experimentalAlgo(photo)
);
```

I intentionally placed `preciseAlgo()` (presumably slowest) first to emphasize that the order of `Observables` passed to `merge()` is rather arbitrary. The `merge()` operator will keep a reference to all of the underlying `Observables`, and as soon as someone subscribes to `Observable<LicensePlate>` `all`, it will automatically subscribe to all upstream `Observables` at once. No matter which one emits a value first, it will be forwarded to the `Observer` of `all`. Of course, the `merge()` operator follows the Rx contract (see "Anatomy of rx.Observable" on page 27), ensuring that events are serialized (do not overlap), even if underlying streams each emit a value at the same time. The following marble diagram illustrates how merge() works:

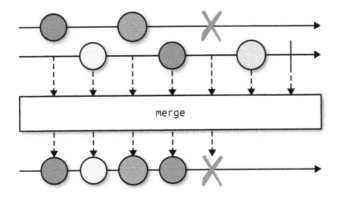

The merge() operator is used extensively when you want to treat multiple sources of events of the same type as a single source.[4] Also, if you have just two Observables you want to merge(), you can use obs1.mergeWith(obs2) instance method.

Keep in mind that errors appearing in any of the underlying Observables will be eagerly propagated to Observers. You can use the mergeDelayError() variant of merge() to postpone any errors until all of the other streams have finished. mergeDe layError() will even make sure to collect all exceptions, not only the first one, and encapsulate them in rx.exceptions.CompositeException.

Pairwise Composing Using zip() and zipWith()

Zipping is the act of taking two (or more) streams and combining them with each other in such a way that each element from one stream is paired with corresponding event from the other. A downstream event is produced by composing the first event from each, second event from each stream, and so on. Therefore, events appear only when all upstream sources emit an event. This is useful when you want to combine results from multiple streams that are somehow related to one another. Or, quite the contrary, when two independent streams emit values but only combining them together has business meaning. The following marble diagram illustrates how this works:

---

4 This is the *join* stage in some types of computation.

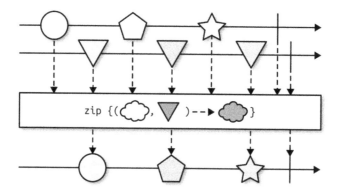

The zip() and zipWith() operators are equivalent. We use the former when we want to fluently compose one stream with another, like so: s1.zipWith(s2, ...). But when we have more than two streams to compose, static zip() on Observable can take up to nine streams:

```
Observable.zip(s1, s2, s3...)
```

There are many other operators that have instance and static variants—for example, merge() and mergeWith(). To understand zip(), imagine that you have two independent streams, yet those streams are entirely synchronized with each other. For example, think about the WeatherStation API that exposes temperature and wind measurements precisely every minute at the same time:

```
interface WeatherStation {
    Observable<Temperature> temperature();
    Observable<Wind> wind();
}
```

We have to make an assumption that events from these two Observables are emitted at the same time and thus with the same frequency. Under this restriction, we can safely join these two streams by combining every pair of events. This means that when an event occurs on one stream, we must hold it until the other appears, and vice versa. The name *zip* implies that there are two flows of events that we join together, one from left, one from right, repeat. But in a more general version, zip() can take up to nine upstream Observables and emit an event only when all of them emit an event.

It seems like a perfect return type for zip() would be tuple or pair (two-element tuple). Unfortunately, Java has no built-in data structure for pairs, and RxJava does not have any external dependencies. Feel free to use the Pair implementation from Apache Commons Lang (*http://bit.ly/2d2BYmQ*), Javaslang (*http://bit.ly/2d2Cm4R*), or Android SDK (*http://bit.ly/2d2BXPS*). Or provide a function or data structure to combine pairs of events together:

```
class Weather {
    public Weather(Temperature temperature, Wind wind) {
        //...
    }
}

//...

Observable<Temperature> temperatureMeasurements = station.temperature();
Observable<Wind> windMeasurements = station.wind();

temperatureMeasurements
    .zipWith(windMeasurements,
        (temperature, wind) -> new Weather(temperature, wind));
```

When a new `Temperature` event occurs, `zipWith()` waits (obviously without block-ing!) for `Wind`, and vice versa. Two events are passed to our custom lambda[5] and com-bined into a `Weather` object. Then, the cycle repeats. `zip()` was described in terms of streams, even infinite ones. However, often you will find yourself using `zipWith()` and `zip()` for `Observable`s that emit exactly one item. Such an `Observable` is typi-cally an asynchronous response to some request or action. We will go into details of how you can use RxJava in real applications in Chapter 4.

For the time being, let's study an example. We will need to produce a *Cartesian prod-uct* of all values from two streams. For example we might have two `Observable`s, one with chessboard's rows (*ranks*, 1 to 8) and one with columns (*files*, a to h). We would like to find all possible 64 squares on a chessboard:

```
Observable<Integer> oneToEight = Observable.range(1, 8);
Observable<String> ranks = oneToEight
    .map(Object::toString);
Observable<String> files = oneToEight
    .map(x -> 'a' + x - 1)
    .map(ascii -> (char)ascii.intValue())
    .map(ch -> Character.toString(ch));

Observable<String> squares = files
    .flatMap(file -> ranks.map(rank -> file + rank));
```

The `squares` `Observable` will emit exactly 64 events: for 1 it generates a1, a2,...a8, followed by b1, b2, and so on until it finally reaches h7 and h8. This is another inter-esting example of `flatMap()`—for each column (*file*), generate all possible squares in that column. Now onto a more realistic example that also employs Cartesian product. Suppose that you would like to plan a one-day vacation in some city when the

---

5 Shorter lambda syntax `Weather::new` is also possible here.

weather is sunny and airfare and hotels are cheap. To do so, we will combine several streams together and come up with all possible results:

```
import java.time.LocalDate;

Observable<LocalDate> nextTenDays =
    Observable
        .range(1, 10)
        .map(i -> LocalDate.now().plusDays(i));

Observable<Vacation> possibleVacations = Observable
    .just(City.Warsaw, City.London, City.Paris)
    .flatMap(city -> nextTenDays.map(date -> new Vacation(city, date))
    .flatMap(vacation ->
        Observable.zip(
            vacation.weather().filter(Weather::isSunny),
            vacation.cheapFlightFrom(City.NewYork),
            vacation.cheapHotel(),
            (w, f, h) -> vacation
        ));
```

Vacation class:

```
class Vacation {
    private final City where;
    private final LocalDate when;

    Vacation(City where, LocalDate when) {
        this.where = where;
        this.when = when;
    }

    public Observable<Weather> weather() {
        //...
    }

    public Observable<Flight> cheapFlightFrom(City from) {
        //...
    }

    public Observable<Hotel> cheapHotel() {
        //...
    }
}
```

Quite a lot is happening in the preceding code. First, we generate all dates from tomorrow to 10 days ahead using a combination of range() and map(). Then, we flatMap() these days with three cities—we do not want to use zip() here, because we need all possible combinations of date versus city pairs. For each such pair, we create an instance of Vacation class encapsulating it. Now the real logic: we zip together three Observables: Observable<Weather>, Observable<Flight>, and Observa

---

ble<Hotel>. The last two are supposed to return a zero or one result depending on whether cheap flight or hotel was found for that city/date. Even though Observable<Weather> always returns something, however, we use filter(Weather::sunny) to discard nonsunny weather. So we end up with zip() operation of three streams, each emitting zero to one items. zip() completes early if any of the upstream Observables complete, discarding other streams early: thanks to this property, if any of weather, flight, or hotel is absent, the result of zip() completes with no items being emitted, as well. This leaves us with a stream of all possible vacation plans matching requirements.

Do not be surprised to see a zip function that does not take arguments into account: (w, f, h) -> vacation. An outer stream of Vacation lists all possible vacation plans for every possible day. However, for each vacation, we want to make sure weather, cheap flight, and hotel are present. If all these conditions are met, we return vacation instance; otherwise, zip will not invoke our lambda expression at all.

When Streams Are Not Synchronized with One Another: combineLatest(), withLatestFrom(), and amb()

In "Pairwise Composing Using zip() and zipWith()" on page 79, we made a very bold assumption that two Observables always produce events with the same frequency and at a similar point in time. However if one of the streams outperforms the other even slightly, events from the faster Observable will need to wait longer and longer for the lagging stream. To illustrate this effect, let's first zip() two streams that are producing items at the exact same pace:

```
Observable<Long> red   = Observable.interval(10, TimeUnit.MILLISECONDS);
Observable<Long> green = Observable.interval(10, TimeUnit.MILLISECONDS);

Observable.zip(
    red.timestamp(),
    green.timestamp(),
    (r, g) -> r.getTimestampMillis() - g.getTimestampMillis()
).forEach(System.out::println);
```

red and green Observables are producing items with the same frequency. For each item, we attach timestamp() so that we know exactly when it was emitted.

timestamp()

The timestamp() operator wraps whatever the event type T was with rx.schedulers.Timestamped<T> class having two attributes: original value of type T and long timestamp when it was created.

In zip() transformation, we simply compare the time difference between creation of events in each stream. When streams are synchronized, this value oscillates around zero. However, if we slightly slow down one Observable, say green becomes Observable.interval(11, MILLISECONDS), the situation is much different. The time difference between red and green keeps going up: red is consumed in real time but it must wait, increasing the amount of time for the slower item. Over time this difference piles up and can lead to stale data or even memory leak (see "Memory Consumption and Leaks" on page 315). In practice zip() must be used carefully.

What we actually expect is emitting a pair every time *any* upstream produces an event, using the latest known value from the other stream. This is where combineLatest() becomes useful, as illustrated by the following marble diagram:

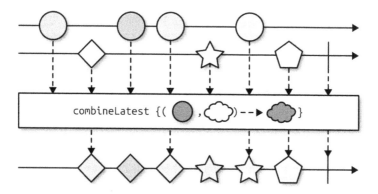

Take the following artificial example. One stream produces S0, S1, S2 values every 17 milliseconds whereas the other F0, F1, F2 every 10 milliseconds (considerably faster):

```
import static java.util.concurrent.TimeUnit.MILLISECONDS;
import static rx.Observable.interval;

Observable.combineLatest(
    interval(17, MILLISECONDS).map(x -> "S" + x),
    interval(10, MILLISECONDS).map(x -> "F" + x),
    (s, f) -> f + ":" + s
).forEach(System.out::println);
```

We combine these two streams and produce a new value every time any of the streams produces something. The output quickly becomes out-of-sync, but at least values are consumed in real time, and the faster stream does not need to wait for the slower one:

```
F0:S0
F1:S0
F2:S0
F2:S1
```

```
F3:S1
F4:S1
F4:S2
F5:S2
F5:S3
...
F998:S586
F998:S587
F999:S587
F1000:S587
F1000:S588
F1001:S588
```

Notice how the new item appears downstream on each new F event: `F0:S0`, `F1:S0`, `F2:S0`. RxJava notices the new event on the fast stream so takes whatever the latest value was of the slow stream (it still has two wait for at least one event!)—`S0` in this case—and produces a new pair. However, neither stream is distinguished: when the new slow `S1` appears, the latest known fast value (`F2`) is taken and combined, as well. After about 10 seconds we encounter the `F1000:S588` event. Everything adds up: during 10 seconds, fast stream produced about 1,000 events, whereas the slow stream only 588 (10 seconds divided by 17 milliseconds).

withLatestFrom() operator

`combineLatest` is symmetric, which means that it does not distinguish between the substreams it combines. Occasionally, however, you want to emit an event every time something appears in one stream with latest value from the second stream, but not vice versa. In other words, events from the second stream do not trigger a downstream event; they are used only when first stream emits. You can achieve such behavior by using the new `withLatestFrom()` operator. Let's illustrate it with the same `slow` and `fast` streams:

```
Observable<String> fast = interval(10, MILLISECONDS).map(x -> "F" + x);
Observable<String> slow = interval(17, MILLISECONDS).map(x -> "S" + x);
slow
    .withLatestFrom(fast, (s, f) -> s + ":" + f)
    .forEach(System.out::println);
```

In the prior example, the `slow` stream is primary, the resulting `Observable` will *always* emit an event when `slow` emits, providing `fast` emitted at least one element so far. Conversely, `fast` stream is just a helper used only when `slow` emits something. The function passed as the second argument to `withLatestFrom()` will combine every new value from `slow` with the most recent value from `fast`. However, new values from `fast` are not propagated downstream; they are just updated internally when the new `slow` appears. The output of the preceding code snippet reveals that all `slow` events appear exactly once, whereas some `fast` events are dropped:

```
S0:F1
S1:F2
S2:F4
S3:F5
S4:F7
S5:F9
S6:F11
...
```

All `slow` events appearing before the first `fast` event are silently dropped because there is nothing with which to combine them. This is by design, but if you truly need to preserve all events from the primary stream, you must ensure that the other stream emits some dummy event as soon as possible. For example, you can prepend said stream with some dummy event emitted immediately. The example that follows artificially slows the `fast` stream by pushing all events 100 milliseconds forward (see "Postponing Events Using the delay() Operator" on page 72). Without a dummy event, we would lose a few `slow` events; however, by using the `startWith()` operator we create a new `Observable` that derives from `fast`. It starts with "FX" immediately and then continues with events from the original `fast` stream:

```
Observable<String> fast = interval(10, MILLISECONDS)
        .map(x -> "F" + x)
        .delay(100, MILLISECONDS)
        .startWith("FX");
Observable<String> slow = interval(17, MILLISECONDS).map(x -> "S" + x);
slow
        .withLatestFrom(fast, (s, f) -> s + ":" + f)
        .forEach(System.out::println);
```

The output reveals that no `slow` events are dropped. However, in the beginning we see dummy "FX" events a few times, until the first "F0" shows up after 100 milliseconds:

```
S0:FX
S1:FX
S2:FX
S3:FX
S4:FX
S5:FX
S6:F1
S7:F3
S8:F4
S9:F6
...
```

`startWith()` basically returns a new `Observable` that, upon subscription, first emits some constant values (like "FX") followed by original `Observable`. For example, the following code block yields 0, 1 and 2, in that order:

```
Observable
    .just(1, 2)
    .startWith(0)
    .subscribe(System.out::println);
```

See also "Slicing and Dicing Using skip(), takeWhile(), and Others" on page 94 for examples of a similar concat() operator.

amb() operator

The last tiny operator that can become useful is amb() (together with ambWith()), which subscribes to all upstream Observables it controls and waits for the very first item emitted. When one of the Observables emits the first event, amb() discards all other streams and just keep forwarding events from the first Observable that woke up, as shown in the following marble diagram:

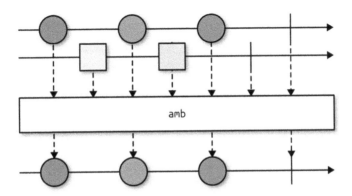

The sample that follows illustrates how amb() works with two streams. Pay attention to initialDelay parameter that controls which Observable starts emitting first:

```
Observable<String> stream(int initialDelay, int interval, String name) {
    return Observable
        .interval(initialDelay, interval, MILLISECONDS)
        .map(x -> name + x)
        .doOnSubscribe(() ->
            log.info("Subscribe to " + name))
        .doOnUnsubscribe(() ->
            log.info("Unsubscribe from " + name));
}

//...

Observable.amb(
        stream(100, 17, "S"),
        stream(200, 10, "F")
).subscribe(log::info);
```

You can write an equivalent program using nonstatic `ambWith()`, but it is less reada-ble because it hides the symmetry of `amb()`. It seems like we are applying the second stream on top of the first, whereas both of them should be treated equally:

```
stream(100, 17, "S")
        .ambWith(stream(200, 10, "F"))
        .subscribe(log::info);
```

No matter which version you prefer, they yield the same results. The `slow` stream produces events less frequently, but the first event appears after 100 milliseconds, whereas the `fast` stream begins after 200 milliseconds. What `amb()` does is first sub-scribe to both `Observables`, and when it encounters the first event in the `slow` stream, it immediately unsubscribes from the fast one and forwards events from only the slow one:

```
14:46:13.334: Subscribe to S
14:46:13.341: Subscribe to F
14:46:13.439: Unsubscribe from F
14:46:13.442: S0
14:46:13.456: S1
14:46:13.473: S2
14:46:13.490: S3
14:46:13.507: S4
14:46:13.525: S5
```

`doOnSubscribe()` and `doOnUnsubscribe()` callbacks are useful for debugging pur-poses (see "doOn...() Callbacks" on page 270). Notice how unsubscription from F occurs roughly 100 millisecond after subscription to S; this is the moment when first event from S `Observable` appeared. At this point, listening for events from F no longer makes any sense.

Advanced Operators: collect(), reduce(), scan(), distinct(), and groupBy()

Some operators allow more advanced transformations such as scanning through the sequence and aggregating some value along the way, like a running average. Some operators are even stateful, managing internal state while the sequence progresses. This is how `distinct` works, caching and discarding already visited values.

Scanning Through the Sequence with Scan and Reduce

All operators we explored so far operated on a per-event basis (e.g., filtering, map-ping, or zipping). But sometimes you want to aggregate events to shrink the initial stream or simplify it. For example, consider an `Observable<Long>` that monitors pro-gress of data transfer. Every time a chunk of data is sent, a single `Long` value appears telling, indicating the size of that chunk. This is a useful bit of information, but what we really want to know is how many bytes were transferred in total. A very bad idea is to use global state modified inside an operator:

```
import java.util.concurrent.atomic.LongAdder;


//BROKEN!
Observable<Long> progress = transferFile();

LongAdder total = new LongAdder();
progress.subscribe(total::add);
```

The preceding code can lead to very unpleasant concurrency bugs, just like any other shared state. Lambda expressions within operators can be executed from arbitrary threads so global state must be thread safe. We must also take laziness into account. RxJava tries to minimize global state and mutability as much as possible by providing composable operators. Modifying global state is tricky, even with Rx guarantees. Moreover, we can no longer rely on Rx operators to further compose total–for example, by periodically updating user interface. Signaling when a transfer is completed is also more complex. What we really want is a way to incrementally accumulate sizes of data chunks and report the current total, every time a new chunk appears. This is what our hypothetical stream should look like:

```
Observable<Long> progress =       // [10, 14, 12, 13, 14, 16]
Observable<Long> totalProgress = /* [10, 24, 36, 49, 63, 79]

    10
    10+14=24
            24+12=36
                    36+13=49
                            49+14=63
                                    63+16=79
    */
```

The first item is propagated *as-is* (10). However, before the second item (14) is passed downstream it is added to the previous emitted item (10), emitting 24 (the sum of the first two items). The third item (12) is again added to the previous item from the resulting stream (24), emitting 36. This iterative process continues until the upstream Observable completes. At this point, the last item emitted is the total of all upstream events. You can implement this relatively complex workflow easily by using the scan() operator:

```
Observable<Long> totalProgress = progress
    .scan((total, chunk) -> total + chunk);
```

scan() takes two parameters: the last generated value (known as the *accumulator*) and current value from upstream Observable. In the first iteration, total is simply the first item from progress, whereas in the second iteration it becomes the result of scan() from the previous one. This is illustrated in Table 3-1.

Table 3-1. Each row represents one scan() iteration

progress	total	chunk	totalProgress
10	-	-	-
14	10	14	24
12	24	12	36
13	36	13	49
14	49	14	63
16	63	16	79

`scan()` is like a bulldozer, going through the source (upstream) `Observable` and accumulating items. Overloaded version of `scan()` can provide an initial value (if it is different than simply the first element):

```
Observable<BigInteger> factorials = Observable
    .range(2, 100)
    .scan(BigInteger.ONE, (big, cur) ->
        big.multiply(BigInteger.valueOf(cur)));
```

`factorials` will generate 1, 2, 6, 24, 120, 720..., and so forth. Notice that the upstream `Observable` starts from 2 but the downstream starts from 1, which was our initial value (`BigInteger.ONE`). The rule of thumb is that the type of resulting `Observable` is always the same as the type of accumulator. So, if you do not provide a custom initial value of accumulator, the type `T` returned from `scan()` will not change. Otherwise (like in our `factorials` example), the result is of type `Observable<BigInteger>` because `BigInteger` was the type of initial value. Obviously, this type cannot change throughout the scanning process.

Sometimes, we do not care about intermediate results, just the final one. For example, we want to calculate total bytes transferred, not intermediate progress. Or, we would like to accumulate all values in some mutable data structure, like `ArrayList`, adding one item at a time. The `reduce()` operator was designed precisely for that. One rather obvious caveat: if your sequence is infinite, `scan()` keeps emitting events for each upstream event, whereas `reduce()` will never emit any event. Imagine that you have a source of `CashTransfer` objects with `getAmount()` method returning `BigDecimal`. We would like to calculate the total amount on all transfers. The following two transformations are equivalent. They iterate over all transfers and add up amounts, beginning at ZERO:

```
Observable<CashTransfer> transfers = //...;
```

```
Observable<BigDecimal> total1 = transfers
    .reduce(BigDecimal.ZERO,
        (totalSoFar, transfer) ->
            totalSoFar.add(transfer.getAmount()));
```

```
Observable<BigDecimal> total2 = transfers
    .map(CashTransfer::getAmount)
    .reduce(BigDecimal.ZERO, BigDecimal::add);
```

Both transformations yield the same result, but the second one seems simpler, despite using two steps. This is another reason to prefer smaller, more composable transformations over a single big one. Also you can probably see that reduce() is basically scan() talking only to the last element. As a matter of fact, you can implement it as follows:

```
public <R> Observable<R> reduce(
        R initialValue,
        Func2<R, T, R> accumulator) {
    return scan(initialValue, accumulator).takeLast(1);
}
```

As you can see, reduce() simply scans through the Observable but discards all but the last item (see "Slicing and Dicing Using skip(), takeWhile(), and Others" on page 94).

Reduction with Mutable Accumulator: collect()

Now, let's transform the finite stream of events of type T into a stream with just a single event of type List<T>. Of course, that event is emitted when upstream Observable<T> completes:

```
Observable<List<Integer>> all = Observable
    .range(10, 20)
    .reduce(new ArrayList<>(), (list, item) -> {
        list.add(item);
        return list;
    });
```

This example of reduce() simply begins with empty ArrayList<Integer> (an accumulator) and adds every emitted item to that ArrayList. The lambda expression responsible for reduction (accumulating) must return a new version of accumulator. Unfortunately, List.add() does not return said List; instead, it returns boolean. An explicit return statement is required. To overcome this verboseness, you can use the collect() operator. It works almost exactly like reduce() but assumes that we use the same mutable accumulator for every event as opposed to returning a new immutable accumulator every time (compare this to the immutable BigInteger example):

```
Observable<List<Integer>> all = Observable
    .range(10, 20)
    .collect(ArrayList::new, List::add);
```

Another useful use case for collect() is aggregating all events into a StringBuilder. In that case, the accumulator is an empty StringBuilder and an operation appends one item to that builder:

```
Observable<String> str = Observable
        .range(1, 10)
        .collect(
                StringBuilder::new,
                (sb, x) -> sb.append(x).append(", "))
        .map(StringBuilder::toString);
```

Just like every Observable operator, both reduce() and collect() are nonblocking, so the resulting List<Integer> containing all numbers emitted from Observable.range(10, 20) will appear when upstream signals completion; exceptions are propagated normally. Transforming Observable<T> into Observable<List<T>> is so common that a built-in toList() operator exists. See "BlockingObservable: Exiting the Reactive World" on page 118 for real life use cases.

Asserting Observable Has Exactly One Item Using single()

By the way, some Observables by definition must emit exactly one value. For example, the preceding code snippet will always emit one List<Integer>, even an empty one. In such circumstances, it is worthwhile to apply a single() operator. It does not change the upstream Observable in any way; however, it makes sure it emits exactly one event. In case this assumption is wrong, you will receive an exception instead of an unexpected result.

Dropping Duplicates Using distinct() and distinctUntilChanged()

An infinite stream of simply random values can be really useful, typically when combined with other streams. The following Observable produces pseudo-random Integer values from 0 to 1,000 exclusive:

```
Observable<Integer> randomInts = Observable.create(subscriber -> {
    Random random = new Random();
    while (!subscriber.isUnsubscribed()) {
        subscriber.onNext(random.nextInt(1000));
    }
});
```

Obviously, duplicates can occur, and take(1001) is guaranteed to have at least one.[6] But what if we want to take a peek at smaller (say, 10) *unique* random values? The built-in distinct() operator automatically discards events from upstream Observable that already occurred, making sure only unique events are passed downstream:

---

6 There are only 1,000 possible unique outcomes of nextInt(1000).

```
Observable<Integer> uniqueRandomInts = randomInts
        .distinct()
        .take(10);
```

Every time a new value is emitted from the upstream Observable (randomInts), the distinct() operator internally makes sure such value did not occur before. The comparison happens by means of equals() and hashCode(), so ensure that you implement them according to Java guidelines (two equal objects *must* have the same hash code). Interestingly, take(1001) would eventually emit every single value from 0 to 999 in random order and never complete because there is no 1,001st unique int between 0 and 999.

In "Use Case: From Callback API to Observable Stream" on page 45, we looked at Observable<twitter4j.Status> that was emitting status updates generated on social media website Twitter. Every time any user posted a status update, new event was pushed from that Observable. The Status object contains several attributes, like get Text(), getUser(), and so on. The distinct() operator makes no sense for Status events, given that duplicates are virtually impossible. But, what if we would like to see the text of only the very first update per each user (status.getUser().getId() returning long)? Obviously, we can extract that unique property and run distinct() on that:

```
Observable<Status> tweets = //...

Observable<Long> distinctUserIds = tweets
        .map(status -> status.getUser().getId())
        .distinct();
```

Unfortunately, by the time we get to execute distinct(), the original Status object is lost. What we really need is a way to extract a property of event used to determine uniqueness. Two events are considered equal (and the latter being discarded as a result) if that extracted property (known as *key*) was already seen:

```
Observable<Status> distinctUserIds = tweets
        .distinct(status -> status.getUser().getId());
```

Whatever we return as *key* is compared using equals() and hashCode() to already seen keys. Be sure to remember that distinct() must keep in mind all events/keys seen so far for eternity. (See "Memory Consumption and Leaks" on page 315. dis tinct() is useful when we want to process unique events only once.)

In practice, distinctUntilChanged() is often more reasonable. In the case of dis tinctUntilChanged(), any given event is discarded only if the previous event was the same (by default using equals() for comparison). distinctUntilChanged() works best when we receive a steady stream of some measurements and we want to be noti fied only when the measured value actually changed. In "Pairwise Composing Using zip() and zipWith()" on page 79 we experimented with Observable<Weather>, with

Weather having two attributes: Temperature and Wind. A new Weather event can appear once every minute, but the weather does not change that often, so we would like to drop duplicated events and focus only on changes:

```
Observable<Weather> measurements = //...

Observable<Weather> tempChanges = measurements
        .distinctUntilChanged(Weather::getTemperature);
```

The preceding code snippet emits a Weather event only when the temperature changes (changes to Wind are not taken into account). Obviously, if we want to an emit event every time either Temperature or Wind changes, parameterless distinctUntilChanged() would work great, assuming that Weather implements equals(). The important difference between distinct() and distinctUntilChanged() is that the latter can produce duplicates but only if they were separated by a different value. For example, the same temperature might occur every day, separated by colder and warmer measurements. Also distinctUntilChanged() must only remember the last seen value, as opposed to distinct(), which must keep track of all unique values since the beginning of the stream. This means that distinctUntilChanged() has a predictable, constant memory footprint, as opposed to distinct().

Slicing and Dicing Using skip(), takeWhile(), and Others

You are never obligated to read the stream fully, especially but not exclusively when dealing with hot infinite Observables. As a matter of fact, it is a common practice to slice Observable and consume just a small subset. Most operators in this section have examples unless they follow the principle of least astonishment. Yet operators such as take or last are too useful to be omitted. Here is a nonexhaustive list of such operators:

take(n) *and* skip(n)

The take(n) operator will truncate the source Observable prematurely after emitting only the first n events from upstream, unsubscribing afterward (or complete earlier if upstream did not have n items). skip(n) is the exact opposite; it discards the first n elements and begins emitting events from the upstream Observable beginning with event n+1. Both operators are quite liberal: negative numbers are treated as zero, exceeding the Observable size is not treated as a bug:

```
Observable.range(1, 5).take(3);  // [1, 2, 3]
Observable.range(1, 5).skip(3);  // [4, 5]
Observable.range(1, 5).skip(5);  // []
```

takeLast(n) *and* skipLast(n)

Another self-descriptive pair of operators. takeLast(n) emits only the last n values from the stream before it completes. Internally, this operator must keep a buffer of the last n values and when it receives completion notification, it immediately emits the entire buffer. It makes no sense to call takeLast() on an infinite stream because it will never emit anything—the stream never ends, so there are no *last events*. skipLast(n), on the other hand, emits all values from upstream Observable except the last n. Internally, skipLast() can emit the first value from upstream only when it received n+1 elements, second when it received n+2, and so on.

```
Observable.range(1, 5).takeLast(2);  // [4, 5]
Observable.range(1, 5).skipLast(2);  // [1, 2, 3]
```

first() *and* last()

The parameterless first() and last() operators can be implement via take(1).single() and takeLast(1).single() accordingly, which should pretty much describe their behavior. The extra single() operator ensures that the downstream Observable emits precisely one value or exception. Additionally, both first() and last() have overloaded versions that take predicates. Rather than returning the very first/last value they emit first/last value, matching a given condition.

takeFirst(predicate)

The takeFirst(predicate) operator can be expressed by filter(predi cate).take(1). The only difference between this one and first(predicate) is that it will not break with NoSuchElementException in case of missing matching values.

takeUntil(predicate) *and* takeWhile(predicate)

takeUntil(predicate) and takeWhile(predicate) are closely related to each other. takeUntil() emits values from the source Observable but completes and unsubscribes after emitting the very first value *matching* predicate. take While(), conversely, emits values as long as they match a given predicate. So the only difference is that takeUntil() will emit the first nonmatching value, whereas takeWhile() will not. These operators are quite important because they provide a means of conditionally unsubscribing from an Observable based on the events being emitted. Otherwise, the operator would need to somehow interact with the Subscription instance (see "Controlling Listeners by Using Subscription and Subscriber<T>" on page 32), which is not available when the operator is invoked.

```
Observable.range(1, 5).takeUntil(x -> x == 3);  // [1, 2, 3]
Observable.range(1, 5).takeWhile(x -> x != 3);  // [1, 2]
```

elementAt(n)

Extracting a specific item by index is rather uncommon, but you can use the built-in elementAt(n) operator for that. It is quite strict, and it can result in an IndexOutOfBoundsException being emitted when upstream Observable is not long enough or the index is negative. Of course, it returns Observable<T> of the same type T as upstream.

...OrDefault() *operators*

Many operators in this section are strict and can result in exceptions being thrown—for example, first() when upstream Observable is empty. Under these circumstances many ...OrDefault operators were introduced to replace exceptions with a default value. All of them are rather self-explanatory: elementAtOrDefault(), firstOrDefault(), lastOrDefault(), and singleOrDefault().

count()

count() is an interesting operator that calculates how many events were emitted by upstream Observable. By the way, if you need to know how many items matching a given predicate that the upstream Observable emitted, filter(predicate).count() can do that idiomatically. Do not worry, all operators are lazy so this will work even for quite large streams. Obviously, count() never emits any value in case of infinite stream. You can implement`count()` easily by using reduce()):

```
Observable<Integer> size = Observable
        .just('A', 'B', 'C', 'D')
        .reduce(0, (sizeSoFar, ch) -> sizeSoFar + 1);
```

all(predicate), exists(predicate), *and* contains(value)

Sometimes, it is useful to ensure that all events from a given Observable match some predicate. The all(predicate) operator will emit true when upstream completes and all values matched the predicate. However, false will be emitted as soon as first nonconforming value is found. exists(predicate) is the exact opposite of all(); it emits true when the first matching value is found but false in case of upstream completing without any matching value found. Often, our predicate in exists() simply compares upstream values with some constants. In that case, you can use the contains() operator:

```
Observable<Integer> numbers = Observable.range(1, 5);

numbers.all(x -> x != 4);    // [false]
numbers.exists(x -> x == 4); // [true]
numbers.contains(4);         // [true]
```

Ways of Combining Streams: concat(), merge(), and switchOnNext()

concat() (and instance method concatWith()) allow joining together two Observa bles: when the first one completes, concat() subscribes to the second one. Importantly, concat() will subscribe to the second Observable if, and only if, the first one is completed (see also "Preserving Order Using concatMap()" on page 75). concat() can even work with the same upstream Observable with different operators applied. For example if we would like to receive only the first few and last few items from a very long stream, we could use the following:

```
Observable<Data> veryLong = //...
final Observable<Data> ends = Observable.concat(
        veryLong.take(5),
        veryLong.takeLast(5)
);
```

Keep in mind that the preceding code example subscribes to veryLong twice, which might be undesirable. Another example of concat() is providing fallback value when first stream did not emit anything:

```
Observable<Car> fromCache = loadFromCache();
Observable<Car> fromDb = loadFromDb();

Observable<Car> found = Observable
        .concat(fromCache, fromDb)
        .first();
```

Observables are lazy, so neither loadFromCache() nor loadFromDb() actually load any data yet. loadFromCache() can complete without emitting any events when cache is empty, but loadFromDb() always emits one Car. concat() followed by first() will initially subscribe to fromCache and if that emits one item, concat() will not subscribe to fromDb. However, if fromCache is empty, concat() will continue with fromDb, subscribe to it, and load data from database.

The concat() operator is actually closely related to merge() and switchMap(). con cat() works like concatenation on ordinary List<T>: first, it takes all items from the first stream and only when it completes, it begins consuming second stream. Of course, like all operators we met so far, concat() is nonblocking, it emits events only when the underlying stream emits something. Now, let's compare concat() with merge() (see "Treating Several Observables as One Using merge()" on page 78) and switchOnNext() just being introduced.

Consider a group of people, each one having microphone. Every microphone is modeled as an Observable<String>, for which an event represents a single word. Obviously, events appear over time, as soon as they are spoken. To simulate this behavior we will construct a simple Observable for demonstration purposes, interesting on its own:

```
Observable<String> speak(String quote, long millisPerChar) {
    String[] tokens = quote.replaceAll("[:,]", "").split(" ");
    Observable<String> words = Observable.from(tokens);
    Observable<Long> absoluteDelay = words
        .map(String::length)
        .map(len -> len * millisPerChar)
        .scan((total, current) -> total + current);
    return words
        .zipWith(absoluteDelay.startWith(0L), Pair::of)
        .flatMap(pair -> just(pair.getLeft())
            .delay(pair.getRight(), MILLISECONDS));
}
```

The preceding code snippet is quite complex, so let's study it first, line by line. We take an arbitrary text in String and split it to words, removing punctuation using a regular expression. Now, for each word we calculate how much it takes to say that word, simply by multiplying the word length by millisPerChar. Then, we would like to spread words over time, so that each word appears in the resulting stream after the delay calculated in the preceding example. Clearly, a simple from operator is not enough:

```
Observable<String> words = Observable.from(tokens);
```

We want words to appear with delay, based on the length of the previous word. The first naive approach simply delays each word, given its length:

```
words.flatMap(word -> Observable
    .just(word)
    .delay(word.length() * millisPerChar, MILLISECONDS));
```

This solution is incorrect. The Observable will first emit all one-letter words at the same time. Then, after a while, all two-letter words followed by all three-letter words. What we want is to have the first word appear immediately and then the second word after a delay, depending on the length of the first word. This sounds terribly complex but turns out to be quite pleasant. First we create a helper stream from words that contains only relative delays induced by each word:

```
words
    .map(String::length)
    .map(len -> len * millisPerChar);
```

Assuming millisPerChar is 100 and words are *Though this be madness*, we first get the following stream: 600, 400, 200, 700. If we were to simply delay() each word by that duration, "*be*" word would appear first and other words would be scrambled as well. What we really want is a cumulative sequence of absolute delays, like this: 600, 600 + 400 = 1,000; 1,000 + 200 = 1,200; 1,200 + 700 = 1,900. This is easy using the scan() operator (see "Scanning Through the Sequence with Scan and Reduce" on page 88):

```
Observable<Long> absoluteDelay = words
    .map(String::length)
    .map(len -> len * millisPerChar)
    .scan((total, current) -> total + current);
```

Now when we have a sequence of words and a sequence of absolute delays for each one of them, we can zip these two streams. This is the kind of a situation in which zip() shines:

```
words
    .zipWith(absoluteDelay.startWith(0L), Pair::of)
    .flatMap(pair -> just(pair.getLeft()))
```

This makes a lot of sense because we know two streams have exact the same size and are entirely in sync with each other. Well…almost. We do not want the first word to be delayed at all. Instead, the length of the first word should influence the delay of the second word, the total length of the first and second word should influence the delay of the third word, and so on. You can achieve such a shift easily by simply prepending absoluteDelay with 0:

```
import org.apache.commons.lang3.tuple.Pair;

words
    .zipWith(absoluteDelay.startWith(0L), Pair::of)
    .flatMap(pair -> just(pair.getLeft())
        .delay(pair.getRight(), MILLISECONDS));
```

We construct a sequence of pair words—absolute delay of that word, making sure the first word is not delayed at all. These pairs might look as follows:

```
(Though, 0)
(this, 600)
(be, 1000)
(madness, 1200)
...
```

This is our speech time line, each word accompanied with its point in time. All we need to do is turn every pair into a one-element Observable shifted in time:

```
flatMap(pair -> just(pair.getLeft())
    .delay(pair.getRight(), MILLISECONDS));
```

After so much preparation, we can finally see how concat(), merge(), and switchOn Next() differ. Suppose that three people were quoting *Hamlet* by William Shakespeare:

```
Observable<String> alice = speak(
        "To be, or not to be: that is the question", 110);
Observable<String> bob = speak(
        "Though this be madness, yet there is method in't", 90);
Observable<String> jane = speak(
```

```
                     "There are more things in Heaven and Earth, " +
                     "Horatio, than are dreamt of in your philosophy", 100);
```

As you can see, each person has a slightly different pace measured in `millisPerChar`. What happens if all people speak at the same time? RxJava can answer this question:

```
Observable
    .merge(
        alice.map(w -> "Alice: " + w),
        bob.map(w   -> "Bob:   " + w),
        jane.map(w  -> "Jane:  " + w)
    )
    .subscribe(System.out::println);
```

The output is very chaotic, words spoken by each person interleave with each other. All we hear is noise, and without prefixing each phrase, it would have been difficult to understand:

```
Alice: To
Bob:    Though
Jane:   There
Alice: be
Alice: or
Jane:   are
Alice: not
Bob:    this
Jane:   more
Alice: to
Jane:   things
Alice: be
Bob:    be
Alice: that
Bob:    madness
Jane:   in
Alice: is
Jane:   Heaven
Alice: the
Bob:    yet
Alice: question
Jane:   and
Bob:    there
Jane:   Earth
Bob:    is
Jane:   Horatio
Bob:    method
Jane:   than
Bob:    in't
Jane:   are
Jane:   dreamt
Jane:   of
Jane:   in
Jane:   your
Jane:   philosophy
```

This is how merge() works: it subscribes to words of each person immediately and forwards them downstream, no matter which person is speaking. If two streams emit an event at more or less the same time, they are both forwarded right away. There is no buffering or halting events within this operator.

The situation is much different if we replace merge() with concat() operator:

```
Alice: To
Alice: be
Alice: or
Alice: not
Alice: to
Alice: be
Alice: that
Alice: is
Alice: the
Alice: question
Bob:   Though
Bob:   this
Bob:   be
Bob:   madness
Bob:   yet
Bob:   there
Bob:   is
Bob:   method
Bob:   in't
Jane:  There
Jane:  are
Jane:  more
Jane:  things
Jane:  in
Jane:  Heaven
Jane:  and
Jane:  Earth
Jane:  Horatio
Jane:  than
Jane:  are
Jane:  dreamt
Jane:  of
Jane:  in
Jane:  your
Jane:  philosophy
```

Now the order is perfect. concat(alice, bob, jane) first subscribes to alice and keeps forwarding events from that first Observable until it is exhausted and completed. Then, concat() switches to bob. Think about hot and cold Observables for a while. In case of merge(), all events from all streams are forwarded because merge() subscribes eagerly to every stream. However, concat() subscribes just to the first stream, so in case of hot Observable, you might expect a different outcome. By the time the first Observable is completed, the second one might be sending an entirely different sequence of events. Keep in mind that concat() does not buffer second Observable until the first one completes; instead, it simply subscribes lazily.

switchOnNext()) is an entirely different way of combining operators. Imagine that you have an Observable<Observable<T>> that is a stream of events for which each event is a stream on its own.[7] This situation actually makes sense, for example, if you have a set of mobile phones connecting and disconnecting to the network (outer stream). Each new connection is an event, but every such event is a stream of independent heartbeat messages (Observable<Ping>). In our case, we will have an Observable<Observable<String>>, where each inner stream is a quote from a different person: alice, bob, or jane:

```
import java.util.Random;

Random rnd = new Random();
Observable<Observable<String>> quotes = just(
                alice.map(w -> "Alice: " + w),
                bob.map(w   -> "Bob:   " + w),
                jane.map(w  -> "Jane:  " + w));
```

First, we wrap alice, bob and jane Observables into an Observable<Observable<String>>. Let us reiterate: quotes Observable emits three events immediately, each event being an inner Observable<String>. Every inner Observable<String> represents words spoken by each person. To illustrate how switchOnNext() works, we shall delay the emission of inner Observables. We are not delaying each word within that Observable (variant A) but the entire Observable (variant B is subtly different):

```
//A
map(innerObs ->
        innerObs.delay(rnd.nextInt(5), SECONDS))

//B
flatMap(innerObs -> just(innerObs)
        .delay(rnd.nextInt(5), SECONDS))
```

In variant A, the Observable appears immediately in the outer stream but begins emitting events with some delay. In variant B, on the other hand, we shift the entire Observable event forward in time so that it appears in the outer Observable much later. Now the reason why we needed such a complex setup. Both static concat() and merge() operators can work with either a fixed list of Observables or Observable of Observables. In the case of switchOnNext(), the ladder makes sense.

---

7 *We Need To Go Deeper*

switchOnNext() begins by subscribing to an outer Observable<Observable<T>>, which emits inner Observable<T>s. As soon as the first inner Observable<T> appears, this operator subscribes to it and begins pushing events of type T downstream. Now what happens if next inner Observable<T> appears? switchOnNext() discards the first Observable<T> by unsubscribing from it and switches to the next one (thus, the name). In other words, when we have a stream of streams, switchOn Next() always forwards downstream events from the last inner stream, even if older streams keep forwarding fresh events.

This is how it looks in our *Hamlet* quoting example:

```
Random rnd = new Random();
Observable<Observable<String>> quotes = just(
            alice.map(w -> "Alice: " + w),
            bob.map(w   -> "Bob:   " + w),
            jane.map(w  -> "Jane:  " + w))
        .flatMap(innerObs -> just(innerObs)
            .delay(rnd.nextInt(5), SECONDS));

Observable
        .switchOnNext(quotes)
        .subscribe(System.out::println);
```

One of the possible outcomes, due to the random nature of this example, could look like this:

```
Jane:  There
Jane:  are
Jane:  more
Alice: To
Alice: be
Alice: or
Alice: not
Alice: to
Bob:   Though
Bob:   this
Bob:   be
Bob:   madness
Bob:   yet
Bob:   there
Bob:   is
Bob:   method
Bob:   in't
```

Each person starts speaking with zero to four seconds random delay. In this particular round, it was Jane's Observable<String>, but after citing few words, Alice's Observable<String> appeared in the outer Observable. At this point switchOn Next() unsubscribes from jane, and we never hear the rest of this quote. This Observ able is discarded and ignored, switchOnNext() only listens to alice at the moment. However, again the inner Observable is interrupted because Bob's quote appears.

Theoretically, `switchOnNext()` could produce all of the events from the inner `Observ` `ables` if they did not overlap, completing before the next one appears.

Now what would happen in the case of delaying only events in every inner `Observa` `ble` (variant *A*, remember?) rather than delaying `Observables` themselves? Well, three inner `Observables` would appear at the same time in outer `Observable`, and `switch` `OnNext()` would only subscribe to one of them.

Criteria-Based Splitting of Stream Using groupBy()

One of the techniques often used together with domain-driven design (for more information about data-driven design, read *Implementing Domain-Driven Design*, by Vaughn Vernon [Addison-Wesley Professional]) is event sourcing. In this architecture style, data is not stored as a snapshot of current state and mutated in place; that is, using SQL UPDATE queries. Instead, a sequence of immutable domain events (facts) about events that already happened are kept in an append-only data store. Using this design, we never overwrite any data, effectively having an audit log for free. Moreover, the only way to see the data in real time is by applying these facts one after another, starting from an empty view.

The process of applying events on top of an initial empty state is known as *projection* in event sourcing.[8] A single source of facts can drive multiple different projections. For example, we might have a stream of facts related to a reservation system, like `Tick` `etReserved`, `ReservationConfirmed`, and `TicketBought`—the past tense is important because facts always reflect actions and events that already occurred. From a single stream of facts (also being the single source of truth), we can derive multiple projections, such as the following:

- List of all confirmed reservations
- List of reservations canceled today
- Total revenue per week

When the system evolves, we can discard old projections and build new ones, taking advantage of data collected eagerly in facts. Suppose that you would like to build a projection containing all reservations together with their status. To do so, you must consume all `ReservationEvents` and apply them to appropriate reservations. Each `ReservationEvent` has a subclass for different types of events, like `TicketBought`. Also, each event has a `UUID` of the reservation to which it applies:

---

8 See the section "Read Model Projections" in Appendix A of *Implementing Domain-Driven Design* (Addison-Wesley).

```
FactStore factStore = new CassandraFactStore();
Observable<ReservationEvent> facts = factStore.observe();
facts.subscribe(this::updateProjection);

//...

void updateProjection(ReservationEvent event) {
    UUID uuid = event.getReservationUuid();
    Reservation res = loadBy(uuid)
        .orElseGet(() -> new Reservation(uuid));
    res.consume(event);
    store(event.getUuid(), res);
}

private void store(UUID id, Reservation modified) {
    //...
}

Optional<Reservation> loadBy(UUID uuid) {
    //...
}

class Reservation {

    Reservation consume(ReservationEvent event) {
        //mutate myself
        return this;
    }

}
```

Obviously, the stream of `facts` is expressed as `Observable`. Some other part of the system receives API calls or web requests, reacts (e.g., charges the customer's credit card) and stores facts (domain events) about what happened. Other parts of the system (or even other systems!) can consume these facts by subscribing to a stream and building a snapshot of current system state from some arbitrary perspective. Our code is quite simple: each `ReservationEvent` loads a `Reservation` from our projection's data store. If `Reservation` was not found, it means that it was the very first event associated with this UUID, so we begin with an empty `Reservation`. Then, we pass `ReservationEvent` to `Reservation` object. It can update itself to reflect any type of fact. Then, we store `Reservation` back.

Remember that projections are independent from facts, they can use any other persistence mechanism or even keep state in-memory. Moreover, you can have multiple projections consuming the same stream of facts but building a different snapshot. For example, you can have an `Accounting` object that consumes the same stream of facts but is only concerned about money coming in and out. Another projection might only be interested in `FraudDetected` facts, summarizing fraudulent situations.

This brief introduction to event sourcing will help us to understand why `groupBy()` operator is useful. After a while, we discovered that updates to `Reservation` projection fall behind, we cannot keep up with the rate of facts being generated. The data store can easily handle concurrent reads and updates, so we can try to parallelize handling of facts:

```
Observable<ReservationEvent> facts = factStore.observe();

facts
        .flatMap(this::updateProjectionAsync)
        .subscribe();

//...

Observable<ReservationEvent> updateProjectionAsync(ReservationEvent event) {
    //possibly asynchronous
}
```

In this case, we consume `facts` in parallel, or to be more precise: receiving is sequential but handling (in `updateProjectionAsync()`) is possibly asynchronous. `update ProjectionAsync()` alters the state of supplied `Reservation` objects inside a projection. But a look at how `updateProjection()` was implemented we quickly see a possible race-condition: two threads can consume different events, modify the same `Reservation` and try to store it—but the first update is overwritten and effectively lost. Technically you can try optimistic locking, but another problem remains: the order of facts is no longer guaranteed. This is not a problem when two unrelated `Res ervation` instances (with different UUID) are touched. But applying facts on the same `Reservation` object in a different order from which they actually occurred can be disastrous.

This is where `groupBy()` comes in handy. It splits a stream based on some key into multiple parallel streams, each holding events with given key. In this case, we want to split one huge stream of all facts regarding reservations into large number of smaller streams, each emitting only events related to a specific UUID:

```
Observable<ReservationEvent> facts = factStore.observe();

Observable<GroupedObservable<UUID, ReservationEvent>> grouped =
        facts.groupBy(ReservationEvent::getReservationUuid);

grouped.subscribe(byUuid -> {
    byUuid.subscribe(this::updateProjection);
});
```

This example contains quite a few new constructs. First, we take upstream `Observa ble<ReservationEvent>` stream and group it by UUID (`ReservationEvent::getRe servationUuid`). You might first expect that `groupBy()` should return a `List<Observable<ReservationEvent>>`—after all we transform a single stream into multiple ones. This assumption breaks when you realize that groupBy() cannot possibly know how many different keys (UUIDs) will generate upstream. Therefore, it must produce them on-the-fly: whenever a new UUID is discovered, the new GroupedOb servable<UUID, ReservationEvent> is emitted, pushing events related to that UUID. So it becomes clear that the outer data structure must be an Observable.

But what is this GroupedObservable<UUID, ReservationEvent> anyway? GroupedOb servable is a simple subclass of Observable that apart from the standard Observable contract returns a key to which all events in that stream belong (UUID, in our case). The number of emitted GroupedObservables can be anything from one (in case of all events having the same key) to the total number of events (if each upstream event has a unique key). This is one of these cases for which nested Observables are not that bad. When we subscribe to the outer Observable, every emitted value is actually another Observable (GroupedObservable) to which you can subscribe. For example, each inner stream can provide events related to one another (like the same correlation ID), however, inner streams are unrelated to one another and can be processed separately.

Where to Go from Here?

There are dozens of other operators built in to RxJava. Many of them will be explained in Chapter 6, but going through the entire API is not very reasonable and quite time consuming. Also such an exhaustive description would become obsolete from version to version. However, you should have a basic understanding of what operators can do for you and how they work. The next logical step is writing custom operators.

Writing Customer Operators

We barely scratched the surface of available operators in RxJava, and you will learn many more throughout the course of this book. Moreover, the true power of operators comes from their composition. Following the UNIX philosophy of "*small, sharp tools*,"[9] each operator is doing one, small transformation at a time. This section will first guide you through the compose() operator, which allows fluent composition of smaller operators, and later introduces the lift() operator, which helps you to write entirely new custom operators.

---

9 Hunt, A. and Thomas, D., *The Pragmatic Programmer: From Journeyman to Master* (Addison-Wesley Professional).

Reusing Operators Using compose()

Let's begin by looking at an example. For some reason, we want to transform an upstream `Observable` so that every other item is discarded and we only receive even items. In "Flow Control" on page 211, we will learn about the `buffer()` operator that makes this task very simple (`buffer(1, 2)` does almost exactly what we want). However, we will pretend that we do not know this operator so far, but we can implement this functionality easily by composing several operators:

```
import org.apache.commons.lang3.tuple.Pair;

//...

Observable<Boolean> trueFalse = Observable.just(true, false).repeat();
Observable<T> upstream = //...
Observable<T> downstream = upstream
        .zipWith(trueFalse, Pair::of)
        .filter(Pair::getRight)
        .map(Pair::getLeft);
```

First, we generate an infinite `Observable<Boolean>` emitting `true` and `false` alternately. We can implement this easily by creating a fixed `[true, false]` stream with just two items and then repeating it infinitely with the `repeat()` operator. `repeat()` simply intercepts completion notification from upstream and rather than passing it downstream it resubscribes. Therefore, it is not guaranteed that `repeat()` will keep cycling through the same sequence of events, but it happens to be the case when upstream is a simple fixed stream. See also "Retrying After Failures" on page 254 for a similar `retry()` operator.

We `zipWith()` our upstream `Observable` with this infinite stream of `true` and `false`. However, zipping requires a function that combines two items. This is simpler in other languages; in Java, we help ourselves by using the Apache Commons Lang library (*http://bit.ly/2cM5gUC*), which provides a simple `Pair` class. At this point, we have a stream of `Pair<T, Boolean>` values, each having `true` or `false` on the right (a pair comprises *left* and *right* components). As a next step, we `filter()` all pairs and keep only those having `true` on the right, effectively discarding every even pair. The last step is to unwrap the pair, throwing out `Boolean` and keeping T only (`getLeft()`). If you want to avoid third-party library, an alternative implementation follows:

```
import static rx.Observable.empty;
import static rx.Observable.just;

//...

upstream.zipWith(trueFalse, (t, bool) ->
                bool ? just(t) : empty())
        .flatMap(obs -> obs)
```

At first glance, flatMap() looks kind of odd and doesn't appear to be doing anything that is actually crucial. From zipWith() transformation we return an Observable (one element or empty), which leads to Observable<Observable<T>>. By using flat Map() this way we get rid of this nesting level—after all, a lambda expression in flat Map() is supposed to return an Observable for each input element, which also happens to be an Observable.

No matter which implementation you choose, this is not very reusable. If you need to reuse "*every odd element*" sequence of operators, you either copy-paste them or create a utility method like this:

```
static <T> Observable<T> odd(Observable<T> upstream) {
    Observable<Boolean> trueFalse = just(true, false).repeat();
    return upstream
            .zipWith(trueFalse, Pair::of)
            .filter(Pair::getRight)
            .map(Pair::getLeft)
}
```

But you can no longer fluently chain operators; in other words, you cannot say: obs.op1().odd().op2(). Unlike C# (where reactive extensions originated) and Scala[10] (via implicits), Java does not allow extension methods. But the built-in com pose() operator comes as close as possible. compose() takes a function as an argument that is supposed to transform the upstream Observable via a series of other operators. This is how it works in practice:

```
private <T> Observable.Transformer<T, T> odd() {
    Observable<Boolean> trueFalse = just(true, false).repeat();
    return upstream -> upstream
            .zipWith(trueFalse, Pair::of)
            .filter(Pair::getRight)
            .map(Pair::getLeft);
}

//...

//[A, B, C, D, E...]
Observable<Character> alphabet =
        Observable
                .range(0, 'Z' - 'A' + 1)
                .map(c -> (char) ('A' + c));

//[A, C, E, G, I...]
alphabet
        .compose(odd())
        .forEach(System.out::println);
```

---

10 Go to *http://reactivex.io/rxscala* for a Scala-specific wrapper for RxJava.

The odd() function returns a `Transformer<T, T>` from `Observable<T>` to `Observable<T>` (of course, types can be different). Thus, `Transformer` is a function on its own, so we can replace it with a lambda expression (`upstream -> upstream...`). Notice that the odd() function is executed eagerly when `Observable` is assembled, not during subscription. Interestingly, if you want to emit even values (2nd, 4th, 6th, etc.) rather than odd (1st, 3rd, 5th, etc.), simply replace `trueFalse` with `trueFalse.skip(1)`.

Implementing Advanced Operators Using lift()

Implementing custom operators is tricky because backpressure (see: "Backpressure" on page 226) and the subscription mechanism need to be taken into account. Therefore, try your best to implement your requirements from existing operators rather than inventing your own. Built-in operators are much better tested and proven. However, if none of the supplied operators work for you, the `lift()` meta-operator will help. `compose()` is only useful for grouping existing operators together. With `lift()`, on the other hand, you can implement almost any operator, altering the flow of upstream events.

Whereas `compose()` transforms `Observables`, `lift()` allows transforming `Subscribers`. Let's recap what we learned in "Mastering Observable.create()" on page 35. When you `subscribe()` to an `Observable`, the `Subscriber` instance wrapping your callback travels up to the `Observable` it subscribed to and causes `Obsevable`'s `create()` method to be invoked with our `subscriber` as an argument (gross simplification). So every time we subscribe, a `Subscriber` travels up through all operators to the original `Observable`. Obviously, between the `Observable` and `subscribe()` there can be an arbitrary number of operators, altering events flowing downstream, as illustrated here:

```
Observable
    .range(1, 1000)
    .filter(x -> x % 3 == 0)
    .distinct()
    .reduce((a, x) -> a + x)
    .map(Integer::toHexString)
    .subscribe(System.out::println);
```

But here is an interesting fact: if you look up the source code of RxJava and replace operator invocations with their body, this quite complex sequence of operators becomes very regular (notice how `reduce()` is implemented using `scan().takeLast(1).single()`:

```
Observable
    .range(1, 1000)
    .lift(new OperatorFilter<>(x -> x % 3 == 0))
    .lift(   OperatorDistinct.<Integer>instance())
```

```
.lift(new OperatorScan<>((Integer a, Integer x) -> a + x))
.lift(    OperatorTakeLastOne.<Integer>instance())
.lift(    OperatorSingle.<Integer>instance())
.lift(new OperatorMap<>(Integer::toHexString))
.subscribe(System.out::println);
```

Almost all operators, excluding those working with multiple streams at once (like flatMap()) are implemented by means of lift(). When we subscribe() at the very bottom, a Subscriber<String> instance is created and passed to the immediate predecessor. It can be "true" Observable<String> that emits events or just the result of some operator, map(Integer::toHexString) in our case. map() itself does not emit events, yet it received a Subscriber that wants to receive them. What map() does (through the lift() helper operator) is it transparently subscribes to its parent (reduce() in the preceding example). However, it cannot pass the same Subscriber instance it received. This is because subscribe() required Subscriber<String>, whereas reduce() expects Subscriber<Integer>. After all, that is what map() is doing here: transforming Integer to String. So instead, map() operator creates a new artificial Subscriber<Integer> and every time this special Subscriber receives anything, it applies Integer::toHexString function and notifies the downstream Sub scriber<String>.

Looking under the hood of the map() operator

This is essentially what OperatorMap class is doing: providing a transformation from downstream (child) Subscriber<R> into upstream Subscriber<T>. Here is the real implementation found in RxJava, with some minor readability simplifications:

```
public final class OperatorMap<T, R> implements Operator<R, T> {

    private final Func1<T, R> transformer;

    public OperatorMap(Func1<T, R> transformer) {
        this.transformer = transformer;
    }

    @Override
    public Subscriber<T> call(final Subscriber<R> child) {
        return new Subscriber<T>(child) {

            @Override
            public void onCompleted() {
                child.onCompleted();
            }

            @Override
            public void onError(Throwable e) {
                child.onError(e);
            }
```

```
            @Override
            public void onNext(T t) {
                try {
                    child.onNext(transformer.call(t));
                } catch (Exception e) {
                    onError(e);
                }
            }
        };
    }
}
```

One unusual detail is the reversed order of T and R generic types. The map() operator transforms values flowing from upstream of type T to type R. However, the operator's responsibility is transforming Subscriber<R> (coming from downstream subscription) to Subscriber<T> (passed to upstream Observable). We expect subscribe via Subscriber<R>, whereas operator map() is used against Observable<T>, requiring Subscriber<T>.

Ensure that you roughly understand the preceding snippet from RxJava's source code. Understanding how map() is implemented (admittedly one of the easiest operators) will enable you to write your own. Every time you map() over a stream, you actually call lift() with a new instance of OperatorMap class, providing the transformer function. This function operates on upstream events of type T and returns downstream events of type R. Every time a user provides any custom function/transformation to your operator, make sure you catch all unexpected exceptions and forward them downstream via the onError() method. This also ensures that you unsubscribe from upstream, preventing it from emitting further events.

Keep in mind that until someone actually subscribes, we barely created a new Observable (lift(), like any other operator, creates new Observable) with a reference to OperatorMap instance underneath, which in turns holds a reference to our function. But only when someone actually subscribes, the call() function of OperatorMap is invoked. This function receives our Subscriber<String> (e.g., wrapping System.out::println) and returns another Subscriber<Integer>. It is the latter Subscriber that travels upstream, to preceding operators.

That is pretty much how all operators work, both built-in and custom. You receive a Subscriber and return another one, enhancing and passing whatever it wishes to downstream Subscriber.

Our first operator

This time we would like to implement an operator that will emit toString() of every odd (1st, 3rd, 5th, etc.) element. It is best explained with some sample code:

```
Observable<String> odd = Observable
        .range(1, 9)
        .lift(toStringOfOdd())
//Will emit: "1", "3", "5", "7" and "9" strings
```

You can achieve the same functionality by using built-in operators, we are writing a custom operator just for educational purposes:

```
Observable
            .range(1, 9)
            .buffer(1, 2)
            .concatMapIterable(x -> x)
            .map(Object::toString);
```

The buffer() will be introduced in "Buffering Events to a List" on page 214, for the time being, all you need to know is that buffer(1, 2) will transform any Observa ble<T> into Observable<List<T>>, where each inner List has exactly one odd element and skips even ones. Having a stream of lists like List(1), List(3), and so on, we reconstruct a flat stream using concatMapIterable(). But for the sake of learning experience, let's implement a custom operator that does that in a single step. The custom operator can be in one of two states:

- It either received odd event (1st, 3rd, 5th, etc.) from upstream which it forwards downstream after applying it to toString().

- It received even event which it simply discards.

Then cycle repeats. The operator might look like this:

```
<T> Observable.Operator<String, T> toStringOfOdd() {
    return new Observable.Operator<String, T>() {

        private boolean odd = true;

        @Override
        public Subscriber<? super T> call(Subscriber<? super String> child) {
            return new Subscriber<T>(child) {
                @Override
                public void onCompleted() {
                    child.onCompleted();
                }

                @Override
                public void onError(Throwable e) {
                    child.onError(e);
                }

                @Override
                public void onNext(T t) {
                    if(odd) {
                        child.onNext(t.toString());
```

```
                } else {
                    request(1);
                }
                odd = !odd;
            }
        };
    }
};
}
```

The `request(1)` invocation will be explained much later in "Honoring the Requested Amount of Data" on page 237. For now you can understand it like this: when a Sub scriber requests just a subset of events—for example, only the first two (`take(2)`)— RxJava takes care of requesting only that amount of data by calling `request(2)` internally. This request is passed upstream and we receive barely 1 and 2. However, we drop 2 (even), yet we were obligated to provide two events downstream. Therefore, we must request one extra event (`request(1)`) in addition to that so that we receive 3, as well. RxJava implements quite a sophisticated mechanism called *backpressure* that allows subscribers to request only the amount of events they can process, protecting from producers outperforming consumers. We devote "Backpressure" on page 226 to this topic.

 Unfortunately, for better or worse, `null` is a valid event value in RxJava; that is, `Observable.just("A", null, "B")` is as good as any other stream. You need to take that into account when designing custom operators as well as when applying operators. However, passing `null` is generally considered nonidiomatic, and you should use wrapper value types, instead.

Another interesting pitfall you might encounter is failing to provide a child Sub scriber as an argument to the new `Subscriber`, like here:

```
<T> Observable.Operator<String, T> toStringOfOdd() {
    //BROKEN
    return child -> new Subscriber<T>() {
        //...
    }
}
```

The parameterless constructor of `Subscriber` is fine, and again our operator seems to work. But let's see how it goes with infinite stream:

```
Observable
        .range(1, 4)
        .repeat()
        .lift(toStringOfOdd())
        .take(3)
        .subscribe(
```

```
        System.out::println,
        Throwable::printStackTrace,
        () -> System.out.println("Completed")
    );
```

We build an infinite stream of numbers (1, 2, 3, 4, 1, 2, 3…), apply our operator ("1", "3", "1", "3"…), and take only the first three values. This is absolutely fine and should never fail; after all, streams are lazy. But remove `child` from `new Sub scriber(child)` constructor and our `Observable` never notifies about completion after receiving 1, 3, 1. What happened?

The `take(3)` operator requested only the first three values and wanted to `unsub scribe()`. Unfortunately, the unsubscription requested never made it to the original stream, which keeps producing values. Even worse, these values are processed by our custom operator and passed to downstream `Subscriber` (`take(3)`), which is not even listening anymore. Implementation details aside, as a rule of thumb, pass the downstream `Subscriber` as a constructor argument to the new `Subscriber` when writing your own operators. A no-argument constructor is used rarely and very unlikely you will need it for simple operators.

This is just the tip of the iceberg with respect to the issues you can encounter when writing your own operators. Luckily, very seldom are we not able to achieve what we want to accomplish with built-in mechanisms.

Summary

The true power of RxJava lies in its operators. Declarative transformations of streams of data is safe yet expressive and flexible. With a strong foundation in functional programming, operators play deciding role in RxJava adoption. Mastering built-in operators is a key to success in this library. But remember we did not see all operators yet —for example, see "Flow Control" on page 211. But at this point, you should have a good overview of what RxJava can do and how to enhance it when it cannot do something directly.

CHAPTER 4

Applying Reactive Programming to Existing Applications

Tomasz Nurkiewicz

Introducing a new library, technology, or paradigm to an application, be it greenfield or legacy codebase, must be a careful decision. RxJava is not an exception. In this chapter, we review some patterns and architectures found in ordinary Java applications and see how Rx can help. This process is not straightforward and requires a significant mindset shift, therefore we will carefully transform from imperative to functional and reactive style. Many libraries in Java projects these days simply add bloat without giving anything in return. However, you will see how RxJava not only simplifies traditional projects, but what kinds of benefits it brings to legacy platforms.

I am pretty sure that you're already very excited about RxJava. Built-in operators and simplicity makes Rx an amazingly powerful tool for transforming streams of events. However, if you go back to your office tomorrow, you will realize that there are no streams, no real-time events from stock exchange. You can hardly find any events in your applications; it's just a mash-up of web requests, databases, and external APIs. You are so eager to try this new RxJava-thing somewhere beyond *Hello world*. Yet it seems that there are simply no use cases in real life that justify using Rx. Yet, RxJava can be a significant step forward in terms of architectural consistency and robustness. You do not need to commit to reactive style top-to-bottom—this is too risky and requires too much work in the beginning. But Rx can be introduced at any layer, without breaking an application as a whole.

We take you through some common application patterns and ways by which you can enhance them with RxJava in noninvasive way, with the focus being on database querying, caching, error handling, and periodic tasks. The more RxJava you add in various places of your stack the more consistent your architecture will become.

From Collections to Observables

Unless your platform was built recently in JVM frameworks like Play (*https://www.playframework.com*), Akka actors (*http://akka.io*), or maybe Vert.x (*http://vertx.io*), you are probably on a stack with a servlet container on one hand, and JDBC or web services on the other. Between them, there is a varying number of layers implementing business logic, which we will not refactor all at once; instead, let's begin with a simple example. The following class represents a trivial repository abstracting us from a database:

```
class PersonDao {

    List<Person> listPeople() {
        return query("SELECT * FROM PEOPLE");
    }

    private List<Person> query(String sql) {
        //...
    }

}
```

Implementation details aside, how is this related to Rx? So far we have been talking about asynchronous events pushed from upstream systems or, at best, when someone subscribes. How is this mundane `Dao` relevant here? `Observable` is not only a pipe pushing events downstream. You can treat `Observable<T>` as a data structure, dual to `Iterable<T>`. They both hold items of type `T`, but providing a radically different interface. So, it shouldn't come as a surprise that you can simply replace one with the other:

```
Observable<Person> listPeople() {
    final List<Person> people = query("SELECT * FROM PEOPLE");
    return Observable.from(people);
}
```

At this point, we made a breaking change to the existing API. Depending on how big your system is, such incompatibility might be a major concern. Thus, it is important to bring RxJava into your API as soon as possible. Obviously, we are working with an existing application so that can't be the case.

BlockingObservable: Exiting the Reactive World

If you are combining RxJava with existing, blocking and imperative code, might need have to *translate* `Observable` to a plain collection. This transformation is rather unpleasant, it requires blocking on an `Observable` waiting for its completion. Until `Observable` completes, we are not capable of creating a collection. `BlockingObservable` is a special type that makes it easier to work with `Observable` in nonreactive environment. BlockingObservable should be your last choice when working with RxJava, but it is inevitable when combining blocking and nonblocking code.

In Chapter 3, we refactored the listPeople() method so that it returns Observable<People> rather than List. Observable is not an Iterable in any sense, so our code no longer compiles. We want to take baby steps rather than massive refactoring, so let's keep the scope of changes as minimal as possible. The client code could look like this:

```
List<Person> people = pesonDao.listPeople();
String json = marshal(people);
```

We can imagine the marshal() method *pulling* data from the people collection and serializing them to JSON. That's no longer the case, we can't simply *pull* items from Observable when we want. Observable is in charge of producing (*pushing*) items and notifying subscribers if any. This radical change can be easily circumvented with BlockingObservable. This handy class is entirely independent from Observable and can be obtained via the Observable.toBlocking() method. The blocking variant of Observable has superficially similar methods like single() or subscribe(). However, BlockingObservable is much more convenient in blocking environments that are inherently unprepared for the asynchronous nature of Observable. Operators on BlockingObservable typically block (wait) until the underlying Observable is completed. This strongly contradicts the main concept of Observables that everything is likely asynchronous, lazy, and processed on the fly. For example, Observable.forEach() will asynchronously receive events from Observable as they come in, whereas BlockingObservable.forEach() will block until all events are processed and stream is completed. Also exceptions are no longer propagated as values (events) but instead are rethrown in the calling thread.

In our case, we want to transform Observable<Person> back into List<Person> to limit the scope of refactoring:

```
Observable<Person> peopleStream = personDao.listPeople();
Observable<List<Person>> peopleList = peopleStream.toList();
BlockingObservable<List<Person>> peopleBlocking = peopleList.toBlocking();
List<Person> people = peopleBlocking.single();
```

I intentionally left all intermediate types explicit in order to explain what happens. After refactoring to Rx, our API returns Observable<Person> peopleStream. This stream can potentially be fully reactive, asynchronous, and event driven, which doesn't match at all what we need: a static List. As the first step, we turn Observable<Person> into Observable<List<Person>>. This lazy operator will buffer all Person events and keep them in memory until the onCompleted() event is received. At this point, a single event of type List<Person> will be emitted, containing all seen events at once, as illustrated in the following marble diagram:

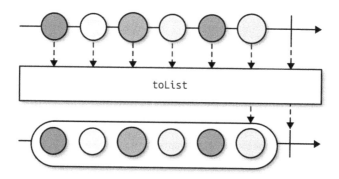

The resulting stream completes immediately after emitting a single List item. Again, this operator is asynchronous; it doesn't wait for all events to arrive but instead lazily buffers all values. The awkward looking Observable<List<Person>> peopleList is then converted to BlockingObservable<List<Person>> peopleBlocking. Blockin gObservable is a good idea only when you must provide a blocking, static view of your otherwise asynchronous Observable. Whereas Observable.from(List<T>) converts normal pull-based collection into Observable, toBlocking() does something quite the opposite. You might ask yourself why we need two abstractions for blocking and nonblocking operators. The authors of RxJava figured out that being explicit about synchronous versus asynchronous nature of underlying operator is too crucial to be left for JavaDoc. Having two unrelated types ensures that you always work with the appropriate data structure. Moreover, BlockingObservable is your weapon of last resort; normally, you should compose and chain plain Observables as long as possible. However, for the purpose of this exercise, let's escape from Observa ble right away. The last operator single() drops observables altogether and extracts one, and only one, item we expect to receive from BlockingObservable<T>. A similar operator, first(), will return a value of T and discard whatever it has left. single(), on the other hand, makes sure there are no more pending events in underlying Observable before terminating. This means single() will block waiting for onCom pleted() callback. Here is the same code snippet as earlier, this time with all operators chained:

```
List<Person> people = personDao
    .listPeople()
    .toList()
    .toBlocking()
    .single();
```

You might think that we went through all this hassle of wrapping and unwrapping Observable for no apparent reason. Remember, this was just the first step. The next transformation will introduce some laziness. Our code as it stands right now always executes query("...") and wraps it with Observable. As you know by now, Observa bles (especially cold ones) are lazy by definition. As long as no one subscribes, they just represent a stream that never had a chance to begin emitting values. Most of the time you can call methods returning `Observable` and as long as you don't subscribe, no work will be done. `Observable` is like a `Future` because it promises a value to appear in the future. But as long as you don't request it, a cold `Observable` will not even begin emitting. From that perspective, `Observable` is more similar to `java.util.function.Supplier<T>`, generating values of type `T` on demand. Hot `Observables` are different because they emit values whether you are listening or not, but we are not considering them right now. The mere existence of `Observable` does not indicate a background job or any side effect, unlike `Future`, which almost always suggests some operation running concurrently.

Embracing Laziness

So how do we make our `Observable` lazy? The simples technique is to wrap an eager `Observable` with `defer()`:

```
public Observable<Person> listPeople() {
    return Observable.defer(() ->
        Observable.from(query("SELECT * FROM PEOPLE")));
}
```

`Observable.defer()` takes a lambda expression (a factory) that can produce `Observable`. The underlying `Observable` is eager, so we want to postpone its creation. `defer()` will wait until the last possible moment to actually create `Observable`; that is, until someone actually subscribes to it. This has some interesting implications. Because `Observable` is lazy, calling `listPeople()` has no side effects and almost no performance footprint. No database is queried yet. You can treat `Observable<Person>` as a promise but without any background processing happening yet. Notice that there is no asynchronous behavior at the moment, just lazy evaluation. This is similar to how values in the Haskell programming language (*https://www.haskell.org/*) are evaluated lazily only when absolutely needed.

If you never programmed in functional languages, you might be quite confused why laziness is so important and groundbreaking. It turns out that such behavior is quite useful and can improve the quality and freedom of your implementation quite a bit. For example, you no longer have to pay attention to which resources are fetched, when, and in what order. RxJava will load them only when they are absolutely needed.

As an example take this trivial fallback mechanism that we have all seen so many times:

```
void bestBookFor(Person person) {
    Book book;
```

```
    try {
        book = recommend(person);
    } catch (Exception e) {
        book = bestSeller();
    }
    display(book.getTitle());
}

void display(String title) {
    //...
}
```

You probably think there is nothing wrong with such a construct. In this example, we try to recommend the best book for a given person, but in case of failures, we degrade gracefully and display the best seller. The assumption is that fetching a bestseller is faster and can be cached. But what if you could add error handling declaratively so that try-catch blocks aren't obscuring real logic?

```
void bestBookFor(Person person) {
    Observable<Book> recommended = recommend(person);
    Observable<Book> bestSeller = bestSeller();
    Observable<Book> book = recommended.onErrorResumeNext(bestSeller);
    Observable<String> title = book.map(Book::getTitle);
    title.subscribe(this::display);
}
```

We are only exploring RxJava so far, thus I left all these intermediate values and types. In real life, bestBookFor() would look more like this:

```
void bestBookFor(Person person) {
    recommend(person)
            .onErrorResumeNext(bestSeller())
            .map(Book::getTitle)
            .subscribe(this::display);
}
```

This code is beautifully concise and readable. First find a recommendation for per son. In case of error (onErrorResumeNext), proceed with a bestseller. No matter which one succeeded, map returns a value by extracting the title and then displays it. onErrorResumeNext() is a powerful operator that intercepts exceptions happening upstream, swallows them, and subscribes to provided *backup* Observable. This is how Rx implements a try-catch clause. We will spend much more time on error handling later in this book (see "Declarative try-catch Replacement" on page 247). For the time being, notice how we can lazily call bestSeller() without worrying that fetching best seller happens even when a real recommendation went fine.

Composing Observables

SELECT * FROM PEOPLE is not really a state-of-the-art SQL query. First, you should not fetch all columns blindly, but fetching all rows is even more damaging. Our old API is not capable of paging results, viewing just a subset of a table. It might look like this, again in traditional enterprise application:

```
List<Person> listPeople(int page) {
    return query(
            "SELECT * FROM PEOPLE ORDER BY id LIMIT ? OFFSET ?",
            PAGE_SIZE,
            page * PAGE_SIZE
    );
}
```

This is not a SQL book, so we're going to set the implementation details aside. The author of this API was merciless: we don't have the freedom to choose any range of records, we can only operate on 0-based page numbers. However in RxJava, due to laziness we can actually simulate reading an entire database starting from given page:

```
import static rx.Observable.defer;
import static rx.Observable.from;


Observable<Person> allPeople(int initialPage) {
    return defer(() -> from(listPeople(initialPage)))
            .concatWith(defer(() ->
                    allPeople(initialPage + 1)));
}
```

This code snippet lazily loads the initial page of database records, for example 10 items. If no one subscribes, even this first query is not invoked. If there is a subscriber that only consumes a few initial elements (e.g., allPeople(0).take(3)), RxJava will unsubscribe automatically from our stream and no more queries are executed. So what happens when we request, say, 11 items but the first listPeople() call returned only 10? Well, RxJava figures out that the initial Observable is exhausted but the consumer is still hungry. Luckily, it sees concatWith() operator, that basically says: when the Observable on the left is completed, rather than propagating completion notification to subscribers, subscribe to Observable on the right and continue as if nothing happened, as depicted in the following marble diagram:

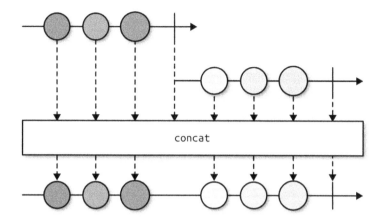

In other words, `concatWith()` can join together two `Observables` so that when the first one completes, the second one takes over. In `a.concatWith(b).subscribe(...)`, subscriber will first receive all events from `a`, followed by all events from `b`. In this case, the subscriber first receives an initial 10 items followed by a subsequent 10. However, look carefully, there is an alleged infinite recursion in our code! `allPeo ple(initialPage)` calls `allPeople(initialPage + 1)` without any stop condition. This is a recipe for `StackOverflowError` in most languages, but not here. Again, calling `allPeople()` is always lazy, therefore the moment you stop listening (unsubscribe), this recursion is over. Technically `concatWith()` can still produce `StackOverflowError` here. Wait until "Honoring the Requested Amount of Data" on page 237, you will learn how to deal with the varying demand for incoming data.

The technique of lazily loading data chunk by chunk is quite useful because it allows you to concentrate on business logic, not on low-level plumbing. We already see some benefits of applying RxJava even on a small scale. Designing an API with Rx in mind doesn't influence the entire architecture, because we can always fall back to `Blockin gObservable` and Java collections. But it's better to have wide range of possibilities that we can further trim down if necessary.

Lazy paging and concatenation

There are more ways to implement lazy paging with RxJava. If you think about it, the simplest way of loading paged data is to load everything and then take whatever we need. It sounds silly, but thanks to laziness it is feasible. First we generate all possible page numbers and then we request loading each and every page individually:

```
Observable<List<Person>> allPages = Observable
        .range(0, Integer.MAX_VALUE)
```

```
.map(this::listPeople)
.takeWhile(list -> !list.isEmpty());
```

If this were not RxJava, the preceding code would take an enormous amount of time and memory, basically loading the entire database to memory. But because `Observable` is lazy, no query to the database appeared yet. Moreover, if we find an empty page it means all further pages are empty, as well (we reached the end of the table). Therefore, we use `takeWhile()` rather than `filter()`. To flatten `allPages` to `Observable<Person>` we can use `concatMap()` (see "Preserving Order Using concatMap()" on page 75):

```
Observable<Person> people = allPages.concatMap(Observable::from);
```

`concatMap()` requires a transformation from `List<Person>` to `Observable<Person>`, executed for each page. Alternatively we can try `concatMapIterable()`, which does the same thing, but the transformation should return an `Iterable<Person>` for each upstream value (happening to be `Iterable<Person>` already):

```
Observable<Person> people = allPages.concatMapIterable(page -> page);
```

No matter which approach you choose, all transformations on `Person` object are lazy. As long as you limit the number of records you want to process (for example with `people.take(15)`), the `Observable<Person>` will invoke `listPeople()` as late as possible.

Imperative Concurrency

I don't often see explicit concurrency in enterprise applications. Most of the time a single request is handled by a single thread. The same thread does the following:

- Accepts TCP/IP connection
- Parses HTTP request
- Calls a controller or servlet
- Blocks on database call
- Processes results
- Encodes response (e.g., in JSON)
- Pushes raw bytes back to the client

This layered model affects user latency when the backend makes several independent requests for instance to database. They are performed sequentially, whereas one could easily parallelize them. Moreover scalability is affected. For example in Tomcat there are 200 threads by default in the executors that are responsible for handling requests. This means that we can't handle more than 200 concurrent connections. In case of a sudden but short burst of traffic, incoming connections are queued and the server responds with higher latency. However, this situation can't last forever, and Tomcat will eventually begin rejecting incoming traffic. We will devote large parts of the next chapter (see "Nonblocking HTTP Server with Netty and RxNetty" on page 169) on how to deal with this rather embarrassing shortcoming. For the time being, let's stay with traditional architecture. Executing every step of request handling within a single thread has some benefits, for example improved cache locality and minimal synchronization overhead.[1] Unfortunately, in classic applications, because overall latency is the sum of each layer's latencies, one malfunctioning component can have a negative impact on total latency.[2] Moreover, sometimes there are many steps that are independent from one another and can be executed concurrently. For example, we invoke multiple external APIs or execute several independent SQL queries.

JDK has quite good support for concurrency, especially since Java 5 with `Executor Service` and Java 8 with `CompletableFuture`. Nonetheless, it is not as widely used as it could be. For example, let's look at the following program with no concurrency whatsoever:

```
Flight lookupFlight(String flightNo) {
    //...
}

Passenger findPassenger(long id) {
    //...
}

Ticket bookTicket(Flight flight, Passenger passenger) {
    //...
}

SmtpResponse sendEmail(Ticket ticket) {
    //...
}
```

And on the client side:

```
Flight flight = lookupFlight("LOT 783");
Passenger passenger = findPassenger(42);
Ticket ticket = bookTicket(flight, passenger);
sendEmail(ticket);
```

Again, quite typical, classic blocking code, similar to what you can find in many applications. But if you look carefully from a latency perspective, the preceding code snippet has four steps; however, the first two are independent from each other. Only the third step (`bookTicket()`) needs results from `lookupFlight()` and `findPassen`

---

[1] In fact, RxJava tries to stay on the same thread via thread affinity in the event loop model to take advantage of this, as well.

[2] See also "Bulkhead Pattern and Fail-Fast" on page 295

ger(). There exists an obvious opportunity to take advantage of concurrency. Yet, very few developers will actually go down this path because it requires awkward thread pools, Futures, and callbacks. What if the API were already Rx-compatible, though? Remember, you can simply wrap blocking, legacy code in Observable, just like we did in the beginning of this chapter:

```
Observable<Flight> rxLookupFlight(String flightNo) {
    return Observable.defer(() ->
            Observable.just(lookupFlight(flightNo)));
}

Observable<Passenger> rxFindPassenger(long id) {
    return Observable.defer(() ->
            Observable.just(findPassenger(id)));
}
```

Semantically, the rx- methods do exactly the same thing and in the same way; that is, they are blocking by default. We didn't gain anything yet, apart from a more verbose API from the client perspective:

```
Observable<Flight> flight = rxLookupFlight("LOT 783");
Observable<Passenger> passenger = rxFindPassenger(42);
Observable<Ticket> ticket =
        flight.zipWith(passenger, (f, p) -> bookTicket(f, p));
ticket.subscribe(this::sendEmail);
```

Both traditional blocking programs and the one with Observable work exactly the same way. It's lazier by default, but the order of operations is essentially the same. First, we create Observable<Flight>, which as you already know, does nothing by default. Unless someone explicitly asks for a Flight, this Observable is just a lazy placeholder. We already learned that this is a valuable property of cold Observables. The same story goes for Observable<Passenger>; we have two placeholders of type Flight and Passenger, however no side-effects were performed yet. No database query or web-service call. If we decide to stop processing here, no superfluous work was done.

To proceed with bookTicket(), we need concrete instances of both Flight and Passenger. It is tempting to just block on these two Observables by using the toBlocking() operator. However, we would like to avoid blocking as much as possible to reduce resource consumption (especially memory) and allow greater concurrency. Another poor solution is to .subscribe() on the flight and passenger Observables and somehow wait for both callbacks to finish. It's fairly straightforward when Observable is blocking, but if callbacks appear asynchronously and you need to synchronize some global state waiting for both of them, this quickly becomes a nightmare. Also a nested subscribe() is nonidiomatic, and typically you want a single subscription for one message flow (use case). The only reason why callbacks work somewhat decently in JavaScript is because there is just one thread. The idiomatic way of subscribing to multiple `Observables` at the same time is `zip` and `zipWith`. You might perceive `zip` as a way to join two independent streams of data pair-wise. But far more often, `zip` is simply used to join together two single-item `Observables`. `ob1.zip(ob2).subscribe(...)` essentially means that receiving an event when both `ob1` and `ob2` are done (emit an event on their own). So whenever you see `zip`, it's more likely that someone is simply making a *join* step on two or more `Observables` that had *forked* paths of execution. `zip` is a way to asynchronously wait for two or more values, no matter which one appears last.

So let's get back to `flight.zipWith(passenger, this::bookTicket)` (a shorter syntax using method reference instead of explicit lambda, as in the code sample). The reason I keep all of the type information rather than fluently joining expressions is because I want you to pay attention to return types. `flight.zipWith(passenger, ...)` doesn't simply invoke callback when both `flight` and `passenger` are done; it returns a new `Observable` which you should immediately recognize as a lazy placeholder for data. Amazingly, at this point in time no computation was yet started, as well. We simply wrapped few data structures together, but no behavior was triggered. As long as no one subscribes to `Observable<Ticket>`, RxJava won't run any backend code. This is what finally happens in last statement: `ticket.subscribe()` explicitly asks for `Ticket`.

Where to Subscribe?

Pay attention to where you see `subscribe()` in domain code. Often your business logic is just composing `Observables` all the way down and returning them to some sort of framework or scaffolding layer. The actual subscription happens behind the scenes in a web framework or some glue code. It is not a bad practice to call `subscribe()` yourself, but try to push it out as far as possible.

To understand the flow of execution, it's useful to look bottom up. We subscribed to `ticket`, thus RxJava must subscribe transparently to both `flight` and `passenger`. At this point the real logic happens. Because both `Observables` are cold and no concurrency is yet involved, the first subscription to `flight` invokes the `lookupFlight()` blocking method right in the calling thread. When `lookupFlight()` is done, RxJava can subscribe to `passenger`. However, it already received a `Flight` instance from synchronous `flight`. `rxFindPassenger()` calls `findPassenger()` in a blocking fashion and receives a `Passenger` instance. At this juncture, data flows back downstream. Instances of `Flight` and `Passenger` are combined using the provided lambda (`bookTicket`) and passed to `ticket.subscribe()`.

This sounds like a lot of work considering it behaves and works essentially just like our blocking code in the beginning. But now we can declaratively apply concurrency without changing any logic. If our business methods returned `Future<Flight>` (or `CompletableFuture<Flight>`, it doesn't really matter), two decisions would have been made for us:

- The underlying invocation of `lookupFlight()` already began and there is no place for laziness. We don't block on such method, but work already started.

- We have no control over concurrency whatsoever, it is the method implementation that decides whether a `Future` task is invoked in a thread pool, new thread per request, and so on.

RxJava gives users more control. Just because `Observable<Flight>` wasn't implemented with concurrency in mind, this does not mean that we cannot apply it later. Real-world `Observables` are typically asynchronous already, but in rare cases you must add concurrency to an existing `Observable`. The consumers of our API, not the implementors, are free to choose the threading mechanism in case of the synchronous `Observable`. All of this is achieved by using the `subscribeOn()` operator:

```
Observable<Flight> flight =
    rxLookupFlight("LOT 783").subscribeOn(Schedulers.io());
Observable<Passenger> passenger =
    rxFindPassenger(42).subscribeOn(Schedulers.io());
```

At any point before subscribing, we can inject `subscribeOn()` operator and provide a so-called `Scheduler` instance. In this case, I used the `Schedulers.io()` factory method, but we can just as well use a custom `ExecutorService` and quickly wrap it with `Scheduler`. When subscription occurs, the lambda expression passed to `Observable.create()` is executed within the supplied `Scheduler` rather than the client thread. It is not necessary yet but we will examine schedulers in depth in "What Is a Scheduler?" on page 141 section. For the time being, treat a `Scheduler` like a thread pool.

How does `Scheduler` change the runtime behavior of our program? Remember that the `zip()` operator subscribes to two or more `Observables` and waits for pairs (or tuples). When subscription occurs asynchronously, all upstream `Observables` can call their underlying blocking code concurrently. If you now run your program, `lookupFlight()` and `findPassenger()` will begin execution immediately and concurrently when `ticket.subscribe()` is invoked. Then, `bookTicket()` will be applied as soon as the slower of the aforementioned `Observables` emits a value.

Talking about slowness, you can declaratively apply a timeout, as well, when a given `Observable` does not emit any value in the specified amount of time:

```
rxLookupFlight("LOT 783")
    .subscribeOn(Schedulers.io())
    .timeout(100, TimeUnit.MILLISECONDS)
```

As always, in case of errors, they are propagated downstream rather than thrown arbitrarily. So if the lookupFlight() method takes more than 100 milliseconds, you will end up with TimeoutException rather than an emitted value sent downstream to every subscriber. The timeout() operator is exhaustively explained in "Timing Out When Events Do Not Occur" on page 251.

We ended up with two methods running concurrently without much effort, assuming that your API is already Rx-driven. But we cheated a little bit with bookTicket() still returning Ticket, which definitely means it is blocking. Even if booking ticket was extremely fast, it is still worth declaring it as such, just to make the API easier to evolve. The evolution might mean adding concurrency or using in fully nonblocking environments (see Chapter 5). Remember that turning a nonblocking API into a blocking one is as easy as calling toBlocking(). The opposite is often challenging and requires lots of extra resources. Also, it is very difficult to predict the evolution of methods like rxBookTicket(), if they ever touch the network or filesystem, not to mention database, it is worth it to wrap them with an Observable indicating possible latency on the type level:

```
Observable<Ticket> rxBookTicket(Flight flight, Passenger passenger) {
    //...
}
```

But now zipWith() returns an awkward Observable<Observable<Ticket>> and the code no longer compiles. A good rule of thumb is that whenever you see double-wrapped type (for example Optional<Optional<...>>) there is a flatMap() invocation missing somewhere. That's the case here, as well. zipWith() takes a pair (or more generally a tuple) of events, applies a function taking these events as arguments, and puts the result into the downstream Observable as-is. This is why we saw Observable<Ticket> first but now it's Observable<Observable<Ticket>>, where Observable<Ticket> is the result of our supplied function. There are two ways to overcome this problem. One way is by using an intermediate pair returned from zipWith:

```
import org.apache.commons.lang3.tuple.Pair;

Observable<Ticket> ticket = flight
        .zipWith(passenger, (Flight f, Passenger p) -> Pair.of(f, p))
        .flatMap(pair -> rxBookTicket(pair.getLeft(), pair.getRight()));
```

If using an explicit Pair from third-party library did not obscure flow enough, method reference would actually work: Pair::of, but again, we decided that visible type information is more valuable than saving a few keystrokes. After all we read code

---

for much more time than we write it. An alternative to an intermediate pair is applying a `flatMap` with an identity function:

```
Observable<Ticket> ticket = flight
        .zipWith(passenger, this::rxBookTicket)
        .flatMap(obs -> obs);
```

This `obs -> obs` lambda expression is seemingly not doing anything, at least if it were a `map()` operator. But remember that `flatMap()` applies a function to each value inside `Observable`, so this function takes `Observable<Ticket>` as an argument in our case. Later, the result is not placed directly in the resulting stream, like with `map()`. Instead, the return value (of type `Observable<T>`) is "flattened," leading to an `Observable<T>` rather than `Observable<Observable<T>>`. When dealing with schedulers, the `flatMap()` operator becomes even more powerful. You might perceive `flatMap()` as merely a syntactic trick to avoid a nested `Observable<Observable<...>>` problem, but it's much more fundamental than this.

Observable.subscribeOn() Use Cases

It is tempting to think that `subscribeOn()` is the right tool for concurrency in RxJava. This operator works but you should not see the usage of `subscribeOn()` (and yet to be described `observeOn()`) often. In real life, `Observables` come from asynchronous sources, so custom scheduling is not needed at all. We use `subscribeOn()` throughout this chapter to explicitly show how to upgrade existing applications to use reactive principles selectively. But in practice, `Schedulers` and `subscribeOn()` are weapons of last resort, not something seen commonly.

flatMap() as Asynchronous Chaining Operator

In our sample application, we must now send a list of `Tickets` via e-mail. But we must keep in mind the following:

1. The list can be potentially quite long.
2. Sending an email might take several milliseconds or even seconds.
3. The application must keep running gracefully in case of failures, but report in the end which tickets failed to be delivered.

The last requirement quickly rules out simple `tickets.forEach(this::sendEmail)` because it eagerly throws an exception and won't continue with tickets that were not yet delivered. Exceptions are actually a nasty back door to the type system and just like callbacks are not very friendly when you want to manage them in a more robust way. That is why RxJava models them explicitly as special notifications, but be patient, we will get there. In light of the error-handling requirement, our code looks more-or-less like that:

```
List<Ticket> failures = new ArrayList<>();
for(Ticket ticket: tickets) {
    try {
        sendEmail(ticket);
    } catch (Exception e) {
        log.warn("Failed to send {}", ticket, e);
        failures.add(ticket);
    }
}
```

However, the first two requirements or guidelines aren't addressed. There is no reason why we keep sending emails from one thread sequentially. Traditionally, we could use an ExecutorService pool for that by submitting each email as a separate task:

```
List<Pair<Ticket, Future<SmtpResponse>>> tasks = tickets
    .stream()
    .map(ticket -> Pair.of(ticket, sendEmailAsync(ticket)))
    .collect(toList());

List<Ticket> failures = tasks.stream()
    .flatMap(pair -> {
        try {
            Future<SmtpResponse> future = pair.getRight();
            future.get(1, TimeUnit.SECONDS);
            return Stream.empty();
        } catch (Exception e) {
            Ticket ticket = pair.getLeft();
            log.warn("Failed to send {}", ticket, e);
            return Stream.of(ticket);
        }
    })
    .collect(toList());

//-----------------------------------

private Future<SmtpResponse> sendEmailAsync(Ticket ticket) {
    return pool.submit(() -> sendEmail(ticket));
}
```

That's a fair amount of code that all Java programmers should be familiar with. Yet it seems too verbose and accidentally complex. First, we iterate over tickets and submit them to a thread pool. To be precise, we call the sendEmailAsync() helper method that submits sendEmail() invocation wrapped in Callable<SmtpResponse> to a thread pool. Even more precise instances of Callable are first placed in an unbounded (by default) queue in front of a thread pool. Lack of mechanisms that slow down too rapid submission of tasks if they cannot be processed on time led to reactive streams and backpressure effort (see "Backpressure" on page 226).

Because later we will need a `Ticket` instance in case of failure, we must keep track of which `Future` was responsible for which `Ticket`, again in a `Pair`. In real production code, you should consider a more meaningful and dedicated container like a `TicketAsyncTask` value object. We collect all such pairs and proceed to the next iteration. At this point, the thread pool is already running multiple `sendEmail()` invocations concurrently, which is precisely what we were aiming at. The second loop goes through all `Future`s and tries to dereference them by blocking (`get()`) and awaiting for completion. If `get()` returns successfully, we skip such a `Ticket`. However, if there is an exception we return `Ticket` instance that was associated with this task—we know it failed and we want to report it later. `Stream.flatMap()` allows us to return zero or one elements (or actually any number), contrary to `Stream.map()`, which always requires one.

You might be wondering why we need two loops instead of just one like this:

```
//WARNING: code is sequential despite utilizing thread pool
List<Ticket> failures = tickets
        .stream()
        .map(ticket -> Pair.of(ticket, sendEmailAsync(ticket)))
        .flatMap(pair -> {
            //...
        })
        .collect(toList());
```

This is an interesting bug that is really difficult to find if you don't understand how `Stream`s in Java 8 work. Because streams—just like `Observables`—are lazy, they evaluate the underlying collection one element at a time and only when terminal operation was requested (e.g., `collect(toList())`). This means that a `map()` operation starting background tasks is not executed on all tickets immediately; rather, it's done one at a time, alternately by using a `flatMap()` operation. Furthermore, we really start one `Future`, block waiting for it, start a second `Future`, block waiting on that, and so on. An intermediate collection is needed to force evaluation, not because of clarity or readability. After all, `List<Pair<Ticket, Future<SmtpResponse>>>` type is hardly more readable.

That's plenty of work and the possibility of mistake is high, so it's no wonder that developers are reluctant to apply concurrent code on a daily basis. The little-known `ExecutorCompletionService` from JDK (*http://bit.ly/2d3eD4x*) is sometimes used when there is a pool of asynchronous tasks and we want to process them as they complete. Moreover, Java 8 brings `CompletableFuture` (see "CompletableFuture and Streams" on page 193) that is entirely reactive and nonblocking. But how can RxJava help here? First, assume that an API for sending an email is already retrofitted to use RxJava:

```
import static rx.Observable.fromCallable;

Observable<SmtpResponse> rxSendEmail(Ticket ticket) {
    //unusual synchronous Observable
    return fromCallable(() -> sendEmail())
}
```

There is no concurrency involved, just wrapping `sendEmail()` inside an `Observable`. This is a rare `Observable`; ordinarily you would use `subscribeOn()` in the implementation so that the `Observable` is asynchronous by default. At this point, we can iterate over all `tickets` as before:

```
List<Ticket> failures = Observable.from(tickets)
    .flatMap(ticket ->
        rxSendEmail(ticket)
            .flatMap(response -> Observable.<Ticket>empty())
            .doOnError(e -> log.warn("Failed to send {}", ticket, e))
            .onErrorReturn(err -> ticket))
    .toList()
    .toBlocking()
    .single();
```

Observable.ignoreElements()

It is easy to see that inner `flatMap()` in our example ignores response and returns an empty stream. In such cases, `flatMap()` is an overkill; the `ignoreElements()` operator is far more efficient. `ignoreElements()` simply ignores all emitted values and forwards `onCompleted()` or `onError()` notifications. Because we are ignoring the actual response and just deal with errors, `ignoreElements()` works great here.

All we are interested in lies inside the outer `flatMap()`. If it were just `flatMap(this::rxSendEmail)`, code would work; however, any failure emitted from `rxSendEmail` would terminate the entire stream. But we want to "catch" all emitted errors and collect them for later consumption. We use a similar trick to `Stream.flatMap()`: if `response` was successfully emitted, we transform it to an empty `Observable`. This basically means that we discard successful tickets. However, in case of failures, we return a `ticket` that raised an exception. An extra `doOnError()` callback allows us to log exception—of course we can just as well add logging to `onErrorReturn()` operator, but I found this separation of concerns more functional.

To remain compatible with previous implementations, we transform `Observable` into `Observable<List<Ticket>>`, `BlockingObservable<List<Ticket>>`, `toBlocking()`, and finally `List<Ticket>` (`single()`). Interestingly, even `BlockingObservable` remains lazy. A `toBlocking()` operator on its own doesn't force evaluation by subscribing to the underlying stream and it doesn't even block. Subscription and thus iteration and sending emails is postponed until `single()` is invoked.

Note that if we replace the outer `flatMap()` with `concatMap()` (see "Ways of Combining Streams: concat(), merge(), and switchOnNext()" on page 97 and "Preserving Order Using concatMap()" on page 75), we will encounter a similar bug as the mentioned with JDK's `Stream`. As opposed to `flatMap()` (or `merge`) that subscribe immediately to all inner streams, `concatMap` (or `concat`) subscribes one inner `Observable` after another. And as long as no one subscribed to `Observable`, no work even began.

So far, a simple `for` loop with a `try—catch` was replaced with less readable and more complex `Observable`. However, to turn our sequential code into multithreaded computation we barely need to add one extra operator:

```
Observable
        .from(tickets)
        .flatMap(ticket ->
                rxSendEmail(ticket)
                        .ignoreElements()
                        .doOnError(e -> log.warn("Failed to send {}", ticket, e))
                        .onErrorReturn(err -> ticket)
                        .subscribeOn(Schedulers.io())))
```

It is so noninvasive that you might find it hard to spot. One extra `subscribeOn()` operator causes each individual `rxSendMail()` to be executed on a specified `Schedu ler` (`io()`, in this case). This is one of the strengths of RxJava; it is not opinionated about threading, defaulting to synchronous execution but allowing seamless and almost transparent multithreading. Of course, this doesn't mean that you can safely inject schedulers in arbitrary places. But at least the API is less verbose and higher level. We will explore schedulers in much more detail later in "Multithreading in RxJava" on page 140. For the time being remember that `Observables` are synchronous by default; however, we can easily change that and apply concurrency in places where it was least expected. This is especially valuable in existing legacy applications, which you can optimize without much hassle.

Wrapping up if you are implementing `Observables` from scratch, making them asynchronous by default is more idiomatic. That means placing `subscribeOn()` directly inside `rxSendEmail()` rather than externally. Otherwise, you risk wrapping already asynchronous streams with yet another layer of schedulers. Of course, if the producer behind `Observable` is already asynchronous, it is even better because your stream does not bind to any particular thread. Additionally, you should postpone subscribing to an `Observable` as late as possible, typically close to the web framework of our outside world. This changes your mindset significantly. Your entire business logic is lazy until someone actually wants to see the results.[3]

Replacing Callbacks with Streams

Traditional APIs are blocking most of the time, meaning they force you to wait synchronously for the results. This approach works relatively well, at least before you heard about RxJava. But a blocking API is particularly problematic when data needs to be pushed from the API producer to consumers—this is anarea where RxJava really shines. There are numerous examples of such cases and various approaches are taken by API designers. Typically, we need to provide some sort of a callback that the API invokes, often called event listeners. One of the most common scenarios like that is Java Message Service (JMS) (*http://bit.ly/2d3hx9m*). Consuming JMS typically involves implementing a class that the application server or container notifies on every incoming messages. We can replace with relative ease such listeners with a composable `Observable`, which is much more robust and versatile. The traditional listener looks similar to this class, here using JMS support in Spring framework (*http://bit.ly/2d3hieL*), but our solution is technology-agnostic:

```
@Component
class JmsConsumer {

    @JmsListener(destination = "orders")
    public void newOrder(Message message) {
        //...
    }
}
```

When a JMS `message` is received, the `JmsConsumer` class must decide what to do with it. Typically, some business logic is invoked inside a message consumer. When a new component wants to be notified about such messages, it must modify `JmsConsumer` appropriately. Coversely, imagine `Observable<Message>` that can be subscribed to by anyone. Moreover, an entire universe of RxJava operators is available, allowing mapping, filtering, and combining capabilities. The easiest way to convert from a push, callback-based API to `Observable` is to use `Subjects`. Every time a new JMS message is delivered, we push that message to a `PublishSubject` that looks like an ordinary hot `Observable` from the outside:

```
private final PublishSubject<Message> subject = PublishSubject.create();

@JmsListener(destination = "orders", concurrency="1")
public void newOrder(Message msg) {
    subject.onNext(msg);
```

---

3 Compare it to lazy evaluation of expressions in Haskell.

```
    }

Observable<Message> observe() {
    return subject;
}
```

Keep in mind that `Observable<Message>` is hot; it begins emitting JMS messages as soon as they are consumed. If no one is subscribed at the moment, messages are simply lost. `ReplaySubject` is an alternative, but because it caches all events since the application startup, it's not suitable for long-running processes. In case you have a subscriber that absolutely must receive all messages, ensure that it subscribes before the JMS message listener is initialized. Additionally, our message listener has a `concurrency="1"` parameter to ensure that `Subject` is not invoked from multiple threads. As an alternative, you can use `Subject.toSerialized()`.

As a side note, `Subjects` are easier to get started but are known to be problematic after a while. In this particular case, we can easily replace `Subject` with the more idiomatic RxJava `Observable` that uses `create()` directly:

```
public Observable<Message> observe(
    ConnectionFactory connectionFactory,
    Topic topic) {
    return Observable.create(subscriber -> {
        try {
            subscribeThrowing(subscriber, connectionFactory, topic);
        } catch (JMSException e) {
            subscriber.onError(e);
        }
    });
}

private void subscribeThrowing(
        Subscriber<? super Message> subscriber,
        ConnectionFactory connectionFactory,
        Topic orders) throws JMSException {
    Connection connection = connectionFactory.createConnection();
    Session session = connection.createSession(true, AUTO_ACKNOWLEDGE);
    MessageConsumer consumer = session.createConsumer(orders);
    consumer.setMessageListener(subscriber::onNext);
    subscriber.add(onUnsubscribe(connection));
    connection.start();
}

private Subscription onUnsubscribe(Connection connection) {
    return Subscriptions.create(() -> {
        try {
            connection.close();
        } catch (Exception e) {
            log.error("Can't close", e);
        }
```

```
        });
    }
```

The JMS API provides two ways of receiving messages from a broker: synchronous via blocking `receive()` method, and nonblocking, using `MessageListener`. The non-blocking API is beneficial for many reasons; for example, it holds less resources like threads and stack memory. Also it aligns beautifully with the Rx style of programming. Rather than creating a `MessageListener` instance and calling our subscriber from within it, we can use this terse syntax with method reference:

```
consumer.setMessageListener(subscriber::onNext)
```

Also, we must take care of resource cleanup and proper error handling. This tiny transformation layer allows us to easily consume JMS messages without worrying about API internals. Here an example using the popular ActiveMQ (*http:// activemq.apache.org*) messaging broker running locally:

```
import org.apache.activemq.ActiveMQConnectionFactory;
import org.apache.activemq.command.ActiveMQTopic;

ConnectionFactory connectionFactory =
    new ActiveMQConnectionFactory("tcp://localhost:61616");
Observable<String> txtMessages =
        observe(connectionFactory, new ActiveMQTopic("orders"))
        .cast(TextMessage.class)
        .flatMap(m -> {
            try {
                return Observable.just(m.getText());
            } catch (JMSException e) {
                return Observable.error(e);
            }
        });
```

JMS, just like JDBC, has a reputation of heavily using checked `JMSException`, even when calling `getText()` on a `TextMessage`. To properly handle errors (see "Error Handling" on page 243 for more details) we use `flatMap()` and wrap exceptions. From that point, you can treat JMS messages flowing in like any other asynchronous and nonblocking stream. And by the way, we used the `cast()` operator that optimistically casts upstream events to a given type, failing with `onError()`, otherwise. `cast()` is basically a specialized `map()` operator that behaves like `map(x -> (TextMessage)x)`.

Polling Periodically for Changes

The worst blocking API that you can work with requires polling for changes. It provides no mechanism to push changes right at you, even with callbacks or by blocking indefinitely. The only mechanism this API gives is asking for the current state, and it is up to you to figure out if it differs from previous state or not. RxJava has few really powerful operators that you can apply to retrofit a given API to Rx style. The first case I want you to consider is a simple method that delivers a single value that represents state, for example `long getOrderBookLength()`. To track changes we must call this method frequently enough and capture differences. You can achieve this in RxJava with a very basic operator composition:

```
Observable
        .interval(10, TimeUnit.MILLISECONDS)
        .map(x -> getOrderBookLength())
        .distinctUntilChanged()
```

First we produce a synthetic `long` value every 10 milliseconds which serves as a basic ticking counter. For each such value (that is every 10 milliseconds), we call `getOrder BookLength()`. However, the aforementioned method doesn't change that often, and we don't want to flood our subscribers with lots of irrelevant state changes. Luckily we can simply say `distinctUntilChanged()` and RxJava will transparently skip `long` values returned by `getOrderBookLength()` that have not changed since last invocation, as demonstrated in the following marble diagram:

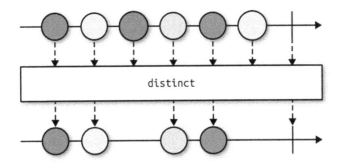

We can apply this pattern even further. Imagine that you are watching for filesystem or database table changes. The only mechanism at your disposal is taking a current snapshot of files or database records. You are building an API that will notify clients about every new item. Obviously, you can use `java.nio.file.WatchService` or database triggers, but take this as an educational example. This time, again, we begin by periodically taking a snapshot of current state:

```
Observable<Item> observeNewItems() {
    return Observable
            .interval(1, TimeUnit.SECONDS)
            .flatMapIterable(x -> query())
            .distinct();
}

List<Item> query() {
    //take snapshot of file system directory
```

```
        //or database table
    }
```

The `distinct()` operator keeps a record of all items that passed through it (see also "Dropping Duplicates Using distinct() and distinctUntilChanged()" on page 92). If the same item appears for the second time, it is simply ignored. That is why we can push the same list of `Items` every second. The first time they are pushed downstream to all subscribers. However, when the exact same list appears one second later, all items were already seen and are therefore discarded. If at some point in time the list returned from `query()` contains one extra `Item`, `distinct()` will let it go but discard it the next time. This simple pattern allows us to replace a bunch of `Thread.sleep()` invocations and manual caching with periodic polling. It is applicable in many areas, like File Transfer Protocol (FTP) (*https://en.wikipedia.org/wiki/File_Transfer_Proto col*) polling, web scraping, and so on.

Multithreading in RxJava

There are third-party APIs that are blocking and there is simply nothing we can do about it. We might not have source code, rewriting might result in too much risk. In that case, we must learn how to deal with blocking code rather than fighting it.

One of the hallmarks of RxJava is declarative concurrency, as opposed to imperative concurrency. Manually creating and managing threads is a thing of the past (compare with "Thread Pool of Connections" on page 331) most of us already use managed thread pools (e.g., with `ExecutorService`). But RxJava goes one step further: `Observable` can be nonblocking just like `CompletableFuture` in Java 8 (see "CompletableFuture and Streams" on page 193), but unlike the other, it is also lazy. Unless you subscribe, a well-behaving `Observable` will not perform any action. But the power of `Observable` goes even beyond that.

An asynchronous `Observable` is the one that calls your `Subscribers` callback methods (like `onNext()`) from a different thread. Recall "Mastering Observable.create()" on page 35 in which we explored when `subscribe()` is blocking, waiting until all notifications arrive? In real life, most `Observables` come from sources that are asynchronous by their nature. Chapter 5 is entirely devoted to such `Observables`. But even our simple JMS example from "Replacing Callbacks with Streams" on page 136, which uses a built-in, nonblocking API from the JMS specification (`MessageListener` interface). This is not enforced or suggested by the type system, but many `Observables` are asynchronous from the very beginning, and you should assume that. A blocking `subscribe()` method happens very rarely, when a lambda within `Observable.create()` is not backed by any asynchronous process or stream. However, by default (with `create()`) everything happens in the client thread (the one that subscribed). If you just poke onNext() directly within your create() callback, no multi-threading and concurrency is involved whatsoever.

Encountering such an unusual Observable, we can *declaratively* select the so-called Scheduler that will be used to emit values. In case of CompletableFuture, we have no control over underlying threads, the API made the decision and in worst case it is impossible to override it. RxJava rarely makes such decisions alone and chooses safe default: client thread and no multithreading involved. For the purposes of this chapter, we will use a really simple logging "library,"[4] which will print a message along with the current thread and number of milliseconds since the start of the program using System.currentTimeMillis():

```
void log(Object label) {
    System.out.println(
        System.currentTimeMillis() - start + "\t| " +
        Thread.currentThread().getName()   + "\t| " +
        label);
}
```

What Is a Scheduler?

RxJava is concurrency-agnostic, and as a matter of fact it does not introduce concurrency on its own. However, some abstractions to deal with threads are exposed to the end user. Also, certain operators cannot work properly without concurrency; see "Other Uses for Schedulers" on page 163 for some of them. Luckily, the Scheduler class, the only one you must pay attention to, is fairly simple. In principle it works similarly to ScheduledExecutorService from java.util.concurrent—it executes arbitrary blocks of code, possibly in the future. However, to meet Rx contract, it offers some more fine-grained abstractions, which you can see more of in the advanced section "Scheduler implementation details overview" on page 146.

Schedulers are used together with subscribeOn() and observeOn() operators as well as when creating certain types of Observables. A scheduler only creates instances of Workers that are responsible for scheduling and running code. When RxJava needs to schedule some code it first asks Scheduler to provide a Worker and uses the latter to schedule subsequent tasks. You will find examples of this API later on, but first familiarize yourself with available built-in schedulers:

Schedulers.newThread()
This scheduler simply starts a new thread every time it is requested via subscribeOn() or observeOn(). newThread() is hardly ever a good choice, not only

---

4 Obviously, for any real project, you will use a production-grade logging system like Logback (*http://logback.qos.ch/*) or Log4J 2 (*http://logging.apache.org/log4j/2.x/*).

because of the latency involved when starting a thread, but also because this thread is not reused. Stack space must be allocated up front (typically around one megabyte, as controlled by the -Xss parameter of the JVM) and the operating system must start new native thread. When the Worker is done, the thread simply terminates. This scheduler can be useful only when tasks are coarse-grained: it takes a lot of time to complete but there are very few of them, so that threads are unlikely to be reused at all. See also: "Thread per Connection" on page 329. In practice, following Schedulers.io() is almost always a better choice.

Schedulers.io()

This scheduler is similar to newThread(), but already started threads are recycled and can possibly handle future requests. This implementation works similarly to ThreadPoolExecutor from java.util.concurrent with an unbounded pool of threads. Every time a new Worker is requested, either a new thread is started (and later kept idle for some time) or the idle one is reused.

The name io() is not a coincidence. Consider using this scheduler for I/O bound tasks which require very little CPU resources. However they tend to take quite some time, waiting for network or disk. Thus, it is a good idea to have a relatively big pool of threads. Still, be careful with unbounded resources of any kind—in case of slow or unresponsive external dependencies like web services, io() scheduler might start an enormous number of threads, leading to your very own application becoming unresponsive, as well. See "Managing Failures with Hystrix" on page 291 for more details how to tackle this problem.

Schedulers.computation()

You should use a computation scheduler when tasks are entirely CPU-bound; that is, they require computational power and have no blocking code (reading from disk, network, sleeping, waiting for lock, etc.) Because each task executed on this scheduler is supposed to fully utilize one CPU core, executing more such tasks in parallel than there are available cores would not bring much value. Therefore, computation() scheduler by default limits the number of threads running in parallel to the value of availableProcessors(), as found in the Runtime.getRuntime() utility class.

If for some reason you need a different number of threads than the default, you can always use the rx.scheduler.max-computation-threads system property. By taking less threads you ensure that there is always one or more CPU cores idle, and even under heavy load, computation() thread pool does not saturate your server. It is not possible to have more computation threads than cores.

computation() scheduler uses unbounded queue in front of every thread, so if the task is scheduled but all cores are occupied, they are queued. In case of load peak, this scheduler will keep the number of threads limited. However, the queue just before each thread will keep growing.

Luckily, built-in operators, especially observeOn() that we are about to discover in "Declarative Concurrency with observeOn()" on page 159 ensure that this Scheduler is not overloaded.

Schedulers.from(Executor executor)

Schedulers are internally more complex than Executors from java.util.con current, so a separate abstraction was needed. But because they are conceptually quite similar, unsurprisingly there is a wrapper that can turn Executor into Sched uler using the from() factory method:

```
import com.google.common.util.concurrent.ThreadFactoryBuilder;
import rx.Scheduler;
import rx.schedulers.Schedulers;

import java.util.concurrent.ExecutorService;
import java.util.concurrent.LinkedBlockingQueue;
import java.util.concurrent.ThreadFactory;
import java.util.concurrent.ThreadPoolExecutor;

//...

ThreadFactory threadFactory = new ThreadFactoryBuilder()
    .setNameFormat("MyPool-%d")
    .build();
Executor executor = new ThreadPoolExecutor(
    10, //corePoolSize
    10, //maximumPoolSize
    0L, TimeUnit.MILLISECONDS, //keepAliveTime, unit
    new LinkedBlockingQueue<>(1000), //workQueue
    threadFactory
);
Scheduler scheduler = Schedulers.from(executor);
```

I am intentionally using this verbose syntax for creating ExecutorService rather than the more simple version:

```
import java.util.concurrent.Executors;

//...

ExecutorService executor = Executors.newFixedThreadPool(10);
```

Although tempting, the Executors factory class hardcodes several defaults that are impractical or even dangerous in enterprise applications. For examples, it uses unbounded LinkedBlockingQueue that can grow infinitely, resulting in OutOfMemor yError for cases in which there are a of large number of outstanding tasks. Also, the default ThreadFactory uses meaningless thread names like pool-5-thread-3.

Naming threads properly is an invaluable tool when profiling or analyzing thread dumps. Implementing `ThreadFactory` from scratch is a bit cumbersome, so we used ThreadFactoryBuilder from Guava (*https://github.com/google/guava*). If you are interested in tuning and properly utilizing thread pools even further, see "Thread Pool of Connections" on page 331 and "Managing Failures with Hystrix" on page 291. Creating schedulers from `Executor` that we consciously configured is advised for projects dealing with high load. However, because RxJava has no control over independently created threads in an `Executor`, it cannot pin threads (that is, try to keep work of the same task on the same thread to improve cache locality). This `Scheduler` barely makes sure a single `Scheduler.Worker` (see "Scheduler implementation details overview" on page 146) processes events sequentially.

`Schedulers.immediate()`

> `Schedulers.immediate()` is a special scheduler that invokes a task within the client thread in a blocking fashion, rather than asynchronously. Using it is pointless unless some part of your API requires providing a scheduler, whereas you are absolutely fine with default behavior of `Observable`, not involving any threading at all. In fact, subscribing to an `Observable` (more on that in a second) via `immediate()` Scheduler typically has the same effect as not subscribing with any particular scheduler at all. In general, avoid this scheduler, it blocks the calling thread and is of limited use.

`Schedulers.trampoline()`

> The `trampoline()` scheduler is very similar to `immediate()` because it also schedules tasks in the same thread, effectively blocking. However, as opposed to `immediate()`, the upcoming task is executed when all previously scheduled tasks complete. `immediate()` invokes a given task right away, whereas `trampoline()` waits for the current task to finish. Trampoline is a pattern in functional programming that allows implementing recursion without infinitely growing the call stack. This is best explained with an example, first involving `immediate()`. By the way, notice that we do not interact directly with a `Scheduler` instance but first create a `Worker`. This makes sense as you will quickly see in "Scheduler implementation details overview" on page 146.

```
Scheduler scheduler = Schedulers.immediate();
Scheduler.Worker worker = scheduler.createWorker();

log("Main start");
worker.schedule(() -> {
    log(" Outer start");
    sleepOneSecond();
    worker.schedule(() -> {
        log("  Inner start");
        sleepOneSecond();
        log("  Inner end");
```

```
    });
    log(" Outer end");
  });
  log("Main end");
  worker.unsubscribe();
```

The output is as expected; you could actually replace `schedule()` with a simple method invocation:

```
1044    | main  | Main start
1094    | main  |  Outer start
2097    | main  |   Inner start
3097    | main  |   Inner end
3100    | main  |  Outer end
3100    | main  | Main end
```

Inside the `Outer` block we `schedule()` `Inner` block that gets invoked immediately, interrupting the `Outer` task. When `Inner` is done, the control goes back to `Outer`. Again, this is simply a convoluted way of invoking a task in a blocking manner indirectly via `immediate()` Scheduler. But what happens if we replace `Schedulers.immediate()` with `Schedulers.trampoline()`? The output is quite different:

```
1030    | main  | Main start
1096    | main  |  Outer start
2101    | main  |  Outer end
2101    | main  |   Inner start
3101    | main  |   Inner end
3101    | main  | Main end
```

Do you see how `Outer` manages to complete before `Inner` even starts? This is because the `Inner` task was queued inside the `trampoline()` Scheduler, which was already occupied by the `Outer` task. When `Outer` finished, the first task from the queue (`Inner`) began. We can go even further to make sure you understand the difference:

```
log("Main start");
worker.schedule(() -> {
    log(" Outer start");
    sleepOneSecond();
    worker.schedule(() -> {
        log("  Middle start");
        sleepOneSecond();
        worker.schedule(() -> {
            log("   Inner start");
            sleepOneSecond();
            log("   Inner end");
        });
        log("  Middle end");
    });
```

```
        log(" Outer end");
    });
    log("Main end");
```

The Worker from immediate() Scheduler outputs the following:

```
1029    | main   | Main start
1091    | main   |  Outer start
2093    | main   |   Middle start
3095    | main   |    Inner start
4096    | main   |    Inner end
4099    | main   |   Middle end
4099    | main   |  Outer end
4099    | main   | Main end
```

Versus the trampoline() worker:

```
1041    | main   | Main start
1095    | main   |  Outer start
2099    | main   |  Outer end
2099    | main   |   Middle start
3101    | main   |   Middle end
3101    | main   |    Inner start
4102    | main   |    Inner end
4102    | main   | Main end
```

Schedulers.test()

This Scheduler is used only for testing purposes, and you will never see it in production code. Its main advantage is the ability to arbitrarily advance the clock, simulating time passing by. TestScheduler is described to a great extent in "Schedulers in Unit Testing" on page 260. Schedulers alone are not very interesting. If you want to discover how they work internally and how to implement your own, check out the next section.

Scheduler implementation details overview

This section is entirely optional, feel free to jump straight to "Declarative Subscription with subscribeOn()" on page 150 if you are not interested in implementation details.

Scheduler not only decouples tasks and their execution (typically by running them in another thread), but it also abstracts away the clock, as we will learn in "Virtual Time" on page 258. The API of the Scheduler is a bit simpler compared to, for example, ScheduledExecutorService:

```
abstract class Scheduler {
    abstract Worker createWorker();
```

```
        long now();

        abstract static class Worker implements Subscription {

            abstract Subscription schedule(Action0 action);

            abstract Subscription schedule(Action0 action,
                                long delayTime, TimeUnit unit);

            long now();
        }
    }
```

When RxJava wants to schedule a task (presumably, but not necessarily in the background), it must first ask for an instance of Worker. It is the Worker that allows scheduling the task without any delay or at some point in time. Both Scheduler and Worker have an overridable source of time (now() method) that it uses to determine when a given task is supposed to run. Naively, you can think of a Scheduler like a thread pool and a Worker like a thread inside that pool.

The separation between Scheduler and Worker is necessary to easily implement some of the guidelines enforced by the Rx contract, namely invoking Subscriber's method sequentially, not concurrently. Worker's contract provides just that: two tasks scheduled on the same Worker will never run concurrently. However, independent Workers from the same Scheduler can run tasks concurrently just fine.

Rather than going through the API, let's analyze the source code of an existing Scheduler, namely HandlerScheduler, as found in the RxAndroid project (*https://github.com/ReactiveX/RxAndroid*). This Scheduler simply runs all scheduled tasks on an Android UI thread. Updating the user interface is only allowed from that thread (see "Android Development with RxJava" on page 277 for more details). This is similar to the Event Dispatch Thread (EDT) (*http://bit.ly/2cMxH4U*) as found in Swing, where most of the updates to windows and components must be executed within dedicated thread (EDT). Unsurprisingly, there is also the RxSwing[5] project for that.

The code snippet that follows is a stripped down and incomplete class from RxAndroid for education purposes only:

```
package rx.android.schedulers;

import android.os.Handler;
import android.os.Looper;
import rx.Scheduler;
import rx.Subscription;
```

---

5 *https://github.com/ReactiveX/RxSwing*

```
import rx.functions.Action0;
import rx.internal.schedulers.ScheduledAction;
import rx.subscriptions.Subscriptions;

import java.util.concurrent.TimeUnit;

public final class SimplifiedHandlerScheduler extends Scheduler {

    @Override
    public Worker createWorker() {
        return new HandlerWorker();
    }

    static class HandlerWorker extends Worker {

        private final Handler handler = new Handler(Looper.getMainLooper());

        @Override
        public void unsubscribe() {
            //Implementation coming soon...
        }

        @Override
        public boolean isUnsubscribed() {
            //Implementation coming soon...
            return false;
        }

        @Override
        public Subscription schedule(final Action0 action) {
            return schedule(action, 0, TimeUnit.MILLISECONDS);
        }

        @Override
        public Subscription schedule(
        Action0 action, long delayTime, TimeUnit unit) {
            ScheduledAction scheduledAction = new ScheduledAction(action);
            handler.postDelayed(scheduledAction, unit.toMillis(delayTime));

            scheduledAction.add(Subscriptions.create(() ->
                    handler.removeCallbacks(scheduledAction)));

            return scheduledAction;
        }
    }
}
```

Details of the Android API are not important at the moment. What happens here is that every time we schedule something on a HandlerWorker, the block of code is passed to a special postDelayed() method that executes it on a dedicated Android thread. There is just one such thread, so events are serialized not only within, but also across Workers.

Before we pass action to be executed, we wrap it with ScheduledAction, which implements both Runnable and Subscription. RxJava is lazy whenever it can be—this also applies to scheduling tasks. If for any reason you decide that a given action should not be executed after all (this makes sense when the action was scheduled in the future, not immediately), simply run unsubscribe() on the Subscription returned from schedule(). It is the responsibility of the Worker to properly handle unsubscription (best effort at least).

Client code can also decide to unsubscribe() from Worker in its entirety. This should unsubscribe all queued tasks as well as release the Worker so that the underlying thread can potentially be reused later. The following code snippet enhances the Sim plifiedHandlerScheduler by adding Worker unsubscription flow (only modified methods are included):

```
private CompositeSubscription compositeSubscription =
    new CompositeSubscription();

@Override
public void unsubscribe() {
    compositeSubscription.unsubscribe();
}

@Override
public boolean isUnsubscribed() {
    return compositeSubscription.isUnsubscribed();
}

@Override
public Subscription schedule(Action0 action, long delayTime, TimeUnit unit) {
    if (compositeSubscription.isUnsubscribed()) {
        return Subscriptions.unsubscribed();
    }

    final ScheduledAction scheduledAction = new ScheduledAction(action);
    scheduledAction.addParent(compositeSubscription);
    compositeSubscription.add(scheduledAction);

    handler.postDelayed(scheduledAction, unit.toMillis(delayTime));

    scheduledAction.add(Subscriptions.create(() ->
            handler.removeCallbacks(scheduledAction)));

    return scheduledAction;
}
```

In "Controlling Listeners by Using Subscription and Subscriber<T>" on page 32, we explored the Subscription interface but never really looked at the implementation details. `CompositeSubscription` is one out of many implementations available that itself is just a container for child `Subscriptions` (a *Composite* design pattern). Unsubscribing from `CompositeSubscription` means unsubscribing from all children. You also can add and remove the children managed by `CompositeSubscription`.

In our custom `Scheduler`, `CompositeSubscription` is used to track all `Subscrip`-`tions` from the previous `schedule()` invocations (see `compositeSubscrip`-`tion.add(scheduledAction)`). On the other hand, the child `ScheduledAction` needs to know about its parent (see: `addParent()`) so that it can remove itself when the action is completed or canceled. Otherwise, `Worker` would accumulate stale child `Sub`-`scriptions` forever. When the client code decides that it no longer needs a `Handler` `Worker` instance, it unsubscribes from it. The unsubscription is propagated to all (if any) outstanding child `Subscriptions`.

That was a very brief introduction to `Schedulers` in RxJava. The details of their internals are not that useful in daily work; as a matter of fac, they are designed in such as way as to make using RxJava more intuitive and predictable. That being said, let's quickly see how `Schedulers` solve many concurrency problems in Rx.

Declarative Subscription with subscribeOn()

In "Mastering Observable.create()" on page 35 we saw that `subscribe()` by default uses the client thread. To recap, here is the most simple subscription that you can come up with where no threading was involved whatsoever:

```
Observable<String> simple() {
    return Observable.create(subscriber -> {
        log("Subscribed");
        subscriber.onNext("A");
        subscriber.onNext("B");
        subscriber.onCompleted();
    });
}

//...

log("Starting");
final Observable<String> obs = simple();
log("Created");
final Observable<String> obs2 = obs
        .map(x -> x)
        .filter(x -> true);
log("Transformed");
obs2.subscribe(
        x -> log("Got " + x),
        Throwable::printStackTrace,
        () -> log("Completed")
```

```
);
log("Exiting");
```

Notice where the logging statements are placed and study the output carefully, especially with regard to which thread invoked the print statement:

```
 33 | main | Starting
120 | main | Created
128 | main | Transformed
133 | main | Subscribed
133 | main | Got A
133 | main | Got B
133 | main | Completed
134 | main | Exiting
```

Pay attention: the order of statements is absolutely predictable. First, every line of code in the preceding code snippet runs in the main thread, there are no thread pools and no asynchronous emission of events involved. Second, the order of execution might not be entirely clear at first sight.

When the program starts, it prints Starting, which is understandable. After creating an instance of Observable<String>, we see the Created message. Notice that Subscribed appears later, when we actually subscribe. Without the subscribe() invocation, the block of code inside Observable.create() is never executed. Moreover, even map() and filter() operators do not have any visible side effects, notice how the Transformed message is printed even before Subscribed.

Later, we receive all emitted events and completion notification. Finally, the Exiting statement is printed and the program can return. This is an interesting observation—subscribe() was supposed to be registering a callback when events appear asynchronously. This is the assumption that you should make by default. However in this case there is no threading involved and subscribe() is actually blocking. How is this so?

There is an inherent but hidden connection between subscribe() and create(). Every time you call subscribe() on an Observable, its OnSubscribe callback method is invoked (wrapping the lambda expression you passed to create()). It receives your Subscriber as an argument. By default, this happens in the same thread and is blocking, so whatever you do inside create() will block subscribe(). If your create() method sleeps for few seconds, subscribe() will block. Moreover, if there are operators between Observable.create() and your Subscriber (lambda acting as callback), all these operators are invoked on behalf of the thread that invoked subscribe(). RxJava does not inject any concurrency facilities by default between Observable and Subscriber. The reason behind that is that Observables tend to be backed by other concurrency mechanisms like event loops or custom threads, so Rx lets you take full control rather than imposing any convention.

This observation prepares the landscape for the subscribeOn() operator. By inserting subscribeOn() anywhere between an original Observable and subscribe(), you declaratively select Scheduler where the OnSubscribe callback method will be invoked. No matter what you do inside create(), this work is offloaded to an independent Scheduler and your subscribe() invocation no longer blocks:

```
log("Starting");
final Observable<String> obs = simple();
log("Created");
obs
        .subscribeOn(schedulerA)
        .subscribe(
                x -> log("Got " + x),
                Throwable::printStackTrace,
                () -> log("Completed")
        );
log("Exiting");

35  | main     | Starting
112 | main     | Created
123 | main     | Exiting
123 | Sched-A-0 | Subscribed
124 | Sched-A-0 | Got A
124 | Sched-A-0 | Got B
124 | Sched-A-0 | Completed
```

Do you see how the main thread exits before Observable even begins emitting any values? Technically, the order of log messages is no longer that predictable because two threads are running concurrently: main, which subscribed and wants to exit, and Sched-A-0, which emits events as soon as someone subscribed. The schedulerA as well as Sched-A-0 thread come from the following sample schedulers we built for illustration purposes:

```
import static java.util.concurrent.Executors.newFixedThreadPool;


ExecutorService poolA = newFixedThreadPool(10, threadFactory("Sched-A-%d"));
Scheduler schedulerA = Schedulers.from(poolA);

ExecutorService poolB = newFixedThreadPool(10, threadFactory("Sched-B-%d"));
Scheduler schedulerB = Schedulers.from(poolB);

ExecutorService poolC = newFixedThreadPool(10, threadFactory("Sched-C-%d"));
Scheduler schedulerC = Schedulers.from(poolC);

private ThreadFactory threadFactory(String pattern) {
    return new ThreadFactoryBuilder()
        .setNameFormat(pattern)
```

```
        .build();
    }
```

These schedulers will be used across all examples, but they are fairly easy to remember. Three independent schedulers, each managing 10 threads from an `ExecutorSer vice`. To make the output nicer, each thread pool has a distinct naming pattern.

Before we begin, you must understand that in mature applications, in terms of Rx adoption, `subscribeOn()` is very seldom used. Normally, `Observables` come from sources that are naturally asynchronous (like RxNetty, see "Nonblocking HTTP Server with Netty and RxNetty" on page 169) or apply scheduling on their own (like Hystrix, see "Managing Failures with Hystrix" on page 291). You should treat `subscri beOn()` only in special cases when the underlying `Observable` is known to be synchronous (`create()` being blocking). However, `subscribeOn()` is still a much better solution than hand-crafted threading within `create()`:

```
//Don't do this
Observable<String> obs = Observable.create(subscriber -> {
    log("Subscribed");
    Runnable code = () -> {
        subscriber.onNext("A");
        subscriber.onNext("B");
        subscriber.onCompleted();
    };
    new Thread(code, "Async").start();
});
```

The preceding code mixes two concepts: producing events and choosing concurrency strategy. `Observable` should be responsible only for production logic, whereas it is only the client code that can make judicious decision about concurrency. Remember that `Observable` is lazy but also immutable, in the sense that `subscribeOn()` affects only downstream subscribers, if someone subscribes to the exact same `Observable` without `subscribeOn()` in between, no concurrency will be involved by default.

Keep in mind that in this chapter our focus is on existing applications and introducing RxJava gradually. The `subscribeOn()` operator is quite useful in such circumstances; however, after you grasp reactive extensions and begin using them on large scale, the value of `subscribeOn()` diminishes. In entirely reactive software stacks, as found for example at Netflix , `subscribeOn()` is almost never used, yet all `Observables` are asynchronous. Most of the time `Observables` come from asynchronous sources and they are treated as asynchronous by default. Therefore, using `subscribeOn()` is very limited, mostly when retrofitting existing APIs or libraries. In Chapter 5, we write write truly asynchronous applications without explicit `subscribeOn()` and `Schedu lers` altogether.

subscribeOn() Concurrency and Behavior

There are several nuances regarding how subscribeOn() works. First, curious reader should be wondering what happens if two invocations of the subscribeOn() appear between Observable and subscribe(). The answer is simple: subscribeOn() closest to the original Observable *wins*. This has important practical implications. If you are designing an API and you use subscribeOn() internally, the client code has no way of overriding the Scheduler of your choice. This can be a conscious design decision; after all, the API designer might know best which Scheduler is appropriate. On the other hand, providing an overloaded version of said API that allows overriding the chosen Scheduler is always a good idea.

Let's study how subscribeOn() behaves:

```
log("Starting");
Observable<String> obs = simple();
log("Created");
obs
        .subscribeOn(schedulerA)
        //many other operators
        .subscribeOn(schedulerB)
        .subscribe(
                x -> log("Got " + x),
                Throwable::printStackTrace,
                () -> log("Completed")
        );
log("Exiting");
```

The output reveals only schedulerA's threads:

```
17 | main    | Starting
73 | main    | Created
83 | main    | Exiting
84 | Sched-A-0 | Subscribed
84 | Sched-A-0 | Got A
84 | Sched-A-0 | Got B
84 | Sched-A-0 | Completed
```

Interestingly, subscribing on schedulerB is not entirely ignored in favor of schedu lerA. schedulerB is still used for a short period of time, but it barely schedules new action on schedulerA, which does all the work. Thus, multiple subscribeOn() are not only ignored, but also introduce small overhead.

Speaking of operators, we said that the create() method used when there is a new Subscriber is executed within the provided scheduler (if any). But which thread executes all these transformations happening between create() and subscribe()? We already know that when all operators are executed by default in the same thread (scheduler), no concurrency is involved by default:

```
log("Starting");
final Observable<String> obs = simple();
log("Created");
obs
        .doOnNext(this::log)
        .map(x -> x + '1')
        .doOnNext(this::log)
        .map(x -> x + '2')
        .subscribeOn(schedulerA)
        .doOnNext(this::log)
        .subscribe(
                x -> log("Got " + x),
                Throwable::printStackTrace,
                () -> log("Completed")
        );
log("Exiting");
```

We sprinkled the pipeline of operators occasionally with doOnNext() to see which thread is in control at this point. Remember that the position of subscribeOn() is not relevant, it can be right after Observable or just before subscribe(). The output is unsurprising:

```
20  | main      | Starting
104 | main      | Created
123 | main      | Exiting
124 | Sched-A-0 | Subscribed
124 | Sched-A-0 | A
124 | Sched-A-0 | A1
124 | Sched-A-0 | A12
124 | Sched-A-0 | Got A12
124 | Sched-A-0 | B
124 | Sched-A-0 | B1
124 | Sched-A-0 | B12
125 | Sched-A-0 | Got B12
```

Watch how create() is invoked and produces A and B events. These events travel sequentially through the scheduler's thread to finally reach the Subscriber. Many newcomers to RxJava believe that using a Scheduler with a large number of threads will automatically fork processing of events concurrently and somehow join all the results together in the end. This is not the case. RxJava creates a single Worker instance (see: "Scheduler implementation details overview" on page 146) for the entire pipeline, mostly to guarantee sequential processing of events.

This means that if one of your operators is particularly slow—for example, map() reading data from disk in order to transform events passing by—this costly operation will be invoked within the same thread. A single broken operator can slow down the entire pipeline, from production to consumption. This is an antipattern in RxJava, operators should be nonblocking, fast, and as pure as possible.

Again, flatMap() comes to the rescue. Rather than blocking within map(), we can invoke flatMap() and asynchronously collect all the results. Therefore, flatMap() and merge() are *the* operators when we want to achieve true parallelism. But even with flatMap() it is not obvious. Imagine a grocery store (let's call it "RxGroceries") that provides an API for purchasing goods:

```
class RxGroceries {

    Observable<BigDecimal> purchase(String productName, int quantity) {
        return Observable.fromCallable(() ->
            doPurchase(productName, quantity));
    }

    BigDecimal doPurchase(String productName, int quantity) {
        log("Purchasing " + quantity + " " + productName);
        //real logic here
        log("Done " + quantity + " " + productName);
        return priceForProduct;
    }

}
```

Obviously, the implementation of doPurchase() is irrelevant here, just imagine it takes some time and resources to complete. We simulate business logic by adding artificial sleep of one second, slightly higher if quantity is bigger. Blocking Observa bles like the one returned from purchase() are unusual in a real application, but let's keep it this way for educational purposes. When purchasing several goods we would like to parallelize as much as possible and calculate total price for all goods in the end. The first attempt is fruitless:

```
Observable<BigDecimal> totalPrice = Observable
        .just("bread", "butter", "milk", "tomato", "cheese")
        .subscribeOn(schedulerA)  //BROKEN!!!
        .map(prod -> rxGroceries.doPurchase(prod, 1))
        .reduce(BigDecimal::add)
        .single();
```

The result is correct, it is an Observable with just a single value: total price, calculated using reduce(). For each product, we invoke doPurchase() with quantity one. However, despite using schedulerA backed by a thread pool of 10, the code is entirely sequential:

```
 144 | Sched-A-0 | Purchasing 1 bread
1144 | Sched-A-0 | Done 1 bread
1146 | Sched-A-0 | Purchasing 1 butter
2146 | Sched-A-0 | Done 1 butter
2146 | Sched-A-0 | Purchasing 1 milk
3147 | Sched-A-0 | Done 1 milk
3147 | Sched-A-0 | Purchasing 1 tomato
4147 | Sched-A-0 | Done 1 tomato
```

```
4147 | Sched-A-0 | Purchasing 1 cheese
5148 | Sched-A-0 | Done 1 cheese
```

Notice how each product blocks subsequent ones from processing. When the purchase of bread is done, butter begins immediately, but not earlier. Strangely, even replacing map() with flatMap() does not help, and the output is exactly the same:

```
Observable
        .just("bread", "butter", "milk", "tomato", "cheese")
        .subscribeOn(schedulerA)
        .flatMap(prod -> rxGroceries.purchase(prod, 1))
        .reduce(BigDecimal::add)
        .single();
```

The code does not work concurrently because there is just a single flow of events, which by design must run sequentially. Otherwise, your Subscriber would need to be aware of concurrent notifications (onNext(), onComplete(), etc.), so it is a fair compromise. Luckily, the idiomatic solution is very close. The main Observable emitting products cannot be parallelized. However, for each product, we create a new, independent Observable as returned from purchase(). Because they are independent, we can safely schedule each one of them concurrently:

```
Observable<BigDecimal> totalPrice = Observable
        .just("bread", "butter", "milk", "tomato", "cheese")
        .flatMap(prod ->
                rxGroceries
                        .purchase(prod, 1)
                        .subscribeOn(schedulerA))
        .reduce(BigDecimal::add)
        .single();
```

Can you spot where subscribeOn() is? The main Observable is not really doing anything, so a special thread pool is unnecessary. However each substream created within flatMap() is supplied with a schedulerA. Every time subscribeOn() is used to the Scheduler gets a chance to return a new Worker, and therefore a separate thread (simplifying a bit):

```
113  | Sched-A-1 | Purchasing 1 butter
114  | Sched-A-0 | Purchasing 1 bread
125  | Sched-A-2 | Purchasing 1 milk
125  | Sched-A-3 | Purchasing 1 tomato
126  | Sched-A-4 | Purchasing 1 cheese
1126 | Sched-A-2 | Done 1 milk
1126 | Sched-A-0 | Done 1 bread
1126 | Sched-A-1 | Done 1 butter
1128 | Sched-A-3 | Done 1 tomato
1128 | Sched-A-4 | Done 1 cheese
```

Finally, we achieved true concurrency. Each purchase operation now begins at the same time and they all eventually finish. The flatMap() operator is carefully designed and implemented so that it collects all events from all independent streams and pushes them downstream sequentially. However, as we already learned in "Order of Events After flatMap()" on page 73, we can no longer rely on the order of downstream events—they neither begin nor complete in the same order as they were emitted (the original sequence began at bread). When events reach the reduce() operator, they are already sequential and well behaving.

By now, you should slowly move away from the classic Thread model and understand how Schedulers work. But if you find it difficult, here is a simple analogy:

- Observable without any Scheduler works like a single-threaded program with blocking method calls passing data between one another.
- Observable with a single subscribeOn() is like starting a big task in the background Thread. The program within that Thread is still sequential, but at least it runs in the background.
- Observable using flatMap() where each internal Observable has subscribeOn() works like ForkJoinPool from java.util.concurrent, where each substream is a *fork* of execution and flatMap() is a safe *join* stage.

Of course, the preceding tips only apply to blocking Observables, which are rarely seen in real applications. If your underlying Observables are already asynchronous, achieving concurrency is a matter of understanding how they are combined and when subscription occurs. For example, merge() on two streams will subscribe to both of them concurrently, whereas the concat() operator waits until the first stream finishes before it subscribes to the second one.

Batching Requests Using groupBy()

Did you notice that RxGroceries.purchase() takes productName and quantity even though the quantity was always one? What if our grocery list had some products multiple times, indicating bigger demand? The first naive implementation simply sends the same request—for example, for egg, multiple times, each time asking for one. Fortunately, we can declaratively batch such requests by using groupBy()—and this still works with declarative concurrency:

```
import org.apache.commons.lang3.tuple.Pair;

Observable<BigDecimal> totalPrice = Observable
    .just("bread", "butter", "egg", "milk", "tomato",
      "cheese", "tomato", "egg", "egg")
    .groupBy(prod -> prod)
    .flatMap(grouped -> grouped
        .count()
        .map(quantity -> {
            String productName = grouped.getKey();
```

```
            return Pair.of(productName, quantity);
        }))
    .flatMap(order -> store
        .purchase(order.getKey(), order.getValue())
        .subscribeOn(schedulerA))
    .reduce(BigDecimal::add)
    .single();
```

This code is quite complex, so before revealing the output, let's quickly go through it. First, we group products simply by their name, thus identity function `prod -> prod`. In return we get an awkward `Observable<GroupedObservable<String, String>>`. There is nothing wrong with that. Next, `flatMap()` receives each `GroupedObserva ble<String, String>`, representing all products of the same name. So, for example, there will be an `["egg", "egg", "egg"]` Observable there with a key "egg", as well. If `groupBy()` used a different key function, like `prod.length()`, the same sequence would have a key 3.

At this point, within `flatMap()` we need to construct an `Observable` of type `Pair<String, Integer>` which represents every unique product and its quantity. Both `count()` and `map()` return an `Observable`, so everything lines up perfectly. Second `flatMap()` receives `order` of type `Pair<String, Integer>` and makes a purchase, this time the quantity can be bigger. The output looks perfect; notice that bigger orders are slightly slower, but still it is much faster than having several repeated requests:

```
 164 | Sched-A-0 | Purchasing 1 bread
 165 | Sched-A-1 | Purchasing 1 butter
 166 | Sched-A-2 | Purchasing 3 egg
 166 | Sched-A-3 | Purchasing 1 milk
 166 | Sched-A-4 | Purchasing 2 tomato
 166 | Sched-A-5 | Purchasing 1 cheese
1151 | Sched-A-0 | Done 1 bread
1178 | Sched-A-1 | Done 1 butter
1180 | Sched-A-5 | Done 1 cheese
1183 | Sched-A-3 | Done 1 milk
1253 | Sched-A-4 | Done 2 tomato
1354 | Sched-A-2 | Done 3 egg
```

If you believe that your system can benefit from batching this way or the other, check out "Batching and Collapsing Commands" on page 297.

Declarative Concurrency with observeOn()

Believe it or not, concurrency in RxJava can be described by two operators: the aforementioned `subscribeOn()` and `observeOn()`. They seem very similar and are confusing to newcomers, but their semantics are actually quite clear and reasonable.

subscribeOn() allows choosing which Scheduler will be used to invoke OnSubscribe (lambda expression inside create()). Therefore, any code inside create() is pushed to a different thread—for example, to avoid blocking the main thread. Conversely, observeOn() controls which Scheduler is used to invoke downstream Subscribers occurring after observeOn(). For example, calling create() happens in the io() Scheduler (via subscribeOn(io())) to avoid blocking the user interface. However, updating the user interface widgets must happen in the UI thread (both Swing and Android have this constraint), so we use observeOn() for example with Android Schedulers.mainThread() before operators or subscribers changing UI. This way we can use one Scheduler to handle create() and all operators up to the first observ eOn(), but other(s) to apply transformations. This is best explained with an example:

```
log("Starting");
final Observable<String> obs = simple();
log("Created");
obs
        .doOnNext(x -> log("Found 1: " + x))
        .observeOn(schedulerA)
        .doOnNext(x -> log("Found 2: " + x))
        .subscribe(
                x -> log("Got 1: " + x),
                Throwable::printStackTrace,
                () -> log("Completed")
        );
log("Exiting");
```

observeOn() occurs somewhere in the pipeline chain, and this time, as opposed to subscribeOn(), the position of observeOn() is quite important. No matter what Scheduler was running operators above observeOn() (if any), everything below uses the supplied Scheduler. In this example, there is no subscribeOn(), so the default is applied (no concurrency):

```
 23 | main     | Starting
136 | main     | Created
163 | main     | Subscribed
163 | main     | Found 1: A
163 | main     | Found 1: B
163 | main     | Exiting
163 | Sched-A-0 | Found 2: A
164 | Sched-A-0 | Got 1: A
164 | Sched-A-0 | Found 2: B
164 | Sched-A-0 | Got 1: B
164 | Sched-A-0 | Completed
```

All of the operators above observeOn are executed within client thread, which happens to be the default in RxJava. But below observeOn(), the operators are executed

within the supplied `Scheduler`. This will become even more obvious when both `sub`
`scribeOn()` and multiple `observeOn()` occur within the pipeline:

```
log("Starting");
final Observable<String> obs = simple();
log("Created");
obs
        .doOnNext(x -> log("Found 1: " + x))
        .observeOn(schedulerB)
        .doOnNext(x -> log("Found 2: " + x))
        .observeOn(schedulerC)
        .doOnNext(x -> log("Found 3: " + x))
        .subscribeOn(schedulerA)
        .subscribe(
                x -> log("Got 1: " + x),
                Throwable::printStackTrace,
                () -> log("Completed")
        );
log("Exiting");
```

Can you predict the output? Remember, everything below `observeOn()` is run within
the supplied `Scheduler`, of course until another `observeOn()` is encountered. Additionally `subscribeOn()` can occur anywhere between `Observable` and `subscribe()`,
but this time it only affects operators down to the first `observeOn()`:

```
21  | main      | Starting
98  | main      | Created
108 | main      | Exiting
129 | Sched-A-0 | Subscribed
129 | Sched-A-0 | Found 1: A
129 | Sched-A-0 | Found 1: B
130 | Sched-B-0 | Found 2: A
130 | Sched-B-0 | Found 2: B
130 | Sched-C-0 | Found 3: A
130 | Sched-C-0 | Got: A
130 | Sched-C-0 | Found 3: B
130 | Sched-C-0 | Got: B
130 | Sched-C-0 | Completed
```

Subscription occurs in `schedulerA` because that is what we specified in `subscri`
`beOn()`. Also "Found 1" operator was executed within that `Scheduler` because it is
before the first `observeOn()`. Later, the situation becomes more interesting. `observ`
`eOn()` switches current `Scheduler` to `schedulerB`, and "Found 2" is using this one,
instead. The last `observeOn(schedulerC)` affects both "Found 3" operator as well as
`Subscriber`. Remember that `Subscriber` works within the context of the last encountered `Scheduler`.

`subscribeOn()` and `observeOn()` work really well together when you want to physically decouple producer (`Observable.create()`) and consumer (`Subscriber`). By
default, there is no such decoupling, and RxJava simply uses the same thread. `sub`

scribeOn() only is not enough, we simply choose a different thread. observeOn() is better, but then we block the client thread in case of synchronous Observables. Because most of the operators are nonblocking and lambda expressions used inside them tend to be short and cheap, typically there is just one subscribeOn() and observeOn() in the pipeline of operators. subscribeOn() can be placed close to the original Observable to improve readability, whereas observeOn() is close to sub scribe() so that only Subscriber uses that special Scheduler, other operators rely on the Scheduler from subscribeOn().

Here is a more advanced program that takes advantage of these two operators:

```
log("Starting");
Observable<String> obs = Observable.create(subscriber -> {
    log("Subscribed");
    subscriber.onNext("A");
    subscriber.onNext("B");
    subscriber.onNext("C");
    subscriber.onNext("D");
    subscriber.onCompleted();
});
log("Created");
obs
    .subscribeOn(schedulerA)
    .flatMap(record -> store(record).subscribeOn(schedulerB))
    .observeOn(schedulerC)
    .subscribe(
            x -> log("Got: " + x),
            Throwable::printStackTrace,
            () -> log("Completed")
    );
log("Exiting");
```

Where store() is a simple nested operation:

```
Observable<UUID> store(String s) {
    return Observable.create(subscriber -> {
        log("Storing " + s);
        //hard work
        subscriber.onNext(UUID.randomUUID());
        subscriber.onCompleted();
    });
}
```

The production of events occurs in schedulerA, but each event is processed independently using schedulerB to improve concurrency, a technique we learned in "subscribeOn() Concurrency and Behavior" on page 154. The subscription in the end happens in yet another schedulerC. We are pretty sure you understand by now which Scheduler/thread will execute which action, but just in case (empty lines added for clarity):

```
  26   | main     | Starting
  93   | main     | Created
 121   | main     | Exiting

 122   | Sched-A-0 | Subscribed
 124   | Sched-B-0 | Storing A
 124   | Sched-B-1 | Storing B
 124   | Sched-B-2 | Storing C
 124   | Sched-B-3 | Storing D

1136   | Sched-C-1 | Got: 44b8b999-e687-485f-b17a-a11f6a4bb9ce
1136   | Sched-C-1 | Got: 532ed720-eb35-4764-844e-690327ac4fe8
1136   | Sched-C-1 | Got: 13ddf253-c720-48fa-b248-4737579a2c2a
1136   | Sched-C-1 | Got: 0eced01d-3fa7-45ec-96fb-572ff1e33587
1137   | Sched-C-1 | Completed
```

observeOn() is especially important for applications with a UI for which we do not want to block the UI event-dispatching thread. On Android (see "Android Development with RxJava" on page 277) or Swing, some actions like updating the UI must be executed within a specific thread. But doing too much in that thread renders your UI unresponsive. In these cases, you put observeOn() close to subscribe() so that code within the subscription is invoked within the context of a particular Scheduler (like UI-thread). However, other transformations, even rather cheap, should be executed outside UI thread. On the server, observeOn() is seldom used because the true source of concurrency is built into most Observables. This leads to an interesting conclusion: RxJava controls concurrency with just two operators (subscribeOn() and observeOn()), but the more you use reactive extensions, the less frequently you will see these in production code.

Other Uses for Schedulers

There are numerous operators that by default use some Scheduler. Typically, Schedulers.computation() is used if none is supplied—JavaDoc always makes it clear. For example, the delay() operator takes upstream events and pushes them downstream after a given time. Obviously, it cannot hold the original thread during that period, so it must use a different Scheduler:

```
Observable
        .just('A', 'B')
        .delay(1, SECONDS, schedulerA)
        .subscribe(this::log);
```

Without supplying a custom schedulerA, all operators below delay() would use the computation() Scheduler. There is nothing inherently wrong with that; however, if your Subscriber is blocked on I/O it would consume one Worker from globally shared computation() scheduler, possibly affecting the entire system. Other important operators that support custom Scheduler are: interval(), range(), timer(), repeat(), skip(), take(), timeout(), and several others that have yet to be introduced. If you do not provide a scheduler to such operators, computation() Scheduler is utilized, which is a safe default in most cases.

Mastering schedulers is essential to writing scalable and safe code using RxJava. The difference between subscribeOn() and observeOn() is especially important under high load where every task must be executed precisely when we expect. In truly reactive applications, for which all long-running operations are asynchronous, very few threads and thus Schedulers are needed. But there is always this one API or dependency that requires blocking code.

Last but not least, we must be sure that Schedulers used downstream can keep up with the load generated by Schedulers upstream. But this danger will be explained in great detail in Chapter 6.

Summary

This chapter described several patterns in traditional applications that can be replaced with RxJava. I hope you understand by now that high-frequency trading or streaming posts from social media are not the only use cases for RxJava. As a matter of fact, almost any API can be seamlessly replaced with Observable. Even if you don't want or need the power of reactive extensions at the moment, it will allow you to evolve implementation without introducing backward-incompatible changes. Moreover, it is the client that eventually harvests all the possibilities offered by RxJava, like laziness, declarative concurrency, or asynchronous chaining. Even better, because of seamless conversion from Observable to BlockingObservable, traditional clients can consume your API as they want, and you can always provide a simple bridge layer.

You should be fairly confident with RxJava and understand the benefits of applying it even in legacy systems. Undoubtedly, working with reactive Observables is more challenging and has a somewhat steep learning curve. But the advantages and possibilities of growth simply can't be exaggerated. Imagine if we could write entire applications using reactive extensions, from top to bottom? Like a greenfield project for which we have control over every API, interface, and external system. Chapter 5 will discuss how you can write such an application and what the implications are.

CHAPTER 5

Reactive from Top to Bottom

Tomasz Nurkiewicz

"Everything is a stream" is an often cited Zen of RxJava. In Chapter 4, we learned how to deploy RxJava in some places throughout our codebase. But what you will quickly discover is that truly reactive applications use streams pretty much from top to bottom. This approach simplifies reasoning and makes our application very consistent. Nonblocking applications tend to provide great performance and throughput for a fraction of the hardware. By limiting the number of threads, we are able to fully utilize CPU without consuming gigabytes of memory.

One of the limiting factors of scalability in Java is the I/O mechanism. The `java.io` package is very well designed with lots of small `Input`/`OutputStream` and `Reader`/`Writer` implementations that decorate and wrap one another, adding one functionality at a time. As much as I like this beautiful separation of concerns, standard I/O in Java is entirely blocking, meaning every thread that wishes to read or write from a `Socket` or `File` must wait indefinitely for the result. Even worse, threads stuck at an I/O operation due to slow network or an even slower spinning disk are hard to interrupt. Blocking on its own is not an issue, when one thread is blocked, others can still interact with remaining open `Socket`s. But threads are expensive to create and manage, and switching between them takes time. Java applications are perfectly capable of handling tens of thousands of concurrent connections, but you must design them carefully. This design effort is greatly reduced when RxJava is combined with some modern event-driven libraries and frameworks.

Beating the C10k Problem

The *C10k problem* was an area of research and optimization that tried to achieve 10,000 concurrent connections on a single commodity server. Even these days, solving this engineering task with the traditional Java toolkit is a challenge. There are many reactive approaches that easily achieve C10k, and RxJava makes them very approachable. In this chapter, we explore several implementation techniques that will improve scalability by several orders of magnitude. All of them will circle around the concept of reactive programming. If you are lucky enough to work on a greenfield project, you might consider implementing your application in a reactive manner top to bottom. Such an application should never synchronously wait for any computation or action. The architecture must be entirely *event-driven* and *asynchronous* in order to avoid blocking. We will go through several examples of a simple HTTP server and observe how it behaves with respect to design choices we made. Admittedly, performance and scalability does have a complexity price tag. But with RxJava the additional complexity will be reduced significantly.

The classic thread per connection model struggles to solve the C10k problem. With 10,000 threads we do the following:

- Consume several gigabytes of RAM for stack space
- Put great pressure on the garbage collection mechanism, despite that stack space is not garbage-collected (lots of GC roots and live objects)
- Waste significant amount of CPU time simply switching cores to run different threads (context switching).

The classic thread-per-Socket model served us really well, and as a matter of fact it works quite good in many applications to this day. However, after you reach certain level of concurrency, the number of threads becomes dangerous. A thousand concurrent connections handled by a single commodity server is not something unusual, especially with long-living TCP/IP connections like HTTP with a Keep-Alive header, server-sent events, or WebSockets. However, each thread occupies a little bit of memory (stack space), regardless of whether it is computing something or just waiting idle for data.

There are two independent approaches to scalability: horizontal and vertical. To handle more concurrent connections we can simply spin up more servers, each managing a subset of the load. This requires a frontend load-balancer and does not solve the original C10k problem that expects just one server. On the other hand, vertical scalability means purchasing bigger and more capable servers. However, with blocking I/O we need a disproportional amount of memory compared to heavily underutilized CPU. Even if a big enterprise server can handle hundreds of thousands of concurrent connections (at very high price), it is far from solving C10M problem—ten million concurrent connections. This number is not a coincidence; a couple of years ago, a properly designed Java application reached that enormous level on a typical server (*http://bit.ly/2d4Z1xu*).

This chapter takes you on a journey through different ways of implementing an HTTP server. From single-threaded servers, through thread pools, to entirely event-driven architectures. The idea behind this exercise is to compare the implementation complexity versus performance and throughput. In the end, you will notice that the version using RxJava combines both relative simplicity and outstanding performance.

Traditional Thread-Based HTTP Servers

The purpose of this section is to compare how blocking servers, even when written properly, behave under high load. This is the exercise that we probably all went through during our education: writing a server on top of raw sockets. We will be implementing an extremely simple HTTP server that responds with 200 OKs for every request. As a matter of fact, for the sake of simplicity we will ignore the request altogether.

Single threaded server

The simplest implementation just opens a ServerSocket and handles client connections as they come. When a single client is served, all other requests are queued up. The following code snippet is actually very simple:

```
class SingleThread {

    public static final byte[] RESPONSE = (
            "HTTP/1.1 200 OK\r\n" +
                    "Content-length: 2\r\n" +
                    "\r\n" +
                    "OK").getBytes();

    public static void main(String[] args) throws IOException {
        final ServerSocket serverSocket = new ServerSocket(8080, 100);
        while (!Thread.currentThread().isInterrupted()) {
            final Socket client = serverSocket.accept();
            handle(client);
        }
    }

    private static void handle(Socket client) {
        try {
            while (!Thread.currentThread().isInterrupted()) {
                readFullRequest(client);
                client.getOutputStream().write(RESPONSE);
            }
        } catch (Exception e) {
            e.printStackTrace();
            IOUtils.closeQuietly(client);
        }
    }

    private static void readFullRequest(Socket client) throws IOException {
        BufferedReader reader = new BufferedReader(
                new InputStreamReader(client.getInputStream()));
```

```
        String line = reader.readLine();
        while (line != null && !line.isEmpty()) {
            line = reader.readLine();
        }
    }

}
```

You will not see similar low-level implementations outside of the university, but it works. For each request we ignore whatever was sent to us and return 200 OK responses. Opening localhost:8080 in the browser succeeds with an OK text reply. The class is named SingleThread for a reason. ServerSocket.accept() blocks until any client establishes a connection with us. Then, it returns a client Socket. While we interact with that Socket (read and write to it), we still listen for incoming connections but no one picks them up because our thread is busy handling first client. It is like at the doctor's office: one patient goes in and everyone else must wait in a queue. Did you notice the extra 100 parameter after 8080 (listening port)? This value (the default is 50) caps the maximum number of pending connections that can wait in a queue. Above that number, they are rejected. To make matters worse, we pretend to implement HTTP/1.1 which uses persistent connections by default. Until the client disconnects we keep the TCP/IP connection open just in case, blocking new clients.

Now, coming back to our client connection, we first must read the entire request and then write the response. Both of these operations are potentially blocking and subject to network slowness and congestion. If one client establishes a connection but then waits a few seconds before sending a request, all other clients must wait. Having just a single thread for handling all incoming connections is clearly not very scalable, we barely solved the C1 (one concurrent connection) problem.

Appendix A contains the source code and a discussion of other blocking servers. Rather than spending more time analyzing nonscalable blocking architectures, we will briefly summarize them so that we can proceed to benchmarks and side-by-side comparisons quicker:

In "fork() Procedure in C Language" on page 327, you will find the source code of a simple server written in C language using fork(). Despite superficial simplicity, forking a new process per each client connection, especially for short-living ones, puts significant load on the operating system. Each process needs quite a bit of memory and initial startup takes some time. Also thousands of processes starting and stopping all the time unnecessarily occupy system resources.

ThreadPerConnection (see "Thread per Connection" on page 329) shows how to implement a blocking server that creates a new thread per each client connection. This presumably scales quite well, but such implementation suffers the same problems as fork() in C: starting a new thread takes some time and resources, which is especially wasteful for short-lived connections. Moreover, there is no limit to the maximum number of client threads running at the same time. And when you do not put a limit on something in the computer system, this limit will be applied for you in the worst and least expected place. For example, our program will become unstable and eventually crash with `OutOfMemoryError` in case of thousands of concurrent connections.

`ThreadPool` (see "Thread Pool of Connections" on page 331) also uses a thread per connection, but threads are recycled when a client disconnects so that we do not pay the price of thread warm up for every client. This is pretty much how all popular servlet containers like Tomcat and Jetty work, managing 100 to 200 threads in a pool by default. Tomcat has the so-called NIO connector that handles some of the operations on sockets asynchronously, but the real work in servlets and frameworks built on top of them is still blocking. This means that traditional applications are inherently limited to a couple thousand connections, even built on top of modern servlet containers.

Nonblocking HTTP Server with Netty and RxNetty

We will now focus on event-driven approaches to writing an HTTP server, which are far more promising in terms of scalability. A blocking processing model involving thread-per-request clearly does not scale. We need a way of managing several client connections with just a handful of threads. This has a lot of benefits:

- Reduced memory consumption
- Better CPU and CPU cache utilization
- Greatly improved scalability on a single node

One caveat is the lost simplicity and clarity. Threads are not allowed to block on any operation, we can no longer pretend that receiving or sending data over the wire is the same as a local method invocation. The latency is unpredictable and response times higher by orders of magnitude. By the time you read this, there will probably still be quite a few spinning hard drives out there, which are even slower than a local area networks. In this section, we will develop a tiny event-driven application with the Netty framework and later refactor it to use RxNetty (*https://github.com/Reacti veX/RxNetty*). Finally, we conclude with a benchmark of all solutions.

Netty (*http://netty.io/*) is entirely event-driven; we never block waiting for data to be sent or received. Instead, raw bytes in the form of `ByteBuf` instances are pushed to our processing pipeline. TCP/IP gives us an impression of connection and data flowing byte after byte between two computers. But in reality TCP/IP is built on top of IP, which can barely transfer chunks of data known as *packets*. It is the operating system's role to assemble them in the correct order and give the illusion of a stream. Netty drops this abstraction and works at a byte-sequence layer, not a stream. Whenever a few bytes arrive to our application, Netty will notify our handler. Whenever we send few bytes, we get a ChannelFuture without blocking (more on futures in a second).

Our example of non-blocking HTTP server has three components. The first simply starts the server and sets up the environment:

```java
import io.netty.bootstrap.ServerBootstrap;
import io.netty.channel.*;
import io.netty.channel.nio.NioEventLoopGroup;
import io.netty.channel.socket.nio.NioServerSocketChannel;

class HttpTcpNettyServer {

    public static void main(String[] args) throws Exception {
        EventLoopGroup bossGroup = new NioEventLoopGroup(1);
        EventLoopGroup workerGroup = new NioEventLoopGroup();
        try {
            new ServerBootstrap()
                    .option(ChannelOption.SO_BACKLOG, 50_000)
                    .group(bossGroup, workerGroup)
                    .channel(NioServerSocketChannel.class)
                    .childHandler(new HttpInitializer())
                    .bind(8080)
                    .sync()
                    .channel()
                    .closeFuture()
                    .sync();
        } finally {
            bossGroup.shutdownGracefully();
            workerGroup.shutdownGracefully();
        }
    }
}
```

This is the most basic HTTP server in Netty. The crucial part is bossGroup pool responsible for accepting incoming connections and workerGroup that processes events. These pools are not very big: one for bossGroup and close to the number of CPU cores for workerGroup but this is more than enough for a well-written Netty server. We did not specify yet what the server should do, apart from listening on port 8080. This is configurable via ChannelInitializer:

```java
import io.netty.channel.ChannelInitializer;
import io.netty.channel.socket.SocketChannel;
import io.netty.handler.codec.http.HttpServerCodec;

class HttpInitializer extends ChannelInitializer<SocketChannel> {

    private final HttpHandler httpHandler = new HttpHandler();

    @Override
    public void initChannel(SocketChannel ch) {
```

```
            ch
                .pipeline()
                .addLast(new HttpServerCodec())
                .addLast(httpHandler);
        }
    }
```

Rather than providing a single function that handles the connection, we build a pipe-line that processes incoming ByteBuf instances as they arrive. The first step of the pipeline decodes raw incoming bytes into higher-level HTTP request objects. This handler is built-in. It is also used for encoding the HTTP response back to raw bytes. In more robust applications you will often see more handlers focused on smaller functionality; for example, frame decoding, protocol decoding, security, and so on. Every piece of data and notification flows through this pipeline.

You're probably beginning to see the analogy with RxJava here. The second step of our pipeline is the business logic component that actually handles the request rather than just intercepting or enriching it. Although HttpServerCodec is inherently state-ful (it translates incoming packets to high-level HttpRequest instances), our custom HttpHandler can be a stateless singleton:

```
import io.netty.channel.*;
import io.netty.handler.codec.http.*;

@Sharable
class HttpHandler extends ChannelInboundHandlerAdapter {

    @Override
    public void channelReadComplete(ChannelHandlerContext ctx) {
        ctx.flush();
    }

    @Override
    public void channelRead(ChannelHandlerContext ctx, Object msg) {
        if (msg instanceof HttpRequest) {
            sendResponse(ctx);
        }
    }

    private void sendResponse(ChannelHandlerContext ctx) {
        final DefaultFullHttpResponse response = new DefaultFullHttpResponse(
                HTTP_1_1,
                HttpResponseStatus.OK,
                Unpooled.wrappedBuffer("OK".getBytes(UTF_8)));
        response.headers().add("Content-length", 2);
        ctx.writeAndFlush(response);
    }

    @Override
    public void exceptionCaught(ChannelHandlerContext ctx, Throwable cause) {
        log.error("Error", cause);
```

```
        ctx.close();
    }
}
```

After constructing the response object, we `write()` back a `DefaultFullHttpRes`
`ponse`. However, `write()` does not block like in ordinary sockets. Instead, it returns a
`ChannelFuture` that we can subscribe via `addListener()` and asynchronously close
the channel:

```
ctx
    .writeAndFlush(response)
    .addListener(ChannelFutureListener.CLOSE);
```

Channel is an abstraction over a communication link—for example, an HTTP connection—therefore closing a channel closes the connection. Again, we do not want to
do this in order to implement persistent connections.

Netty uses just a handful of threads to process possibly thousands of connections. We
do not keep any heavyweight data structures or threads per each connection. This is
much closer to what actually happens close to the metal. The computer receives an IP
packet and wakes up process listening on the destination port. TCP/IP connections
are just an abstraction often implemented using threads. However, when the application is much more demanding in terms of load and the number of connections, operating directly at the packet level is much more robust. We still have channels
(lightweight representation of threads) and pipelines with possibly stateful handlers.

Observable server with RxNetty

Netty is an important backbone behind plenty of successful products and frameworks
such as Akka (*http://akka.io*), Elasticsearch (*https://www.elastic.co*), HornetQ (*http://
hornetq.jboss.org*), Play framework (*https://www.playframework.com*), Ratpack (*http://
ratpack.io*) and Vert.x (*http://vertx.io*) to name a few. There is also a thin wrapper
around Netty that bridges between its API and RxJava. Let's rewrite the nonblocking
Netty server into RxNetty (*https://github.com/ReactiveX/RxNetty*). But we will begin
with a simple currency server to become familiar with the API:

```
import io.netty.handler.codec.LineBasedFrameDecoder;
import io.netty.handler.codec.string.StringDecoder;
import io.reactivex.netty.protocol.tcp.server.TcpServer;

class EurUsdCurrencyTcpServer {

    private static final BigDecimal RATE = new BigDecimal("1.06448");

    public static void main(final String[] args) {
        TcpServer
            .newServer(8080)
            .<String, String>pipelineConfigurator(pipeline -> {
                pipeline.addLast(new LineBasedFrameDecoder(1024));
```

```
            pipeline.addLast(new StringDecoder(UTF_8));
        })
        .start(connection -> {
            Observable<String> output = connection
                .getInput()
                .map(BigDecimal::new)
                .flatMap(eur -> eurToUsd(eur));
            return connection.writeAndFlushOnEach(output);
        })
        .awaitShutdown();
    }

    static Observable<String> eurToUsd(BigDecimal eur) {
        return Observable
            .just(eur.multiply(RATE))
            .map(amount -> eur + " EUR is " + amount + " USD\n")
            .delay(1, TimeUnit.SECONDS);
    }
}
```

This is a self-sufficient, standalone TCP/IP server written on top of RxNetty. You should have a rough understanding of its major parts. First, we create a new TCP/IP server listening on port 8080. Netty provides rather low-level abstraction of `ByteBuf` messages flowing through a pipeline. We must configure such a pipeline, as well. The first handler rearranges (splits and joins when needed) `ByteBuf` sequences into sequences of lines using built-in `LineBasedFrameDecoder`. Second, the decoder transforms a `ByteBuf` containing full lines into actual `String` instances. From this point, we are working exclusively with `Strings`.

Every time a new connection arrives, the callback is executed. The `connection` object allows us to asynchronously send and receive data. First, we begin with `connection.getInput()`. This object is of type `Observable<String>` and emits a value every time a new line of the client's request appears on the server. The `getInput()` `Observable` notifies us asynchronously about new input. First, we parse the `String` into `BigDecimal`. Then, using the helper method `eurToUsd()`, we fake calling some currency exchange service. To make the example more realistic, we artificially applied `delay()` so that we must wait a little bit for the response. Obviously `delay()` is asynchronous and does not involve any sleeping. In the meantime, we keep receiving and transforming requests along the way.

After all these transformations the `output` `Observable` is fed directly into `writeAndFlushOnEach()`. I believe this is quite understandable—we receive a sequence of inputs, transform them, and use the transformed sequence as a sequence of outputs. Now, let's interact with this server using `telnet`. Notice how some responses appear after several requests were consumed due to faked currency server latency:

```
$ telnet localhost 8080
Trying 127.0.0.1...
```

```
Connected to localhost.
Escape character is '^]'.
2.5
2.5 EUR is 2.661200 USD
0.99
0.99 EUR is 1.0538352 USD
0.94
0.94 EUR is 1.0006112 USD
20
30
40
20 EUR is 21.28960 USD
30 EUR is 31.93440 USD
40 EUR is 42.57920 USD
```

We treat our server like a function of request data into response data. Because the TCP/IP connection is not just a simple function but a stream of sometimes interdependent chunks of data, RxJava works amazingly well in this scenario. A rich set of operators makes it easy to transform input to output in nontrivial ways. Of course, the output stream does not have to be based on input; for example, if you are implementing server-sent events, the server simply publishes data irrespective of incoming data.

The `EurUsdCurrencyTcpServer` is reactive because it only acts when data comes in. We do not have a dedicated thread per each client. This implementation can easily withstand thousands of concurrent connections, and vertical scalability is limited only by the amount of traffic it must handle, not the number of more-or-less idle connections.

Knowing how RxNetty works in principle, we can go back to the original HTTP server that returns OK responses. RxNetty has built-in support for HTTP clients and servers, but we will begin from a plain implementation based on TCP/IP:

```java
import io.netty.handler.codec.LineBasedFrameDecoder;
import io.netty.handler.codec.string.StringDecoder;
import io.reactivex.netty.examples.AbstractServerExample;
import io.reactivex.netty.protocol.tcp.server.TcpServer;

import static java.nio.charset.StandardCharsets.UTF_8;

class HttpTcpRxNettyServer {

    public static final Observable<String> RESPONSE = Observable.just(
            "HTTP/1.1 200 OK\r\n" +
            "Content-length: 2\r\n" +
            "\r\n" +
            "OK");

    public static void main(final String[] args) {
        TcpServer
```

```
        .newServer(8080)
        .<String, String>pipelineConfigurator(pipeline -> {
            pipeline.addLast(new LineBasedFrameDecoder(128));
            pipeline.addLast(new StringDecoder(UTF_8));
        })
        .start(connection -> {
            Observable<String> output = connection
                .getInput()
                .flatMap(line -> {
                    if (line.isEmpty()) {
                        return RESPONSE;
                    } else {
                        return Observable.empty();
                    }
                });
            return connection.writeAndFlushOnEach(output);
        })
        .awaitShutdown();
    }
}
```

Having `EurUsdCurrencyTcpServer` in mind understanding `HttpTcpRxNettyServer` should be fairly simple. Because for educational purposes we are always returning static `200 OK` responses, there is no point in parsing the request. However, a well-behaving server should not send a response before it read a request. Therefore, we begin by looking for an empty line in `getInput()`, marking the end of the HTTP request. Only then do we produce the `200 OK` line. The output `Observable` built this way is passed to `connection.writeString()`. In other words, the response will be sent to the client as soon as the request contains the first empty line.

Implementing an HTTP server using TCP/IP is an entertaining exercise that helps you to understand the intricacies of HTTP. Luckily, we are not forced to implement HTTP and RESTful web services using TCP/IP abstraction all the time. Similar to Netty, RxNetty also has a bunch of built-in components to serve HTTP:

```
import io.reactivex.netty.protocol.http.server.HttpServer;

class RxNettyHttpServer {

    private static final Observable<String> RESPONSE_OK =
        Observable.just("OK");

    public static void main(String[] args) {
        HttpServer
            .newServer(8086)
            .start((req, resp) ->
                resp
                    .setHeader(CONTENT_LENGTH, 2)
                    .writeStringAndFlushOnEach(RESPONSE_OK)
            ).awaitShutdown();
```

```
        }

    }
```

If you are bored with just returning a static 200 OK, we can build nonblocking REST-ful web service with relative ease, again for currency exchange:

```
class RestCurrencyServer {

    private static final BigDecimal RATE = new BigDecimal("1.06448");

    public static void main(final String[] args) {
        HttpServer
                .newServer(8080)
                .start((req, resp) -> {
                    String amountStr = req.getDecodedPath().substring(1);
                    BigDecimal amount = new BigDecimal(amountStr);
                    Observable<String> response = Observable
                            .just(amount)
                            .map(eur -> eur.multiply(RATE))
                            .map(usd ->
                                    "{\"EUR\": " + amount + ", " +
                                    "\"USD\": " + usd + "}");
                    return resp.writeString(response);
                })
                .awaitShutdown();
    }
}
```

We can interact with this server using a web browser or curl. The initial sub string(1) is required to strip the first slash from the request:

```
$ curl -v localhost:8080/10.99

> GET /10.99 HTTP/1.1
> User-Agent: curl/7.35.0
> Host: localhost:8080
> Accept: */*
>

< HTTP/1.1 200 OK
< transfer-encoding: chunked
<

{"EUR": 10.99, "USD": 11.6986352}
```

Having a handful of implementations of this simple HTTP server we can compare them in terms of performance, scalability, and throughput. This is the reason why we abandoned the familiar thread-based model and began using RxJava and asynchronous APIs in the first place.

Benchmarking Blocking versus Reactive Server

To illustrate why writing nonblocking, reactive HTTP server is valuable and pays off, we will run a series of benchmarks for each implementation. Interestingly, the benchmarking tool wrk (*https://github.com/wg/wrk*) of our choice is also nonblocking; otherwise, it would fail to simulate the load equivalent to tens of thousands of concurrent connections. Another interesting alternative is Gatling (*http://gatling.io*), which is built on top of the Akka toolkit. Traditional thread-based load tools like JMeter and ab (*http://bit.ly/2cOdAmX*) fail to simulate such excessive load and become a bottleneck themselves.

Every JVM-based implementation[1] was benchmarked against 10,000, 20,000, and 50,000 concurrent HTTP clients, thus TCP/IP connections. We were interested in the number of requests per second (throughput) as well as median and 99th percentile response time. Just as a reminder: median means 50% of the requests were as fast, whereas 99th percentile tells us that 1% of the requests was slower than given number.

 Benchmark Environment

All benchmarks were executed on home laptops running Linux 3.13.0-62-generic kernel with an Intel i7 CPU 2.4 GHz, 8 GB of RAM, and a solid-state drive (SSD) drive. The client machine was running official wrk, Gatling and JMeter tools were connected to the server machine via a single Gigabit ethernet router. Average ping between client and server machine is 289 µs (deviation 42 µs, minimum 160 µs).

Every benchmark was running for at least one minute with 30 seconds of warm-up on JDK 1.8.0_66. RxJava 1.0.14, RxNetty 0.5.1, and Netty 4.0.32.Final. The system load was measured using htop.

Benchmarks were executed using the following command (with varying -c parameter representing number of concurrent clients):

```
wrk -t6 -c10000 -d60s --timeout 10s --latency http://server:8080
```

Plain server returning 200 OKs

The first benchmark compares how various implementations are performing when they simply return 200 OKs and perform no backend tasks. This is a somewhat unrealistic benchmark but it will give us a notion of the server and Ethernet upper limits. In subsequent tests we will add some arbitrary sleep inside every server.

---

1 We exclude C programs but also other reactive platforms like Node.js.

The following chart depicts number of requests per second handled by each implementation (note the logarithmic scale):

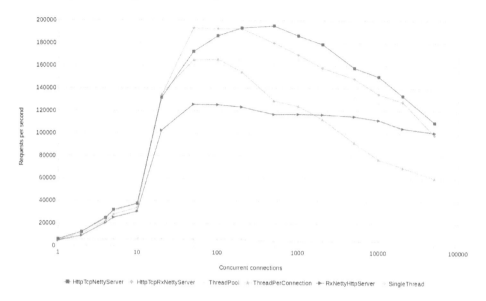

Keep in mind that this benchmark is just a warm-up before real scenarios involving some work on the server side. But we can already see a few interesting trends:

- Netty and RxNetty-based implementations using raw TCP/IP have the best throughput, almost reaching 200,000 requests per second.

- Unsurprisingly, SingleThread implementation is significantly slower, being able to handle about 6,000 requests per second, irrespective of the concurrency level.

- However, SingleThread is the fastest implementation when there is just one client. The overhead of thread pools, event-driven (Rx)Netty, and pretty much any other implementation is visible. This advantage quickly diminishes when the number of clients grow. Moreover throughput of the server is highly dependent on the performance of the client.

- Surprisingly, ThreadPool performs really well, but it becomes unstable under high load (lots of errors reported by wrk) and fails entirely when confronted with 50,000 concurrent clients (10-second timeout reached).

- ThreadPerConnection is also performing very well, but above 100–200 threads, the server quickly drops throughput. Also 50,000 threads put a lot of pressure on the JVM, especially a few extra gigabytes of stack space is troublesome.

We will not spend too much time analyzing this artificial benchmark. After all our servers rarely return a response immediately. Instead, we want to simulate some work happening upon each request.

Simulating server-side work

To simulate some work on the server-side, we will simply inject `sleep()` invocation in between request and response. This is fair: often servers are not performing any CPU-intensive work to fulfill a request. Traditional servers block on external resources, consuming one thread. Reactive servers, on the other hand, simply wait for an external signal (like event or message containing response), releasing underlying resources in the meantime.

For that reason, for blocking implementations we simply added `sleep()`, whereas for nonblocking servers we will use `Observable.delay()` and similar to simulate non-blocking, slow response of some external service, as demonstrated in the following example

```
public static final Observable<String> RESPONSE = Observable.just(
        "HTTP/1.1 200 OK\r\n" +
        "Content-length: 2\r\n" +
        "\r\n" +
        "OK")
    .delay(100, MILLISECONDS);
```

There was no point in using a nonblocking delay in blocking implementations because they would still have to wait for the response, even if the underlying implementation was nonblocking. That being said we injected a 100-millisecond delay to each request so that each interaction with the server takes at least a tenth of a second. The benchmark is now much more realistic and interesting. The number of requests per second versus client connections is shown in the following graphic:

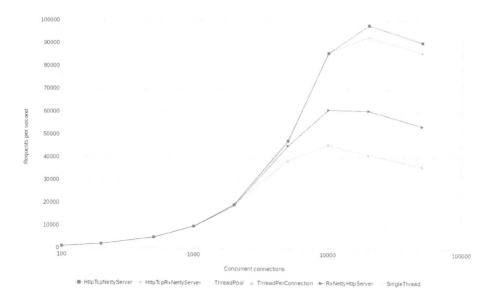

Requests per second

100000
90000
80000
70000
60000
50000
40000
30000
20000
10000
0

100   1000   10000   100000

Concurrent connections

■ HttpTcpNettyServer   ○ HttpTcpRxNettyServer   ThreadPool   ▲ ThreadPerConnection   ◆ RxNettyHttpServer   SingleThread

The results more closely follow what one could expect from a real life load. The two Netty-based implementations (HttpTcpNettyServer and HttpTcpRxNettyServer) on the top are by far the fastest, easily reaching 90,000 requests per second (RPS). As a matter of fact, up until about 10,000 concurrent clients, the server scales linearly. It is very simple to prove: one client generates about 10 RPS (each request takes around 100 milliseconds, so 10 requests fit in 1 second). Two clients generate up to 20 RPS, 5 clients up to 50 RPS, and so on. At about 10,000 concurrent connections we should expect 100,000 RPS and we are close to that theoretical limit (90,000 RPS).

On the bottom, we see the SingleThread and ThreadPool servers. Their performance results are miserable, which does not come as a surprise. Having one thread processing requests, each request taking at least 100 milliseconds clearly cannot handle more than 10 RPS. ThreadPool is much better, having 100 threads, each processing 10 RPS, totaling at 1,000 RPS. These results are worse by a few orders of magnitude compared to reactive Netty and RxJava implementations. Also, the SingleThread implementation was rejecting almost every request under high load. At around 50,000 concurrent connections, it was accepting a marginal number of requests but almost never met the 10-second timeout imposed by wrk.

You might ask, why restrict ThredPool to just 100 threads? This number is similar to what popular HTTP servlet containers are defaulting to, but surely we can specify more. Because all connections are persistent and keep thread from a pool for the duration of the entire connection, you can treat ThreadPerConnection like a thread pool with an unlimited number of threads. Surprisingly, such an implementation works quite well, even when JVM must manage 50,000 concurrent threads, each representing one connection. As a matter of fact, `ThreadPerConnection` is not much worse than `RxNettyHttpServer`. It turns out that throughput measured in RPS is not sufficient, we must also look at the response times for each individual request. It depends on your requirements but typically you need both great throughput to utilize the server and low response times so that *perceived* performance is great, as well.

Average response time is rarely a good indicator. On one hand, average hides outliers (the few requests that are unacceptably slow), on the other, *typical* response time (those observed by most clients) is smaller compared to average, again due to outliers. Percentiles proved to be much more indicative, effectively describing the distribution of a particular value. The following diagram shows 99th percentile of response time for each implementation versus the number of concurrent connections (or clients). The value on the Y axis tells us that 99% of the requests were faster than a given value. Obviously, we want these numbers to be as low as possible (but they cannot be lower than 100 milliseconds of simulated delay) and grow as little as possible with increasing load, as depicted in the following chart:

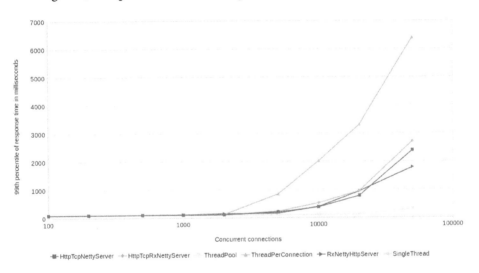

`ThreadPerConnection` implementation badly stands out. Up to 1,000 concurrent connections of all implementations go side by side. But at some point `ThreadPerConnection` becomes really slow to respond, several times slower than competitors. There are a couple of primary reasons for that: first, excessive context switches between thousands of threads, and second, more frequent garbage collection cycles. Basically JVM spends a lot of time housekeeping and not much is left for actual work. Thousands of concurrent connections are sitting idle, waiting for their turn.

You might be surprised why the `ThreadPool` implementation has such an outstanding 99th percentile of response time? It outperforms all other implementations and remains stable even under high load. Let's quickly recap what the implementation of `ThreadPool` looked like:

```
BlockingQueue<Runnable> workQueue = new ArrayBlockingQueue<>(1000);
executor = new ThreadPoolExecutor(100, 100, 0L, MILLISECONDS, workQueue,
        (r, ex) -> {
            ((ClientConnection) r).serviceUnavailable();
        });
```

Rather than using the `Executors` builder, we built `ThreadPoolExecutor` directly, taking control of `workQueue` and `RejectedExecutionHandler`. The latter is executed when the former runs out of space. Basically, we prevent server overload, ensuring that requests that cannot be served quickly are rejected immediately. No other implementation has a similar safety feature, often called *fail-fast*. We will briefly cover fail-fast in "Managing Failures with Hystrix" on page 291; for the time being, let's confront `ThreadPool` responsiveness with the error rate it exposes, as shown here:

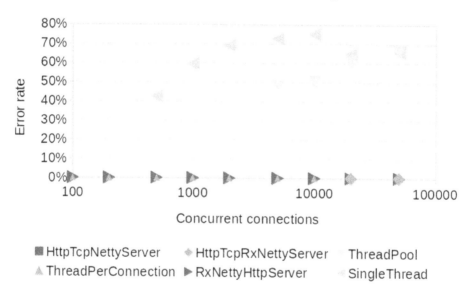

Errors, as reported by the `wrk` load test tool are nonexistent to marginal for all of the implementations except `SingleThread` and `ThreadPool`. This is an interesting trade-off: `ThreadPool` always responds as soon as possible, much faster than competitors. However, it is also very eager to reject requests immediately when it is being overwhelmed. Of course, you can implement a similar mechanism on top of a reactive implementation with Netty/RxJava.

Wrapping up, using thread pools and independent threads can no longer keep up with throughput and response time requirements that are easily met with reactive implementation.

Reactive HTTP Servers Tour

TCP/IP and HTTP built on top of it are inherently event driven. Despite providing an illusion of input and output pipes, underneath one can see asynchronous packets of data arriving asynchronously. As with nearly every abstraction in computer science, treating the network stack as a blocking stream of bytes becomes leaky. Especially when we want to take the full advantage of the hardware.

Classic approaches to networking are just fine, even under moderate load. But to scale up to the limits unheard of in traditional Java applications, you must go reactive. Although Netty is a wonderful framework for building reactive, event-driven network applications, it is rarely used directly. Instead, it is part of a wide range of libraries and frameworks, including RxNetty. RxNetty is especially interesting because it combines the power of event-driven networking with the simplicity of RxJava's operators. We still treat network communication as a flow of messages (packets) but abstracted away with `Observable<ByteBuf>`.

Remember how we defined the problem of 10,000 concurrent connections in "Beating the C10k Problem" on page 165? We managed to solve this problem using numerous Netty and RxNetty implementations. As a matter of fact, we successfully implemented servers that withstood C50k, handling 50,000 concurrent HTTP persistent connections. With more client hardware (because the server was doing just fine) and less frequent requests going through the wire, the same implementations could easily survive C100k and more—using about dozen lines of code.

Obviously, implementing the server part of HTTP (or any other protocol for that matter; HTTP was chosen due to its ubiquity) is just one side of the story. It is equally important what the server is doing, and most of the time it becomes a client of another server. So far in this chapter, we focused on reactive, nonblocking HTTP servers. This is reasonable, but there are multiple, sometimes surprising places where blocking code can sneak in. First of all we paid a lot of attention to the server side, whereas we entirely skipped the client part. But modern servers, especially in large distributed systems, serve the role of client, as well, requesting and pushing data to many downstream services. It is safe to assume that a single request to a popular search engine can span hundreds or even thousands of downstream components, thus making plenty of client requests. It is obvious that if these requests were blocking and sequential, the search engine's response time would be unbearably slow.

No matter how perfectly we implement the server's infrastructure code, if it still has to deal with blocking APIs, the scalability will be harmed, just like our benchmarks have shown. There are a few known sources of blocking in the Java ecosystem in particular, which we will explore briefly.

HTTP Client Code

Servers that simply make several requests to downstream services and combine the responses together are not unheard of. In fact, you can probably find dozens of start-ups that managed to cleverly mash up several available data sources and provide a valuable service simply on top of that. Today's APIs are mostly RESTful with SOAP playing a diminishing role—but both based on the ever-prevalent HTTP.

Even a single blocking request can bring a server down, significantly degrading performance. Fortunately, there is a wide range of mature HTTP clients that are non-blocking and we already met the first one: Netty. There are two classes of problems that a nonblocking HTTP client tries to solve:

- Large number of independent concurrent requests, each requiring a few client calls to third-party APIs. This is typical for service-oriented architectures for which one request spans multiple services.

- A server is making a large number of HTTP client requests, probably during batch operations. Think about web crawlers or indexing services that constantly keep thousands of connections open.

Regardless of the nature of the server, the problem remains the same: maintaining large (tens of thousands and more) open HTTP connections introduces significant overhead. This is especially painful when services we connect to (this time as a client) are slow, therefore requiring us to hold the resources for a long time.

In contrast, a TCP/IP connection is actually quite lightweight. The operating system must keep a socket descriptor for each open connection (around one kilobyte) and that is pretty much it. When a packet (message) arrives, the kernel dispatches it to the appropriate process, like JVM. One kilobyte is a quite a small memory footprint compared to the roughly one megabyte consumed by the stack of each thread blocked on a socket. That being said, the classic thread per connection model does not scale in the case of high-performance servers, and we need to embrace the underlying networking model rather than trying to abstract it using blocking code. The good news is that RxJava + Netty provide a much better abstraction, still relatively close to the metal.

Nonblocking HTTP Client with RxNetty

RxJava together with Netty provides an abstraction that is sufficiently close to the way networks work. Rather than pretending that an HTTP request is almost like an ordinary method call within JVM, it embraces asynchrony. Moreover, we can no longer pretend that HTTP is just a request–response protocol. The emergence of server-sent events (one request, multiple responses), WebSockets (full-duplex communication), and finally HTTP/2 (many parallel requests and responses over the same wire, interleaving with one another) reveals many different usage scenarios for HTTP.

RxNetty on the client side provides quite a concise API for the simplest use cases. You make a request and get back easily composable `Observables`:

```
Observable<ByteBuf> response = HttpClient
        .newClient("example.com", 80)
        .createGet("/")
        .flatMap(HttpClientResponse::getContent);
response
        .map(bb -> bb.toString(UTF_8))
        .subscribe(System.out::println);
```

Calling the `createGet()` method returns a subclass of `Observable<HttpClientResponse>`. Obviously, the client does not block waiting for the response, so the `Observable` seems like a good choice. But this is just the beginning. `HttpClientResponse` itself has a `getContent()` method that returns `Observable<ByteByf>`. If you recall from "Nonblocking HTTP Server with Netty and RxNetty" on page 169, `ByteBuf` is an abstraction over a chunk of data received over the wire. From the client perspective, this is *part* of the response. That is right, RxNetty goes a bit further compared to other nonblocking HTTP clients and does not simply notify us when the entire response arrives. Instead, we get a stream of `ByteBuf` messages, optionally followed by `Observable` completion when the server decides to drop the connection.

Such a model is much closer to how the TCP/IP stack works and scales better in terms of use cases. It can work with a simple request/response flow as well as complex streaming scenarios. But beware that even in case of a single response—for example, one containing HTML—it will most likely arrive in multiple chunks. Of course, RxJava has plenty of ways to assemble them back such as `Observable.toList()` or `Observable.reduce()`. But it is your choice: if you want to consume data as it comes in small bits, that is absolutely fine. In that regard, RxNetty is quite low-level, but because the abstraction does not impose a major performance bottleneck like excessive buffering or blocking, it turns out to be extremely scalable. If you are looking for a reactive and robust but more high-level HTTP client, see "Retrofit with Native RxJava Support" on page 280.

As opposed to callback-based reactive APIs, RxNetty plays very nicely with other `Observables`, you can easily parallelize, combine, and split work. For example, imagine that you have a stream of URLs to which you must connect and consume data in real time. This stream can be fixed (built from a simple `List<URL>`) or dynamic, with new URLs appearing all the time. If you want a steady stream of packets flowing through all of these sources, you can simply `flatMap()` over them:

```
Observable<URL> sources = //...

Observable<ByteBuf> packets =
```

```
sources
.flatMap(url -> HttpClient
    .newClient(url.getHost(), url.getPort())
    .createGet(url.getPath()))
.flatMap(HttpClientResponse::getContent);
```

This is a slightly contrived example because it mixes together `ByteBuf` messages from different sources, but you get the idea. For each `URL` in the upstream `Observable`, we produce an asynchronous stream of `ByteByf` instances from that `URL`. If you want to first transform incoming data, perhaps by combining chunks of data into a single event—you can do this easily, for example with `reduce()`. Here is the upshot: you can easily have tens of thousands of open HTTP connections, idle or receiving data. The limiting factor is no longer memory, but the processing power of your CPU and network bandwidth. JVM does not need to consume gigabytes of memory to process a reasonable number of transactions.

HTTP APIs are one of the major bottlenecks in modern applications. They are not expensive in terms of CPU, but blocking HTTP behaving like an ordinary procedural call substantially limits scalability. Even if you carefully remove the blocking HTTP, communication, synchronous code can appear in the most surprising places. It is a pitfall of the `equals()` method in `java.net.URL` that it makes a network request. That's right: when you compare two instances of the URL class, this seemingly fast method makes a network roundtrip (call sequence, read top to bottom):

```
java.net.URL.equals(URL.java)
java.net.URLStreamHandler.equals(URLStreamHandler.java)
java.net.URLStreamHandler.sameFile(URLStreamHandler.java)
java.net.URLStreamHandler.hostsEqual(URLStreamHandler.java)
java.net.URLStreamHandler.getHostAddress(URLStreamHandler.java)
java.net.InetAddress.getByName(InetAddress.java)
java.net.InetAddress.getAllByName(InetAddress.java)
java.net.InetAddress.getAllByName0(InetAddress.java)
java.net.InetAddress.getAddressesFromNameService(InetAddress.java)
java.net.InetAddress$2.lookupAllHostAddr(InetAddress.java)
[native code]
```

To determine whether two URLs are equal, JVM calls `lookupAllHostAddr()`, which (in `native` code) calls `gethostbyname` (or similar), which can make a synchronous request to DNS server. This can have a disastrous effect when you have just a handful of threads and a few of them are unexpectedly blocked. Remember our RxNetty-based servers? They were using a few dozen threads at most. Another disastrous sitation can happen when `URL.equals()` is invoked frequently such as in `Set<URL>`. This unexpected behavior of URL is rather well known, just like the fact that its `equals()` can actually yield different results depending on Internet connectivity.

We bring up this fact just to illustrate how writing fully reactive applications is difficult and filled with traps. In the next section, we look at another, more obvious source of blocking: database access code.

Relational Database Access

In previous parts, we concluded that every server eventually becomes a client of some different service. Another interesting observation is that pretty much every computer system we've had a chance to work with was distributed. When two machines separated by a network cable need to communicate with each other, they are already spatially distributed. Taking that to the extreme, you might even consider every computer as a distributed system, with independent CPU core's caches that are not always consistent and must synchronize with one another via message-passing protocol. But let's stick to application server versus database server architecture.

The long-existing standard for relational database access in Java is called *Java Database Connectivity* (JDBC). From the consumer perspective, JDBC provides a set of APIs for communicating with any relational database like PostgreSQL, Oracle Database, and many others. The core abstractions are `Connection` (TCP/IP, wire connection), `Statement` (a database query), and `ResultSet` (view over the database result). Today, developers very rarely use this API directly because more user-friendly abstractions exist, from lightweight `JdbcTemplate` in Spring framework, through code generation libraries like jOOQ (*http://www.jooq.org*), to object-relational mapping solutions like JPA. JDBC has a notorious reputation for difficult error handling combined with checked exceptions (much simpler with try-with-resources since Java 7):

```
import java.sql.*;

try (
        Connection conn = DriverManager.getConnection("jdbc:h2:mem:");
        Statement stat = conn.createStatement();
        ResultSet rs = stat.executeQuery("SELECT 2 + 2 AS total")
) {
    if (rs.next()) {
        System.out.println(rs.getInt("total"));
        assert rs.getInt("total") == 4;
    }
}
```

The preceding example uses an embedded H2 database, often utilized during integration tests. But in production, you rarely see a database instance running on the same machine as the application. Every interaction with the database requires a network roundtrip. The core part of JDBC is the API, which every database vendor must implement.

When asking the JDBC API for a new `Connection`, the implementation must make a physical connection to the database by opening a client socket, authorizing, and so on. Databases have different wire protocols (almost universally binary) and the responsibility of the JDBC implementation (also known as `Driver`) is to translate this low-level network protocol into a consistent API. This works quite well (putting aside different SQL dialects), unfortunately when the JDBC standard was released with JDK 1.1 around 1997, nobody predicted how important reactive and asynchronous programming would be two decades later. Surely, the API went through many versions, but all of them are inherently blocking, waiting for each database operation to complete.

This is precisely the same problem as we had with HTTP. You must have as many threads in your application as active database operations (queries). JDBC is the only mature standard for accessing the variety of relational databases in a portable way (again, SQL dialects differences put aside). The servlet specification was significantly revamped in version 3.0 by introducing the `HttpServletRequest.startAsync()` method several years ago. It's too bad that the JDBC standard still holds the classic model.

There are reasons for JDBC to remain blocking. Web servers can easily handle hundreds of thousands of open connections; for example, if they just occasionally stream small bits of data. Database systems, on the other hand, perform several more or less similar steps for each client query:

1. *Query parsing* (CPU-bound) translates a `String` containing a query into a parse tree

2. *Query optimizer* (CPU-bound) evaluates the query against various rules and statistics, trying to build an execution plan

3. *Query executor* (I/O-bound) traverses database storage and finds appropriate tuples to return

4. *Result set* (network-bound) is serialized and pushed back to the client

Clearly, every database needs a lot of resources to perform a query. Typically, the majority of time is actually spent executing the query and disks (spinning or SSD) are not very parallel by design. Therefore, there is a limited amount of concurrent queries that a database system can and should perform until it saturates. This limit largely depends on the actual database engine being used and the hardware on which it's running. There are also many other less-obvious aspects like locks, context switches, and CPU cache lines exhaustion. You should expect around a few hundred queries per second. This is very little compared to, for example, the hundreds of thousands of open HTTP connections, easily achievable with nonblocking APIs.

Knowing that throughput of the database is severely limited by hardware, having fully and entirely reactive drivers does not make that much sense after all. Technically, you can implement a wire protocol on top of Netty or RxNetty and never block the client thread. In fact, there are numerous nonstandard, independently developed approaches (see postgresql-async (*http://bit.ly/2d5649l*), postgres-async-driver (*http://bit.ly/2d56QTS*), adbcj (*https://github.com/mheath/adbcj*), and finagle-mysql (*http://bit.ly/2d56nB2*)), all trying to implement a wire protocol of a particular database with a nonblocking networking stack. But knowing that JVM can handle hundreds to thousands of threads without much hassle (see "Thread per Connection" on page 329), there does not seem to be much benefit derived from rewriting the well-established JDBC API from the ground up. Even Slick (*http://bit.ly/2d562i3*) from commonly used Lightbend reactive stack powered by Akka toolkit uses JDBC underneath. There are also community-led projects bridging between RxJava and JDBC, such as rxjava-jdbc (*http://bit.ly/2d56jS7*).

The advice for interacting with relational databases is to actually have a dedicated, well-tuned thread pool and isolate the blocking code there. The rest of your application can be highly reactive and operate on just a handful of threads, but from a pragmatic point of view, just deal with JDBC because trying to replace it with something more reactive could bring a lot of pain for no apparent gain. We already gave a few hints in "From Collections to Observables" on page 118 for how to interact with JDBC in classic software stacks. Still, we can still experiment a little bit with RxJava, even on top of blocking JDBC.

NOTIFY AND LISTEN on PostgreSQL Case Study

PostgreSQL has a peculiar built-in messaging mechanism available through the LIS TEN and NOTIFY extended SQL statements. Every PostgreSQL client can send a notification to virtual *channel* via a SQL statement, as shown here:

```
NOTIFY my_channel;
NOTIFY my_channel, '{"answer": 42}';
```

In this example, we send an empty notification followed by an arbitrary string (it can be JSON, XML, or data in any other encoding) to channel named my_channel. A channel is basically a queue managed inside the PostgreSQL database engine. Interestingly, sending a notification is part of a transaction, so delivery happens after the commit, and in the case of rollback, the message is discarded.

To consume notifications from a particular channel, we first must LISTEN on that channel. When we begin listening on a given connection, the only way to obtain notifications is by periodic polling by using the getNotifications() method. This introduces random latency and unnecessary CPU load and context switches; unfortunately, that is how the API was designed. The complete blocking example follows:

```
try (Connection connection =
        DriverManager.getConnection("jdbc:postgresql:db")) {
    try (Statement statement = connection.createStatement()) {
        statement.execute("LISTEN my_channel");
    }
    Jdbc4Connection pgConn = (Jdbc4Connection) connection;
    pollForNotifications(pgConn);
}
}

//...

void pollForNotifications(Jdbc4Connection pgConn) throws Exception {
    while (!Thread.currentThread().isInterrupted()) {
        final PGNotification[] notifications = pgConn.getNotifications();
        if (notifications != null) {
            for (final PGNotification notification : notifications) {
                System.out.println(
                        notification.getName() + ": " +
                        notification.getParameter());
            }
        }
        TimeUnit.MILLISECONDS.sleep(100);
    }
}
```

Not only do we block the client thread, we are also forced to keep one JDBC connection open because listening is tied to a particular connection. At least we can listen on many channels at the same time. The preceding code is quite verbose but straightforward. After calling LISTEN, we enter an endless loop asking for new notifications. Calling getNotifications() is destructive, meaning that it discards returned notifications, so calling it twice will not return the same events. getName() is the channel name (for example, my_channel), whereas getParameter() returns optional event contents such as a JSON payload.

The API is horribly old-fashioned, using null to signal no pending notifications, and arrays rather than collections. Let's make it more Rx-friendly. In the absence of any push-based mechanism for notifications, we are forced to reimplement polling using the nonblocking interval() operator. There are many tiny details that allow our custom Observable to behave properly, which we will discuss further after the example (which is not yet complete):

```
Observable<PGNotification> observe(String channel, long pollingPeriod) {
    return Observable.<PGNotification>create(subscriber -> {
        try {
            Connection connection = DriverManager
                    .getConnection("jdbc:postgresql:db");
            subscriber.add(Subscriptions.create(() ->
                    closeQuietly(connection)));
            listenOn(connection, channel);
```

```
                Jdbc4Connection pgConn = (Jdbc4Connection) connection;
                pollForNotifications(pollingPeriod, pgConn)
                        .subscribe(Subscribers.wrap(subscriber);
            } catch (Exception e) {
                subscriber.onError(e);
            }
        }).share();
    }

    void listenOn(Connection connection, String channel) throws SQLException {
        try (Statement statement = connection.createStatement()) {
            statement.execute("LISTEN " + channel);
        }
    }

    void closeQuietly(Connection connection) {
        try {
            connection.close();
        } catch (SQLException e) {
            e.printStackTrace();
        }
    }
}
```

It's amazing how much shorter this example could have been if there were no SQLEx017ception. Never mind. Our goal is to produce robust Observable<PGNotification>. First, we postpone opening a connection to a database until someone actually subscribes. Also, to avoid connection leaks (serious problem in any application that deals with JDBC directly) we ensure that the connection is closed when the Subscriber unsubscribes. Moreover, when an error occurs in the stream, the unsubscription and therefore closing the connection happens.

Now we are ready to call listenOn() and begin receiving notifications over an open connection. If an exception is thrown when this statement is executed, it will be caught and handled by calling subscriber.onError(e). Not only does it seamlessly propagate the error to the subscriber but it also forces the closing of the connection. But if the LISTEN request succeeds, the next invocation of getNotifications() will return all events sent afterward.

We do not want to block any thread so instead, we create an inner Observable with interval() inside pollForNotifications(). We subscribe to that Observable with the same Subscriber but wrapped with Subscribers.wrap() so that onStart() is not executed twice on that Subscriber.

```
Observable<PGNotification> pollForNotifications(
            long pollingPeriod,
            AbstractJdbc2Connection pgConn) {
    return Observable
            .interval(0, pollingPeriod, TimeUnit.MILLISECONDS)
            .flatMap(x -> tryGetNotification(pgConn))
```

```
            .filter(arr -> arr != null)
            .flatMapIterable(Arrays::asList);
    }

    Observable<PGNotification[]> tryGetNotification(
            AbstractJdbc2Connection pgConn) {
        try {
            return Observable.just(pgConn.getNotifications());
        } catch (SQLException e) {
            return Observable.error(e);
        }
    }
}
```

Periodically, we examine the contents of getNotifications() by first wrapping it in an awkward Observable<PGNotification[]>. Because the returned array PGNotifi cation[] can be null, we then filter() out nulls and via flatMapIterable() unwrap the array, first converting it to a List<PGNotification> with Arrays::asL ist. I encourage you to walk carefully through all of these steps, tracking types of intermediate Observables. The only reason for including closeQuietly() and try GetNotification() is for handling checked SQLException. Notice, that we swallow this exception in closeQuietly() because it is called from the context where we can do nothing about it; for example, when someone just unsubscribed and there is no way of forwarding it.

One last tiny bit of implementation is publish() and refCount(), close to the end of the first method. These two methods make it possible to share a single JDBC connection among multiple subscribers. Without them, every new subscriber would open a new connection and listen on it, which is quite wasteful. Additionally refCount() keeps track of the number of subscribers and when the last one unsubscribes it physically closes the database connection. See "Single Subscription with publish().refCount()" on page 54 for more details about publish() and refCount(), especially how it changes the behavior of a lambda expression inside Observable.cre ate().

Remembering that a single connection can listen on multiple channels, as an exercise try to implement observe() so that it reuses the same connection among all subscribers and all channels in which they are interested. The current implementation shares a connection if you call observe() once and subscribe multiple times, whereas it could easily reuse the same connection all the way down, even for subscribers interested in different channels.

There is no practical reason for exploring LISTEN and NOTIFY in PostgreSQL; there are faster, more robust and reliable message queues on the market. But this case study was showing how to exploit JDBC in more reactive scenario, even when it still requires a little bit of blocking or polling.

CompletableFuture and Streams

Java 8, apart from lambda expressions, new `java.time` API, and multiple smaller additions also brought us `CompletableFuture` class. This utility significantly improves the `Future` interface known since Java 5. Pure `Future` represents asynchronous operation running in the background, typically obtained from `ExecutorService`. However `Future`'s API is overly simplistic, forcing developers to block on `Future.get()` invocation pretty much all the time. It is not possible to efficiently implement waiting for the first of the `Future`s to complete without busy waiting. Other options to compose `Future`s are nonexistent. The following section will briefly describe how `CompletableFuture` works. Later, we will implement thin interoperability layer between `CompletableFuture` and `Observable`.

A Short Introduction to CompletableFuture

`CompletableFuture` successfully bridges that gap by providing dozens of useful methods, almost all of which are nonblocking and composable. We got used to that `map()` asynchronously transforms input events on the fly. Moreover, `Observable.flatMap()` allows us to replace single event with another `Observable`, chaining asynchronous tasks. A similar operation is possible with `CompletableFuture`s. Imagine a service that needs two unrelated pieces of information: `User` and `GeoLocation`. Knowing both of these, we ask several independent travel agencies to find `Flight` and we book the `Ticket` in whichever provider was first to return—promoting the fastest and most reactive one. This last requirement is especially difficult to implement, and prior to Java 8 required `ExecutorCompletionService` to effectively find the fastest task:

```
User findById(long id) {
    //...
}

GeoLocation locate() {
    //...
}

Ticket book(Flight flight) {
    //...
}

interface TravelAgency {
    Flight search(User user, GeoLocation location);
}
```

And usage:

```
ExecutorService pool = Executors.newFixedThreadPool(10);
List<TravelAgency> agencies = //...
```

```
User user = findById(id);
GeoLocation location = locate();
ExecutorCompletionService<Flight> ecs =
    new ExecutorCompletionService<>(pool);
agencies.forEach(agency ->
    ecs.submit(() ->
        agency.search(user, location)));
Future<Flight> firstFlight = ecs.poll(5, SECONDS);
Flight flight = firstFlight.get();
book(flight);
```

ExecutorCompletionService was not particularly popular among Java developers, and with CompletableFuture it is no longer needed. But first notice how we wrap ExecutorService with ExecutorCompletionService so that we can later poll for completed tasks as they arrive. With vanilla ExecutorService we would get a bunch of Future objects having no idea which one will complete first, so ExecutorComple tionService was useful. Yet, we still have to sacrifice one extra thread to block waiting for TravelAgencies response. Also, we do not take advantage of concurrency where it is possible (loading User and GeoLocation at the same time).

Our refactoring will turn all methods into their asynchronous counterparts and later combine CompletableFutures appropriately. This way our code is fully nonblocking (main thread completes almost immediately) and we parallelize as much as possible:

```
CompletableFuture<User> findByIdAsync(long id) {
    return CompletableFuture.supplyAsync(() -> findById(id));
}

CompletableFuture<GeoLocation> locateAsync() {
    return CompletableFuture.supplyAsync(this::locate);
}

CompletableFuture<Ticket> bookAsync(Flight flight) {
    return CompletableFuture.supplyAsync(() -> book(flight));
}

@Override
public CompletableFuture<Flight> searchAsync(User user, GeoLocation location) {
    return CompletableFuture.supplyAsync(() -> search(user, location));
}
```

We simply wrapped blocking methods with an asynchronous CompletableFuture. The supplyAsync() method takes an optional Executor as an argument. If not specified, it uses the globally defined one in ForkJoinPool.commonPool(). It is advised to always use custom Executor, but for the purpose of this sample, we take advantage of the default one. Just keep in mind that the default is shared among all CompletableFu tures, parallel streams (see "Java 8 Streams and CompletableFuture" on page 310), and a few other less obvious places.

```
import static java.util.function.Function.identity;


List<TravelAgency> agencies = //...
CompletableFuture<User> user = findByIdAsync(id);
CompletableFuture<GeoLocation> location = locateAsync();

CompletableFuture<Ticket> ticketFuture = user
    .thenCombine(location, (User us, GeoLocation loc) -> agencies
        .stream()
        .map(agency -> agency.searchAsync(us, loc))
        .reduce((f1, f2) ->
            f1.applyToEither(f2, identity())
        )
        .get()
    )
    .thenCompose(identity())
    .thenCompose(this::bookAsync);
```

Quite a bit is happening in the preceding code example. Explaining CompletableFu
ture in its entirety is beyond the scope of this book, but some parts of the API are
going to be useful in the context of RxJava. First, we asynchronously begin fetching
User and GeoLocation. These two operations are independent and can run concurrently. However, we need the results of both in order to proceed, of course without
blocking and wasting the client thread. This is what thenCombine() is doing—it takes
two CompletableFutures (user and location) and invokes a callback when both are
completed, asynchronously. Interestingly, the callback can return a value, which will
become the new content of resulting CompletableFuture, as demonstrated here:

```
CompletableFuture<Long> timeFuture = //...
CompletableFuture<ZoneId> zoneFuture = //...

CompletableFuture<Instant> instantFuture = timeFuture
        .thenApply(time -> Instant.ofEpochMilli(time));

CompletableFuture<ZonedDateTime> zdtFuture = instantFuture
        .thenCombine(zoneFuture, (instant, zoneId) ->
                ZonedDateTime.ofInstant(instant, zoneId));
```

CompletableFuture shares a lot of similarities with Observable. The thenApply()
performs on-the-fly transformation of whatever the Future brings, just like Observa
ble.map(). In our example, we transform CompletableFuture<Long> to Completable
Future<Instant> by supplying a function from Long to Instant
(Instant::ofEpochMilli). Later, we take two Futures (instantFuture and zoneFu
ture) and run a transformation on their future values, namely Instant and ZoneId,
using the thenCombine() method. This transformation returns ZoneDateTime, but
because most of the CompletableFuture operators are nonblocking, we get Completa
bleFuture<ZonedDateTime> in return—again, very similar to zip() in Observable.

Going back to the previous example with booking tickets, the following snippet of code is probably quite obscure:

```
List<TravelAgency> agencies = //...

agencies
    .stream()
    .map(agency -> agency.searchAsync(us, loc))
    .reduce((f1, f2) ->
            f1.applyToEither(f2, identity())
    )
    .get()
```

We need to start asynchronous operation on each TravelAgency by calling searchA sync(). We immediately get back a List<CompletableFuture<Flight>>; this is a very inconvenient data structure if all we need is the first Future to complete. There are methods like CompletableFuture.allOf() and CompletableFuture.anyOf(). The latter is exactly what we need from a semantic point of view—it takes a group of CompletableFutures and returns a CompletableFuture that completes when the very first underlying CompletableFuture completes, discarding all the others. This is very similar to) Observable.amb() (see "When Streams Are Not Synchronized with One Another: combineLatest(), withLatestFrom(), and amb()" on page 83). Unfortunately the syntax of anyOf() is very awkward. First, it accepts an array (varargs) and it always returns CompletableFuture<Object>, not of whatever the type that the underlying Futures was such as Flight. We can use it, but it becomes quite messy:

```
.thenCombine(location, (User us, GeoLocation loc) -> {
    List<CompletableFuture<Flight>> fs = agencies
        .stream()
        .map(agency -> agency.searchAsync(us, loc))
        .collect(toList());
    CompletableFuture[] fsArr = new CompletableFuture[fs.size()];
    fs.toArray(futuresArr);
    return CompletableFuture
        .anyOf(futuresArr)
        .thenApply(x -> ((Flight) x));
})
```

The trick with Stream.reduce() is as follows. There exists a CompletableFu ture.applyToEither() operator that accepts two CompletableFutures and applies a given transformation on the first one to complete. The applyToEither() transformation is extremely useful when you have two homogeneous tasks and you only care about the first one to complete. In the following example, we query User on two different servers: primary and secondary. Whichever finishes first, we apply a simple transformation that extracts date of the user's birth. The second CompletableFuture is not interrupted, but its result is discarded. Obviously, we end up with Completable Future<LocalDate>:

```
CompletableFuture<User> primaryFuture = //...
CompletableFuture<User> secondaryFuture = //...

CompletableFuture<LocalDate> ageFuture =
    primaryFuture
        .applyToEither(secondaryFuture,
            user -> user.getBirth());
```

applyToEither() can only work on two CompletableFutures, whereas the quirky anyOf() can take an arbitrary number. Fortunately, we can call applyToEither() on the first two Futures and then take the result (fastest out of the first two) and apply it with the third upstream Future (fastest out of the first three). By iteratively calling applyToEither(), we get the CompletableFuture representing the fastest overall. This handy trick can be efficiently implemented using the reduce() operator. One last caveat is the identity() method from Function. This is a requirement of apply ToEither(); we must provide a transformation that deals with the first result to come. If the result is supposed to be left *as-is*, we can use an identity function, which can also be written as f -> f or (Flight f) -> f.

Finally, we implemented CompletableFuture<Flight> that completes when the fastest TravelAgency responds, asynchronously. There is still a tiny issue with the result of thenCombine(). Whatever the transformation passed to thenCombine() returns is then wrapped back into CompletableFuture. In our case, we return CompletableFuture<Flight>, so the type of the thenCombine() result is: CompletableFuture<CompletableFuture<Flight>>. Double wrapping is a common issue with Observable as well, and we can use the same trick to fix it in both cases: flatMap()! (See "Wrapping Up Using flatMap()" on page 67.) But remember that just like map() is called thenApply() in Futures, flatMap() is called thenCompose():

```
Observable<Observable<String>> badStream = //...
Observable<String> goodStream = badStream.flatMap(x -> x);

CompletableFuture<CompletableFuture<String>> badFuture = //...
CompletableFuture<String> goodFuture = badFuture.thenCompose(x -> x);
```

Normally, we use flatMap()/thenCompose() to chain an asynchronous computation, but here we simply unwrap the incorrect type. Keep in mind that thenCompose() expects the return type of the supplied transformation to be CompletableFuture. But because the internal type is already a Future, using an identity() function, or simply x -> x, fixes the type by unwrapping the internal Future.

Finally, when we have CompletableFuture<Flight> (abbreviated to flightFuture), we can call bookAsync(), which takes a Flight as an argument:

```
CompletableFuture<Ticket> ticketFuture = flightFuture
        .thenCompose(flight -> bookAsync(flight));
```

This time, thenCompose() was used more naturally when calling bookAsync(). That method returns CompletableFuture<Ticket>, so to avoid double wrapping, we choose thenCompose() instead of thenApply().

Interoperability with CompletableFuture

The factory method Observable.from(Future<T>) that returns Observable<T> already exists. However, because of the limitations of the old Future<T> API, it has several shortcomings, the biggest one being blocking on Future.get() internally. Classic Future<T> implementations have no way of registering callbacks and processing them asynchronously, therefore they are quite useless in reactive applications.

CompletableFuture, in contrast, is a totally different story. Semantically, you can treat CompletableFuture like an Observable that has the following characteristics:

It is hot.
> The computation behind CompletableFuture starts eagerly, regardless of whether someone registered any callbacks like thenApply() or not.

It is cached.
> The background computation behind CompletableFuture is triggered once eagerly and the result is forwarded to all registered callbacks. Moreover, if a callback is registered after completion, it is immediately invoked with completed value (or exception)

It emits exactly one element or exception.
> In principle, Future<T> completes exactly once (or never) with a value of type T or an exception. This matches the contract of Observable.

Turning CompletableFuture into Observable with single item

First, we would like to write a utility function that takes a CompletableFuture<T> and returns a properly behaving Observable<T>:

```
class Util {
    static <T> Observable<T> observe(CompletableFuture<T> future) {
        return Observable.create(subscriber -> {
            future.whenComplete((value, exception) -> {
                if (exception != null) {
                    subscriber.onError(exception);
                } else {
                    subscriber.onNext(value);
                    subscriber.onCompleted();
                }
            });
        });
    }
}
```

To be notified about both successful and failed completion, we use the `Completable`
`Future.whenComplete()` method. It receives two parameters excluding each other. If
`exception` is not `null`, it means that the underlying `Future` failed. Otherwise, we take
the successful `value`. In both cases, we notify the incoming `subscriber`. Notice that if
the subscription appears after the `CompletableFuture` completed (one way or the
other), the callbacks are executed immediately. `CompletableFuture` caches the result
as soon as it completes so that callbacks registered afterward are invoked immediately
within the calling thread.

It is tempting to register an unsubscription handler that tries to cancel `Completable`
`Future` in case of unsubscription:

```
//Don't do this!
subscriber.add(Subscriptions.create(
        () -> future.cancel(true)));
```

This is a bad idea. We can create many `Observables` based on one `CompletableFu`
`ture`, and every `Observable` can have multiple `Subscribers`. If just one `Subscriber`
decides to unsubscribe prior to `Future`'s completion, cancellation will affect all other
`Subscribers`.

Remember that `CompletableFuture` is *hot* and *cached* using Rx terminology. It begins
computation immediately, whereas `Observable` will not start computation until
someone actually subscribes. Having that in mind, with the following tiny utility we
can further improve our API:

```
Observable<User> rxFindById(long id) {
    return Util.observe(findByIdAsync(id));
}

Observable<GeoLocation> rxLocate() {
    return Util.observe(locateAsync());
}

Observable<Ticket> rxBook(Flight flight) {
    return Util.observe(bookAsync(flight));
}
```

Obviously, if the API you are consuming supports `Observable` from the beginning,
you do not need all these extra layers of adapters. However, if all you have at your
disposal are `CompletableFutures`, converting them to `Observables` is efficient and
safe. The advantage of RxJava is much more concise implementation of our initial
problem:

```
Observable<TravelAgency> agencies = agencies();
Observable<User> user = rxFindById(id);
Observable<GeoLocation> location = rxLocate();

Observable<Ticket> ticket = user
```

```
        .zipWith(location, (us, loc) ->
            agencies
                .flatMap(agency -> agency.rxSearch(us, loc))
                .first()
    )
    .flatMap(x -> x)
    .flatMap(this::rxBook);
```

The client code using RxJava API seems less noisy and easier to read. Rx naturally supports "futures with multiple values" in the form of streams. If you still find identity transformation x -> x inside flatMap() little bit intimidating, we can always split zipWith() using a Pair helper container:

```
import org.apache.commons.lang3.tuple.Pair;

//...
Observable<Ticket> ticket = user
        .zipWith(location, (usr, loc) -> Pair.of(usr, loc))
        .flatMap(pair -> agencies
                .flatMap(agency -> {
                    User usr = pair.getLeft();
                    GeoLocation loc = pair.getRight();
                    return agency.rxSearch(usr, loc);
                }))
        .first()
        .flatMap(this::rxBook);
```

At this point, you should understand why extra x -> x is no longer needed. zip With() takes two independent Observables and asynchronously waits for both of them. Java has no built-in pairs and tuples, thus we must provide a transformation that will take the events from both streams and combine them into a single Observa ble<Pair<User, Location>> object. That object will be the input for the down-stream Observable. Later, we use flatMap() to search every travel agency concurrently for a given User and Location. flatMap() does the unwrapping for us (from a syntactic perspective), so the resulting stream is a simple Observa ble<Flight>. Naturally, in both cases we do first() to process only the first Flight occurring upstream (fastest TravelAgency).

From Observable to CompletableFuture

In some cases, the API you are using might support CompletableFuture but not RxJava. Such a situation can be quite common, especially taking into account that the former is part of JDK, whereas the latter is a library. Under these circumstances it would be nice to convert Observable into CompletableFuture. There are two ways to implement this transformation:

Observable<T> *to* CompletableFuture<T>

Use this when you expect just a single item emitted from stream—for example, when Rx wraps a method invocation or request/response pattern. The Completa bleFuture<T> completes successfully when stream completes with exactly one emitted value. Obviously, future completes with an exception when stream completed in such a way or when it did not complete with exactly one item emitted.

Observable<T> *to* CompletableFuture<List<T>>

In this scenario, the CompletableFuture completes when all events from upstream Observable are emitted and the stream completes. This is just a special case of the first transformation, as you will see later.

You can implement the first scenario easily using the following utility:

```
static <T> CompletableFuture<T> toFuture(Observable<T> observable) {
    CompletableFuture<T> promise = new CompletableFuture<>();
    observable
            .single()
            .subscribe(
                    promise::complete,
                    promise::completeExceptionally
            );
    return promise;
}
```

Before diving into the implementation, keep in mind that this transformation has an important side effect: it subscribes to Observable, thus forcing evaluation and computation of cold Observables. Moreover, each invocation of this transformer will subscribe again; it is just a design choice that you must be aware of.

Apart from that, the implementation is quite interesting. First, we force Observable to emit precisely one element using single(), throwing an exception otherwise. If this single event is emitted and a stream completes, we invoke CompletableFu ture.complete(). It turns out one can create CompletableFuture from scratch without any backing thread pool and asynchronous task. It is still a CompletableFu ture, but the only way to complete it and signal all registered callbacks is by calling complete() explicitly. This is an efficient way of exchanging data asynchronously, at least when RxJava is not available.

In case of failure, we can trigger an error in all registered callbacks by calling Comple tableFuture.completeExceptionally(). As surprising as it is, this is the entire implementation. Future returned from toFuture behaves as if it had some task attached in the background, whereas in reality we explicitly complete it.

The transformation from Observable<T> to CompletableFuture<List<T>> is embarrassingly simple:

```
static <T> CompletableFuture<List<T>> toFutureList(Observable<T> observable) {
    return toFuture(observable.toList());
}
```

Interoperability between `CompletableFuture` and `Observable` is quite useful. The former is properly designed but lacks the expressiveness and richness of the latter. Therefore, if you are forced to deal with `CompletableFuture` in an otherwise RxJava-based application, apply these simple transformations as soon as possible to provide a consistent and predictable API. Make sure you understand the difference between eager (hot) `Future` and `Observable` lazy by default.

Observable versus Single

I often see people afraid of RxJava because it looks so stream oriented. `Observable` is a stream, potentially infinite, and all operators are described in terms of streams. But similar to a `List<T>`, which can have one element, certain `Observable<T>` can by definition always emit one event. It is quite confusing to have a `List<T>` to hold exactly one element all the time; therefore, we simply use `T` or `Optional<T>` for that. In the land of RxJava there is a special abstraction for `Observables` emitting exactly one element, and it is called `rx.Single<T>`.

`Single<T>` is basically a container for a future value of type `T` or `Exception`. In that regard `CompletableFuture` from Java 8 is the closest cousin of `Single` (see "CompletableFuture and Streams" on page 193). But unlike `CompletableFuture`, `Single` is lazy and does not begin producing its value until someone actually subscribes. `Single` is typically used for APIs known to return a single value (duh!) asynchronously and with high probability of failure. Obviously, `Single` is a great candidate for request–response types of communication involving I/O, like a network call. The latency is typically high compared to normal method invocation and failures are inevitable. Moreover, because `Single` is lazy and asynchronous, we can apply all sorts of tricks to improve latency and resilience, such as invoking independent actions concurrently and combining responses together (see "Combining Responses Using zip, merge, and concat" on page 205). `Single` reduces the confusion of APIs returning `Observable` by providing a type-level guidance:

```
Observable<Float> temperature() {
    //...
}
```

It's difficult to predict the contract of the preceding method. Does it return just one temperature measurement and complete? Or maybe it streams temperatures infinitely? Even worse, it might complete without any events under some circumstances. If `temperature()` returned `Single<Float>`, we would have known immediately what output to expect.

Creating and Consuming Single

`Single` is fairly similar to `Observable` in terms of the operators it supports, so we will not spend much time on them here. Instead, we will briefly compare them to `Observable`'s counterparts and focus on use cases for `Single`. There are few ways to create a `Single`, beginning with the constant `just()` and `error()` operators:

```
import rx.Single;


Single<String> single = Single.just("Hello, world!");
single.subscribe(System.out::println);

Single<Instant> error =
        Single.error(new RuntimeException("Opps!"));
error
        .observeOn(Schedulers.io())
        .subscribe(
                System.out::println,
                Throwable::printStackTrace
        );
```

There are no overloaded versions of `just()` that take multiple values—after all, `Single` can hold only one value by definition. Also the `subscribe()` method takes two arguments rather than three. There is simply no point in having an `onComplete()` callback; `Single` completes with either a value (first callback) or exception (second callback). Listening on completion alone is equivalent to subscribing for a single value. Additionally, we included the `observeOn()` operator, which works exactly the same as its `Observable` peer. The same applies to `subscribeOn()` (see "Imperative Concurrency" on page 125 for more details). Finally, you can use the `error()` operator to create a `Single` that always completes with a given `Exception`.

Let's implement a more real-life scenario of making an HTTP request. In "Nonblocking HTTP Client with RxNetty" on page 184, we learned how to use RxNetty to build an asynchronous HTTP clients. This time we will use async-http-client (*http://bit.ly/UbSPq1*) that happens to use Netty underneath, as well. After making an HTTP request we can provide a callback implementation that will be invoked asynchronously whenever a response or error comes back. This fits very nicely into how `Single` is created:

```
import com.ning.http.client.AsyncCompletionHandler;
import com.ning.http.client.AsyncHttpClient;
import com.ning.http.client.Response;


AsyncHttpClient asyncHttpClient = new AsyncHttpClient();

Single<Response> fetch(String address) {
```

```
            return Single.create(subscriber ->
                    asyncHttpClient
                            .prepareGet(address)
                            .execute(handler(subscriber)));
        }

        AsyncCompletionHandler handler(SingleSubscriber<? super Response> subscriber) {
            return new AsyncCompletionHandler() {
                public Response onCompleted(Response response) {
                    subscriber.onSuccess(response);
                    return response;
                }

                public void onThrowable(Throwable t) {
                    subscriber.onError(t);
                }
            };
        }
```

`Single.create()` looks similar to `Observable.create()` (see "Mastering Observable.create()" on page 35) but it has some important constraints; you must call either `onSuccess()` once or `onError()` once. Technically, it is also possible to have a `Single` that never completes, but multiple `onSuccess()` invocations are not allowed. Speaking of `Single.create()` you can also try `Single.fromCallable()` that accepts `Callable<T>` and returns `Single<T>`. As simple as that.

Going back to our HTTP client example, when a response is back, we let subscribers know by calling `onSuccess()` or propagate the exception with `onError()` in case of asynchronous failure callback. You can use `Single` in similar fashion to `Observable`:

```
Single<String> example =
    fetch("http://www.example.com")
        .flatMap(this::body);

String b = example.toBlocking().value();

//...

Single<String> body(Response response) {
    return Single.create(subscriber -> {
        try {
            subscriber.onSuccess(response.getResponseBody());
        } catch (IOException e) {
            subscriber.onError(e);
        }
    });
}

//Same functionality as body():
Single<String> body2(Response response) {
    return Single.fromCallable(() ->
```

```
          response.getResponseBody());
   }
```

Unfortunately, `Response.getResponseBody()` throws an `IOException`, so we cannot simply say: `map(Response::getResponseBody)`. But at least we see how `Single.flatMap()`) works. By wrapping the potentially dangerous `getResponseBody()` method with `Single<String>`, we make sure potential failure is encapsulated and clearly expressed in type system. `Single.flatMap()` works as you might expect, knowing `Observable.flatMap()`: if the second stage of computation (`this::body` in our case) fails, the entire `Single` fails, as well. Interestingly, `Single` has `map()` and `flatMap()` but no `filter()`. Can you guess why? `filter()` could potentially filter out content of `Single<T>` if it did not meet certain `Predicate<T>`. But `Single<T>` *must* have exactly one item inside whereas `filter()` could result with `Single` having none.

Just like `BlockingObservable` (see "BlockingObservable: Exiting the Reactive World" on page 118), `Single` has its very own `BlockingSingle` created with `Single.toBlocking()`. Analogously, creating `BlockingSingle<T>` does not yet block. However, calling `value()` on it blocks until value of type `T` (the `String` containing the response body in our example) is available. In case of exception, it will be rethrown from `value()` method.

Combining Responses Using zip, merge, and concat

`rx.Single` would be useless if it did not provide composable operators. The most important operator you will come across is `Single.zip()`, which works the same way as `Observable.zip()` (see "Pairwise Composing Using zip() and zipWith()" on page 79) but has simpler semantics. `Single` always emits precisely one value (or exception) so the result of `Single.zip()` (or a `Single.zipWith()` instance version) is always exactly one pair/tuple. `zip()` is basically a way of creating a third `Single` when two underlying `Singles` complete.[2]

Suppose that you are rendering an article to be displayed on your website. Three independent operations need to be made to fulfill the request: reading the article content from the database, asking a social media website for a number of likes collected so far, and updating the read count metric. Naive implementation not only performs these three actions sequentially, but also risks unacceptable latency if any of the steps are slow. With `Single` every step is modeled separately:

```
import org.springframework.jdbc.core.JdbcTemplate;

//...
```

---

2 In `CompletableFuture`, this operator is called `thenCombine()`.

```
Single<String> content(int id) {
    return Single.fromCallable(() -> jdbcTemplate
        .queryForObject(
            "SELECT content FROM articles WHERE id = ?",
            String.class, id))
        .subscribeOn(Schedulers.io());
}

Single<Integer> likes(int id) {
    //asynchronous HTTP request to social media website
}

Single<Void> updateReadCount() {
    //only side effect, no return value in Single
}
```

As an example, we show how `Single` can be created using `fromCallable` by passing a lambda expression. This utility is quite useful because it manages error handling for us (see "Where Are My Exceptions?" on page 244). The `content()` method uses a handy `JdbcTemplate` from Spring framework to unobtrusively load the article content from the database. JDBC is inherently blocking the API, so we explicitly call `sub scribeOn()` to make `Single` asynchronous. The implementation of `likes()` and `updateReadCount()` is omitted. You can imagine `likes()` making an asynchonous HTTP request to some API using RxNetty (see "Nonblocking HTTP Client with RxNetty" on page 184). `updateReadCount()` is interesting because it has a `Sin gle<Void>` type. This suggest it performs some side effect that has no return value but significant latency. Yet, we still might want to be notified about possible failures that happened asynchronously. RxJava has a special type for such cases, as well: `Completa ble`. This specifies that either complete without result or yield exception asynchronously.

Combining these three operations with `zip` is quite straightforward:

```
Single<Document> doc = Single.zip(
        content(123),
        likes(123),
        updateReadCount(),
        (con, lks, vod) -> buildHtml(con, lks)
);

//...

Document buildHtml(String content, int likes) {
    //...
}
```

`Single.zip()` takes three `Singles` (it has overloaded versions for anything between two and nine instances) and invokes our custom function when all three are completed. The outcome of this custom function is then placed back in a `Single<Document>`

---

instance that we can further transform. You should be aware that Void result is never used by the transformation. This means that we wait until updateReadCount() completes, yet we do not need its (empty) result. This might be a requirement or can suggest possible optimization: building an HTML document might work just as well if updateReadCount() is executed asynchronously without waiting for its completion or failure.

Now imagine what happens if invoking likes() fails or takes an unacceptably long time to complete (which is actually much worse). Without reactive extensions rendering, HTML fails entirely or takes a considerable amount of time. However, our implementation is not much better in that regard. Single supports multiple operators like timeout(), onErrorReturn(), and onErrorResumeNext() that enhance resiliency and error handling. All of these operators behave the same way as their Observable counterparts.

Interoperability with Observable and CompletableFuture

From the perspective of the type system, Observable and Single are unrelated. This basically means when Observable is required, you cannot use Single and vice versa. However there are two situations for which conversion between the two makes sense:

- When we use Single as an Observable that emits one value and completion notification (or error notification)
- When Single is missing certain operators available in Observable, cache() is one such example[3]

Let's take the second reason as an example:

```
Single<String> single = Single.create(subscriber -> {
    System.out.println("Subscribing");
    subscriber.onSuccess("42");
});

Single<String> cachedSingle = single
        .toObservable()
        .cache()
        .toSingle();

cachedSingle.subscribe(System.out::println);
cachedSingle.subscribe(System.out::println);
```

---

3 As of this writing (RxJava 1.1.6). The set of available operators grows fast so ensure that you use newest release and check again.

We use the cache() operator here so that Single generates "42" only once for the first subscriber. Single.toObservable() is a safe and easy to understand operator. It takes a Single<T> instance and converts it to an Observable<T>, emitting one element immediately followed by a completion notification (or error notification if that is how Single completed). The opposite Observable.toSingle() (do not confuse with the single() operator; see "Asserting Observable Has Exactly One Item Using single()" on page 92) requires more attention. Just like single(), toSingle() will throw an exception saying that "*Observable emitted too many elements*" if the underlying Observable emits more than one element. Similarly, expect "*Observable emitted no items*" if Observable is empty:

```
Single<Integer> emptySingle =
        Observable.<Integer>empty().toSingle();
Single<Integer> doubleSingle =
        Observable.just(1, 2).toSingle();
```

Now you might think that when the toObservable() and toSingle() operators are used close to each other, the latter is safe, but it does not need to be the case. For example, intermediate Observable might duplicate or discard an event emitted by Single:

```
Single<Integer> ignored = Single
        .just(1)
        .toObservable()
        .ignoreElements()    //PROBLEM
        .toSingle();
```

In the preceding code, ignoreElements() from Observable simply discards a single value emitted from Single. Therefore, when the toSingle() operator is used, all it can see is an Observable is that the completes without any elements. One thing to keep in mind that toSingle() operator, just like all of the other operators we discovered so far, is lazy. The exception about Single not emitting precisely one event will appear only when someone actually subscribes.

When to Use Single?

Having two abstractions, Observable and Single, it is important to distinguish between them and understand when to use which one. Just like with data structures, one size does not fit all. You should use Single in the following scenarios:

- An operation must complete with some particular value or an exception. For example, calling a web service always results with either a response from an external server or some sort of exception.

- There is no such thing as a *stream* in your problem domain; using Observable would be misleading and an overkill.

- `Observable` is too heavyweight and you *measured* that `Single` is faster in your particular problem.

On the other hand, you should prefer `Observable` for these circumstances:

- You model some sort of events (messages, GUI events) which are by definition occurring several times, possibly infinite.
- Or entirely the opposite, you expect the value to occur or not before completion.

The latter case is quite interesting. Do you think it makes sense for `findById(int)` method on some repository to return `Single<Record>` rather than `Record` or `Observable<Record>`? Well, it sounds reasonable: we look up an item by ID (which suggests there is just one such `Record`). However, there is no guarantee that a `Record` exists for every ID we supply. Therefore, this method can technically return *nothing*, modeled as `null`, `Optional<Record>`, or `Observable<Record>`, which are perfectly capable of handling empty streams followed by a completion notification. What about `Single`? It must either complete with a single value (`Record`) or with an exception. It is your design choice if you want to model a nonexisting record with an exception, but this often is considered a bad practice. Deciding whether a missing record for a given ID is a truly *exceptional* situation is not a responsibility of repository layer.

Summary

Chapters 2 and 3 gave you an overview and feel of RxJava. In this chapter, we covered quite advanced topics related to designing entirely reactive applications. This part was much more advanced, showing real-life techniques for implementing event-driven systems without introducing accidental complexity. We have shown several benchmarks proving that RxJava together with a nonblocking networking stack like Netty. You are not forced to use such advanced libraries but it certainly pays off when you strive for maximum throughput on a commodity servers.

CHAPTER 6

Flow Control and Backpressure

Tomasz Nurkiewicz

So far, we've become very familiar with the push-based nature of RxJava. Events are produced somewhere up in the stream to be consumed later by all subscribers. We never really paid much attention to what happens if `Observer` is slow and cannot keep up with events emitted from within `Observable.create()`. This entire chapter is devoted to this problem.

RxJava has two ways of dealing with producers being more active than subscribers:

- Various flow-control mechanisms such as sampling and batching are implemented via built-in operators

- Subscribers can propagate their demand and request only as many items as they can process by using a feedback channel known as backpressure.

These two mechanisms are described in this chapter.

Flow Control

Before RxJava began implementing backpressure (see the section "Backpressure" on page 226), dealing with producers (`Observables`) outperforming consumers (`Observers`) was a difficult task. There are quite a few operators that were invented to deal with producers pushing too many events, and most of them are quite interesting on their own. Some are useful for batching events; others are dropping some events. This section walks you through these operators, including some examples.

Taking Periodic Samples and Throttling

There are cases for which you definitely want to receive and process every single event pushed from the upstream `Observable`. But, there are some scenarios for which periodic sampling is enough. The most obvious case is receiving measurements from some device; for example, temperature (compare with "Dropping Duplicates Using distinct() and distinctUntilChanged()" on page 92). The frequency at which the device produces new measurements is often irrelevant for us, especially when the measurements appear often but are very similar to one another. The `sample()` operator looks at the upstream `Observable` periodically (for example, every second) and emits the last encountered event. If there were no event at all in the last one-second period, no sample is forwarded downstream and the next sample will be taken after one second, as illustrated in this sample:

```
long startTime = System.currentTimeMillis();
Observable
    .interval(7, TimeUnit.MILLISECONDS)
    .timestamp()
    .sample(1, TimeUnit.SECONDS)
    .map(ts -> ts.getTimestampMillis() - startTime + "ms: " + ts.getValue())
    .take(5)
    .subscribe(System.out::println);
```

The preceding code snippet will print something similar to the following:

```
1088ms: 141
2089ms: 284
3090ms: 427
4084ms: 569
5085ms: 712
```

The first column shows relative time from subscription to sample emission. You can clearly see that the first sample appears a little bit over one second (as requested by the `sample()` operator) and subsequent samples are roughly one second after one another. More important, notice what the values are. The `interval()` operator emits natural numbers starting from zero every seven milliseconds. Thus, by the time the first sample is taken, we can expect about 142 (1,000/7) events to appear, where 142nd value is 141 (0-based).

Let's explore a sample that's a little bit more complex. Imagine that you have a list of names that appear with some absolute delays, like so:

```
Observable<String> names = Observable
    .just("Mary", "Patricia", "Linda",
        "Barbara",
        "Elizabeth", "Jennifer", "Maria", "Susan",
        "Margaret", "Dorothy");

Observable<Long> absoluteDelayMillis = Observable
    .just(0.1, 0.6, 0.9,
```

```
          1.1,
          3.3, 3.4, 3.5, 3.6,
          4.4, 4.8)
      .map(d -> (long)(d * 1_000));

Observable<String> delayedNames = names
    .zipWith(absoluteDelayMillis,
        (n, d) -> Observable
                    .just(n)
                    .delay(d, MILLISECONDS))
    .flatMap(o -> o);

delayedNames
    .sample(1, SECONDS)
    .subscribe(System.out::println);
```

First, we construct a sequence of names followed by a sequences of absolute delays (in seconds, later mapped to milliseconds). Using the `zipWith()` operator, we `delay()` the occurrence of certain names; for example, *Mary* appears after 100 milliseconds from subscription, whereas *Dorothy* appears after 4.8 seconds. The `sample()` operator will periodically (every second) pick the last seen name from the stream within the last period. So, after the first second, we `println` *Linda*, followed by *Barbara* a second later. Now between 2,000 and 3,000 milliseconds since subscription, no name appeared, so `sample()` does not emit anything. Two seconds after *Barbara* was emitted, we see *Susan*. `sample()` will forward completion (and errors, as well) discarding the last period. If we want to see *Dorothy* appearing as well, we can artificially postpone the completion notification, as is done here:

```
static <T> Observable<T> delayedCompletion() {
    return Observable.<T>empty().delay(1, SECONDS);
}

//...

delayedNames
    .concatWith(delayedCompletion())
    .sample(1, SECONDS)
    .subscribe(System.out::println);
```

`sample()` has a more advanced variant taking `Observable` as an argument rather than a fixed period. This second `Observable` (known as sampler) basically dictates when to take a sample from the upstream source: every time sampler emits any value, a new sample is taken (if any new value appeared since the last sample). You can use this overloaded version of `sample()` to dynamically change the sampling rate or take samples only at very specific points in time. For example, taking a snapshot of some value when a new frame is redrawn or when a key is pressed. A trivial example can simply emulate the fixed period by using the `interval()` operator:

```
//equivalent:
obs.sample(1, SECONDS);
obs.sample(Observable.interval(1, SECONDS));
```

As you can see, there are some subtleties regarding `sample()`'s behavior. Rather than relying on our understanding of documentation or manual verification, it is great to have automated tests. Testing time-sensitive operators like `sample()` is covered in the section "Virtual Time" on page 258.

`sample()` has an alias in RxJava called `throttleLast()`. Symmetrically, there is also the `throttleFirst()`) operator that emits the very first event that appeared in each period. So, applying `throttleFirst()` instead of `sample()` in our name stream yields rather expected results:

```
Observable<String> names = Observable
    .just("Mary", "Patricia", "Linda",
        "Barbara",
        "Elizabeth", "Jennifer", "Maria", "Susan",
        "Margaret", "Dorothy");

Observable<Long> absoluteDelayMillis = Observable
    .just(0.1, 0.6, 0.9,
        1.1,
        3.3, 3.4, 3.5, 3.6,
        4.4, 4.8)
    .map(d -> (long)(d * 1_000));

//...

delayedNames
    .throttleFirst(1, SECONDS)
    .subscribe(System.out::println);
```

The output looks like this:

```
Mary
Barbara
Elizabeth
Margaret
```

Just like `sample()` (aka `throttleLast()`), `throttleFirst()` does not emit any event when no new name appeared between *Barbara* and *Elizabeth*.

Buffering Events to a List

Buffering and moving windows are among the most exciting built-in operators offered by RxJava. They both traverse input stream through a window that captures several consecutive elements and moves forward. On one hand, they allow batching values from an upstream source to handle them more effectively. In practice, they are flexible and versatile tools that allow various aggregations of data on the fly.

The `buffer()` operator aggregates batches of events in real time into a `List`. However, unlike the `toList()` operator, `buffer()` emits several lists grouping some number of subsequent events as opposed to just one containing all events (like `toList()`). The simplest form of `buffer()` groups values from upstream `Observable` into a lists of equal size:

```
Observable
    .range(1, 7)  //1, 2, 3, ... 7
    .buffer(3)
    .subscribe((List<Integer> list) -> {
            System.out.println(list);
        }
    );
```

Of course, `subscribe(System.out::println)` would work as well; we left the type information for educational purposes. The output shows three events emitted from the `buffer(3)` operator:

```
[1, 2, 3]
[4, 5, 6]
[7]
```

`buffer()` keeps receiving upstream events and buffers them (hence the name) internally until the buffer reaches a size of 3. When that happens, the entire buffer (`List<Integer>`) is pushed downstream. When the completion notification appears and internal buffer was not empty (but not yet of size 3), it is pushed downstream anyway. That is the reason we see a one-element list in the end.

By using the `buffer(int)` operator you can replace several fine-grained events with less but bigger batches. For example, if you want to reduce database load, you might want to replace storing each event individually by storing them in batches:

```
interface Repository {
    void store(Record record);
    void storeAll(List<Record> records);
}

//...

Observable<Record> events = //...

events
        .subscribe(repository::store);
//vs.
events
        .buffer(10)
        .subscribe(repository::storeAll);
```

The latter subscription calls `storeAll` on `Repository`, storing batches of 10 elements at once. This can potentially improve throughput in your application.

`buffer()` has many overloaded variants. A slightly more complex version allows you to configure how many oldest values from internal buffer to drop when `buffer()` pushes the list downstream. That sounds complex, but put in more basic terms, it makes it possible for you to look at your event stream through the moving window of a certain size:

```
Observable
        .range(1, 7)
        .buffer(3, 1)
        .subscribe(System.out::println);
```

This yields several overlapping lists:

```
[1, 2, 3]
[2, 3, 4]
[3, 4, 5]
[4, 5, 6]
[5, 6, 7]
[6, 7]
[7]
```

You can use `buffer(N, 1)` variant if you want to compute a moving average of some time-series data.[1] The code example that follows generates 1,000 random values from normal distribution. Later, we take a sliding window of 100 elements (advancing one element at a time) and compute the average of such a window.[2] Run this program yourself and notice how the moving average is much smoother than the random unordered values.

```
import java.util.Random;
import java.util.stream.Collectors;

//...

Random random = new Random();
Observable
        .defer(() -> just(random.nextGaussian()))
        .repeat(1000)
        .buffer(100, 1)
        .map(this::averageOfList)
        .subscribe(System.out::println);

//...

private double averageOfList(List<Double> list) {
    return list
            .stream()
```

---

1 *https://en.wikipedia.org/wiki/Moving_average*

2 Keep in mind that this is not the most efficient algorithm because it adds the same number multiple times.

```
        .collect(Collectors.averagingDouble(x -> x));
    }
```

You can probably imagine that calling `buffer(N)` is in fact equivalent to `buffer(N, N)`. The simplest form of `buffer()` drops the entire internal buffer when it becomes full. Interestingly, the second parameter of `buffer(int, int)` (that specifies how many elements to skip when the buffer is pushed downstream) can be bigger than the first argument, effectively skipping some elements!

```
Observable<List<Integer>> odd = Observable
        .range(1, 7)
        .buffer(1, 2);
odd.subscribe(System.out::println);
```

This setup forwards the first element but then skips two: the first and the second one. Then the cycle repeats: `buffer()` forwards the third element but then skips the third and fourth. Effectively, the output is: `[1] [3] [5] [7]`. Notice that each element in the odd `Observable` is actually a one-element list. You can use `flatMap()` or `flatMapIterable()` to get back a simple `Observable<Integer>`:

```
Observable<Integer> odd = Observable
        .range(1, 7)
        .buffer(1, 2)
        .flatMapIterable(list -> list);
```

`flatMapIterable()` expects a function that transforms each value in the stream (one-element `List<Integer>`) into a `List`. Identity transformation (`list -> list`) is enough here.

Buffering by time periods

`buffer()` is actually a broad family of operators. Rather than batching upstream events based on size (so that each batch has the same size), another variant of `buffer()` batches events by time period. While `throttleFirst()` and `throttleLast()` were taking first and last events within a given period of time accordingly, one of the overloaded versions of buffer batches all events in each time period. Coming back to our names example:

```
Observable<String> names = just(
        "Mary",     "Patricia", "Linda", "Barbara", "Elizabeth",
        "Jennifer", "Maria",    "Susan", "Margaret", "Dorothy");
Observable<Long> absoluteDelays = just(
        0.1, 0.6, 0.9, 1.1, 3.3,
        3.4, 3.5, 3.6, 4.4, 4.8
).map(d -> (long) (d * 1_000));

Observable<String> delayedNames = Observable.zip(names,
        absoluteDelays,
        (n, d) -> just(n).delay(d, MILLISECONDS)
).flatMap(o -> o);
```

```
delayedNames
        .buffer(1, SECONDS)
        .subscribe(System.out::println);
```

An overloaded version of `buffer()` that accepts time period (one second in the preceding example) aggregates all upstream events within that period. Therefore, `buffer()` collects all events that happened during first time period, second time period, and so on:

```
[Mary, Patricia, Linda]
[Barbara]
[]
[Elizabeth, Jennifer, Maria, Susan]
[Margaret, Dorothy]
```

The third `List<String>` is empty because no events appeared in that time frame. One of the use cases for `buffer()` is counting the number of events per each time period; for example, number of key events per second:

```
Observable<KeyEvent> keyEvents = //...

Observable<Integer> eventPerSecond = keyEvents
        .buffer(1, SECONDS)
        .map(List::size);
```

Luckily, because no events within a one-second period yields an empty list, we do not have gaps in our measurements. However, this is not the most efficient way, as we will soon discover with the `window()` operator.

The most comprehensive overload of `buffer()` allows you to take full control over when this operator begins buffering events and when the buffer should be flushed downstream. In other words, you choose in which periods of time upstream events should be grouped. Imagine that you are monitoring some industrial device that pushes telemetric data very often. The amount of data is overwhelming, so to save some computational capacity, you decided to look only at certain samples. The algorithm follows:

- During business hours (9:00–17:00), we take 100-millisecond long snapshots every second (processing approximately 10% of data)
- Outside business hours we look only at 200-millisecond long snapshots taken every 5 seconds (4%)

In other words, once every second (or 5 seconds) we buffer all events for 100 milliseconds (or 200 accordingly) and emit lists of all of the events within that period. This will become clear when you see the entire example. First, we need an `Observable` that emits any value whenever we want to begin buffering (grouping) upstream events. This `Observable` can literally push any type of value, but this is irrelevant because only timing matters. The fact that we are returning `Duration` from the `java.time` package is a coincidence, RxJava does not use this value in any way:

```
Observable<Duration> insideBusinessHours = Observable
    .interval(1, SECONDS)
    .filter(x -> isBusinessHour())
    .map(x -> Duration.ofMillis(100));
Observable<Duration> outsideBusinessHours = Observable
    .interval(5, SECONDS)
    .filter(x -> !isBusinessHour())
    .map(x -> Duration.ofMillis(200));

Observable<Duration> openings = Observable.merge(
    insideBusinessHours, outsideBusinessHours);
```

First using the `interval()` operator we generate timer ticks every second but exclude those that are not within business hours. This way, we get a steady clock ticking every second between 9:00 and 17:00. Recall that `interval()` returns growing natural Long numbers; however, we do not need them, so for convenience we replace them with fixed duration of `100` milliseconds. Symmetrical code creates a steady stream of events every 5 seconds between 17:00 and 9:00. If you are curious how `isBusinesHour()` is implemented, it uses the `java.time` package:

```
private static final LocalTime BUSINESS_START = LocalTime.of(9, 0);
private static final LocalTime BUSINESS_END = LocalTime.of(17, 0);

private boolean isBusinessHour() {
    ZoneId zone = ZoneId.of("Europe/Warsaw");
    ZonedDateTime zdt = ZonedDateTime.now(zone);
    LocalTime localTime = zdt.toLocalTime();
    return !localTime.isBefore(BUSINESS_START)
        && !localTime.isAfter(BUSINESS_END);
}
```

The `openings` stream *merges* together `insideBusinessHours` and `outsideBusinesHours` streams. It is basically a trigger that instructs the `buffer()` operator when to begin collecting samples from upstream rather than discarding them. Whatever the value is emitted from the `openings` stream is entirely irrelevant. But we must also specify when to stop aggregating (buffering) events and push them downstream as one batch in a `List`. The most obvious solution is to treat each event emitted from `openings` stream as a signal to stop the current batch, emit it downstream, and start another batch:

```
Observable<TeleData> upstream = //...

Observable<List<TeleData>> samples = upstream
    .buffer(openings);
```

Notice how we pass carefully crafted `openings` stream to the `buffer()` operator. The preceding code example slices the `upstream` source of `TeleData` values. The ticking clock of `openings` stream batches events from `upstream`. Within business hours, a new batch is created every second, outside business hours, batches group values in five-second periods. Importantly in this version, all events from `upstream` are preserved because they either land in one batch or the other. However, an overloaded version of the `buffer()` operator also allows marking the end of a batch:

```
Observable<List<TeleData>> samples = upstream
    .buffer(
        openings,
        duration -> empty()
            .delay(duration.toMillis(), MILLISECONDS));
```

First recall that `openings` is an `Observable<Duration>`, but the actual value of events from `openings` is not important. RxJava merely uses this event to start buffering `Tele Data` instances. But this time we have full control when buffering and emission of this buffer should occur. The second parameter is an `Observable` that must complete whenever we want to stop sampling. Completion of this second stream marks the end of a given batch. Look carefully: the `openings` stream emits an event every time we would like to start a new batch. For each event emitted from `openings` we return a new `Observable` that should complete some time in the future. So, for example, when the `openings` stream emits an event of `Duation.ofMillis(100)` value, we transform it to an `Observable` that completes when a given batch should end, after 100 milliseconds. Notice that in this case some events might be dropped or duplicated in consecutive batches. If second, the `Observable`—which is responsible for marking the end of a given batch, appears before an opening event of the next batch, within this time gap events are discarded by `buffer()`. This is our case: we begin buffering events every second (or every other second outside business hours), but the buffer closes and is being forwarded after 100 milliseconds (or 200, accordingly). The majority of events fall between buffering periods and therefore are discarded.

The `buffer()` operator is extremely flexible and quite complex. Make sure that you experiment a little bit with it and understand the preceding example. It is used to smartly batch events from the upstream source to achieve grouping, sampling, or moving window functionality. But because `buffer()` requires creating an intermediate `List` before the current buffer is closed and passed downstream, it might unnecessarily put pressure on garbage collection and memory usage (see the section "Memory Consumption and Leaks" on page 315). Therefore, the `window()` operator was introduced.

Moving window

When working with `buffer()` we build `List` instances over and over. Why do we build these intermediate `List`s rather then somehow consume events on the fly? This is where the `window()` operator becomes useful. You should prefer `window()` over buffer() if possible because the latter is less predictable in terms of memory usage. The window() operator is very similar to buffer(): it has similar overloaded versions including the one that does the following:

- Receive int, grouping events from source into fixed-size lists
- Receive time unit, grouping events within fixed-time periods
- Receive custom Observables marking the beginning and end of each batch

What is the difference, then? Remember the example that was counting how many events occurred per second in given source? Let's take another look at it:

```
Observable<KeyEvent> keyEvents = //...

Observable<Integer> eventPerSecond = keyEvents
    .buffer(1, SECONDS)
    .map(List::size);
```

We batch all events from Observable<KeyEvent> that occurred in each second into Observable<List<KeyEvent>>. In the next step, we map List into its size. This is quite wasteful, especially if the number of events in each second is significant:

```
Observable<Observable<KeyEvent>> windows = keyEvents.window(1, SECONDS);
Observable<Integer> eventPerSecond = windows
    .flatMap(eventsInSecond -> eventsInSecond.count());
```

window(), as opposed to buffer(), returns an Observable<Observable<KeyEvent>>. Think about it for a moment. Rather than receiving fixed lists with each one containing one batch (or buffer), we receive a stream of streams. Every time a new batch begins (every one second in the preceding example), a new Observable<KeyEvent> value appears in the outer stream. We can further transform all of these inner streams, but to avoid double-wrapping we use flatMap(). flatMap() receives each buffer (an Observable<KeyEvent>) as an argument and is suppose to return another Observable. The count() operator (see the section "Slicing and Dicing Using skip(), takeWhile(), and Others" on page 94) transforms an Observable<T> into an Observable<Integer> that emits just one item representing the number of events in the original Observable. Therefore, for each one-second batch we produce, the number of events occurred within that second. But there is no internal buffering; the count() operator counts events on the fly as they pass through.

Skipping Stale Events by Using debounce()

buffer() and window() group several events together so that you can process them in batches. sample() picks one fairly arbitrary event once in a while. These operators do not take into account how much time elapsed between events. But in many cases, the event can be discarded if it is shortly followed by another event. For example, imagine a stream of stock prices flowing from a trading platform:

```
Observable<BigDecimal> prices = tradingPlatform.pricesOf("NFLX");
Observable<BigDecimal> debounced = prices.debounce(100, MILLISECONDS);
```

debounce() (alias: throttleWithTimeout()) discards all of the events that are shortly followed by another event. In other words, if a given event is not followed by another event within a time window, that event is emitted. In the preceding example, the pri ces stream pushes prices of "NFLX" stock every time they change. Prices sometimes change very frequently, dozens of times per second. For each price change we would like to run some computation that takes a significant amount of time to complete. However, if a new price arrives, the result of this computation is irrelevant; it must begin from scratch with this new price. Therefore, we would like to discard events if they are followed (suppressed by) a new event shortly after.

debounce() waits a little bit (100 milliseconds in the preceding example) just in case second event appears later on. This process repeats itself so that if a second event appears in less than 100 milliseconds from the first one, RxJava will postpone its emission, hoping for the third one to appear. This time, again, you have an option to flexibly control for how long to wait on a per-event basis. For example, you might want to ignore stock price changes if they are followed by an update in less than 100 milliseconds. However, if the price goes above $150, we would like to forward such an update downstream much faster without hesitation. Maybe because some types of events need to be handled straight away; for example, because they are great market opportunities. you can implement this easily by using an overloaded version of debounce():

```
prices
    .debounce(x -> {
        boolean goodPrice = x.compareTo(BigDecimal.valueOf(150)) > 0;
        return Observable
            .empty()
            .delay(goodPrice? 10 : 100, MILLISECONDS);
    })
```

For each new update of price x, we apply sophisticated logic (> $150) to figure out if the price is good. Then, for each such update we return a unique Observable, which is empty. It does not need to emit any items; it is important when it completes. For good prices, it emits a completion notification after 10 milliseconds. For other prices, this Observable completes after 100 milliseconds. The debounce() operator for each event it receives subscribes to this Observable waiting for its completion. If it completes first, the event is passed downstream. Otherwise, if more recent upstream event appeared in the meantime, the cycle repeats.

In our example, when a price x of $140 appears, the debounce() operator creates a new Observable with completion delayed by 100 milliseconds via the expression we provided. If no events appear before the completion of this event, the $140 event will be forwarded downstream. However, imagine another price update x of $151 came along. This time when the debounce() operator asks us to provide an Observable (called debounceSelector in the API) we return a stream that completes much faster, after 10 milliseconds. So in case of good prices (greater than $150), we are willing to wait only 10 milliseconds for a subsequent update. If you still struggle to understand how debounce() works, here is a stock price simulator you can try:

```
Observable<BigDecimal> pricesOf(String ticker) {
    return Observable
            .interval(50, MILLISECONDS)
            .flatMap(this::randomDelay)
            .map(this::randomStockPrice)
            .map(BigDecimal::valueOf);
}

Observable<Long> randomDelay(long x) {
    return Observable
            .just(x)
            .delay((long) (Math.random() * 100), MILLISECONDS);
}

double randomStockPrice(long x) {
    return 100 + Math.random() * 10 +
            (Math.sin(x / 100.0)) * 60.0;
}
```

The preceding code nicely composes several streams. First, we generate a sequence of long values emitted in fixed 50-millisecond intervals. Then, we delay each event independently by some random value between 0 and 100 milliseconds. Last but not least, we transform infinitely growing long numbers into a sine wave (using Math.sin()) with random jitter. This simulates stock price fluctuation over time. If you run this stream against the debounce() operator, you will notice that as long as prices are low, events are generally infrequent because we are willing to wait as much as 100 milliseconds for subsequent event, which often occurs. But when the price goes above $150, the debounce() tolerance goes down to 10 milliseconds, so effectively every good price update is forwarded downstream.

Avoid starvation in debounce()

It is quite easy to imagine a situation in which the debounce() operator prevents emission of all events because they simply appear too often and there is never a moment of silence:

```
Observable
    .interval(99, MILLISECONDS)
    .debounce(100, MILLISECONDS)
```

Such a source will never emit any event because debounce() waits as much as 100 milliseconds to wnsure that there is no more recent event. Unfortunately, just 1 millisecond before this timeout, a new event appears, starting debounce's timer all over. This leads to an Observable that produces events so often that we may never get to see any of them (!) You can call this a feature, but in practice you might want to see *some* event from time to time, even in case of flood. To prevent such a situation we must get a little bit creative.

First, we must discover a situation in which no new event appeared for a long time. We already played with timeout() operator in the section "Timing Out When Events Do Not Occur" on page 251, so we know that part is easy:

```
Observable
        .interval(99, MILLISECONDS)
        .debounce(100, MILLISECONDS)
        .timeout(1, SECONDS);
```

Now, we at least get an exception signaling an idle upstream source. Bizarrely it is the opposite—the upstream interval() operator produces events too often and because of that, debounce() never passes them downstream—but we digress. If events appear too often, we hold them back waiting for a moment of silence. But if this silence is too long (more than one second), we fail and throw a TimeoutException. Rather than failing permanently, we would actually like to see an arbitrary value from upstream Observable and continue. The first part of the task is simple:

```
ConnectableObservable<Long> upstream = Observable
        .interval(99, MILLISECONDS)
        .publish();
upstream
        .debounce(100, MILLISECONDS)
        .timeout(1, SECONDS, upstream.take(1));
upstream.connect();
```

The timeout() operator has an overloaded version that accepts a fallback Observable upon timeout. Unfortunately, there is a subtle bug here. In case of timeout, we naively take the first encountered item from upstream and then complete. What we really want is to continue emitting events from upstream, still with debounce() support.

ConnectableObservable

ConnectableObservable together with the publish() and con
nect() pair is needed here to turn the cold Observable.inter
val() into hot one (see the section "Hot and Cold Observables" on
page 43 for details why interval() is cold and what that means).
By calling publish() followed by connect() (see the section "ConnectableObservable Lifecycle" on page 56) we force the interval()
operator to begin producing events right away, even without anyone subscribing. This means that if we subscribe to such an Observ
able many seconds later, it begins receiving events in the middle,
and all subscribers get the same events at the same time. By default,
interval() is a cold Observable, so each subscriber, no matter
when subscribed, starts from 0, from the beginning.

Another approach is seemingly better:

```
upstream
    .debounce(100, MILLISECONDS)
    .timeout(1, SECONDS, upstream
        .take(1)
        .concatWith(
            upstream.debounce(100, MILLISECONDS)))
```

It looks somewhat OK at first sight. The original source, after applying debounce()
has a timeout. When timeout occurs, we emit the very first item we encountered and
continue with the same source, also by using the debounce() operator. However, in
the case of a first timeout, we switch to the fallback Observable that no longer has a
timeout() operator applied. A quick, dirty, and short-sighted fix:

```
upstream
    .debounce(100, MILLISECONDS)
    .timeout(1, SECONDS, upstream
        .take(1)
        .concatWith(
            upstream
                .debounce(100, MILLISECONDS)
                .timeout(1, SECONDS, upstream)))
```

Yet again, we forgot to put a fallback Observable in the inner timeout() operator.
Enough is enough, you should already see a recurring pattern here. Rather than infinitely repeating the same form of upstream → debounce → timeout() → upstream →
…we can use recursion!

```
import static rx.Observable.defer;


Observable<Long> timedDebounce(Observable<Long> upstream) {
    Observable<Long> onTimeout = upstream
```

```
            .take(1)
            .concatWith(defer(() -> timedDebounce(upstream)));
    return upstream
            .debounce(100, MILLISECONDS)
            .timeout(1, SECONDS, onTimeout);
}
```

The definition of onTimeout fallback Observable in timedDebounce is tricky. We declare that it first takes one sample event from upstream (which is the original source) followed by a recursively invoked timedDebounce() method. We must use the defer() operator to avoid infinite recursion. The rest of the timedDebounce() basically takes the original upstream source, applies the debounce() operator, and adds fallback onTimeout. This fallback does the exact same thing: applies debounce(), adds a timeout(), and fallback—recursively.

 Do not become depressed if you find it difficult to grasp at first. This is a rather complex example showing the power of stream composition together with laziness and recursion. You hardly ever need that level of complexity, but after you grasp how it works, it is quite satisfying. Play around with this code and observe how tiny changes drastically alter the way streams interact with one another.

Backpressure

Backpressure is quite essential to build robust and responsive applications. In essence, it is a feedback channel from the consumer to producer. The consumer has a certain level of control over how much data it can process at any time. This way consumers or messaging middleware are not becoming saturated and unresponsive under high load. Instead, they request fewer messages, letting the producer decide how to slow down.

In every system that exchanges data via message passing (or events for that matter), a problem of consumers not keeping up with producers can arise. Depending on the underlying implementation, it can manifest in different ways. If the communication channel somehow synchronizes producers and consumers (for example, by using ArrayBlockingQueue), the producer is throttled (blocked) when the consumer is not keeping up with the load. This leads to coupling between the producer and consumer which should otherwise be entirely independent. Message passing typically means asynchronous processing, an assumption that fails when the producer suddenly must wait for the consumer. Even worse, the producer might be a consumer of a different producer higher in the hierarchy, cascading increased latency up.

Conversely, if the medium in between these two parties is unbounded, well…it is still bound by factors over which we have less control. An infinite queue like LinkedBlock ingQueue allows the producer to greatly outperform consumers without blocking.

That is, until `LinkedBlockingQueue` does not consume all memory and crash entire application. If the medium is persistent—for example a JMS message broker—the same problem can technically manifest as well with disk space, but this is less probable. Far more common is a situation in which the messaging middleware finds it difficult to manage thousands if not millions of unconsumed messages. Some specialized brokers such as Kafka (*http://kafka.apache.org:*) can technically store hundreds of millions of messages until lagging consumers get a hold of them. But this leads to an enormous increase in latencies, measured as a time between message production and consumption.

Although message-driven systems are generally considered more robust and scalable, the problem of too eager producers remains unsolved. However, there are some efforts to solve this integration issue. Sampling and throttling (using `sample()` and others) and batching (using `window()` and `buffer()`) are manual ways of reducing producer load in RxJava. When `Observable` generates more events that can be consumed, we can apply sampling or batching to increase subscription throughput. Yet, more robust and systematic approach was needed, hence the Reactive Streams (*http://www.reactive-streams.org:*) initiative was born out of necessity. This small set of interfaces and semantics aims to formalize the problem and provide a systematic algorithm for producer–consumer coordination, known as *backpressure*.

Backpressure is a simple protocol that allows the consumer to request how much data it can consume at a time, effectively providing a feedback channel to a producer. Producers receive requests from consumers, avoiding message overflow. Of course, this algorithm can work only with producers that are capable of throttling themselves; for example, when they are backed by static collection or source that can be pulled from something like `Iterator`. When the producer has no control over the frequency of data it produces (the source is external or hot), backpressure can not help much.

Backpressure in RxJava

Even though Reactive Streams solve a very general problem in technology-agnostic way, we will focus on RxJava and how it approaches the problem of backpressure. Throughout this chapter we will use an example of continually washing dishes in a small restaurant.[3] Dishes are modeled as large objects with an identifier:

```
class Dish {
    private final byte[] oneKb = new byte[1_024];
    private final int id;

    Dish(int id) {
```

---

3 This example was inspired by *https://www.lightbend.com/blog/7-ways-washing-dishes-and-message-driven-reactive-systems*.

```
            this.id = id;
            System.out.println("Created: " + id);
        }

        public String toString() {
            return String.valueOf(id);
        }
    }
```

The oneKb buffer simulates some extra memory utilization. Dishes are passed to the kitchen by waiters and are modeled as an Observable:

```
Observable<Dish> dishes = Observable
        .range(1, 1_000_000_000)
        .map(Dish::new);
```

The range() operator produces new values as fast as it possibly can. So what happens if washing dishes takes a little bit of time and is clearly slower than the pace of production?

```
Observable
        .range(1, 1_000_000_000)
        .map(Dish::new)
        .subscribe(x -> {
            System.out.println("Washing: " + x);
            sleepMillis(50);
        });
```

Surprisingly nothing bad. If you study the output you will notice that range() is perfectly aligned with subscription:

```
Created: 1
Washing: 1
Created: 2
Washing: 2
Created: 3
Washing: 3
...
Created: 110
Washing: 110
...
```

This should not come as a surprise to you. The range() operator is not asynchronous by default, so every item it produces is passed to a Subscriber directly within the context of the same thread. If the Subscriber is slow, it effectively prevents Observable from producing more elements. range() cannot call onNext() of the Subscriber until the previous one finished. This is possible because both producer and consumer work in the same thread and are transparently coupled. In some sense, there is an implicit queue between them with a maximum capacity of one. A *rendezvous* algorithm that we did not anticipate. Imagine a waiter in a restaurant who cannot leave new dishes for cleaning as long as the ones currently being washed are not done. But when a waiter stands still waiting for dish washing to be done, customers are not served. And when they are not served, new customers cannot enter the restaurant. This is how one blocking component can bring the entire system to a stall. However, in real life there is typically a thread boundary between producer and consumer: `Observable` produces events in one thread, whereas `Subscriber` consumes in another:

```
dishes
    .observeOn(Schedulers.io())
    .subscribe(x -> {
        System.out.println("Washing: " + x);
        sleepMillis(50);
    });
```

Stop for a moment and think about what could happen without actually compiling and running the code. One might think that a disaster should occur because `dishes` produces events very fast from the `range()` operator, whereas `Subscriber` is quite slow, consuming only 20 dishes per second. The `observeOn()` operator keeps consuming events in quick succession but the `Subscriber` is consuming them way to slow. Therefore you might conclude that `OutOfMemoryError` is unavoidable with unprocessed events piling up somewhere. Luckily backpressure saves the day in this case and RxJava protects us to some degree. The output of the program is somewhat unexpected:

```
Created: 1
Created: 2
Created: 3
...
Created: 128

Washing: 1
Washing: 2
...
Washing: 128

Created: 129
...
Created: 223
Created: 224

Washing: 129
Washing: 130
...
```

First, a batch of 128 dishes is being produced by `range()` pretty much instantaneously. Later, there is a slow process of washing dishes, one by one. Somehow the `range()` operator becomes idle. When the last dish out of these 128 is washed, another batch of 96 dishes is produced by `range()`, followed by a slow process of washing.[4] Apparently, there must be some clever mechanism that prevents `range()` from producing too many events, controlled by subscriber. If you do not see where such mechanism is deployed, let's try to implement `range()` ourselves:

```java
Observable<Integer> myRange(int from, int count) {
    return Observable.create(subscriber -> {
        int i = from;
        while (i < from + count) {
            if (!subscriber.isUnsubscribed()) {
                subscriber.onNext(i++);
            } else {
                return;
            }
        }
        subscriber.onCompleted();
    });
}
```

Here, we're using `myRange()` in the same example together with `observeOn()`:

```java
myRange(1, 1_000_000_000)
        .map(Dish::new)
        .observeOn(Schedulers.io())
        .subscribe(x -> {
                    System.out.println("Washing: " + x);
                    sleepMillis(50);
                },
                Throwable::printStackTrace
        );
```

This ends with catastrophe, and we never even get to wash any dish:

```
Created: 1
Created: 2
Created: 3
...
Created: 7177
Created: 7178

rx.exceptions.MissingBackpressureException
    at rx.internal.operators...
    at rx.internal.operators...
```

`MissingBackpressureException` will be explained later on. For the time being, I'm guessing that this convinces you that there is some background mechanism that our custom implementation of `range()` is lacking.

---

4 Do not pay much attention to these exact sizes, what matters is that something requests batches of events periodically.

Built-in Backpressure

For the past several chapters we watched how events were flowing downstream from the source Observable, through a sequence of operators, down to a Subscriber. There was never any feedback channel past a subscription request. The moment we invoked subscribe() (which in some sense propagates up) all events and notifications are traveling down without any apparent feedback loop. This lack of feedback can lead to producers (uppermost Observable) emitting a number of events overwhelming the subscriber. As a consequence, your application can crash with OutOfMemoryError or at best become very latent.

Backpressure is a mechanism that allows terminal subscribers as well as all intermediate operators to request only a certain number of events from the producer. By default, an upstream cold Observable produces events as fast it can. But in the presence of such requests coming from downstream, it should in a way "slow down" and produce exactly the number requested. This is the reason behind the magic number of 128 seen with observeOn(). But, first let's see how the final subscriber can control backpressure.

When subscribing, we have a possibility to implement onNext(), onCompleted(), and onError() (see the section "Subscribing to Notifications from Observable" on page 30). Turns out there is another callback method to implement: onStart().

```
Observable
    .range(1, 10)
    .subscribe(new Subscriber<Integer>() {

        @Override
        public void onStart() {
            request(3);
        }

        //onNext, onCompleted, onError follows...
    });
```

onStart() is invoked by RxJava exactly when you think it should—before any event or notification is propagated to Subscriber. You can technically use a constructor of your Subscriber, but for anonymous inner classes in Java, constructors look really eerie:

```
    .subscribe(new Subscriber<Integer>() {

        {{
            request(3);
        }}

        //onNext, onCompleted, onError follows...
    });
```

But we digress. The `request(3)` invocation inside a `Subscriber` instructs the upstream source how many items we are willing to receive at first. Skipping this invocation entirely (or calling `request(Long.MAX_VALUE)`) is equivalent to requesting as many events as possible. This is the reason why we must invoke `request()` very early; otherwise, the stream begins to emit events and we cannot decrease our demand later on. But when we request only three events, the `range()` operator will obediently stop emitting events temporarily after pushing 1, 2, and 3. Our `onNext()` callback method will be invoked three times and no more, despite `range()` operator not being completed yet. However, we, as a `Subscriber`, have full control over how much data we want to receive. For example, we might want to request items individually:

```
Observable
    .range(1, 10)
    .subscribe(new Subscriber<Integer>() {

        @Override
        public void onStart() {
            request(1);
        }

        @Override
        public void onNext(Integer integer) {
            request(1);
            log.info("Next {}", integer);
        }

        //onCompleted, onError...
    });
```

This example is a bit silly because it behaves just like an ordinary `Subscriber` without any backpressure whatsoever. But it illustrates how you can use backpressure. You can probably imagine a `Subscriber` that prebuffers some number of events and then requests chunks when it finds it convenient. `Subscriber` might decide that it wants to wait a little bit before receiving more events, despite being idle, for example to reduce stress on some downstream dependency. In our restaurant example, the waiter is an `Observable<Dish>` that keeps pushing new dirty dishes whereas `request(N)` is a readiness of the kitchen staff to wash a certain number of dishes. A good waiter should not deliver new dishes without a request from the kitchen's staff.

That being said, calling `request(N)` directly in client code is rare. More often, the various operators that we put between source and final `Subscriber` take advantage of backpressure to control how much data flows through our pipeline. For example `observeOn ()` must subscribe to the upstream `Observable` and schedule each event it receives on a particular `Scheduler`, such as `io()`. But what if upstream produces events at such a pace that the underlying `Scheduler` and `Subscriber` can no longer keep up? The `Subscriber` that is being created by the `observeOn()` operator is backpressure-enabled, it requests only 128 values to begin with.[5] The upstream Observable, which understands backpressure, emits only a given number of events and remains idle—this is what range() does, for example. When observeOn() finds that this batch of events was successfully processed by downstram Subscriber, it requests more. This way, despite crossing a thread boundary and the asynchronous nature of both producer and consumer side, the consumer is never flooded with events.

observeOn() is not the only operator that is backpressure friendly. As a matter of fact, dozens of other operators take advantage of it. For example, zip() buffers only a fixed number of events from each underlying Observable. Thanks to this zip() is not affected in case of only one of zipped streams being very active. The same logic applies to most of the operators we use.

Producers and Missing Backpressure

We already came across a MissingBackpressureException in our custom implementation of range(). What does it actually mean and how do you interpret this exception? Imagine a Subscriber (yours but more often the one create by some operator) that knows exactly how many items it wants to receive; for example, buffer(N) or take(N). Another example of such an operator is observeOn(). It must be very strict in that regard, if upstream Observable pushes more items for some reason, the internal buffer inside observeOn() overflows and it is signaled with MissingBackpressureException. But why does an upstream Observable push more items than requested? Well, because it simply ignores the request() invocations. Let's revisit our simple range() reimplementation:

```
Observable<Integer> myRange(int from, int count) {
    return Observable.create(subscriber -> {
        int i = from;
        while (i < from + count) {
            if (!subscriber.isUnsubscribed()) {
                subscriber.onNext(i++);
            } else {
                return;
            }
        }
        subscriber.onCompleted();
    });
}
```

---

5 You can change this value via the rx.ring-buffer.size system property.

The only way to stop it is by unsubscribing, but we do not want to unsubscribe, just slow it down a little bit. Downstream operators know precisely how many events they want to receive, but our source ignores these requests. The low-level mechanism for honoring the requested number of events is implemented via the `rx.Producer`. This interface is plugged in within `create()`. To recap, `OnSubscribeRange` is a callback that is executed every time someone subscribes to this `Observable`. Normally, you would see calling `onNext()` directly from within this interface, but not when backpressure is taken into account:

```
Observable<Integer> myRangeWithBackpressure(int from, int count) {
    return Observable.create(new OnSubscribeRange(from, count));
}

class OnSubscribeRange implements Observable.OnSubscribe<Integer> {

    //constructor...

    @Override
    public void call(final Subscriber<? super Integer> child) {
        child.setProducer(new RangeProducer(child, start, end));
    }

}

class RangeProducer implements Producer {

    @Override
    public void request(long n) {
        //calling onNext() on child subscriber here
    }
}
```

This is the skeleton of code you will find in RxJava's implementation of `range()`. Implementing `Producer` is quite a challenging task: it must be stateful, thread-safe, and extremely fast. Thus, we do not normally implement producers ourselves but it is useful to understand how they work (see the section "Honoring the Requested Amount of Data" on page 237 for details on how to implement backpressure yourself).[6] Backpressure internally turns Rx principles upside down. `Observable` produced by `range()` (and many other built-in operators) no longer pushes data eagerly to `Subscribers`. Instead, it wakes up and reacts on data requests (`request(N)` invocations within `Subscriber`) and only then produces events. Also, it makes sure not to produce more than was requested.

---

6 See, for example, *https://github.com/ReactiveX/RxJava/blob/1.x/src/main/java/rx/internal/operators/OnSubscri beRange.java* to get a feeling for how optimized and complex even the simplest producer can be.

Look how we set a Producer on child Subscriber—this Producer will later be invoked indirectly within Subscriber whenever it calls request(). This is how we set up a feedback channel from Subscriber to the source Observable. An Observable instructs its Subscriber how it can request certain amount of data. Effectively Observable switches from push to pull–push model, where clients can optionally request only limited number of events. So, what to do if some foreign Observable does not set up such a channel? Well, when RxJava discovers that it;s dealing with a source that does not support backpressure, it can fail with MissingBackpressureException at any time. However, there are operators from the onBackpressure*() family that can simulate backpressure to some extent.

The simplest onBackpressureBuffer() operator unconditionally buffers all upstream events and serves only the requested amount of data to downstream subscribers:

```
myRange(1, 1_000_000_000)
        .map(Dish::new)
        .onBackpressureBuffer()
        .observeOn(Schedulers.io())
        .subscribe(x -> {
                System.out.println("Washing: " + x);
                sleepMillis(50);
        });
```

As always, reading from bottom to top: first subscribe() propagates up to the observeOn() operator. observeOn() must subscribe, as well, but it cannot simply begin consuming arbitrary number of events. Thus, it requests only a fixed number at the beginning (128) to avoid overflow of the io() Scheduler's queue. The onBack pressureBuffer() operator acts as a guard against sources ignoring backpressure. When it receives request(128) from the downstream Subscriber, it passes the request up and does nothing if only 128 flow through it. But, in the event that the Observable that ignored that request and simply pushed data irrespective to back-pressure, onBackpressureBuffer() keeps an unbounded buffer internally. When another request comes from a downstream Subscriber, onBackpressureBuffer() first drains its internal buffer, and only when it is almost empty does it ask upstream for more. This clever mechanism allows observeOn() to work as if myRange() was backpressure-enabled, whereas in reality it is onBackpressureBuffer() that does the throttling. Unfortunately, infinite internal buffer is not something that you can treat lightheartedly:

```
Created: 1
Created: 2
Created: 3
Created: 4
Created: 8
Created: 9
Washing: 1
Created: 10
```

```
Created: 11
...
Created: 26976
Created: 26977
Washing: 15
Exception in thread "main" java.lang.OutOfMemoryError: ...
Washing: 16
    at java.util.concurrent.ConcurrentLinkedQueue.offer...
    at rx.internal.operators.OperatorOnBackpressureBuffer...
...
```

Of course, your mileage may vary, and with smaller events and sufficient amount of memory, onBackpressureBuffer() can technically work. But in reality, you should never rely on unbounded resources. Neither memory nor your solid state drive are inifnite. Luckily there is an overloaded version of onBackpressureBuffer(N) that accepts the maximum buffer size:

```
.onBackpressureBuffer(1000, () -> log.warn("Buffer full"))
```

The second parameter is optional; it is a callback invoked when the bounded buffer of 1,000 elements is full—when despite buffering Subscriber still cannot process events at a satisfying pace. It does not allow any recovery, so expect MissingBackpressureEx ception immediately following the warning message. We do at least we have control over the buffer, but not the limits of the hardware or operating system.

An alternative to onBackpressureBuffer() is onBackpressureDrop(), which simply discards all events that appeared without prior request(). Imagine a waiter in a restaurant who keeps delivering new dishes to the kitchen. onBackpressureBuffer() is a finite/infinite table with dishes waiting to be washed. onBackpressureDrop(), on the other hand, is a waiter who simply throws away dirty dishes if there is no washing capacity at the moment. This is not a very sustainable business model, but at least the restaurant can keep serving clients:

```
.onBackpressureDrop(dish -> log.warn("Throw away {}", dish))
```

The callback is optional and it notifies us every time an event had to be discarded because it appeared without being requested. It is a good idea to keep track of how many events we dropped; this can be an important metric. Finally, there is onBack pressureLatest() which is quite similar to onBackpressureDrop(), but keeps a reference to the very last dropped element so that in case of a late request() from downstream, the last seen value from upstream is served.

The onBackpressure*() family of methods is used to bridge between operators and subscribers requesting backpressure and Observables that are not supporting it. However, it is better to either use or create sources that support it natively.

Honoring the Requested Amount of Data

There are many ways to construct an Observable that supports downstream back-pressure requests. The easiest solution is to use built-in factory methods like range() or from(Iterable<T>). The latter creates a source backed by Iterable but with backpressure built-in. This means that such an Observable will not emit all values from Iterable at once; rather, it will do so gradually as requests are flowing from consumers. Note that this does not imply loading all data to List<T> (extending Iterable<T>) first. Iterable is basically a factory of Iterators, so we can safely load data on the fly.

An interesting example of a backpressure-enabled Observable is wrapping Result Set from JDBC onto a stream. Notice that ResultSet is pull-based, just like the backpressure-enabled Observable. But it is not an Iterable or Iterator, so we must first convert it to Iterator<Object[]>—an Object[] is a loosely-typed representation of a single row from a database:

```java
public class ResultSetIterator implements Iterator<Object[]> {

    private final ResultSet rs;

    public ResultSetIterator(ResultSet rs) {
        this.rs = rs;
    }

    @Override
    public boolean hasNext() {
        return !rs.isLast();
    }

    @Override
    public Object[] next() {
        rs.next();
        return toArray(rs);
    }
}
```

The preceding converter is a very simplified version without error handling, extracted from ResultSetIterator, as found in Apache Commons DbUtils open source utility library.[7] This class also provides a simplistic conversion to Iterable<Object[]>:

```java
public static Iterable<Object[]> iterable(final ResultSet rs) {
    return new Iterable<Object[]>() {
```

---

[7] https://commons.apache.org/proper/commons-dbutils/apidocs/org/apache/commons/dbutils/ResultSetIterator.html

```
        @Override
        public Iterator<Object[]> iterator() {
            return new ResultSetIterator(rs);
        }

    };
}
```

ResultSet handling

Keep in mind that treating ResultSet as an Iterator (and especially Iterable) is a leaky abstraction. First, ResultSet is destructive like Iterator, but unlike Iterable. You can traverse Iterator
only once, often this applies to ResultSet, as well. Secondly Itera
ble is a factory of fresh Iterators, whereas preceding converter
always returns an Iterator backed by the same ResultSet. This
means that calling iterator() twice will not yield the same values
—both iterators will compete over the same ResultSet. Finally,
ResultSet must be closed when done, but Iterator has no such
lifecycle. Relying on client code reading Iterator in its entirety to
perform cleanup in the end is too optimistic.

Having all of these converters in place, we can finally build Observable<Object[]>
backed by ResultSet with backpressure support:

```
Connection connection = //...
PreparedStatement statement =
        connection.prepareStatement("SELECT ...");
statement.setFetchSize(1000);
ResultSet rs = statement.executeQuery();
Observable<Object[]> result =
    Observable
        .from(ResultSetIterator.iterable(rs))
        .doAfterTerminate(() -> {
            try {
                rs.close();
                statement.close();
                connection.close();
            } catch (SQLException e) {
                log.warn("Unable to close", e);
            }
        });
```

The result Observable supports backpressure out of the box because the built-in
from() operator supports it. Therefore, the throughput of Subscriber is not relevant
anymore and we will no longer see MissingBackpressureException. Notice that set
FetchSize() is necessary; otherwise, some JDBC drivers might try to load all records
into memory, quite inefficient if we want to stream over a large result set.

As we already mentioned, the low-level mechanism for supporting backpressure is a custom implementation of `Producer`. However, this task is quite error-prone, thus a helper class was created, namely `SyncOnSubscribe`. This implementation of `Observable.OnSubscribe` is pull-based and has backpressure transparently built in. Let's begin from the simplest case of stateless `Observable`—which is hardly ever found in real life. This type of `Observable` does not hold any state in between `onNext()` invocations. But even the simplest `range()` or `just()` must remember which items were already emitted. One of the few useful `Observables` without state emits random numbers:

```
import rx.observables.SyncOnSubscribe;


Observable.OnSubscribe<Double> onSubscribe =
    SyncOnSubscribe.createStateless(
        observer -> observer.onNext(Math.random())
    );

Observable<Double> rand = Observable.create(onSubscribe);
```

The `rand` `Observable` is an ordinary `Observable` that you can transform, combine, and subscribe to. But underneath, it has full-fledged backpressure support. If `Subscriber` or any other operator in the pipeline requests a limited number of events, this `Observable` will correctly obey the orders. The only thing we must provide to `createStateless()` is a lambda expression that is invoked for each requested event; so if downstream calls `request(3)`, this custom expression is invoked three times, assuming that each invocation emits just one event. There is no context (state) in between invocations, thus it is called stateless.

Now let's build a stateful operator. This variation of `SyncOnSubscribe` allows an immutable state variable that is passed between invocations. Also, each invocation must return a new state value. As an example, we will build an unbounded generator of natural numbers, beginning at zero. Such an operator is actually quite useful if you want to zip an arbitrarily long sequence with monotonically increasing natural numbers. `range()` will work as well, but it requires providing an upper limit, which is not always practical:

```
Observable.OnSubscribe<Long> onSubscribe =
        SyncOnSubscribe.createStateful(
                () -> 0L,
                (cur, observer) -> {
                    observer.onNext(cur);
                    return cur + 1;
                }
        );

Observable<Long> naturals = Observable.create(onSubscribe);
```

This time we provide two lambda expressions to the `createStateful()` factory method. The first lazily creates initial state—zero in this case. The second expression is more important: it is supposed to push one item downstream somehow based on current state and return new state value. The state is expected to be immutable, thus this method allows returning a new state as opposed to mutating it. You can easily rewrite `naturals` `Observable` so that it returns `BigInteger` instead and prevents hypothetical overflow. This `Observable` can produce an infinite number of increasing natural numbers, but fully supports backpressure. This means that it can adjust the speed at which it produces events based on `Subscribers` preferences. Compare this to naive implementation that is undeniably much simpler, but falls short in the case of slow `Subcribers`:

```
Observable<Long> naturals = Observable.create(subscriber -> {
    long cur = 0;
    while (!subscriber.isUnsubscribed()) {
        System.out.println("Produced: " + cur);
        subscriber.onNext(cur++);
    }
});
```

If you prefer a single state variable that mutates while you traverse it (like `ResultSet` from JDBC), `SyncOnSubscribe` has a method for you as well. The following code does *not* compile due to checked exceptions, but we want to first highlight the overall usage pattern:

```
ResultSet resultSet = //...

Observable.OnSubscribe<Object[]> onSubscribe = SyncOnSubscribe.createSingleState(
        () -> resultSet,
        (rs, observer) -> {
            if (rs.next()) {
                observer.onNext(toArray(rs));
            } else {
                observer.onCompleted();
            }
            observer.onNext(toArray(rs));
        },
        ResultSet::close
);

Observable<Object[]> records = Observable.create(onSubscribe);
```

There are three callbacks to implement:

- Generator of state. This lambda is invoked once to produce state variable that will be passed as an argument to subsequent expressions.

- Callback to generate next value, typically based on state. This callback is free to mutate state given as the first argument.

- Third callback is invoked on unsubscription. This is the place to clean up `Result Set`.

The more complete implementation with error handling looks as follows. Note that errors occurring during unsubscription are really difficult to propagate properly downstream:

```
Observable.OnSubscribe<Object[]> onSubscribe = SyncOnSubscribe.createSingleState(
    () -> resultSet,
    (rs, observer) -> {
        try {
            rs.next();
            observer.onNext(toArray(rs));
        } catch (SQLException e) {
            observer.onError(e);
        }
    },
    rs -> {
        try {
            //Also close Statement, Connection, etc.
            rs.close();
        } catch (SQLException e) {
            log.warn("Unable to close", e);
        }
    }
);
```

`SyncOnSubscribe` is a handy utility that allows you to write backpressure-enabled Observables.[8] It is slightly more complex compared to `Observable.create()`, but the benefits of backpressure controlled by each `Subscriber` are difficult to underestimate. You should avoid using the `create()` operator directly and instead consider built-in factories like `from()` or `SyncOnSubscribe`.

Backpressure is an amazingly powerful mechanism for controlled throttling of `Observables` by `Subscribers`. The feedback channel obviously brings some overhead, but the advantages of loosely coupled yet managed producers and consumers are enormous. Backpressure is often batched, so the overhead is minimal, but if `Subscriber` is really slow (even briefly), this slowness is immediately reflected and the overall system stability is preserved. Missing backpressure can be mitigated to some extent by using the `onBackpressure*()` family of methods, but not on the long term.

When creating your `Observables`, think about correctly handling the backpressure requests. After all, you have no control over the throughput of `Subscribers`. Another technique is to avoid the heavyweight work in `Subscriber`, instead off-loading it to

---

8 If you need an even more reactive toolkit, check out `AsyncOnSubscribe` that in principle is quite similar, but callbacks generating the next item for `Observer` are allowed to be asynchronous as well.

`flatMap()`. For example, rather than storing events in a database within `subscribe()` try doing this:

```
source.subscribe(this::store);
```

Consider making `store` more reactive (let it return `Observable<UUID>` of saved record) and subscribing only to trigger subscription and side-effects:

```
source
    .flatMap(this::store)
    .subscribe(uuid -> log.debug("Stored: {}", uuid));
```

Or even further, batch UUIDs to reduce logging framework overhead:

```
source
    .flatMap(this::store)
    .buffer(100)
    .subscribe(
        hundredUuids -> log.debug("Stored: {}", hundredUuids))
```

By avoiding long-running work in `subscribe()` we reduce the need for backpressure, but it is still a good idea to think about it in advance. Consult JavaDocs for an indication as to whether the operator supports backpressure or not. If such information is missing, most likely the operator is not affected by backpressure in any way, like `map()`.

Summary

One important takeaway from this chapter is to avoid `Observable.create()` and manually emitting events. If you must implement `Observable` yourself, consider the many factory methods that support backpressure for you. Also, pay attention to your domain, maybe you can safely skip or batch incoming events to reduce overall load on the consuming side.

CHAPTER 7

Testing and Troubleshooting

Tomasz Nurkiewicz

By now you should understand the basic principles of programming with reactive extensions. So far, we've mastered subscription, most commonly used operators, taking advantage of RxJava in existing applications, and writing entirely reactive software stacks. But to make the best of reactive programming, we must dive a little bit deeper. This chapter focuses on a few nontrivial but important aspects and principles, among them:

- Declarative error handling, including retries (see "Error Handling")
- Virtual time and testing (see "Virtual Time" on page 258)
- Monitoring and debugging of your `Observable` streams (see "Monitoring and Debugging" on page 270)

Understanding a library or framework is not enough to successfully deploy it to production. The aforementioned aspects are crucial if you want to build solid, stable, and resilient applications.

Error Handling

The Reactive Manifesto (*http://www.reactivemanifesto.org*) enumerates four traits that reactive systems should embrace. Such systems should be: responsive, resilient, elastic, and message driven. Let's take a look at a couple of these:

Responsive
 The system responds in a timely manner if at all possible. [...] responsiveness means that problems may be detected quickly and dealt with effectively. [...] rapid and consistent response times, [...] simplifies error handling."

Resilient

> The system stays responsive in the face of failure. [...] parts of the system can fail and recover without compromising the system as a whole. [...] The client of a component is not burdened with handling its failures.

This section explains why the first two, responsiveness and resiliency, are important and how RxJava helps to achieve them. You are already familiar with `onError()` callback when subscribing to an `Observable`. But this is just the tip of the iceberg and often not the best approach to handle errors.

Where Are My Exceptions?

Traditionally in Java, errors are indicated by using exceptions. There are two flavors of exceptions in this language:

- Unchecked exceptions, which are not required in method declaration. If a method throws an unchecked exception (like `NullPointerException`), it can indicate this in its declaration, but it is not obligatory.

- Checked exceptions, which must be declared and handled in order for the code to compile. Basically, this is every `Throwable` that does not extend `RuntimeException` or `Error`. Example: `IOException`.

There are pros and cons to both of these types of traditional error handling. Unchecked exceptions are easy to add and do not break compile-time backward compatibility. Also, with unchecked exceptions, client code seems cleaner because it does not need to deal with error handling (although it can). Checked exceptions, on the other hand, are more explicit about the outcome that we can expect from a method. Of course, every method can throw other arbitrary types but checked exceptions are considered part of the API and suggest errors that must be handled explicitly. Although checked exceptions are impossible to miss and might seem superior in terms of writing error-free code, they proved to be quite unwieldy and obscure. Even official Java APIs are migrating to unchecked exceptions, for example, old `JMSException` (checked) versus new in JMS 2.0 `JMSRuntimeException` (unchecked).

RxJava takes an entirely different approach. First, in standard Java, exceptions are a new dimension in the type system. There is a method return type and there are exceptions that are completely orthogonal. When a method opens a `File`, it can either return `InputStream` or throw `FileNotFoundException`. But what if `FileNotFoundException` is not declared? Or are there any other exceptions we should expect? Exceptions are like an alternative execution path, as if failures were always unexpected and never part of ordinary business flow. In RxJava, failures are just another type of notification. Every `Observable<T>` is a sequence of events of type `T` optionally followed by completion or error notification. This means that errors are implicitly a part of every stream, and even though we are not required to handle them, there are plenty of operators that declaratively handle errors in a more elegant way. Also, an obtrusive `try-catch` around `Observable` will not capture any errors, they are only propagated through the aforementioned error notifications.

But, before we explore a handful of RxJava operators to declaratively handle errors, first we must understand the heuristics that apply when errors are not handled at all. In Java, exceptions can occur almost everywhere, and library creators must ensure they are appropriately handled or at least reported if not otherwise dealt with. The most common problem is a `subscribe()` that does not define an `onError` callback:

```
Observable
    .create(subscriber -> {
        try {
            subscriber.onNext(1 / 0);
        } catch (Exception e) {
            subscriber.onError(e);
        }
    })
    //BROKEN, missing onError() callback
    .subscribe(System.out::println);
```

Within `create()`, we forcibly throw `ArithmeticException` and invoke an `onError()` callback on each `Subscriber`. Unfortunately, `subscribe()` does not provide `onError()` implementation. Fortunately, RxJava tries to save the day by throwing `OnErrorNotImplementedException` wrapping the original `ArithmeticException`. But which thread throws this exception? This is a difficult question. If `Observable` is synchronous (as in the preceding example), the client thread indirectly invokes `create()` and thus throws `OnErrorNotImplementedException` in case of unhandled `onError()`. This means that the thread that invoked `subscribe()` will receive `OnErrorNotImplementedException`.

The situation becomes more complex if you forget to subscribe for errors and `Observable` is asynchronous. In that case, the thread that invoked `subscribe()` might be long gone when `OnErrorNotImplementedException` is thrown. Under these circumstances, an exception is thrown from whichever thread was about to invoke `onError()` callback. This can be a thread from `Scheduler` selected via `subscribeOn()` or the last `observeOn()`. `Scheduler` is free to manage such an unexpected exception in any way it likes, most of the time it simply prints a stack trace to the standard error stream. This is far from perfect: such exceptions bypass your normal logging code, and in a worst-case scenario can go unnoticed. Therefore, `subscribe()` only listening for values and not errors is often a bad sign and possibly missed errors. Even if you do not expect any exceptions to happen (which is rarely the case), at least place error logging that plugs into your logging framework:

```
private static final Logger log = LoggerFactory.getLogger(My.class);

//....

.subscribe(
        System.out::println,
        throwable -> log.error("That escalated quickly", throwable));
```

There are many other places where exceptions can occur and sneak in. First of all, it is a good practice to surround a lambda expression within `create()` with a try-catch() block, just like in the previous example:

```
Observable.create(subscriber -> {
    try {
        subscriber.onNext(1 / 0);
    } catch (Exception e) {
        subscriber.onError(e);
    }
});
```

However, if you forget about the `try-catch` and let `create()` throw an exception, RxJava does its best and propagates such an exception as an `onError()` notification:

```
Observable.create(subscriber -> subscriber.onNext(1 / 0));
```

The two preceding code examples are semantically equivalent. Exceptions thrown from `create()` are caught internally by RxJava and translated to error notification. Yet, it is advised to explicitly propagate exceptions via `subscriber.onError()` if possible. Even better, use `fromCallable()`):

```
Observable.fromCallable(() -> 1 / 0);
```

Other places where exceptions can generally occur are any operators that accept user code. In simpler words, any operator that takes a lambda expression as an argument, like `map()`, `filter()`, `zip()`, and many, many more. These operators should not only deal with error notifications coming from an upstream `Observable`, but also with exceptions thrown from custom mapping functions or predicates. Take this broken mapping and filtering as an example:

```
Observable
        .just(1, 0)
        .map(x -> 10 / x);

Observable
        .just("Lorem", null, "ipsum")
        .filter(String::isEmpty);
```

The first example throws the familiar `ArithmeticException` for some elements. The second example will lead to `NullPointerException` while the `filter()` predicate is invoked. All lambda expressions passed to higher-order functions like `map()` or `fil ter()` should be pure, whereas throwing an exception is an impure side effect. RxJava again does its best to handle unexpected exceptions here and the behavior is exactly what you would expect. If any operator in the pipeline throws an exception, it is translated to error notification and passed downstream. Despite RxJava making an effort to fix broken user code, if you suspect your lambda expression to potentially throw an exception, make it explicit by using `flatMap()`:

```
Observable
        .just(1, 0)
        .flatMap(x -> (x == 0) ?
                Observable.error(new ArithmeticException("Zero :-(")) :
                Observable.just(10 / x)
        );
```

`flatMap()` is a very versatile operator, it does not need to manifest the next step of asynchronous computation. `Observable` is a container for values or errors, so if you want to declaratively express even very fast computation that can result in an error, wrapping it with `Observable` is a good choice, as well.

Declarative try-catch Replacement

Errors are very much like normal events flowing through our `Observable` pipeline. We now understand where they come from, so we should learn how to handle them declaratively. The `Observables` we program against most often are a combination of several operators and upstream `Observables`. Take this simple example of constructing an insurance agreement based on some data:

```
Observable<Person> person = //...
Observable<InsuranceContract> insurance = //...
Observable<Health> health = person.flatMap(this::checkHealth);
Observable<Income> income = person.flatMap(this::determineIncome);
Observable<Score> score = Observable
    .zip(health, income, (h, i) -> asses(h, i))
    .map(this::translate);
Observable<Agreement> agreement = Observable.zip(
    insurance,
    score.filter(Score::isHigh),
    this::prepare);
Observable<TrackingId> mail = agreement
    .filter(Agreement::postalMailRequired)
    .flatMap(this::print)
    .flatMap(printHouse::deliver);
```

This contrived example shows several steps of some business process: loading a Per son, looking up an available `InsuranceContract`, determining `Health` and `Income` based on `Person` (concurrently forking execution), and then joining these two results to compute and translate `Score`. Finally, the `InsuranceContract` is joined with `Score` (but only if it is high) and some post-processing like sending postal mail is per formed. You know by now that no processing was performed so far; we barely declared operations to be invoked but until someone subscribes, no business logic is involved. But, what happens if any of these upstream sources result in error notification? There is no error handling visible here but errors are propagated quite conveniently.

All of the operators we've encountered so far worked primarily with values, entirely ignoring errors. This is fine: ordinary operators transform values flowing through but skip completion and error notifications, letting them flow downstream. This means that a single error from any upstream Observable will propagate with a cascading failure to all downstream subscribers. Again, this is fine if your business logic requires absolutely all steps to succeed. But sometimes you can safely ignore failures and replace them with fallback values or secondary sources.

Replacing errors with a fixed result using onErrorReturn()

The simplest error handling operator in RxJava is onErrorReturn(): when encountered, an error simply replaces it with a fixed value:

```
Observable<Income> income = person
    .flatMap(this::determineIncome)
    .onErrorReturn(error -> Income.no())

//...

private Observable<Income> determineIncome(Person person) {
    return Observable.error(new RuntimeException("Foo"));
}

class Income {
    static Income no() {
        return new Income(0);
    }
}
```

The onErrorReturn() operator probably goes without explanation. As long as normal events are flowing through, this operator does nothing. However, the moment it encounters an error notification from upstream, it immediately discards it and replaces it with a fixed value—Income.no(), in this example. onErrorReturn() is a fluent and very pleasant to read alternative to a try-catch block that returns fixed result in the catch statement known from imperative style:

```
try {
    return determineIncome(Person person)
} catch(Exception e) {
    return Income.no();
}
```

In this example, you might have noticed that this catch swallows the original exception and just returns a fixed value. This can be by design but it is generally a good idea to at least log an exception when it occurs. All error handling operators in RxJava behave this way—if you declaratively handle some exception, it will be swallowed. This is something you should definitely take into account; there is nothing worse than a malfunctioning system with a log file that does not reveal any issues. `onErrorReturn()` passes error as an argument, which we happily ignore. You can either log an exception within `onErrorReturn()` or use the more specialized diagnostics operators, which are covered in "Monitoring and Debugging" on page 270. For the time being, just remember that all error handling operators in RxJava leave exception logging and monitoring up to you.

Lazily computing fallback value using onErrorResumeNext()

Returning a fixed stub result with `onErrorReturn()` might sometimes be a good approach, but more often than not you would actually like to lazily compute some fallback value in case of error. There are two possible scenarios here:

- The primary way of generating a stream of data failed (`onError()` event, so we switch to a secondary source that is just as good, but for some reason we treat it as backup (slower, more expensive, and so on)

- In the presence of a failure, we would like to replace real data with some less expensive, more stable, maybe stale information. For example, when retrieval of fresh data fails we choose possibly a stale stream from cache. Another common example is delivering a slightly worse user experience; for example, returning a list of global best-sellers rather than personalized recommendations in an online shop.

Clearly, the logic required when an error occurs can be expensive on its own and can lead to errors. Therefore, we must somehow encapsulate the fallback logic in a lazy, preferably asynchronous wrapper. What can it be? Of course: an `Observable`!

```
Observable<Person> person = //...
Observable<Income> income = person
    .flatMap(this::determineIncome)
    .onErrorResumeNext(person.flatMap(this::guessIncome));

//...

private Observable<Income> guessIncome(Person person) {
        //...
}
```

The `onErrorResumeNext()` operator basically replaces error notification with another stream. If you subscribe to an an `Observable` guarded with `onErrorResumeNext()` in case of failure, RxJava transparently switches from main `Observable` to the fallback one, specified as an argument. In our example, if `income` stream fails, the error notification is captured and the library automatically subscribes to guessIncome() stream that is probably less precise, but more reliable, faster, or cheaper. Interestingly, you can replace onErrorResumeNext() with the concatWith() operator, assuming determineIncome always emits exactly one value or error:

```
Observable<Income> income = person
    .flatMap(this::determineIncome)
    .flatMap(
        Observable::just,
        th -> Observable.empty(),
        Observable::empty)
    .concatWith(person.flatMap(this::guessIncome))
    .first();
```

There is something unfamiliar with the flatMap() operator here: it accepts three lambda expressions instead of one:

- The first argument allows replacing each element from the upstream Observable with new Observable—this is exactly how flatMap() was used so far throughout this book

- The second argument replaces the optional error notification with another stream. We want to ignore upstream errors so we simply switch to an empty Observable

- Finally, when upstream completes normally, we can replace the completion notification with another stream

The usage of the first() operator is crucial here. By applying the first() operator, we wait only for the very first event to appear. In case of success, we get back a result of determineIncome and RxJava never really subscribes to guessIncome()'s result. But, in case of failure, the first Observable essentially yields no events, so the first() operator asks for another item, this time by subscribing to the fallback stream passed as an argument to concatWith().

I hope you realized by now that concatWith() is not needed at all in this example; flatMap() in its most complex form is enough. Even the first() operator is no longer needed. Think about it:

```
Observable<Income> income = person
    .flatMap(this::determineIncome)
    .flatMap(
        Observable::just,
        th -> person.flatMap(this::guessIncome),
        Observable::empty);
```

The preceding example has an interesting feature: we can return a different Observable from onError() mapping based on th of type Throwable. So, theoretically we can

return a different fallback stream based on the exception message or type. The `onEr`
`rorResumeNext()` operator has an overloaded version that allows just that:

```
Observable<Income> income = person
    .flatMap(this::determineIncome)
    .onErrorResumeNext(th -> {
        if (th instanceof NullPointerException) {
            return Observable.error(th);
        } else {
            return person.flatMap(this::guessIncome);
        }
    });
```

Although `flatMap()` is versatile enough to provide flexible error handling, `onErrorRe`
`sumeNext()` is more expressive and easier to read, so you should prefer it.

Timing Out When Events Do Not Occur

RxJava provides some operators to handle exception notifications from an upstream
`Observable`. But do you know what is even worse than an error? Silence. When a system you connect to fails with an exception, this is relatively simple to predict, handle,
unit test, and so on. But what if you subscribe to an `Observable` and it simply never
emits anything, even though you expected to get a result almost immediately? This
scenario is much worse than simply having an error. The latency of the system is
greatly affected, and it appears as if it was hanging with no clear indication in the logs
whatsoever.

Luckily, RxJava provides a built-in `timeout()` operator that listens to the upstream
`Observable`, constantly monitoring how much time elapsed since the last event or
subscription. If it so happens that the silence between consecutive events is longer
than a given period, the `timeout()` operator publishes an error notification that contains `TimeoutException`. To better understand how `timeout()` works, first let's consider an `Observable` that emits only one event after a certain time. For the purposes
of this demonstration, we will create an `Observable` that returns some `Confirmation`
event after 200 milliseconds. We simulate the latency by adding `delay(100, MILLI`
`SECONDS)`. Moreover, we would like to simulate additional latency between the event
and completion notification. That is the purpose of `empty()` `Observable` that normally just completes immediately but with the extra `delay()` it waits before sending a
completion. Combining these two streams looks as follows:

```
Observable<Confirmation> confirmation() {
    Observable<Confirmation> delayBeforeCompletion =
        Observable
            .<Confirmation>empty()
            .delay(200, MILLISECONDS);
    return Observable
            .just(new Confirmation())
```

```
            .delay(100, MILLISECONDS)
            .concatWith(delayBeforeCompletion);
    }
```

Now, let's test drive the `timeout()` operator in its simplest overloaded version:

```
import java.util.concurrent.TimeoutException;

//...

confirmation()
    .timeout(210, MILLISECONDS)
    .forEach(
        System.out::println,
        th -> {
            if ((th instanceof TimeoutException)) {
                System.out.println("Too long");
            } else {
                th.printStackTrace();
            }
        }
    );
```

The 210-millisecond timeout is not a coincidence. The delay between subscription and arrival of `Confirmation` instance is exactly 100 milliseconds, so less than the timeout threshold. Also, the delay between this event and completion notification is 200 milliseconds, also less than 210. Therefore, in this example, the `timeout()` operator is transparent and does not influence the overall flow of messages. But decrease the `timeout()` threshold to slightly less than 200 milliseconds (say, 190) and it becomes visible. The `Confirmation` is displayed but rather than a completion callback we receive an error notification holding `TimeoutException`. The first event arrived considerably less than 200 milliseconds but the latency between the first event and the second one (completion notification actually) exceeded 190 milliseconds and instead an error notification was propagated downstream. Of course, if the timeout threshold is less than 100 milliseconds, you will not even see the first event.

This was the simplest use case for `timeout()`; you'll find it useful when you want to limit the time you wish to wait for a response or responses. However, sometimes a fixed timeout threshold is too strict and you would like to adjust timeouts at runtime. Suppose that we built an algorithm for predicting the next solar eclipse. The interface of that algorithm is an `Observable<LocalDate>` (of course!) which streams future dates of these kinds of events. Imagine for a second that this algorithm is really computationally intensive, which again we are going to simulate, this time by using the `interval()` operator (see "Timing: timer() and interval()" on page 43) by zipping a fixed list of dates with a slowly progressing stream generated by `interval()`. The first date available appears after 500 milliseconds, and every subsequent one after 50 milliseconds, thanks to `interval(500, 50, MILLISECONDS)`. This is quite common in real-life systems: the initial element of the response has relatively high latency as a result of establishing the connection, SSL handshake, query optimization, or whatever the server is doing. But subsequent responses are either readily available or easily retrievable, so latency between them is much lower:

```
Observable<LocalDate> nextSolarEclipse(LocalDate after) {
    return Observable
        .just(
            LocalDate.of(2016, MARCH, 9),
            LocalDate.of(2016, SEPTEMBER, 1),
            LocalDate.of(2017, FEBRUARY, 26),
            LocalDate.of(2017, AUGUST, 21),
            LocalDate.of(2018, FEBRUARY, 15),
            LocalDate.of(2018, JULY, 13),
            LocalDate.of(2018, AUGUST, 11),
            LocalDate.of(2019, JANUARY, 6),
            LocalDate.of(2019, JULY, 2),
            LocalDate.of(2019, DECEMBER, 26))
        .skipWhile(date -> !date.isAfter(after))
        .zipWith(
            Observable.interval(500, 50, MILLISECONDS),
            (date, x) -> date);
}
```

In these types of scenarios, having one fixed threshold is problematic. The first event should have a pessimistic limit, whereas subsequent limits should be much more aggressive. The overloaded version of `timeout()` does just that: it accept two factories of `Observables`, one marking the timeout of the first event, and the second one for each subsequent element. An example is worth a thousand words:

```
nextSolarEclipse(LocalDate.of(2016, SEPTEMBER, 1))
    .timeout(
        () -> Observable.timer(1000, TimeUnit.MILLISECONDS),
        date -> Observable.timer(100, MILLISECONDS))
```

Here, the first `Observable` emits exactly one event after one second—this is the acceptable latency threshold for the first event. The second `Observable` is created for each event that appears on the stream and allows fine tuning of the timeout for the subsequent event. Notice that we do not use the `date` parameter. You can imagine a timeout value that is adaptive in some sense; for example, we can wait a little bit more for the next event if the previous one was bigger than usual. Or, vice versa, each subsequent event has a lower timeout, adapting to our subscriber's performance.

It is sometimes useful to also track the latency of each event, even if we do not timeout. The handy `timeInterval()` operator does just that: it replaces each event of type `T` with `TimeInterval<T>` that encapsulates the event but also shows how much time has elapsed since the previous event (or subscription in case of first event):

```
Observable<TimeInterval<LocalDate>> intervals =
        nextSolarEclipse(LocalDate.of(2016, JANUARY, 1))
                .timeInterval();
```

Apart from getValue() that returns LocalDate, TimeInterval<LocalDate> also has getIntervalInMilliseconds() but it is easier to see how it looks studying the output of the preceding program after subscription. You can clearly see that it took 533 milliseconds for the first event to arrive but only around 50 milliseconds for each one subsequently:

```
TimeInterval [intervalInMilliseconds=533, value=2016-03-09]
TimeInterval [intervalInMilliseconds=49, value=2016-09-01]
TimeInterval [intervalInMilliseconds=50, value=2017-02-26]
TimeInterval [intervalInMilliseconds=50, value=2017-08-21]
TimeInterval [intervalInMilliseconds=50, value=2018-02-15]
TimeInterval [intervalInMilliseconds=50, value=2018-07-13]
TimeInterval [intervalInMilliseconds=50, value=2018-08-11]
TimeInterval [intervalInMilliseconds=50, value=2019-01-06]
TimeInterval [intervalInMilliseconds=51, value=2019-07-02]
TimeInterval [intervalInMilliseconds=49, value=2019-12-26]
```

The timeout() operator has yet another overloaded version that accepts the fallback Observable replacing the original source in case of error. It is very similar in behavior to onErrorResumeNext() (see "Lazily computing fallback value using onErrorResumeNext()" on page 249).

Retrying After Failures

The onError notification is terminal; no other event can ever appear in such stream. Therefore, if you want to signal business conditions that are potentially nonfatal, avoid onError. This is not much different from a common recommendation to avoid controlling the program flow by using exceptions. Instead, in Observables consider wrapping errors in special types of events that can emerge multiple times next to ordinary events. For example, if you are providing a stream of transaction results and some transactions can fail due to business reasons such as insufficient funds, do not use onError notification for that. Instead, consider creating a TransactionResult abstract class with two concrete subclasses, each representing either success or failure. onError notification in such a stream signals that something is going terribly wrong, like a catastrophic failure preventing further emission of any event.

That being said, onError can represent transient failures of external components or systems. Surprisingly, often simply retrying one more time can lead to success. Other systems might be experiencing a brief load spike, GC pause, or restart. Retrying is an essential mechanism in building robust and resilient applications. RxJava has first-class support for retry.

The simplest version of the `retry()` operator resubscribes to a failed `Onservable` hoping that it will keep producing normal events rather than failures. For educational purposes, we will create an `Observable` that misbehaves severely:

```
Observable<String> risky() {
    return Observable.fromCallable(() -> {
        if (Math.random() < 0.1) {
            Thread.sleep((long) (Math.random() * 2000));
            return "OK";
        } else {
            throw new RuntimeException("Transient");
        }
    });
}
```

In 90 percent of the cases, subscribing to `risky()` ends with a `RuntimeException`. If you somehow make it to the `"OK"` branch an artificial delay between zero and two seconds is injected. Such a risky operation will serve as a demonstration of `retry()`:

```
risky()
    .timeout(1, SECONDS)
    .doOnError(th -> log.warn("Will retry", th))
    .retry()
    .subscribe(log::info);
```

Remember that a slow system is generally indistinguishable from a broken one, but often it is even worse because we experience additional latency. Having timeouts, sometimes even aggressive ones with a retry mechanism is desirable—of course, as long as retrying has no side effects or the operation is idempotent. The behavior of `retry()` is fairly straightforward: it pushes all events and completion notification downstream, but not `onError()`. The error notification is swallowed (so no exception is logged whatsoever), thus we use `doOnError()` callback (see "doOn...() Callbacks" on page 270). Every time `retry()` encounters a simulated `RuntimeException` or `Time outException`, it tries subscribing again.

A word of caution here: if your `Observable` is cached or otherwise guaranteed to always return the same sequence of elements, `retry()` will not work:

```
risky().cached().retry()   //BROKEN
```

If `risky()` emits errors once, it will continue emitting them forever, no matter how many times you resubscribe. To overcome this issue, you can delay the creation of `Observable` even further by using) `defer()`:

```
Observable
    .defer(() -> risky())
    .retry()
```

Even if an `Observable` returned from `risky()` is cached, `defer()` calls `risky()` multiple times, possibly getting a new `Observable` each time.

Retrying by using delay and limited attempts

A plain `retry()` method is useful, but blindly resubscribing with no throttling or limiting attempts is dangerous. We can quickly saturate the CPU or network, generating a lot of load. Basically, parameterless `retry()` is a `while` loop with a `try` block within it, followed by an empty `catch`. First, we should limit the number of attempts, which happens to be built in:

```
risky()
    .timeout(1, SECONDS)
    .retry(10)
```

The integer parameter to `retry()` instructs how many times to resubscribe, thus `retry(0)` is equivalent to no retry at all. If the upstream `Observable` failed for the tenth time, the last seen exception is propagated downstream. A more flexible version of `retry()` leaves you with a decision about retry, based on the attempt number and the actual exception:

```
risky()
    .timeout(1, SECONDS)
    .retry((attempt, e) ->
        attempt <= 10 && !(e instanceof TimeoutException))
```

This version not only limits the number of resubscription attempts to 10, but also drops retrying prematurely if the exception happens to be `TimeoutException`.

If failures are transient, waiting a little bit prior to a resubscription attempt sounds like a good idea. The `retry()` operator does not provide such a possibility out of the box, but it is relatively easy to implement. A more robust version of `retry()` called `retryWhen()` takes a function receiving an `Observable` of failures. Every time an upstream fails, this `Observable` emits a `Throwable`. Our responsibility is to transform this `Observable` in such a way that it emits some arbitrary event when we want to retry (hence the name):

```
risky()
    .timeout(1, SECONDS)
    .retryWhen(failures -> failures.delay(1, SECONDS))
```

The preceding example of `retryWhen()` receives an `Observable` that emits a `Throwable` every time the upstream fails. We simply delay that event by one second so that it appears in the resulting stream one second later. This is a signal to `retryWhen()` that it should attempt retry. If we simply returned the same stream (`retryWhen(x -> x)`), `retryWhen()` would behave exactly like `retry()`, resubscribing immediately when an error occurs. With `retryWhen()`, we can also easily simulate `retry(10)` (well, almost… keep reading):

```
.retryWhen(failures -> failures.take(10))
```

We receive an event each time a failure occurs. The stream we return is supposed to emit an arbitrary event when we want to retry. Thus, we simply forward the first 10 failures, causing each one of them to be retried immediately. But what happens when eleventh failure occurs in a `failures` Observable? This is where it becomes tricky. The `take(10)` operator emits an `onComplete` event immediately following the 10th failure. Therefore, after the 10th retry, `retryWhen()` receives a completion event. This completion event is interpreted as a signal to stop retrying and complete downstream. It means that after 10 failed attempts, we simply emit nothing and complete. However, if we complete `Observable` returned inside `retryWhen()` with an error, this error will be propagated downstream.

In other words, as long as we emit any event from an `Observable` inside `retry When()`, they are interpreted as retry requests. However, if we send a completion or error notification, retry is abandoned and this completion or error is passed downstream. Doing just `failures.take(10)` *will* retry 10 times, but in case of yet another failure, we do not propagate the last error but the successful completion, instead. Let's have a look at it:

```
static final int ATTEMPTS = 11;

//...

.retryWhen(failures -> failures
        .zipWith(Observable.range(1, ATTEMPTS), (err, attempt) ->
                attempt < ATTEMPTS ?
                        Observable.timer(1, SECONDS) :
                        Observable.error(err))
        .flatMap(x -> x)
)
```

This looks quite complex, but it is also really powerful. We `zip` failures with sequence numbers from 1 to 11. We would like to perform as many as 10 retry attempts, so if the attempt sequence number is smaller than 11, we return `timer(1, SECONDS)`. The `retryWhen()` operator will capture this event and retry one second after failure. However, when the 10th retry ends with a failure, we return an `Observable` with that error, completing the retry mechanism with the last seen exception.

This gives us a lot of flexibility. We can stop retrying when a certain exception appears or when too many attempts were already performed. Moreover, we can adjust the delay time between attempts! For example, the first retry can appear immediately but the delays between subsequent retries should grow exponentially:[1]

```
.retryWhen(failures -> failures
    .zipWith(Observable.range(1, ATTEMPTS),
```

---

1 *https://en.wikipedia.org/wiki/Exponential_backoff*

```
        this::handleRetryAttempt)
    .flatMap(x -> x)
)

//...

Observable<Long> handleRetryAttempt(Throwable err, int attempt) {
    switch (attempt) {
        case 1:
            return Observable.just(42L);
        case ATTEMPTS:
            return Observable.error(err);
        default:
            long expDelay = (long) Math.pow(2, attempt - 2);
            return Observable.timer(expDelay, SECONDS);
    }
}
```

On the first retry attempt, we return an Observable emitting an arbitrary event immediately, so that retry happens right away. It makes no difference what type and value of event we return (only the moment counts), so 42 is as good as any other value. On the last retry attempt, we forward an exception to the downstream Sub scriber containing the last seen failure reason. Finally, for attempts 2 through 10, we calculate the delay using the following exponential formula:

$$delay(attempt) = \begin{cases} 0 & \text{if } attempt = 1 \\ 2^{attempt-2} & \text{if } attempt\{2, 3, 4 \cdots 10\} \end{cases}$$

Testing and Debugging

Stream composition, especially involving time, can become difficult. Happily, RxJava has great support for unit testing. You can use a TestSubscriber to assert emitted events, but more importantly, RxJava has a concept of virtual time. In essence, we have full control over the elapsing of time so that tests relying on time are both fast and predictable.

Virtual Time

Time is an important factor in almost any application we deal with, and we are not talking about latency and response times here. Everything happens at some point in time, the order of events is important, jobs are scheduled in the future. Therefore, we spend countless hours looking for bugs occurring only at certain dates or timezones. There does not seem to be any established way of testing time-related code. One of the practices, known as *property-based testing*, aims at generating hundreds of test cases (sometimes randomized) to test a wide spectrum of input arguments. For exam-

---

ple, let's validate a very simple property: for any given date, adding and subsequently subtracting one month gives back the same date:

```
import spock.lang.Specification
import spock.lang.Unroll

import java.time.LocalDate
import java.time.Month

class PlusMinusMonthSpec extends Specification {

    static final LocalDate START_DATE =
            LocalDate.of(2016, Month.JANUARY, 1)

    @Unroll
    def '#date +/- 1 month gives back the same date'() {
        expect:
            date == date.plusMonths(1).minusMonths(1)
        where:
            date << (0..365).collect {
                day -> START_DATE.plusDays(day)
            }
    }

}
```

We used the Spock framework (*http://spockframework.org:*) in Groovy language to rapidly generate 366 different test cases. The code in the expect block is executed for each value generated in the where block. In the where block, we iterate over integers from 0 to 365 and generate all possible dates beginning on 2016-01-01 to 2016-12-31. The assertion is fairly obvious and straightforward: if we add and then subtract one month for pretty much any date we should get that date back. Yet 6 out of 366 test cases fail:

```
date == date.plusMonths(1).minusMonths(1)
|    | |   |            |
|    | |   2016-02-29   2016-01-29
|    | 2016-01-30
|    false
2016-01-30


date == date.plusMonths(1).minusMonths(1)
|    | |   |            |
|    | |   2016-02-29   2016-01-29
|    | 2016-01-31
|    false
2016-01-31


date == date.plusMonths(1).minusMonths(1)
```

```
|  |  |     |          |
|  |  |     2016-04-30  2016-03-30
|  |  2016-03-31
|  false
2016-03-31
```

. . .

We bet that you can work out the other dates that fail yourself. The reason to show this contrived example is to make you realize how complex the time domain is. But the peculiarities of the calendar are not the root cause of the headaches we have when dealing with time in computer systems. RxJava tries to tackle the complexity of concurrency by avoiding state and using pure functions as often as possible. Being pure means that a function (or operator) should explicitly declare all inputs and output. This makes testing much easier. However, the dependency on time is almost always hidden and concealed. Every time you see new Date(), Instant.now(), System.currentTimeMillis(), and many others, you are depending on an external value that changes...well, over time. We know depending on singletons is bad for your design, especially from a testability point of view. But, reading current time is effectively relying on a system-wide singleton available everywhere.

One of the patterns to make dependency on time more explicit involves a fake system clock. This pattern requires all programmers to be very rigorous and delegate time-related code to a special service that can be mocked. Java 8 formalizes this method by introducing the Clock abstraction, which boils down to the following:

```
public abstract class Clock {

    public static Clock system(ZoneId zone) { /* ... */ }

    public long millis() {
        return instant().toEpochMilli();
    }

    public abstract Instant instant();

}
```

Interestingly, RxJava has a very similar abstraction that we already explored in great detail: Schedulers (see: "What Is a Scheduler?" on page 141). How are Schedulers related to the passage of time, you might ask? Well, everything that happens in RxJava either happens immediately or is scheduled in some *time* in the future. It is the Scheduler that has full control over when to execute every single line of code in RxJava.

Schedulers in Unit Testing

Various Schedulers like io() or computation() have no special capabilities apart from running tasks at given points in time. However, there is one special test()

`Scheduler` that has two intriguing methods: `advanceTimeBy()` and `advanceTimeTo()`. These methods of `TestScheduler` are capable of advancing the time manually; otherwise, it's frozen forever. This means that no tasks scheduled in the future on this `Scheduler` are ever executed until we manually advance time whenever we find it useful.

As an example, let's look at a sequence of events appearing over time:

```
TestScheduler sched = Schedulers.test();
Observable<String> fast = Observable
    .interval(10, MILLISECONDS, sched)
    .map(x -> "F" + x)
    .take(3);
Observable<String> slow = Observable
    .interval(50, MILLISECONDS, sched)
    .map(x -> "S" + x);

Observable<String> stream = Observable.concat(fast, slow);
stream.subscribe(System.out::println);
System.out.println("Subscribed");
```

When subscribed, we should see three events F0, F1, and F2, each preceded with 10 ms delay, followed by an infinite number of S0, S1... events, each after 50 ms delay. How can we test that we combined all these streams together, that events appear in the correct order and, more importantly, at the correct time? The key is the explicit `TestScheduler` that we passed wherever it was possible:

```
TimeUnit.SECONDS.sleep(1);
System.out.println("After one second");
sched.advanceTimeBy(25, MILLISECONDS);

TimeUnit.SECONDS.sleep(1);
System.out.println("After one more second");
sched.advanceTimeBy(75, MILLISECONDS);

TimeUnit.SECONDS.sleep(1);
System.out.println("...and one more");
sched.advanceTimeTo(200, MILLISECONDS);
```

The output you can expect is absolutely predictable and repeatable, entirely independent from system time, and experiences transient load spikes, GC pauses, and so on:

```
Subscribed
After one second
F0
F1
After one more second
F2
S0
...and one more
```

```
S1
S2
```

Here is what happens:

1. After we subscribed to `stream Observable`, it began by scheduling `F0` task 10 ms in the future. However, it used `TestScheduler` that sits absolutely idle unless we manually advance time.

2. Sleeping one second is actually irrelevant and could be omitted, `TestScheduler` is independent from system time, thus no events are emitted at all. Sleeping here is only to prove that `TestScheduler` works. If this were not a `TestScheduler` but an ordinary (default) one, you could expect several events to appear on the console by now.

3. Calling `advanceTimeBy(25ms)` forces everything that was scheduled up to 25th millisecond to be triggered and executed. This causes events `F0` (10th ms) and `F1` (20th ms) to appear on the console.

4. Sleeping another second does nothing to the output; `TestScheduler` ignores real time. However, calling `advanceTimeBy(75ms)` (so the logical time is now 100th ms) further triggers `F2` (30th ms) and `S0` (80th ms). Nothing more happens

5. After one more second of real time elapsed, we advance time to absolute value of 200 ms (`advanceTimeTo(200ms)`, `advanceTimeBy()` uses relative time). `Test Scheduler` realizes that `S1` (130th ms) and `S2` (180th ms) should have been triggered by that time. But no other event is triggered, even if we wait for eternity.

As you can see, `TestScheduler` is actually much more clever than an ordinary fake `Clock` abstraction. Not only do we have full control over current time, but we can also arbitrarily postpone all events. One caveat is that you must pass `TestScheduler` everywhere, basically to every operator that has an optional `Scheduler` argument. For your convenience, all such operators use a default `computation()` `Scheduler`, but from a testability point of view, you should prefer passing an explicit `Scheduler`. Moreover, consider dependency injection and provide `Scheduler`s from the outside.

But having `TestScheduler` alone is not enough. It works very well in unit tests for which predictability is a must and flickering tests failing sporadically are quite frustrating. Chapter 8 explores tools and techniques that enable unit testing of inherently asynchronous `Observable`s.

Unit Testing

Writing testable code and having a solid suite of tests has been a necessity for a long time, not a novel approach. Whether you write tests first in test-driven development (TDD) spirit or hack around and confirm your assumptions with few integration tests later, automated testing is something you should be comfortable with. Therefore, the tools you use (frameworks, libraries, platforms) must support automated tests, and this ability should be one of the aspect when making technology decisions. Fear no more, RxJava has excellent support for unit testing, despite a quite complex domain of asynchronous, event-driven architecture. Explicitness of time, combined with focus on pure functions and function composition (well grounded in functional programming) greatly improve the testing experience.

Verifying emitted events

First, we need to define our goals for testing `Observables`. Having a method returning an `Observable` we probably want to make sure of the following:

- Events are emitted in correct order
- Errors are properly propagated
- Various operators are composed together as predicted
- Events appear at right moments in time
- Backpressure is supported

And much more. The first two requirements are simple and do not require any special support from RxJava. Basically, collect everything that was emitted and execute assertions using whichever library you prefer:

```
import org.junit.Test;
import static org.assertj.core.api.Assertions.assertThat;


@Test
public void shouldApplyConcatMapInOrder() throws Exception {
    List<String> list = Observable
        .range(1, 3)
        .concatMap(x -> Observable.just(x, -x))
        .map(Object::toString)
        .toList()
        .toBlocking()
        .single();

    assertThat(list).containsExactly("1", "-1", "2", "-2", "3", "-3");
}
```

The preceding simple test case transforms an `Observable<Integer>` into `List<Integer>` by using the well-known `toList()` → `toBlocking()` → `single()` construct (see "BlockingObservable: Exiting the Reactive World" on page 118). Normally, an `Observable` is asynchronous, so to have predictable and fast tests, we must perform such transformation. We can also easily assert `onError()` notifications when `BlockingObservable` is used. Exceptions are simply rethrown upon subscription. Notice that checked exceptions are wrapped with RuntimeExceptions—something only a good test can prove:

```java
import com.google.common.io.Files;
import static java.nio.charset.StandardCharsets.UTF_8;
import static org.assertj.core.api.Assertions.failBecauseExceptionWasNotThrown;


File file = new File("404.txt");
BlockingObservable<String> fileContents = Observable
    .fromCallable(() -> Files.toString(file, UTF_8))
    .toBlocking();

try {
    fileContents.single();
    failBecauseExceptionWasNotThrown(FileNotFoundException.class);
} catch (RuntimeException expected) {
    assertThat(expected)
        .hasCauseInstanceOf(FileNotFoundException.class);
}
```

The fromCallable() operator is handy when you want to lazily create an Observable that emits at most one element. It also handles error handling and backpressure, so you should prefer it over Observable.create() for one-element streams. You can use another type of unit test to prove our understanding of various operators and their behavior. For example, what does the concatMapDelayError() operator actually do? You are free to try it once, but having an automated test that everyone can read and quickly grasp is a great advantage:

```java
import static rx.Observable.fromCallable;

Observable<Notification<Integer>> notifications = Observable
    .just(3, 0, 2, 0, 1, 0)
    .concatMapDelayError(x -> fromCallable(() -> 100 / x))
    .materialize();

List<Notification.Kind> kinds = notifications
    .map(Notification::getKind)
    .toList()
    .toBlocking()
    .single();

assertThat(kinds).containsExactly(OnNext, OnNext, OnNext, OnError);
```

With the standard concatMap(), the transformation of the second element (0) would fail and terminate the entire stream. However, we clearly see that our final stream has four elements: three OnNext notifications followed by OnError. Another assertion could actually show that indeed the final values are 33 (100 / 3), 50, and 100. This nicely explains how concatMapDelayError() works—if any error is generated from transformation, it is not passed downstream but the operator continues. Only when the upstream source completes, we instead pass onError notification that we found along the way. In this last test case, we could no longer convert Observable to List because it would throw an exception immediately. materialize() is useful in such cases: each kind of event (onNext, onCompleted, and onError) is wrapped in a homogeneous Notification object. These objects can later be examined, but this is tedious and not very readable. This is where TestSubscriber becomes handy:

```
Observable<Integer> obs = Observable
        .just(3, 0, 2, 0, 1, 0)
        .concatMapDelayError(x -> Observable.fromCallable(() -> 100 / x));

TestSubscriber<Integer> ts = new TestSubscriber<>();
obs.subscribe(ts);

ts.assertValues(33, 50, 100);
ts.assertError(ArithmeticException.class);  //Fails (!)
```

The TestSubscriber class is quite simple: it stores all events and notifications it received internally so that we can later query it. TestSubscriber also provides a set of assertions that are very useful in a test case. All we need to do is create an instance of TestSubscriber, subscribe to an Observable-under-test, and examine the contents of it. Strangely, the preceding test actually fails. assertError() fails because we expect the stream to complete with ArithmeticException, whereas in reality we got CompositeException that aggregates all three ArithmeticExceptions found along the way. This is yet another reason why discovering operators by running them and testing automatically is quite useful.

TestSubscriber is extremely effective when working hand in hand with TestScheduler. A typical scenario involves interleaving assertions and advancing time to observe how events are flowing over time. Imagine that you have a service that returns an Observable. The details of its implementation are entirely irrelevant:

```
interface MyService {
    Observable<LocalDate> externalCall();
}
```

Rather than mixing different concerns, we decided to build a decorator over MyService that adds timeout functionality to whatever the underlying implementation of MyService is. For the reasons that you can probably guess by now, we also go the extra mile of externalizing the Scheduler used by the timeout() operator:

```
class MyServiceWithTimeout implements MyService {

    private final MyService delegate;
    private final Scheduler scheduler;

    MyServiceWithTimeout(MyService d, Scheduler s) {
        this.delegate = d;
```

```
            this.scheduler = s;
        }

        @Override
        public Observable<LocalDate> externalCall() {
            return delegate
                    .externalCall()
                    .timeout(1, TimeUnit.SECONDS,
                        Observable.empty(),
                        scheduler);
        }
    }
```

MyServiceWithTimeout wraps another MyService instance and adds a one-second timeout with fallback. In the spirit of RxJava, every class has one responsibility which you can combine, just like operators are very focused but are easy to compose. Suppose that we would like to test whether the timeout actually works. Unit tests should ideally be extremely fast. Do you remember PlusMinusMonthSpec from the beginning of "Virtual Time" on page 258? Invoking it for all possible days in 21st century (more than 36 thousand test cases) takes about one second. A good unit test should not take more than few milliseconds.

Our one-second timeout does not sound like much but it is an eternity when there are hundreds of such scenarios. We can externalize the timeout (which is a good idea anyway) and shrink it to, for example, 100 milliseconds for unit testing. In such a test, we can sleep for 90 milliseconds, assert that the timeout did not yet kick in, sleep for another 20 milliseconds, and verify the timeout returned an empty Observable. Unfortunately, such a setup is very brittle, prone to context switches, garbage-collection pauses, system load variability, and so on. Long story short, your test can be either relatively stable or relatively fast. But the faster you make it, the more often it will spuriously fail. Flickering tests are worse than no tests at all because they are frustrating, you have no trust in them, and they are eventually removed.

The RxJava approach involves a synthetic, controlled clock that is entirely predictable. 100 percent accurate but also extremely fast tests are achieved by artificially advancing time. First, we setup a mock of MyService (using Mockito (*http://mockito.org*)) that can return any Observable:

```
import static org.mockito.BDDMockito.given;
import static org.mockito.Mockito.mock;

private MyServiceWithTimeout mockReturning(
            Observable<LocalDate> result,
            TestScheduler testScheduler) {
    MyService mock = mock(MyService.class);
    given(mock.externalCall()).willReturn(result);
    return new MyServiceWithTimeout(mock, testScheduler);
}
```

We will now write two unit tests. The first ensures that in case of an externalCall() that never finishes, we receive a timeout precisely after one second:

```
@Test
public void timeoutWhenServiceNeverCompletes() throws Exception {
    //given
    TestScheduler testScheduler = Schedulers.test();
    MyService mock = mockReturning(
            Observable.never(), testScheduler);
    TestSubscriber<LocalDate> ts = new TestSubscriber<>();

    //when
    mock.externalCall().subscribe(ts);

    //then
    testScheduler.advanceTimeBy(950, MILLISECONDS);
    ts.assertNoTerminalEvent();
    testScheduler.advanceTimeBy(100, MILLISECONDS);
    ts.assertCompleted();
    ts.assertNoValues();
}
```

The never() operator returns an Observable that never completes and never emits any value. This simulates MyService's call that is painfully slow. Then, we make a sequence of two assertions. First, we advance time just before the timeout threshold (950 milliseconds) and make sure that the TestSubscriber did not yet complete or fail. After 100 more milliseconds—that is, after the timeout threshold—we assert that the stream completed (assertCompleted()) with no values (assertNoValues()). We can also take advantage of assertError().

The second test should ensure that the timeout does not kick in before the configured threshold:

```
@Test
public void valueIsReturnedJustBeforeTimeout() throws Exception {
    //given
    TestScheduler testScheduler = Schedulers.test();
    Observable<LocalDate> slow = Observable
            .timer(950, MILLISECONDS, testScheduler)
            .map(x -> LocalDate.now());
    MyService myService = mockReturning(slow, testScheduler);
    TestSubscriber<LocalDate> ts = new TestSubscriber<>();

    //when
    myService.externalCall().subscribe(ts);

    //then
    testScheduler.advanceTimeBy(930, MILLISECONDS);
    ts.assertNotCompleted();
    ts.assertNoValues();
    testScheduler.advanceTimeBy(50, MILLISECONDS);
```

```
        ts.assertCompleted();
        ts.assertValueCount(1);
    }
```

advanceTimeBy() is equivalent to sleeping in test, waiting for some action to happen, but without actually sleeping. You can test all sorts of operators like buffer(), sample(), and so on, as long as you meticulously allow passing a custom Scheduler. Speaking of schedulers, it is tempting to use Schedulers.immediate() (see "What Is a Scheduler?" on page 141) as opposed to standard ones. This Scheduler avoids concurrency by invoking all actions in the context of the caller thread. Such an approach works in some scenarios, but in general you should prefer TestScheduler because its use cases are far more versatile.

Following the dependency injection principle is very important. Otherwise, you will not be able to replace various Schedulers with test one. There are some techniques that can help you; for example, the RxJavaSchedulersHook plug-in. RxJava has a set of plug-ins that can globally alter the behavior of the library. RxJavaSchedulersHook, for example, can override the standard computation() Scheduler (and other) with test one:

```
    private final TestScheduler testScheduler = new TestScheduler();

    @Before
    public void alwaysUseTestScheduler() {
        RxJavaPlugins
            .getInstance()
            .registerSchedulersHook(new RxJavaSchedulersHook() {
                @Override
                public Scheduler getComputationScheduler() {
                    return testScheduler;
                }

                @Override
                public Scheduler getIOScheduler() {
                    return testScheduler;
                }

                @Override
                public Scheduler getNewThreadScheduler() {
                    return testScheduler;
                }
            });
    }
```

This global approach has many shortcomings. You can register only RxJavaSchedulersHook once across all of JVM, so invoking this @Before method for the second time fails. You can work around this, but it becomes increasingly complex. Also running unit tests in parallel (normally, unit tests are independent from one another so it should not be an issue) becomes impossible. Therefore, the only scalable solution for controlling time is explicitly passing TestScheduler whenever possible.

The one last thing that you can exercise with TestSubscriber is backpressure. In "Honoring the Requested Amount of Data" on page 237, we examined two implementations of an infinite Observable that produces subsequent natural numbers. One was using an old-fashioned raw Observable.create(), which does not support backpressure:

```
Observable<Long> naturals1() {
    return Observable.create(subscriber -> {
        long i = 0;
        while (!subscriber.isUnsubscribed()) {
            subscriber.onNext(i++);
        }
    });
}
```

The more advanced but recommended implementation fully supports backpressure:

```
Observable<Long> naturals2() {
    return Observable.create(
        SyncOnSubscribe.createStateful(
            () -> 0L,
            (cur, observer) -> {
                observer.onNext(cur);
                return cur + 1;
            }
    ));
}
```

From a functionality point of view, these two are the same, both are infinite but you can, for example, just take only a selected subset. However, with TestSubscriber we can easily unit-test whether a given Observable also supports backpressure:

```
TestSubscriber<Long> ts = new TestSubscriber<>(0);

naturals1()
        .take(10)
        .subscribe(ts);

ts.assertNoValues();
ts.requestMore(100);
ts.assertValueCount(10);
ts.assertCompleted();
```

The crucial part of this example is the TestSubscriber<>(0) constructor. Without it, TestSubscriber simply receives everything at the velocity dictated by the source. But, if we request no data prior to subscription, TestSubscriber does not request any data from an Observable. This is the reason why we see assertNoValues() despite the source Observable clearly emitting 10 values. Later, we request as much as 100 items (just to be safe) but obviously the source `Observable` emits only 10—as many as it can possibly produce. This test fails for `naturals1` almost immediately, and the following message appears:

```
AssertionError: No onNext events expected yet some received: 10
```

Our naive `Observable`, of course, knows to stop emitting events after receiving 10, despite being infinite. The `take(10)` operator eagerly unsubscribes ending the internal `while` loop. However, `naturals1` ignores the backpressure requests issued by `TestSubscriber`, the latter receives items it never wanted. If you replace source with `naturals2`, now the test passes. This is another reason to avoid plain `Observable.cre ate()` in favor of the built-in factories and `SyncOnSubscribe`.

`TestSubscriber` has many other assertions. Some of them block waiting for completion; for example, `awaitTerminalEvent()`. Most of them, however, assert the state of the subscriber at the current moment, so that we can observe events flowing over time.

Monitoring and Debugging

Monitoring the behavior of various streams interacting with one another and troubleshooting when issues arise is a difficult subject in RxJava. As a matter of fact, every asynchronous event-driven system is inherently more difficult to troubleshoot compared to blocking architectures. When a synchronous operation fails, the exception flows all the way up the call stack, exposing the exact sequence of operations that caused it, from HTTP server, through all filters, aspects, business logic, and so on. In an asynchronous system, the call stack is of limited use because when an event crosses the thread boundary, we no longer have the original call stack available. The same applies to distributed systems. This section gives you few tips on how to make monitoring and debugging easier in applications using RxJava.

doOn...() Callbacks

Every `Observable` has a set of callback methods that you can use to peek into various events, namely:

- `doOnCompleted()`
- `doOnEach()`
- `doOnError()`
- `doOnNext()`
- `doOnRequest()`
- `doOnSubscribe()`

- doOnTerminate()

- doOnUnsubscribe()

What they all have in common is that they are not allowed to alter the state of an Observable in any way and they all return the same Observable, which makes them an ideal place to sprinkle some logging logic. For example, many newcomers forget that the code within Observable.create() is executed for each new Subscriber. This is important especially when a subscription triggers side effects like a network call. To detect such problems, it is a good practice to log every subscription to critical sources:

```
Observable<Instant> timestamps = Observable
    .fromCallable(() -> dbQuery())
    .doOnSubscribe(() -> log.info("subscribe()"));

timestamps
    .zipWith(timestamps.skip(1), Duration::between)
    .map(Object::toString)
    .subscribe(log::info);
```

The preceding program queries the database (dbQuery()) and retrieves some time series data in the form of Observable<Instant>. We would like to transform this stream a little bit by calculating the duration (using Duration class from the java.time package) between each subsequent pairs of Instants: first and second, second and third, and so on. One way to do this is to zip() stream with itself shifted by one element. This way we tie together the first with the second element, the second with the third, up to the end. What we did not anticipate is that zipWith() actually subscribes to all of the underlying streams, effectively subscribing to the same time stamps Observable twice. This is a problem that you can discover by observing doOn Subscribe() is being invoked twice. This leads to duplicated database query, which is the problem we discussed in great lengths in Chapter 2.

Speaking of zip(), thanks to backpressure it no longer buffers faster stream infinitely, waiting for a slower one to emit events. Instead, it asks for a fixed batch of values from each Observable, throwing MissingBackpressureException if it received more:

```
.doOnSubscribe(() -> log.info("subscribe()"))
.doOnRequest(c -> log.info("Requested {}", c))
.doOnNext(instant -> log.info("Got: {}", instant));
```

doOnRequest() logs Requested 128, the value chosen by zip operator. Even when the source is infinite or very large, we should see at most 128 messages such as Got: ... afterward from a well-behaving Observable. doOnNext() is another callback that we can take advantage of. Another useful operator that you should use fairly often is doO nError(). It invokes callback every time an error notification flows from upstream.

You cannot use doOnError() for any error handling; it is for logging only. It does not consume the error notification, which keeps propagating downstream:

```
Observable<String> obs = Observable
    .<String>error(new RuntimeException("Swallowed"))
    .doOnError(th -> log.warn("onError", th))
    .onErrorReturn(th -> "Fallback");
```

As clean as onErrorReturn() looks, it is very easy to swallow exceptions with it. It does provide the exception that we want to replace with a fallback value, but logging it is our responsibility. To keep functions small and composable, logging the error first in doOnError() and then handling the exception in the following line silently is a little bit more robust. Forgetting to log the exception is rarely a good idea and must be a careful decision, not an oversight.

Other operators are rather self-explanatory, with the possible exception of this pair:

doOnEach()

This is invoked for each Notification, namely onNext(), onCompleted(), and onError(). It can accept either a lambda invoked for each Notofication or an Observer.

doOnTerminate()

This is invoked when either onCompleted() or onError() occurs. It is impossible to distinguish between them, so it might be better to use doOnCompleted() and doOnError() independently.

Measuring and Monitoring

Callbacks are not only useful for logging. Having various telemetric probes built into your application (like simple counters, timers, distribution histograms, and so on) and available externally can greatly reduce troubleshooting time as well as give great insight into what an application is doing. There are many libraries that simplify collecting and publishing metrics, one of them being Dropwizard metrics (*http://metrics.dropwizard.io:*). Before you begin using this library, you need to do a little bit of setup:

```
import com.codahale.metrics.MetricRegistry;
import com.codahale.metrics.Slf4jReporter;
import org.slf4j.LoggerFactory;


MetricRegistry metricRegistry = new MetricRegistry();
Slf4jReporter reporter = Slf4jReporter
    .forRegistry(metricRegistry)
    .outputTo(LoggerFactory.getLogger(SomeClass.class))
    .build();
reporter.start(1, TimeUnit.SECONDS);
```

`MetricRegistry` is a factory for various metrics. Additionally, we set up a `Slf4jRe porter` that will push a current snapshot of statistics to a given SLF4J logger. Other reporters publishing to Graphite (*http://graphite.readthedocs.org:*) and Ganglia (*http:// ganglia.info*) are available. Having this basic setup you can being monitoring your streams.

One of the simplest metrics you can think of is a simple `Counter` that can be incremented or decremented. You can use it to measure the number of events that flew through the stream:

```
final Counter items = metricRegistry.counter("items");
observable
        .doOnNext(x -> items.inc())
        .subscribe(...);
```

After you subscribe to this `Observable`, `Counter` will being showing how many items were generated so far. This information becomes even more useful when you publish it to an external monitoring server like Graphite and put it on a chart over time.

Another important metric that you might want to capture is how many items are being concurrently processed right at that moment. For example, `flatMap()` can easily spin hundreds and more concurrent `Observables` and subscribe to all of them. Knowing how many such `Observables` we have (think about open database connections, web sockets, and so on) can give significant insight into the system:

```
Observable<Long> makeNetworkCall(long x) {
    //...
}


Counter counter = metricRegistry.counter("counter");
observable
        .doOnNext(x -> counter.inc())
        .flatMap(this::makeNetworkCall)
        .doOnNext(x -> counter.dec())
        .subscribe(...);
```

When an event appears from upstream, we increment the counter. When an event appears after `flatMap()` (which means one of the asynchronous operations just emitted something), we decrement it. In an idle system, the counter is always zero, but when an upstream `observable` produces a lot of events and `makeNetworkCall()` is relatively slow, this counter skyrockets, clearly indicating where the bottleneck is.

The preceding example assumes that `makeNetworkCall()` always returns just one item and never fails (never completes with `onError()`). If instead you want to measure the time between subscription to the internal `Observable` (when the work actually began) and its completion, it is equally straightforward:

```
observable
    .flatMap(x ->
        makeNetworkCall(x)
            .doOnSubscribe(counter::inc)
            .doOnTerminate(counter::dec)
    )
    .subscribe(...);
```

One of the most complex metrics is `Timer`, which measures the duration between two points in time. I cannot overstate the value of such a metric—we can measure network call latency, database query time, user response time, and much more. The way we typically measure time is by taking a snapshot of the current time, doing some lengthy operation, and then noting the difference between the time now and then. This is encapsulated in the Metrics library like this:

```
import com.codahale.metrics.Timer;

Timer timer = metricRegistry.timer("timer");
Timer.Context ctx = timer.time();
//some lengthy operation...
ctx.stop();
```

The API keeps the operation start time encapsulated in `Timer.Context` and assumes that the code we are benchmarking is blocking. But what if we want to measure the time between subscription to an `Observable` for which we have no control and its termination? `doOnSubscribe()` and `doOnTerminate()` are insufficient here because we cannot pass `Timer.Context` between them. Luckily, RxJava is flexible enough to tackle this problem anyway by one extra layer of composition:

```
Observable<Long> external = //...

Timer timer = metricRegistry.timer("timer");

Observable<Long> externalWithTimer = Observable
        .defer(() -> Observable.just(timer.time()))
        .flatMap(timerCtx ->
                external.doOnCompleted(timerCtx::stop));
```

We use a little trick. First, we lazily start time with a help of the `defer()` operator. This way, the timer starts exactly when subscription happens. Later, we (in a way) replace the `Timer.Context` instance with the actual `Observable` that we want to benchmark (`external`). However, before we return `external` `Observable`, we stop our running timer. You can use this technique to measure the time between subscription and termination of any `Observable` over which you have no control.

If you need more comprehensive and enterprise-ready solutions for your monitoring layer, consider using RxJava-powered Hystrix. This library will be one of the case studies in the Chapter 8 (see "Managing Failures with Hystrix" on page 291).

Summary

Every reactive library or framework, due to their asynchronous and event-driven nature, is challenging when it comes to debugging and troubleshooting. RxJava is no exception here, but it provides a handful of tools that make developers' and operations' life easier.

- First, RxJava embraces errors and make it easy to handle and manage.
- Secondly, it provides facilities for monitoring and debugging streams in real-time.
- Finally, it has excellent unit-testing support.

As a matter of fact, being able to take full control over the system clock is immensely useful for time-sensitive operators. RxJava can be difficult to troubleshoot at first. Yet it provides a clear API and strict contract as opposed to superficially simpler blocking code that has hidden race conditions and poor throughput.

CHAPTER 8

Case Studies

Tomasz Nurkiewicz

This chapter shows examples of selected use cases of RxJava in real-life applications. The API of Reactive Extensions is very powerful but there must be a source of `Observables` somewhere. Creating an `Observable` from scratch can be challenging due to backpressure and the Rx contract, which must be followed. The good news is that there are many libraries and frameworks out there that support RxJava natively. Also RxJava turned out to be very useful on some platforms that are inherently asynchronous.

Throughout this chapter, you will see how RxJava improves the design and enhances the capabilities of existing architectures. We will also explore more complex topics that can arise when deploying reactive applications to production, such as memory leaks. When you've finished this chapter, you should be convinced that RxJava is mature and versatile enough to implement a variety of use cases in real, modern applications.

Android Development with RxJava

RxJava is very popular among Android developers. First, graphic user interfaces are inherently event driven, with events coming from various actions like key presses or mouse movements. Second, Android, just like Swing or many other GUI environments, is very unforgiving when it comes to threads. The main Android thread should not be blocked to avoid freezing the user interface; however, all updates to the user interface must happen in that main thread. These issues will be addressed in "Schedulers in Android" on page 285. But if there is just one thing you should try to learn about RxJava in Android, be sure to go through the next section that explains memory leaks and how to avoid them easily.

Avoiding Memory Leaks in Activities

One pitfall unique to Android is `Activity`-related memory leak. It happens when an `Observer` holds a strong reference to any GUI component that in turn references the entire parent `Activity` instance. When you rotate the screen of your mobile device or press the back button, the Android operating system destroys the current `Activity` and eventually tries to garbage collect it. Activities are fairly large objects, so eagerly cleaning them up is important. However if your `Observer` holds a reference to such an `Activity`, it might never be garbage-collected, leading to memory leak and device killing your application in its entirety. Take the following innocent code:

```
public class MainActivity extends AppCompatActivity {

    private final byte[] blob = new byte[32 * 1024 * 1024];

    @Override
    protected void onCreate(Bundle savedInstanceState) {
        super.onCreate(savedInstanceState);
        TextView text = (TextView) findViewById(R.id.textView);
        Observable
                .interval(100, TimeUnit.MILLISECONDS)
                .observeOn(AndroidSchedulers.mainThread())
                .subscribe(x -> {
                    text.setText(Long.toString(x));
                });
    }

}
```

The `blob` field is there just to speed up the memory-leak effects; imagine `MainActiv ity` being quite a complex tree of objects, instead. This simple application superficially looks fine. Every 100 milliseconds it updates a text field with the current counter value. But if you rotate your device a couple of times it crashes with `OutOfMe moryError` for some reason. Here is what happens:

1. `MainActivity` is created, and during `onCreate()` we subscribe to `interval()`.

2. Every 100 milliseconds, we update `text` with the current counter value. Ignore `mainThread()` Scheduler for a second, it will be explained in "Schedulers in Android" on page 285.

3. The device changes orientation.

4. `MainActivity` is destroyed, a new one is created, and `onCreate()` is executed again.

5. We currently have two `Observable.interval()` running because we never unsubscribed from the first one.

The fact that we have two intervals running at the same time, the first one being a leftover from the destroyed `Activity` is not the worst part. The `interval()` operator uses a background thread (via `computation()` `Scheduler`) to emit counter events. These events are subsequently propagated to `Observer`, one of them holding a reference to `TextView` which in turn holds a reference to old `MainActivity`. The thread emitting `interval()` events becomes the new GC root; therefore, everything it references directly or indirectly is not eligible for garbage collection. That being said, even though the first instance of `MainActivity` was destroyed, it cannot be garbage-collected and the memory of our `blob` cannot be reclaimed. Every change of orientation (or whenever Android decides to destroy a particular `Activity`) increases memory leak. The solution is simple: let `interval()` know when it is no longer needed by unsubscribing from it (see "Controlling Listeners by Using Subscription and Subscriber<T>" on page 32). Just like `onCreate()`, Android has a callback on destruction called `onDestroy()`:

```
private Subscription subscription;

@Override
protected void onCreate(Bundle savedInstanceState) {
    //...
    subscription = Observable
        .interval(100, TimeUnit.MILLISECONDS)
        .observeOn(AndroidSchedulers.mainThread())
        .subscribe(x -> {
            text.setText(Long.toString(x));
        });
}

@Override
protected void onDestroy() {
    super.onDestroy();
    subscription.unsubscribe();
}
```

That is all there is to it. When an `Observable` is created as part of `Activity`'s lifecycle, make sure to unsusbcribe from it when the `Activity` is destroyed. Calling `unsusb cribe()` will detach `Observer` from `Observable` so that it is eligible for garbage collection. Together with `Observer`, the entire `MainActivity` can be collected, as well. Also the `interval()` itself will stop emitting events because no one is listening to them. Double win.

When you create multiple `Observables` together with some `Activity`, holding a reference to all `Subscriptions` can become tedious. A `CompositeSubscription` is a handy container in such cases. Each `Subscription` can simply be inserted into `Compo siteSubscription` and on destruction we can unsubscribe all of them in one easy step:

```
    private CompositeSubscription allSubscriptions = new CompositeSubscription();

    @Override
    protected void onCreate(Bundle savedInstanceState) {
          //...
        Subscription subscription = Observable
            .interval(100, TimeUnit.MILLISECONDS)
            .observeOn(AndroidSchedulers.mainThread())
            .subscribe(x -> {
                text.setText(Long.toString(x));
            });
        allSubscriptions.add(subscription);
    }

    @Override
    protected void onDestroy() {
        super.onDestroy();
        allSubscriptions.unsubscribe();
    }
}
```

It is worth mentioning that unsubscribing from an Observable that is no longer in use is a good practice in any environment. But on resource-constrained mobile devices, this becomes particularly important. Now that you are aware of the pitfalls of memory management on Android, it is time to redesign your mobile applications. First, we will explore Retrofit, an HTTP client with built-in RxJava support that is particularly popular on mobile environments.

Retrofit with Native RxJava Support

Retrofit (*http://square.github.io/retrofit/*) is a popular library for making HTTP requests, especially in the Android ecosystem. It is neither Android-specific nor the only choice for an HTTP client. However, because it natively supports RxJava, it is a good choice for mobile applications, both written with RxJava in mind or only willing to properly handle HTTP code. The main advantage of using RxJava in network-related code is its ability to jump between threads easily. Before we begin experimenting with Retrofit, you will need the following dependencies. The library itself, an adapter for RxJava, and a converter for Jackson JSON parser:

```
compile 'com.squareup.retrofit2:retrofit:2.0.1'
compile 'com.squareup.retrofit2:adapter-rxjava:2.0.1'
compile 'com.squareup.retrofit2:converter-jackson:2.0.1'
```

Retrofit promotes a type-safe way of interacting with RESTful services by asking you to first declare a Java interface without implementation. This interface is later translated into an HTTP request transparently. For the purpose of the exercise, we will be interacting with Meetup API (*http://www.meetup.com/meetup_api/*), a popular service for organizing events. One of the endpoints returns a list of cities near a given location:

```
import retrofit2.http.GET;
import retrofit2.http.Query;


public interface MeetupApi {

    @GET("/2/cities")
    Observable<Cities> listCities(
        @Query("lat") double lat,
        @Query("lon") double lon
    );

}
```

Retrofit will translate the method call to `listCities()` into a network call. Under the hood, we will be making an HTTP GET request to /2/cities?lat=...&lon=... resource. Notice the return type. First, we have the strongly typed `Cities` rather than `String` or weakly typed *map-of-maps*. But more important, `Cities` comes from an `Observable` that will emit this object when a response arrives. `Cities` class maps most of the fields found in JSON received from the server, getters, and setters omitted:

```
public class Cities {
    private List<City> results;
}

public class City {
    private String city;
    private String country;
    private Double distance;
    private Integer id;
    private Double lat;
    private String localizedCountryName;
    private Double lon;
    private Integer memberCount;
    private Integer ranking;
    private String zip;
}
```

Such an approach provides a good balance between abstraction (using high-level concepts like method calls and strongly-typed responses) and low-level details (asynchronous nature of network call). Although HTTP has request-response semantics, we model inevitable latency with `Observable` so that it is not hidden behind a leaky blocking RPC (remote procedure call) abstraction. Unfortunately, there is quite a bit of glue code that you must configure in order to interact with this particular API. Your mileage may vary, but it is important to see the steps required to properly parse the JSON response:

```
import com.fasterxml.jackson.databind.DeserializationFeature;
import com.fasterxml.jackson.databind.ObjectMapper;
```

```
import com.fasterxml.jackson.databind.PropertyNamingStrategy;
import retrofit2.Retrofit;
import retrofit2.adapter.rxjava.RxJavaCallAdapterFactory;
import retrofit2.converter.jackson.JacksonConverterFactory;


ObjectMapper objectMapper = new ObjectMapper();
objectMapper.setPropertyNamingStrategy(
    PropertyNamingStrategy.CAMEL_CASE_TO_LOWER_CASE_WITH_UNDERSCORES);
objectMapper.configure(
    DeserializationFeature.FAIL_ON_UNKNOWN_PROPERTIES, false);

Retrofit retrofit = new Retrofit.Builder()
        .baseUrl("https://api.meetup.com/")
        .addCallAdapterFactory(
            RxJavaCallAdapterFactory.create())
        .addConverterFactory(
            JacksonConverterFactory.create(objectMapper))
        .build();
```

First, we need to tune `ObjectMapper` from the Jackson library to seamlessly convert the underscore field names to camel-case convention used in Java Beans—for example, `localized_country_name` in JSON to `localizedCountryName` in `City` class. Second, we want to avoid fields that are not mapped in our bean classes. Especially JSON APIs tend to evolve by adding new fields that clients did not support earlier. A reasonable default is to ignore such fields and use only those that are meaningful to us. Therefore, the server can add new fields to response as the system grows without breaking existing clients.

Having an instance of `Retrofit`, we can finally synthesize `MeetupApi` implementation to be used throughout the client code:

```
MeetupApi meetup = retrofit.create(MeetupApi.class);
```

At last, with our `MeetupApi` we can make some HTTP requests and use the power of RxJava. Let's build a more comprehensive example. Using the Meetup API, we first grab a list of all cities and towns nearby a given location:

```
double warsawLat = 52.229841;
double warsawLon = 21.011736;
Observable<Cities> cities = meetup.listCities(warsawLat, warsawLon);
Observable<City> cityObs = cities
        .concatMapIterable(Cities::getResults);
Observable<String> map = cityObs
        .filter(city -> city.distanceTo(warsawLat, warsawLon) < 50)
        .map(City::getCity);
```

First, we expand an `Observable<Cities>` with just one item into `Observable<City>` with one item per found city using `concatMapIterable()`. Then, we filter out only cities closer than 50 kilometers to the initial location. Finally, we extract a city name.

Our next goal is to find the population of each city found in the vicinity of Warsaw to see how many people live within a radius of 50 kilometers. To achieve that, we must consult another API delivered by GeoNames (*http://bit.ly/2d5e7TL*). One method searches for location by a given name and, among other attributes, returns its population. We will again use Retrofit to connect to that API:

```java
public interface GeoNames {

    @GET("/searchJSON")
    Observable<SearchResult> search(
            @Query("q") String query,
            @Query("maxRows") int maxRows,
            @Query("style") String style,
            @Query("username") String username);

}
```

A JSON object must be mapped to data objects (getters and setters omitted):

```java
class SearchResult {
    private List<Geoname> geonames = new ArrayList<>();
}

public class Geoname {
    private String lat;
    private String lng;
    private Integer geonameId;
    private Integer population;
    private String countryCode;
    private String name;
}
```

The way to instantiate `GeoNames` is similar to `MeetupApi`:

```java
GeoNames geoNames = new Retrofit.Builder()
        .baseUrl("http://api.geonames.org")
        .addCallAdapterFactory(RxJavaCallAdapterFactory.create())
        .addConverterFactory(JacksonConverterFactory.create(objectMapper))
        .build()
        .create(GeoNames.class);
```

Suddenly our sample application uses two different APIs and mashes them together very uniformly. For each city name, we would like to consult the GeoNames API and extract the population:

```java
Observable<Long> totalPopulation = meetup
        .listCities(warsawLat, warsawLon)
        .concatMapIterable(Cities::getResults)
        .filter(city -> city.distanceTo(warsawLat, warsawLon) < 50)
        .map(City::getCity)
        .flatMap(geoNames::populationOf)
        .reduce(0L, (x, y) -> x + y);
```

If you think about it for a while, the preceding program is doing quite a lot of work in this concise form. First it asks MeetupApi for a list of cities and later for each city it fetches the population. Population responses (possibly coming asynchronously) are later totaled using reduce(). In the end, this whole computational pipeline ends up as Observable<Long>, emitting one long value whenever the population from all cities is accumulated. This shows the true power of RxJava, how streams from different sources can be seamlessly combined. For example, the populationOf() method is actually quite a complex chain of operators making an HTTP request to GeoNames and extracting population by city name:

```java
public interface GeoNames {

    default Observable<Integer> populationOf(String query) {
        return search(query)
            .concatMapIterable(SearchResult::getGeonames)
            .map(Geoname::getPopulation)
            .filter(p -> p != null)
            .singleOrDefault(0)
            .doOnError(th ->
            log.warn("Falling back to 0 for {}", query, th))
            .onErrorReturn(th -> 0)
            .subscribeOn(Schedulers.io());
    }

    default Observable<SearchResult> search(String query) {
        return search(query, 1, "LONG", "some_user");
    }

    @GET("/searchJSON")
    Observable<SearchResult> search(
        @Query("q") String query,
        @Query("maxRows") int maxRows,
        @Query("style") String style,
        @Query("username") String username
    );

}
```

A generic search() method at the bottom is wrapped using default methods so that it is easier to use. After receiving a SearchResult object wrapped in JSON, we unwrap all individual search results, make sure the population was not absent in the response, and in case of any errors we simply return 0. Finally, we make sure each population request is invoked on an io() scheduler to allow better concurrency. subscribeOn() is actually crucial here. Without it, every request for population for each city would be sequential, drastically increasing the overall latency. However, because for each city flatMap() will invoke the populationOf() method and subscribe to it when needed, data about each city is fetched concurrently. In fact, we can also add a timeout() operator to each population request, as well, to achieve an even better response time at the cost of incomplete data. Without RxJava, implementing this scenario would require a lot of manual thread-pool integration. Even with `CompletableFuture` (see "CompletableFuture and Streams" on page 193) the task is nontrivial. Yet RxJava with noninvasive concurrency and powerful operators make it possible to write both fast and easy to understand, concise code.

Combining two different APIs, both driven by Retrofit, works like a charm. However, there is nothing that prevents us from combining entirely unrelated `Observables`; for example, one coming from Retrofit, another from a JDBC call, and yet another one receiving a JMS message. All these use cases are fairly easy to implement, neither leaking the abstraction nor giving too many details about the nature of the underlying stream implementation.

Schedulers in Android

One of the very first mistakes that every Android developer makes is blocking the UI thread. On Android there is one designated main thread that interacts bi-directionally with the user interface (UI). Callbacks from native widgets invoke our handlers on main thread but also widget updates (changing labels, drawing) must occur within that thread. This restriction greatly simplifies the UI internal architecture but also has serious downsides:

- Attempting any time-consuming operation (typically blocking network call) within callback handling, a UI event will prevent other events from being handled, causing the UI to freeze. Eventually, the operating system will kill such misbehaving applications

- Updating the UI—for example, when a blocking network call completed—must occur on the main thread. We must somehow ask the operating system to invoke updating code within that main thread.

Amazingly, RxJava has two built-in mechanisms for that. You can run side-effecting tasks in the background using `subscribeOn()`, whereas jumping back to the main thread is easy with `observeOn()`. These two operators were explained in "Declarative Subscription with subscribeOn()" on page 150, and they fit perfectly on Android. All you need is a special `Scheduler` that is aware of the Android environment and its main thread. This `Scheduler` was already partially implemented in "Scheduler implementation details overview" on page 146, but luckily we do not have to implement it ourselves. You begin your journey with RxJava on Android by adding this small dependency:

```
compile 'io.reactivex:rxandroid:1.1.0'
```

This small library will add the `AndroidSchedulers` class to your CLASSPATH, which is essential for writing concurrent code on Android with RxJava. Using the Android

Schedulers is best explained by means of an example. We would like to make a call to the Meetup API (see "Retrofit with Native RxJava Support" on page 280), fetch a list of cities nearby a given location, and then display them:

```
button.setOnClickListener(new View.OnClickListener() {
    @Override
    public void onClick(View view) {
        meetup
            .listCities(52.229841, 21.011736)
            .concatMapIterable(extractCities())
            .map(toCityName())
            .toList()
            .subscribeOn(Schedulers.io())
            .observeOn(AndroidSchedulers.mainThread())
            .subscribe(
                    putOnListView(),
                    displayError());
    }

    //...

});
```

This chapter is the only place in the book that does not use any lambda expressions from Java 8. As of this writing, Android supports Java 7 and does not allow closures natively.[1] Therefore, we extracted anonymous inner classes into separate methods to improve readability. If you find this syntax too verbose (even if you are not using RxJava), you can experiment with retrolambda (*https://github.com/orfjackal/retro lambda*) that backports lambdas to older versions of Java and works on Android. On vanilla Android, all transformations and callbacks look as follows:

```
//Cities::getResults
Func1<Cities, Iterable<City>> extractCities() {
    return new Func1<Cities, Iterable<City>>() {
        @Override
        public Iterable<City> call(Cities cities) {
            return cities.getResults();
        }
    };
}

//City::getCity
Func1<City, String> toCityName() {
    return new Func1<City, String>() {
        @Override
        public String call(City city) {
```

---

1 This can change with the release of Android N; for more information, check out this guide to using Java 8 features (*http://bit.ly/2d5eAFw*).

```
                return city.getCity();
            }
        };
    }

    //cities -> listView.setAdapter(...)
    Action1<List<String>> putOnListView() {
        return new Action1<List<String>>() {
            @Override
            public void call(List<String> cities) {
                listView.setAdapter(new ArrayAdapter(
        MainActivity.this, R.layout.list, cities));
            }
        };
    }

    //throwable -> {...}
    Action1<Throwable> displayError() {
        return new Action1<Throwable>() {
            @Override
            public void call(Throwable throwable) {
                Log.e(TAG, "Error", throwable);
                Toast.makeText(MainActivity.this,
                                "Unable to load cities",
                                Toast.LENGTH_SHORT)
                        .show();
            }
        };
    }
```

Here is what happens. When a button is clicked (we will get rid of callbacks in "UI Events as Streams" on page 288), we make an HTTP request via Retrofit. Retrofit produces an `Observable<Cities>` that we further transform by extracting only relevant information. We end up with `List<String>` representing nearby cities. This list is eventually displayed on screen.

The use of two schedulers is actually crucial. Without `subscribeOn()`, Retrofit will use a caller thread to make an HTTP call, causing `Observable` to become blocking. This means that the HTTP request will attempt to block the main Android thread, which is immediately picked up by an operating system and fails with `NetworkOnMain ThreadException`. The traditional way of running network code in the background is by either creating a new `Thread` or using `AsyncTask`. The advantages of `subscri beOn()` are obvious: code is much cleaner, less invasive, and has built-in declarative error handling via `onError` notification.

The `observeOn()` invocation is equally important. When all transformations are done, we invoke a UI update only on the main thread because we want to carry out as little processing as possible there. Without `observeOn()` that shifts execution to `main Thread()` our `Observable` would attempt updating `listView` from a background thread, which fails immediately with `CalledFromWrongThreadException`. Again, `observeOn()` is much more convenient than `postDelayed()` from the `android.os.Handler` class (that `AndroidSchedulers.mainThread()` uses under the hood).

Flexibility of schedulers combined with the API simplicity is very compelling to many Android developers. RxJava offers a simpler, cleaner but also safer way of tackling the complexity of concurrent programming on mobile devices.

On Memory Leaks

The preceding example has one major flaw that can lead to memory leak. The `Observer` keeps a reference to the enclosing Android `Activity` and can outlive it. This problem was explained and dealt with in "Avoiding Memory Leaks in Activities" on page 278.

UI Events as Streams

From the syntax level, RxJava aims to avoid *callback hell* by replacing nested callbacks with declarative transformations. Therefore, `setOnClickListener()` enclosing `Observable` looked a bit disturbing. Fortunately, there is a library that translates Android UI events into streams.[2] Simply add the following dependency to your project:

```
compile 'com.jakewharton.rxbinding:rxbinding:0.4.0'
```

From this point, we can replace an imperative callback registration with a handy pipeline:

```
RxView
        .clicks(button)
        .flatMap(listCities(52.229841, 21.011736))
        .delay(2, TimeUnit.SECONDS)
        .concatMapIterable(extractCities())
        .map(toCityName())
        .toList()
        .subscribeOn(Schedulers.io())
        .observeOn(AndroidSchedulers.mainThread())
        .subscribe(
                putOnListView(),
                displayError());

Func1<Void, Observable<Cities>> listCities(final double lat, final double lon) {
    return new Func1<Void, Observable<Cities>>() {
        @Override
```

---

2 A similar utility exists for Swing (*https://github.com/ReactiveX/RxSwing*).

```
            public Observable<Cities> call(Void aVoid) {
                return meetup.listCities(lat, lon);
            }
        };
    }
```

Rather than registering a callback that creates and transforms `Observable` locally, we begin with `Observable<Void>` representing button clicks. Clicking a button does not convey any information; thus, it is `Void`. Each click event triggers an asynchronous HTTP request returning `Observable<Cities>`. Everything else stays pretty much the same. If you think this is just a minor readability improvement, consider composing multiple GUI event streams.

Imagine that you have two text fields; one for entering latitude and another one for longitude. Any time either of them changes, you would like to make an HTTP request looking for all cities nearby that location. However, to avoid unnecessary network traffic when the user is still typing, we want to implement a certain delay. The network request is initiated only when no changes occurred to any text field for one second. This is very similar to autocomplete text fields that have a slight delay to avoid excessive network usage, but in this case we have to take two inputs together into account. The implementation using RxJava and RxBinding is very elegant:

```
import android.widget.EditText;
import com.jakewharton.rxbinding.widget.RxTextView;
import com.jakewharton.rxbinding.widget.TextViewAfterTextChangeEvent;


EditText latText = //...
EditText lonText = //...

Observable<Double> latChanges = RxTextView
    .afterTextChangeEvents(latText)
    .flatMap(toDouble());
Observable<Double> lonChanges = RxTextView
    .afterTextChangeEvents(lonText)
    .flatMap(toDouble());

Observable<Cities> cities = Observable
    .combineLatest(latChanges, lonChanges, toPair())
    .debounce(1, TimeUnit.SECONDS)
    .flatMap(listCitiesNear());
```

And all transformations (note how verbose the code is when lambda expressions are not an option):

```
Func1<TextViewAfterTextChangeEvent, Observable<Double>> toDouble() {
    return new Func1<TextViewAfterTextChangeEvent, Observable<Double>>() {
        @Override
        public Observable<Double> call(TextViewAfterTextChangeEvent e) {
            String s = e.editable().toString();
```

```
                try {
                    return Observable.just(Double.parseDouble(s));
                } catch (NumberFormatException e) {
                    return Observable.empty();
                }
            }
        };
    }


    //return Pair::new
    Func2<Double, Double, Pair<Double, Double>> toPair() {
        return new Func2<Double, Double, Pair<Double, Double>>() {
            @Override
            public Pair<Double, Double> call(Double lat, Double lon) {
                return new Pair<>(lat, lon);
            }
        };
    }


    //return latLon -> meetup.listCities(latLon.first, latLon.second)
    Func1<Pair<Double, Double>, Observable<Cities>> listCitiesNear() {
        return new Func1<Pair<Double, Double>, Observable<Cities>>() {
            @Override
            public Observable<Cities> call(Pair<Double, Double> latLon) {
                return meetup.listCities(latLon.first, latLon.second);
            }
        };
    }
```

First, RxTextView.afterTextChangeEvents() transforms the imperative callbacks invoked by EditText whenever the content changes. We create two such streams for latitude and longitude separately. On the fly, we transform TextViewAfterTextChan geEvent into a double, silently dropping the malformed inputs. Having two streams of doubles, we combine them using combineLatest() so that we receive a stream of pairs every time either of the inputs change. The final piece is debounce() (see "Skipping Stale Events by Using debounce()" on page 221), which waits one second before forwarding such pairs just in case another edit (either of latitude or longitude) follows shortly. Thanks to debounce(), we avoid unnecessary network calls while the user is typing. The rest of the application remains the same.

This example nicely shows how reactive programming propagates up from Retrofit to user components so that everything in the application becomes a composition of streams. Just make sure that you unsubscribe from afterTextChangeEvents(); failing to do so can lead to memory leak.

Managing Failures with Hystrix

> A distributed system is one in which the failure of a computer you didn't even know existed can render your own computer unusable.
>
> —Leslie Lamport, *1987*

RxJava has many operators that support writing scalable, reactive, and resilient applications:

- Declarative concurrency with `Schedulers` ("Multithreading in RxJava" on page 140)
- Timeouts ("Timing Out When Events Do Not Occur" on page 251) and various error handling mechanisms ("Error Handling" on page 243, "Retrying After Failures" on page 254)
- Parallelizing work with `flatMap()` ("flatMap() as Asynchronous Chaining Operator" on page 131) and limiting the concurrency at the same time ("Controlling the concurrency of flatMap()" on page 76).

Yet, to write robust and resilient applications, especially in the cloud environment or when using microservices architecture, more features are needed that do not belong to core RxJava. In this section, we take a quick look at Hystrix (*https://github.com/Netflix/Hystrix*), a library for managing, isolating, and handling failures in distributed environments. Hystrix allows you to wrap actions that can potentially fail and apply clever logic around such code. This includes:

- Bulkhead pattern by cutting off misbehaving actions entirely for a certain time
- Failing fast by applying timeouts, limiting concurrency, and implementing a so-called *circuit breaker*
- Batching requests by collapsing small orders into one big order
- Collecting, publishing, and visualizing performance statistics

One of the greatest strengths of Hystrix is a circuit breaker, a mechanism for turning off temporarily broken dependencies so that their failures do not cascade. If failures are not handled properly in a distributed system, they tend to propagate to downstream dependencies, just like exceptions propagate throughout the stack. In a distributed system, one end user request can easily require making tens if not hundreds of requests to various upstream dependencies. One broken service, even nonessential, can take down the entire system, failing every single request.

Interestingly, slow service can be even worse than a failing one. If every single user request is failing instantaneously with a friendly error message, the situation is bad. But if your users do not get any response at all and simply wait infinitely, the situation is much worse. The typical reaction (admit it!) is trying to refresh a web page. This rarely helps but more often it just starts another request, further overflowing the system. One slow service causes delays to further cascade, bringing the entire system to a stall. Suddenly, all services using the slow one become slow and the situation cascades recursively. Hystrix attempts to shield such broken dependencies and stop cascading of failures.

The First Steps with Hystrix

There are several reasons to study Hystrix in this book. First, it is built on top of RxJava, which makes it a great practical example of reactive extensions in real life. Second, we can invoke the Hystrix command and get Observable in return. Finally, but most important, Hystrix supports nonblocking commands (see "Nonblocking Commands with HystrixObservableCommand" on page 294).

Before we proceed, let's explore how to use Hystrix in the simplest, blocking scenario. A rule of thumb is to use Hystrix whenever execution escapes our process or machine. Making a network call (but also accessing I/O) significantly increases the risk of failure: risks can include unpredictable latencies, network partitions, and packet loss. When we identify such a potentially dangerous block of code, we wrap it in a HystrixCommand:

```
import org.apache.commons.io.IOUtils;
import com.netflix.hystrix.HystrixCommand;
import com.netflix.hystrix.HystrixCommandGroupKey;

class BlockingCmd extends HystrixCommand<String> {

    public BlockingCmd() {
        super(HystrixCommandGroupKey.Factory.asKey("SomeGroup"));
    }

    @Override
    protected String run() throws IOException {
        final URL url = new URL("http://www.example.com");
        try (InputStream input = url.openStream()) {
            return IOUtils.toString(input, StandardCharsets.UTF_8);
        }
    }

}
```

Blocking code that can potentially fail is wrapped inside a run() method. The resulting type T of that method is defined by a generic type of HystrixCommand<T>. If we would like to parameterize the action (e.g., use a different URL), it must be passed via constructor. HystrixCommand is an implementation of the *Command* design pattern, as defined in the seminal *Design Patterns: Elements of Reusable Object-Oriented Software* by Erich Gamma et al. (Addison-Wesley).

Having an instance of `HystrixCommand`, we must now somehow execute it. There are a couple of ways to block: on-command execution or by obtaining a pre-Java 8 `Future`, neither which are very interesting to us:

```
String string        = new BlockingCmd().execute();
Future<String> future = new BlockingCmd().queue();
```

The `execute()` method invokes the `run()` method indirectly through a safety net of timeouts, advanced error handling, and so on. You can read more about that in "Bulkhead Pattern and Fail-Fast" on page 295. The method blocks and returns only when the underlying `run()` completes or throws an exception. In that case, the exception is propagated to the caller. `queue()`, on the other hand, is nonblocking but returns `Future<T>`, instead. The old `Future` interface is not particularly reactive, thus we are not very interested in both `execute()` and `queue()` throughout this book.

> Notice that we always create a new instance of `BlockingCmd`—you cannot reuse a command instance for multiple executions. `Hystrix Commands` are supposed to be created directly before execution and never reused. In practice, you typically parametrize command upon construction so reusability of instance is questionable anyway.

Hystrix supports `Observable` as a first-class citizen,[3] being able to return command result as a stream:

```
Observable<String> eager = new BlockingCmd().observe();
Observable<String> lazy  = new BlockingCmd().toObservable();
```

The semantic difference between `observe()` and `toObservable()` is quite important. `toObservable()` converts a command to a lazy and cold `Observable`—the command will not be executed until someone actually subscribes to this `Observable`. Moreover, the `Observable` is not cached, so each `subscribe()` will trigger command execution. `observe()`, in contrast, invokes the command asynchronously straight away, returning a hot but also cached `Observable`. As we learned in "Embracing Laziness" on page 121, lazy `Observables` are quite handy; for example, we can create them at any point in time but skip subscription and avoid any side effects like making network call. We can also very effectively batch requests. However, with a cold `Observable` there is a risk of accidentally invoking an action multiple times in case of more than one subscriber. The `cache()` operator can help in these circumstances. In general laziness allows the most efficient concurrency so you should prefer `toObservable()` over `observe()` unless you have a very valid point to eagerly invoke a command.

---

3 In fact, `execute()` is implemented in terms of `queue()`, which in turn is implemented with `toObservable()`.

Having an `Observable`, you can apply all sorts of operators; for example, you can retry failed commands using `retry()`:

```
Observable<String> retried = new BlockingCmd()
    .toObservable()
    .doOnError(ex -> log.warn("Error ", ex))
    .retryWhen(ex -> ex.delay(500, MILLISECONDS))
    .timeout(3, SECONDS);
```

The preceding pipeline invokes a command, but in case of failure retries after 500 milliseconds. However, retrying can take up to three seconds; above that `TimeoutEx ception` is thrown (see "Timing Out When Events Do Not Occur" on page 251). Later we will see how timeouts built into Hystrix can help, as well.

Nonblocking Commands with HystrixObservableCommand

If your application was designed with RxJava in mind, the chances are that your actions involving third-party services or unknown libraries are already modeled as `Observables`. The basic `HystrixCommand` supports only blocking code. If your inter‐ actions with the outside world are already an `Observable` that you want to further protect via Hystrix, the `HystrixObservableCommand` is much better suited:

```
public class CitiesCmd extends HystrixObservableCommand<Cities> {

    private final MeetupApi api;
    private final double lat;
    private final double lon;

    protected CitiesCmd(MeetupApi api, double lat, double lon) {
        super(HystrixCommandGroupKey.Factory.asKey("Meetup"));
        this.api = api;
        this.lat = lat;
        this.lon = lon;
    }

    @Override
    protected Observable<Cities> construct() {
        return api.listCities(lat, lon);
    }
}
```

The `MeetupApi` was introduced in "Retrofit with Native RxJava Support" on page 280, and it can return `Observable<Cities>`. Hystrix transparently wraps this `Observable` by adding fault-tolerance features that we will discover shortly. The `CitiesCmd` com‐ mand is also much more typical compared to `BlockingCmd` because it accepts a few parameters in its constructor. We can also pass a stubbed `MeetupApi` instance in unit tests to verify the behavior of command.

The advantage of the `HystrixObservableCommand` over `HystrixCommand` is that the former does not require a thread pool to operate. `HystrixCommands` are always executed in a bound thread pool, whereas `Observable` commands do not require any extra threads. Of course, `Observable` returned from `construct()` (notice that it is no longer named `run()`) can still use some threads, depending on the underlying implementation.

Knowing how to create commands in Hystrix and how they fit into the RxJava ecosystem, it's time to see in action what features Hystrix actually does provide.

Bulkhead Pattern and Fail-Fast

Bulkheads are large walls across a ship's hull that create watertight compartments. In case of water leak, bulkheads keep water in just one compartment, preventing the ship from sinking. The same engineering principle can be applied to distributed systems. When one component in your architecture fails, it should be isolated. The system should work even if an individual component is broken broken.

Another engineering pattern that works great in software is the *circuit breaker*. The responsibility of a circuit breaker is to interrupt flow of electricity and protect various devices from overload or even catching fire. The circuit breaker can be reset (manually or automatically) when the danger is gone. But, wouldn't this cause the power to be cut off your lights or heat or (in worst case scenario) your router? Not necessarily. Those other electrical networks might be protected by other circuit breakers, and thus they will still work. And most important, your house did not catch fire.

Hystrix implements both of these patterns in the area of system integration. Every single command has a timeout (by default 1 second) and limited concurrency (by default up to 10 concurrent commands from a given group). These rather aggressive limits ensure that commands are not consuming too many resources like threads and memory. Also, by applying timeouts we do not introduce excessive latency. We can compare this behavior to the bulkhead in ship, because if one of our dependencies begins to fail (remember, excessively high latency is indistinguishable from failure), this problem will not affect our entire system. Timeouts and limited concurrency significantly reduce the number of threads blocked on an external system.

A circuit breaker, on the other hand, is even more clever. What if we discover that a dependency that used to respond within 100 milliseconds times-out after 1 second almost all the time. If calling this misbehaving dependency was part of some broader request processing, nearly every transaction is now one second slower. Without Hystrix, the latency could have been much bigger but timeouts can be achieved with pure RxJava. Hystrix does much more than that. If it discovers that a particular command keeps failing (either with an exception or timeout) too often (by default 50% of all invocations) within certain time window (by default 10 seconds) it opens a circuit.

What happens then is very interesting. Hystrix no longer invokes your failing command, at all. Instead, it throws an exception immediately, failing fast.

It's time to see Hystrix in action. First we need to mock-up MeetupApi using Mockito so that it always fails with some unacceptable latency:

```
import static org.mockito.BDDMockito.given;
import static org.mockito.Matchers.anyDouble;
import static org.mockito.Mockito.mock;


MeetupApi api = mock(MeetupApi.class);
given(api.listCities(anyDouble(), anyDouble())).willReturn(
    Observable
        .<Cities>error(new RuntimeException("Broken"))
        .doOnSubscribe(() -> log.debug("Invoking"))
        .delay(2, SECONDS)
);
```

The default timeout is one second, so in fact you will never really see the "Broken" exception because timeout will kick in first. Now, we would like to invoke MeetupApi multiple times concurrently and see how Hystrix behaves:

```
Observable
    .interval(50, MILLISECONDS)
    .doOnNext(x -> log.debug("Requesting"))
    .flatMap(x ->
            new CitiesCmd(api, 52.229841, 21.011736)
                .toObservable()
                .onErrorResumeNext(ex -> Observable.empty()),
        5)
```

Using the interval() operator, we emit an event every 50 milliseconds. On each event, we invoke CitiesCmd and swallow errors. Remember that in real projects you will most likely want to at least log them using the doOnError() callback. Every 50 milliseconds Hystrix invokes our command and notices it times out after 1 second. The command is actually even slower, but Hystrix prematurely interrupts it. When you subscribe and run this program you will notice that CitiesCmd is invoked several times but then suddenly stops. Although the "Requesting" message still appears every 50 milliseconds, the command is no longer invoked.

Hystrix figured out via some heuristics that CitiesCmd is somewhat broken and thus no longer calls it. Instead, whenever you attempt to call this command, the resulting Observable fails immediately with an exception. This is a circuit breaker kicking in and failing fast. Your command is no longer invoked because Hystrix realized it keeps failing and there is no point in further calling it. When the failure rate exceeds 50%, the circuit breaker opens and every subsequent attempt to call a command fails instantaneously. By failure, Hystrix assumes either an exception or a timeout.

The advantages of the circuit breaker are twofold. From the perspective of the application invoking the command, it would have failed anyway, but we get a response faster, thus leading to better user experience. But it is even more interesting from the server perspective—or whatever was the target of the request made within a command. If your command keeps failing or timing out, it might be a sign that your dependency (another service, database) is having difficulties. This can be a restart, peak of traffic, or a very long GC pause. By cutting off this command with a circuit breaker, you give the system room to breathe for a while. Maybe when the load spike ends or internal job queue empties, the system will become responsive and healthy again. This prevents your system from performing a distributed denial of service (DDoS) attack on itself.

So how will Hystrix recognize that a downstream dependency is fine again and close the circuit? Luckily, this process is automatic. In the previous example, at some point in time we stopped seeing the "Invoking" log message, which implied that the circuit was open and the command is no longer executed at all. This is not entirely true. Once in a while (by default every five seconds), Hystrix will let one request and invoke the command, checking whether it is fine this time. All other clients in the meantime are still failing fast. If this single request succeeds, Hystrix assumes the command is now healthy and closes the circuit; otherwise, the circuit remains open.

This property is known as *self-healing* and it is an important concept in computer systems. Hystrix helps in two fronts. By temporarily turning off broken commands, it allows downstream dependencies to recover. After they recover, the system returns back to normal operations. Without mechanisms like this, even a minor glitch can lead to cascading failures and manual restarts in order to restore the stability of various components.

Batching and Collapsing Commands

One of the most advanced features of Hystrix is the batching requests. Imagine that you are making several small downstream requests throughout the course of handling one single upstream request. For example, suppose that you are displaying a list of books, and for each book you must ask an external system for its rating:

```
Observable<Book> allBooks() { /* ... */ }
Observable<Rating> fetchRating(Book book) { /* ... */ }
```

The allBooks() method returns a stream of Books that we want to process, whereas fetchRating() retrieves a Rating for each and every Book. Naive implementation would simply iterate over all books and retrieve Rating one after another. Fortunately, running subtasks asynchronously in RxJava is very simple:

```
Observable<Rating> ratings = allBooks()
        .flatMap(this::fetchRating);
```

The diagrams that follow compare calling `fetchRatings()` sequentially versus using `flatMap()`. The phases are `send` for transferring request, `proc` for server-side processing, and `recv` for transferring the response. The following image illustrates fetching sequentially:[4]

The following image illustrates fetching using `flatMap()`:

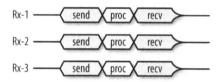

This works great and generally we see a satisfying performance. All `fetchRating()` invocations are executed concurrently and greatly improve latency. However if you consider that each invocation of `fetchRating()` implies a fixed amount of network latency, calling it for dozens of books seems wasteful. Making one batch request for all books and receiving one response with all ratings sounds much more productive:

Rx-1 ——(send(3))(proc(3))(recv(3))——

Notice that all phases: sending, processing, and receiving, are slightly slower. All of them either transfer or process more data, so this is understandable. Therefore, the total latency is actually higher compared to multiple small requests. The improvement is questionable. But you must look at a bigger picture.

Although the latency of an individual request increased, system throughput is probably greatly improved. The number of concurrent connections we can perform, network throughput and JVM threads are limited and scarce resources. If the dependency you request has limited throughput, it is easy to saturate it with relatively few transactions that take advantage of concurrency. A selfishly utilized `flatMap()` improves latency of single request but can degrade performance of all other requests by saturating resources. Therefore, we might want to sacrifice a little bit of latency in order to achieve much better overall throughput without generating too much load on downstream dependencies. In the end, the latency is actually improved, as well: requests are more fair in sharing resources, so the latency is more predictable.

---

4 Diagrams generated using this GitHub repo (*https://github.com/drom/wavedrom*).

So how do we achieve batching? Hystrix knows about every single command you execute. When it discovers that you are about to start two similar commands at the same time (e.g., to fetch two Ratings) at the same time it can collapse these two commands into one bigger batch command. This batch command is invoked, and when batch response arrives, replies are mapped back to individual requests. First, we need an implementation of the batch command that can retrieve multiple Ratings at once:

```
class FetchManyRatings extends HystrixObservableCommand<Rating> {

    private final Collection<Book> books;

    protected FetchManyRatings(Collection<Book> books) {
        super(HystrixCommandGroupKey.Factory.asKey("Books"));
        this.books = books;
    }

    @Override
    protected Observable<Rating> construct() {
        return fetchManyRatings(books);
    }

}
```

The fetchManyRatings() method takes several books as an argument and emits several Rating instances. Internally, it can make a single batch HTTP request asking for several ratings, as opposed to the fetchRating(book) method, which always retrieves just one. Asking for more than one Rating is surely slower but definitely faster than asking for ratings sequentially. But we do not want to go through the hassle of manually batching several individual requests and then unzipping the batch response. This might be easy when dealing with a single transaction, but what if we have multiple concurrent clients, each asking for some Rating? When two independent requests from two browsers hit our server, we would still like to batch these two requests together and make just one downstream call. However, this would require interthread synchronization and some global registry of all requests. Imagine one thread trying to invoke a given command and another thread invoking the same command (with different arguments) just milliseconds later. We would like to wait a little bit after the first request attempted to start a command, just in case another thread wants to invoke the same command shortly thereafter. In that case, we want to capture these two requests, merge them together, make just one batch request, and map batch response back to individual requests. This is precisely what Hystrix is doing with a little help from us:

```
public class FetchRatingsCollapser
    extends HystrixObservableCollapser<Book, Rating,
Rating, Book> {

    private final Book book;
```

```
    public FetchRatingsCollapser(Book book) {
        //Explained below
    }

    public Book getRequestArgument() {
        return book;
    }

    protected HystrixObservableCommand<Rating> createCommand(
        Collection<HystrixCollapser.CollapsedRequest<Rating, Book>> requests) {
        //Explained below
    }

protected void onMissingResponse(
        HystrixCollapser.CollapsedRequest<Rating, Book> r)
{
        r.setException(new RuntimeException("Not found for: "
+ r.getArgument())));
}

    protected Func1<Book, Book> getRequestArgumentKeySelector() {
        return x -> x;
    }

    protected Func1<Rating, Rating> getBatchReturnTypeToResponseTypeMapper() {
        return x -> x;
    }

    protected Func1<Rating, Book> getBatchReturnTypeKeySelector() {
        return Rating::getBook;
    }

}
```

There is a lot of code here, so let's dissect it step by step. When we want to retrieve one Rating for a given Book, we create an instance of FetchRatingsCollapser like that:

```
Observable<Rating> ratingObservable =
    new FetchRatingsCollapser(book).toObservable();
```

The client code is entirely oblivious to the batching and collapsing that's happening, thanks to HystrixObservableCollapser. From the outside, we use it as if it were retrieving one Rating for one Book. But internally, there are a few interesting details that allow batching. First, in the constructor, apart from storing Book for this request we configure the collapsing of requests:

```
public FetchRatingsCollapser(Book book) {
    super(withCollapserKey(HystrixCollapserKey.Factory.asKey("Books"))
            .andCollapserPropertiesDefaults(HystrixCollapserProperties.Setter()
                    .withTimerDelayInMilliseconds(20)
                    .withMaxRequestsInBatch(50)
```

```
        )
            .andScope(Scope.GLOBAL));
    this.book = book;
}
```

20 milliseconds configured with `withTimerDelayInMilliseconds()` is the length of time window during which collapsing occurs (the default is 10 milliseconds). When the first individual request occurs, a 20 millisecond timer delays its actual invocation. Within that time, Hystrix waits for other requests to come, possibly from other threads. Hystrix speculatively delays the first request to see if more commands of the same type arrive. When this time elapses or as many as 50 requests are already queued up (`withMaxRequestsInBatch(50)` parameter), the gate is opened. At this point, the library is supposed to invoke all queued commands in a single batch. But Hystrix will not magically batch your command into one; you must instruct it how to do this. Here's how to do that:

```
protected HystrixObservableCommand<Rating>
createCommand(
    Collection<HystrixCollapser.CollapsedRequest<Rating,
Book>> requests) {
    List<Book> books = requests.stream()
            .map(c -> c.getArgument())
            .collect(toList());
    return new FetchManyRatings(books);
}
```

The responsibility of the `createCommand()` method is to translate individual requests into one batch command. It receives a collection of all `requests` that were gathered within the 20 milliseconds time frame and should now be merged into a single, batch request. In our case, we construct an instance of `FetchManyRatings` command that takes all `Books` for which we requested `Ratings`. Hystrix then invokes our batch command and subscribes for multiple responses. Notice that `HystrixObservableCommand` is allowed to return multiple values, which is exactly what we are looking for.

When values begin to emerge from `FetchManyRatings`, we must somehow map the `Rating` instances to independent requests. Remember that at this point we might have several individual threads and transactions, each waiting for just one `Rating`. This routing and dispatching of batch response to small individual requests occurs more or less automatically with the help of the following methods:

`getRequestArgumentKeySelector()`

This maps from an individual request argument (`Book`) into a key that will later be used to map a batch response. In our case, we simply use the same `Book` instance, thus the identity `x -> x` transformation.

`getBatchReturnTypeToResponseTypeMapper()`

This maps one item from the batch response to one individual response. Again, the identity `x -> x` transformation is sufficient in our case.

`getBatchReturnTypeKeySelector()`

You use this to instruct Hystrix which request key (`Book`) this particular response (`Rating`) answers. For simplicities sake, each `Rating` returned from a batch response has a `getBook()` method that indicates to which `Book` it is related.

Having all these methods in place (especially the last one: `getBatchReturnTypeKeySelector()`), Hystrix prepares a map of individual requests by request key (`Book`) and whenever a new `Rating` appears from batch response it can automatically map that response to request.

That's quite a bit of plumbing to get batching to work, but it pays off quickly. When multiple clients access the same downstream dependency—for example, a cache server—we can collect many requests into one. This significantly cuts bandwidth costs. When our dependency is a bottleneck and throughput is limited, collapsing requests greatly reduces load on that dependency. However, batching introduces extra latency on the client side. With a default configuration of 10 milliseconds (`withTimerDelayInMilliseconds(10)`), under high load each request is delayed on average by 5 milliseconds. The actual delay depends on whether the request just started a new timer or appeared just before current batch is about to collapse.

Notice that batching makes no sense under low load. If very rarely more than one request forms a batch, you barely added an extra delay of 10 milliseconds to each request. This is the time Hystrix pointlessly waits, hoping for other requests to come. Thus, tuning of request batching is important. First, if your timer delay is 10 milliseconds, batching makes sense only when you make at least 100 requests per second. Otherwise, very rarely more than one request forms a batch.

Tuning `withTimerDelayInMilliseconds`

It's tempting to have a very long timer delay to let as many requests into a single batch as possible. Values like 100 milliseconds or even 1 second are fine but will work best in offline systems that generate a lot of traffic and where latency is not an issue.

Batching is a feature that works best under high load. Thus Hystrix provides quite comprehensive monitoring mechanism that helps you to understand the overall system performance.

Monitoring and Dashboards

To work properly, Hystrix must collect a lot of statistics internally for each command over time, like counting successful and failed invocations and response time distribution. It would be kind of selfish to keep this precious data inside of the library, but not to worry: Hystrix provides several ways to digest it. You can subscribe to several types of streams prepared by Hystrix that emit events about occurrences within the library. For example, the following code creates a stream of `HystrixCommandCompletion` events emitted every time a command `FetchRating` completes:

```
import com.netflix.hystrix.metric.HystrixCommandCompletion;
import com.netflix.hystrix.metric.HystrixCommandCompletionStream;


Observable<HystrixCommandCompletion> stats =
    HystrixCommandCompletionStream
    .getInstance(HystrixCommandKey.Factory.asKey("FetchRating"))
    .observe();
```

`HystrixCommandCompletionStream` is a factory of such streams, but there are many others like `HystrixCommandStartStream` or `HystrixCollapserEventStream`. Having these streams inside your application allows you to build more sophisticated monitoring mechanisms. For example, if you want to know how many times given command failed per second, try this:

```
import static com.netflix.hystrix.HystrixEventType.FAILURE;


HystrixCommandCompletionStream
        .getInstance(HystrixCommandKey.Factory.asKey("FetchRating"))
        .observe()
        .filter(e -> e.getEventCounts().getCount(FAILURE) > 0)
        .window(1, TimeUnit.SECONDS)
        .flatMap(Observable::count)
        .subscribe(x -> log.info("{} failures/s", x));
```

But building a monitoring infrastructure on top of these streams requires a bit of design and work. Also you might want to externalize monitoring from the actual application. Hystrix, via the `hystrix-metrics-event-stream` module, supports pushing all aggregated metrics via HTTP. If your application already runs on top of or has an embedded servlet container, it is enough to add a built-in `HystrixMetrics StreamServlet` to your mappings. Otherwise, you can start a tiny container yourself:

```
import
 com.netflix.hystrix.contrib.metrics.eventstream.
    HystrixMetricsStreamServlet;
import org.eclipse.jetty.server.Server;
import org.eclipse.jetty.servlet.ServletContextHandler;
import org.eclipse.jetty.servlet.ServletHolder;
import static org.eclipse.jetty.servlet.ServletContextHandler.NO_SESSIONS;
```

```
//...

ServletContextHandler context = new ServletContextHandler(NO_SESSIONS);
HystrixMetricsStreamServlet servlet = new HystrixMetricsStreamServlet();
context.addServlet(new ServletHolder(servlet), "/hystrix.stream");
Server server = new Server(8080);
server.setHandler(context);
server.start();
```

Whether you mapped a servlet to an existing container or started your own, you can now access Hystrix statistics streamed in real time. Notice that this connection is not plain request-response but rather a server-sent events (SSEs) stream. Every second, a new packet of statistics in JSON format is pushed to the client:

```
$ curl -v localhost:8080/hystrix.stream
> GET /hystrix.stream HTTP/1.1
...
< HTTP/1.1 200 OK
< Content-Type: text/event-stream;charset=UTF-8

ping:

data: {
    "currentConcurrentExecutionCount": 2,
    "errorCount": 0,
    "errorPercentage": 0,
    "group": "Books",
    "isCircuitBreakerOpen": false,
    "latencyExecute": {/* ... */},
    "latencyExecute_mean": 0,
    "latencyTotal": {"0":18, "25":80, "50":98, "75":120, "90":138,
                     "95":146, "99":159, "99.5":159, "100":167},
    "latencyTotal_mean": 0,
    "name": "FetchRating",
    "propertyValue_circuitBreakerErrorThresholdPercentage": 50,
    "propertyValue_circuitBreakerSleepWindowInMilliseconds": 5000,
    "propertyValue_executionIsolationSemaphoreMaxConcurrentRequests": 10,
    "propertyValue_executionTimeoutInMilliseconds": 1000,
    "requestCount": 334
    ...
}

data: { ...
```

Even in this stripped down sample, you can see which command is measured, what is the latency distribution (from 0th to 100th percentile), is a circuit breaker open, and what are its parameters (error threshold, timeouts, and so on). This continuous stream of data can further be consumed by custom monitoring tools and dashboards. Yet again, Hystrix comes to the rescue and provides a very robust dashboard written almost entirely in JavaScript that runs in the browser. All this standalone application

—implemented in `hystrix-dashboard`—needs is a URL to your `hystrix.stream`. The following graphic shows a sample dashboard:

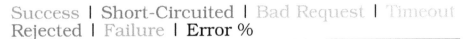

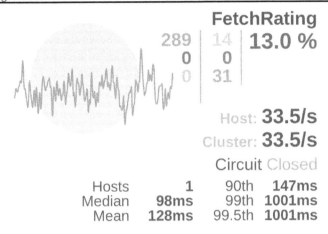

For each command, there is a similar tile, each presenting several important telemetric details, including the following

- Number of commands executed, grouped by: success (289), timeout (14), failure (31), short-circuited (0), and so on
- Latency percentiles (for example, we see that 90% of all requests took no longer than 147 milliseconds) and short-term history on the chart
- Circuit breaker status and overall throughput
- Thread pool statistics if we use blocking `HystrixCommand`

The dashboard also can display streams aggregated from multiple servers via Turbine (*https://github.com/Netflix/Turbine*). That is the reason why we see the number of hosts and cluster throughput as well, even though the stream comes from just one machine. An Hystrix dashboard is very useful because it can quickly show status of multiple commands in near real time. It is also color coded, so if some commands begin to fail, their corresponding tiles become red.

Hystrix is a useful tool in distributed systems where failures are inevitable. The command pattern allows us to encapsulate and isolate error domains. Great integration with RxJava make it a good choice in reactive applications that require better error handling.

Querying NoSQL Databases

A typical application these days has two high-latency origins of data: network calls (mostly HTTP) and database queries. Retrofit (see "Retrofit with Native RxJava Support" on page 280) is a fantastic source of Observables that are backed by an asynchronous HTTP call. When it comes to database access, we spent quite some time looking at SQL databases (see "Relational Database Access" on page 187) that are historically blocking due to the JDBC API design. NoSQL databases are more modern in that regard and often provide asynchronous, nonblocking client drivers. In this chapter, we will briefly explore Couchbase and MongoDB drivers that have native RxJava support and can return Observable for each external call.

Couchbase Client API

Couchbase Server (*http://www.couchbase.com*) is a modern document database in the NoSQL family. What is interesting is that Couchbase supports RxJava as first-class citizen in its client API. Reactive extensions are not only used as a wrapper but are officially supported and idiomatic when interacting with the database. Many other storage engines have a nonblocking, asynchronous API but the creators of Couchbase chose RxJava as the best foundation for the client layer.

As an example, let's query the example dataset called travel-sample, which happens to have a document for ID route_14197. In a sample dataset, the route document looks as follows:

```
{
  "id": 14197,
  "type": "route",
  "airline": "B6",
  "airlineid": "airline_3029",
  "sourceairport": "PHX",
  "destinationairport": "BOS",
  "stops": 0,
  "equipment": "320",
  "schedule": [
    {
      "day": 0,
      "utc": "22:12:00",
      "flight": "B6928"
    },
    {
      "day": 0,
      "utc": "06:40:00",
      "flight": "B6387"
    },
    ...
    {
      "day": 1,
```

```
    "utc": "08:16:00",
    "flight": "B6922"
  }
  ...
```

Every query returns an `Observable`, and from this point, we can safely transform retrieved records in whatever way we find suitable:

```
CouchbaseCluster cluster = CouchbaseCluster.create();
cluster
    .openBucket("travel-sample")
    .get("route_14197")
    .map(AbstractDocument::content)
    .map(json -> json.getArray("schedule"))
    .concatMapIterable(JsonArray::toList)
    .cast(Map.class)
    .filter(m -> ((Number)m.get("day")).intValue() == 0)
    .map(m -> m.get("flight").toString())
    .subscribe(flight -> System.out.println(flight));
```

An `AsyncBucket.get()` returns an `Observable<JsonDocument>`. JSON documents are inherently loosely typed so in order to extract meaningful information we must traverse them with prior knowledge of their structure.

Knowing what the document looks like in advance, it is easy to understand transformations on `JsonDocument`. The sequence of transformations first extracts the `"schedule"` element and further pulls all of the `"flight"` nodes that are for the `"day"` node equal to 0. The `Observer` eventually receives strings of `"B6928"`, `"B6387"`, and so on. Amazingly, RxJava works equally good for the following:

- Data retrieval, including timeouts, caching, and error handling
- Data transformation, like extracting, filtering, drilling down into data, and aggregating

This shows the power of the `Observable` abstraction that you can use in very different scenarios while still exposing the same concise API.[5]

MongoDB Client API

Just like Couchbase, MongoDB (*https://www.mongodb.org*) allows storing arbitrary JSON-like documents without any predefined schema. The client library has first-class support for RxJava allowing both asynchronous storing and querying of data. The following example does both of these. It first inserts 12 documents into the database; as soon as the batch insert is done, it queries them back:

---

5 This characteristic is similar to Language Integrated Query (LINQ) on .NET platform.

```
import com.mongodb.rx.client.*;
import org.bson.Document;
import java.time.Month;


MongoCollection<Document> monthsColl = MongoClients
    .create()
    .getDatabase("rx")
    .getCollection("months");

Observable
    .from(Month.values())
    .map(month -> new Document()
        .append("name", month.name())
        .append("days_not_leap", month.length(false))
        .append("days_leap", month.length(true))
    )
    .toList()
    .flatMap(monthsColl::insertMany)
    .flatMap(s -> monthsColl.find().toObservable())
    .toBlocking()
    .subscribe(System.out::println);
```

The Month class is an enum having values from January to December. Also, we can easily obtain any month's length in both leap and nonleap years. First, we create twelve BSON (binary JSON) documents, each representing one month with its length. Then we batch insert List<Document> using insertMany() in MongoCollec tion. This yields an Observable<Success> (the value itself does not contain any meaningful information; it is a singleton). When the Success event appears, we can query the database by calling find().toObservable(). Hopefully, the 12 documents we just inserted are found. Excluding the automatically assigned _id property for clarity, this is what is printed at the very end:

```
Document{{name=JANUARY, days_not_leap=31, days_leap=31}}
Document{{name=FEBRUARY, days_not_leap=28, days_leap=29}}
Document{{name=MARCH, days_not_leap=31, days_leap=31}}
...
```

Again, the true power comes from composition. With MongoDB's RxJava driver, you can easily query multiple collections at the same time and achieve concurrency without really thinking about it much. The code snippet that follows makes two con current requests to MongoDB and another one to some pricing service. Note that first() is not an operator on Observable; rather, it is a MongoDB operator that returns an Observable after constructing a query. find() is equivalent to the WHERE clause in SQL, whereas projection() represent SELECT. first() is like LIMIT 1:

```
Observable<Integer> days = db.getCollection("months")
    .find(Filters.eq("name", APRIL.name())))
    .projection(Projections.include("days_not_leap"))
    .first()
```

```
        .map(doc -> doc.getInteger("days_not_leap"));
Observable<Instant> carManufactured = db.getCollection("cars")
    .find(Filters.eq("owner.name", "Smith"))
    .first()
    .map(doc -> doc.getDate("manufactured"))
    .map(Date::toInstant);

Observable<BigDecimal> pricePerDay = dailyPrice(LocalDateTime.now());
Observable<Insurance> insurance = Observable
    .zip(days, carManufactured, pricePerDay,
        (d, man, price) -> {
            //Create insurance
        });
```

Technically, you can mix and match any `Observables`, irrespective of their nature and source. The preceding example makes two queries to MongoDB to two different collections and another query in `dailyPrice()` that can—for example, return an `Observable` from Retrofit making an HTTP call. The bottom line is this: the source of `Observable` is irrelevant, you can compose asynchronous computations and requests any way you like. Do you plan on querying multiple databases combined with web services and local file system operation? All of these can run concurrently and be composed together with the same ease. After you grasp how RxJava behaves in general, every source of `Observable` is the same on the surface.

Camel Integration

In "Retrofit with Native RxJava Support" on page 280 we learned how to make an HTTP request with excellent RxJava support. However, there are many other ways to integrate systems, and a lot of them are built into the Apache Camel (*http://camel.apache.org*) framework. Camel has an astounding set of integration components with which you can connect and exchange abstract messages with more than two hundred platforms. These include technologies like AMQP, Amazon Web Services, Cassandra, ElasticSearch, file system, FTP, Google APIs, JDBC, Kafka, MongoDB, SMTP, XMP, and much, much more. Most of these components are capable of pushing abstract messages to the client; for example, when new email arrives or a new file appears on the file system.

Camel also provides an RxJava adapter so that you can work with incoming messages in a more declarative, reactive way.

Consuming Files with Camel

We can integrate with hundreds of systems in the same, uniform way, using RxJava's `Observables` and operators. For example, suppose that you want to monitor a filesystem for new files (compare with "Polling Periodically for Changes" on page 138). With Camel's support for RxJava, this task is very simple:

```
CamelContext camel = new DefaultCamelContext();
ReactiveCamel reactiveCamel = new ReactiveCamel(camel);

reactiveCamel
    .toObservable("file:/home/user/tmp")
    .subscribe(e ->
        log.info("New file: {}", e));
```

This is it. After creating `DefaultCamelContext` and `ReactiveCamel`, we are ready to begin consuming messages. Every integration platform supported by Camel is encoded via URI, `file:/home/user` in our case. By calling `toObservable()` with such a URI, we create generic `Observable<Message>` that will emit an event every time a new file appears in the designated directory. The URI itself for each type of integration has dozens of configuration options. For example, by adding `?recursive=true&noop=true` to `file` URI, we are asking Camel to look for files recursively and to not delete them after discovery.

Receiving Messages from Kafka

Consuming data by polling the filesystem for changes is a surprisingly popular integration technique, just like polling an FTP directory. But if you need a more robust, faster, and reliable communication protocol, you should instead choose message brokers based on the JMS specification or Kafka. Kafka (*http://kafka.apache.org*) is an open source publish–subscribe message broker. It was designed to be fault tolerant and capable of handling hundreds of thousands of messages per second. Kafka has a native Java API, but using it from the `Observable` perspective is very tempting. The Camel integration is pretty much the same, apart from a different URI:

```
reactiveCamel
        .toObservable("kafka:localhost:9092?topic=demo&groupId=rx")
        .map(Message::getBody)
        .subscribe(e ->
                log.info("Message: {}", e));
```

The idea that you can consume abstract messages from virtually any platform using the same `Observable` API is astonishingly powerful. Camel provides the necessary physical connection behind a consistent interface, whereas RxJava further enhances this API with a plethora of operators. Camel and Retrofit (see "Retrofit with Native RxJava Support" on page 280) are great starting points for reactive extensions in your application. After you have a stable source of `Observables`, it is much easier to propagate reactive behavior further and further down in your stack.

Java 8 Streams and CompletableFuture

Sometimes there is a confusion as to which abstraction to use for concurrent programming, especially since Java 8. There are a few competing APIs that allow you to express asynchronous computation in a clean way. This section compares all of them to help you choose the right tool for the job. The available abstractions include the following:

CompletableFuture

CompletableFuture introduced in Java 8 is a much more powerful extension to the well-recognized Future from the java.util.concurrent package. Completa bleFuture allows registering an asynchronous callback when Future completes or fails rather than blocking and waiting for the result. But the true strength comes from the composition and transformation capabilities, similar to what Observable.map() and flatMap() offer. Despite being introduced in standard JDK, not a single class in standard Java library depends or uses CompletableFu ture. It is perfectly usable but not very well integrated into the Java ecosystem. To learn about portability concerns with RxJava, see "A Short Introduction to CompletableFuture" on page 193.

Parallel Stream

Just like CompletableFutures, streams in java.util.stream were introduced in JDK 8. Streams are a way to declare a sequence of operations like mapping, filtering, and so on prior to execution. All operations on a stream are lazy until a terminal operation is used, like collect() or reduce(). Also JDK can automatically parallelize some operations on all available cores, which sounds very compelling. Parallel streams promise transparent mapping, filtering, or even sorting of large datasets on multiple cores. Streams are typically generated from a collection but can just as well be created on the fly and infinite.

rx.Observable

An Observable represents a stream of events appearing in unpredictable moments in time. It can represent zero, one, fixed, or infinite number of events, available immediately or over time. Observable can terminate with completion or error event. You should be fairly comfortable with what Observable is by now.

rx.Single

When RxJava matured it became apparent that a specialized type that represents exactly one result is beneficial. The Single type is a stream that either completes with exactly one value or with an error. In that sense, it is much like Completable Future, but Singles are lazy, meaning that they do not begin computation until subscribed. Single was described in "Observable versus Single" on page 202.

rx.Completable

Sometimes we invoke a certain computation purely for side effects, not expecting any result. Sending an email or storing a record in a database are examples of such operations that involve I/O (this can benefit from asynchronous processing)

but do not return any meaningful result. Traditionally, CompletableFu
ture<Void> or Observable<Void> was used in such scenarios. However, the even
more specific Completable type better expresses the intent of asynchronous computation without result. Completable can notify about completion or error in
concurrent execution and just like all other Rx types, it is lazy.

Obviously, there are other ways of expressing asynchronous computation, such as the
following:

- Flux and Mono from project Reactor (*https://projectreactor.io*). These types are
  somewhat similar to Observable and Single, respectively.

- ListenableFuture from Guava (*http://bit.ly/2d3XllF*).

However, we will keep our list of choices short by limiting it to JDK and RxJava.
Before we continue, let me state that if your application already uses CompletableFu
ture rather consistently, you should probably stick to it. Some APIs provided by Com
pletableFuture are a bit awkward, but in general this class delivers quite good
support for reactive programming. Moreover, we can expect more and more frameworks to take advantage and idiomatically support it. Supporting RxJava in third-
party libraries is more difficult because it requires additional dependency, whereas
CompletableFuture is part of JDK.

Usefulness of Parallel Streams

Let's shift for a moment and discuss parallel streams from the standard JDK. In Java
8, when you transform a moderately big collection of objects you can transform them
declaratively with optional parallelism:

```
List<Person> people = //...

List<String> sorted = people
    .parallelStream()
    .filter(p -> p.getAge() >= 18)
    .map(Person::getFirstName)
    .sorted(Comparator.comparing(String::toLowerCase))
    .collect(toList());
```

Notice the parallelStream() rather than conventional stream() in the preceding
code snippet. By using parallelStream(), we ask for terminal operation like col
lect() to be performed in parallel rather than sequentially. Of course, this should not
have any impact on the result but is supposed to be much faster. Under the hood,
what parallelStream() does is split an input collection into multiple chunks, invoke
operations on each one of them in parallel, and then combine the results in a divide-
and-conquer spirit.

Many operators are very straightforward to parallelize—for example, map() and fil
ter()—others are a bit more difficult (like sorted()) because after sorting every
chunk separately we must combine them together, which in the case of sorting means
merging two sorted sequences. Some operations are inherently difficult or impossible
to parallelize without further assumptions. For example, reduce() can be performed
only if the accumulating function is associative.

Same Results?

There are operators that can yield different results under sequential
stream() and parallelStream(). For example, findFirst() operator returns the very first element encountered in a stream. On the
other hand, a findAny() operator exists that seemingly does the
same thing. But whereas findFirst() always returns the very first
value from the stream, findAny() is free to return any value when
executed on parallel stream.

This can occur for example when the filter() operator was used
prior to findFirst() or findAny(). Execution of parallel
Stream() is free to split the input stream—for example, into two
halves and perform filtering in parallel on each half independently.
If filtering the second half yields any matching value first, fin
dAny() will return it, even if some matching values exist in first half
as well. findFirst() guarantees to return the first matching value
globally, so it must wait for the result of filtering of both halves.
Both methods have their merits and should be used deliberately.

Ideally, taking Amdahl's law (*https://en.wikipedia.org/wiki/Amdahl%27s_law*) into
account on a four-CPU machine, we can expect up to four times faster execution. But
parallel streams have their drawbacks. To begin with, for small streams and short
pipelines of transformations the cost of context switching can be significant to the
point at which parallel streams are slower than their sequential counterparts. The
problem of too fine-grained a concurrency can potentially occur in RxJava as well,
therefore it supports declarative concurrency via Schedulers (see "What Is a Scheduler?" on page 141). The situation with parallel streams is different.

Ever wondered why this framework is called *parallel* and not *concurrent* streams? Parallel streams were only designed for CPU-intensive work and have a hardcoded
thread pool (ForkJoinPool, to be precise) that is aligned with the number of CPUs
we have. This pool is available statically and globally under ForkJoinPool.common
Pool(). Every parallel stream, as well as some CompletableFuture callbacks within
JVM share this ForkJoinPool. All parallel streams in the entire JVM (so in multiple
applications if you are deploying WAR files onto application server) share the same
small pool. This is generally fine because parallel streams were designed for parallel

tasks, which really need the CPU 100% of the time. Thus, if multiple parallel streams are invoked concurrently they do compete for CPU, no matter what.

But imagine one selfish application running an I/O operation within a parallel stream:

```
//DON'T DO THIS
people
        .parallelStream()
        .forEach(this::publishOverJms);
```

publishOverJms() sends a JMS message for each person in a stream. We intentionally chose JMS sending. It seems fast, but due to delivery guarantees a JMS send will most likely touch either network (to notify message broker) or disk (to persist message locally). This tiny amount of I/O latency is enough to hold precious ForkJoin Pool.commonPool() threads for an excessively long time. Even though this program is not using CPU, no other code within JVM is allowed to execute parallel stream. Now imagine if this were not sending over JMS but retrieving data from web service or making an expensive database query. parallelStream() can only ever be used for entirely CPU-bound tasks, otherwise the performance of the JVM takes a significant hit.

This does not imply that parallel streams are bad. However, due to the fixed thread pool powering them they are of very limited use. Certainly, parallel streams from JDK are not a replacement for Observable.flatMap() or other concurrency mechanisms. Parallel streams work best when executed, well...in parallel. But concurrent tasks that do not require the CPU 100% of the time—for example, being blocked on network or disk—are better off using other mechanisms.

Knowing the limitations of streams lets us compare futures and RxJava to see where they fit best.

Choosing the Appropriate Concurrency Abstraction

The closest equivalent to CompletableFuture in RxJava is Single. You can also use Observable, keeping in mind that it can emit any number of values. One big difference between futures and RxJava types is the laziness of the latter. When you have a reference to CompletableFuture, you can be sure that background computation already began, whereas Single and Observable will most likely begin to work only when you subscribe to them. Knowing this semantic discrepancy, you can fairly easily interchange CompletableFuture with Observable (see "CompletableFuture and Streams" on page 193) and Single (see "Interoperability with Observable and CompletableFuture" on page 207).

For rare cases in which the result of asynchronous computation is unavailable or irrelevant, CompletableFuture<Void> or Observable<Void> was used. Whereas the former is quite straightforward, the latter might suggest a potentially infinite stream of empty events, whatever that means. Using rx.Single<Void> sounds as bad as a future of Void. Thus, rx.Completable was introduced. Use Completable when your architecture has many operations that have no meaningful result (but might result in an exception). One example of such architecture is command-query separation (CQS) (*http://bit.ly/2d5sFTj*) wherein commands are asynchronous and by definition have no result.

When to Choose Observable?

When your application deals with a stream of events appearing over time (e.g., user logins, GUI events, and push notifications), Observable is unbeatable. We never mentioned it, but since version 1.0, Java has offered java.util.Observable, which allows registering Observers and notifying them at the same time. Yet it lacks the following:

- Composition capabilities (no operators)
- Generics (Observer has one update() method taking the Object representing an arbitrary notification payload)
- Performance (synchronized keyword used everywhere, java.util.Vector internally)
- Separation of concerns (in some sense, it combines Observable and PublishSub ject under the same interface)
- Concurrency support (all observers are notified sequentially)
- Immutability

Observable from JDK is the best of what we can get in standard Java for declarative modeling of events, right after addListener() methods in the GUI packages. If your domain explicitly mentions events or flow of data, rx.Observable<T> is hard to beat. The declarative expressiveness combined with a broad family of operators can solve many of the problems you can come across. For cold Observables, you can take advantage of backpressure to control the throughput, whereas in case of hot Observa bles, you can use many flow control operators like buffer().

Memory Consumption and Leaks

RxJava is all about streams of events being processed in memory and on the fly. It provides a consistent, rich API abstracting away the details of the event source. Ideally, we should keep only a very limited, fixed set of events in memory, between the producer emitting events and the consumer storing them or forwarding to another component. In reality, some components, especially when misused, can consume an unlimited amount of memory. Obviously, memory *is* limited and we will eventually encounter either `OutOfMemoryError` or a never-ending garbage collection loop. This sections shows you a few examples of uncontrolled consumption and memory leaks in RxJava and how to prevent them. A special type of memory leak, related to missing unsubscriptions, was described in "Avoiding Memory Leaks in Activities" on page 278, in the Android section.

Operators Consuming Uncontrolled Amounts of Memory

There are operators that can consume any amount of memory depending only on the nature of your stream. We will look at just few of them and try to take some safety measures to avoid leaks.

distinct() caching all seen events

For example, `distinct()`, by definition, must store all encountered keys since the subscription. The default overload of `distinct()` compares all seen events so far with an internal cache set. If the same event (with respect to `equals()`) did not appear yet in the stream, it is emitted and added to the cache for the future. This cache is never evicted[6] to guarantee that the same event never again appears. You can easily imagine that if events are fairly big or frequent, this internal cache will just keep growing, leading to memory leak.

For the purpose of this demonstration, we will use the following event simulating a big chunk of data:

```
class Picture {
    private final byte[] blob = new byte[128 * 1024];
    private final long tag;

    Picture(long tag) { this.tag = tag; }

    @Override
    public boolean equals(Object o) {
        if (this == o) return true;
        if (!(o instanceof Picture)) return false;
        Picture picture = (Picture) o;
        return tag == picture.tag;
    }

    @Override
    public int hashCode() {
        return (int) (tag ^ (tag >>> 32));
    }
```

---

6 In RxJava 1.1.6, it is actually a `HashSet`.

```
    @Override
    public String toString() {
        return Long.toString(tag);
    }
}
```

The following program is executed against a very memory constraint environment (-mx32M: 32 MB of heap), emitting fairly large events as fast as it can:

```
Observable
        .range(0, Integer.MAX_VALUE)
        .map(Picture::new)
        .distinct()
        .sample(1, TimeUnit.SECONDS)
        .subscribe(System.out::println);
```

After running this, OutOfMemoryError appears very quickly because the internal cache of distinct() can no longer hold more Picture instances. The CPU usage shortly before crash is also quite severe due to the garbage collector being determined to free some space. But even if rather than using the entire Picture as a key used to distinguish events we use only Picture.tag the program still crashes, only much later:

```
distinct(Picture::getTag)
```

This type of leak is even more dangerous. The problem slowly escalates without us noticing, until it finally explodes in the least expected moment, often under high load. To prove that distinct() is the root of memory leak, check out a similar program that does not use distinct() but instead counts how many events were emitted per second without any buffering. Your mileage may vary, but you can expect hundreds of thousands of large messages per second processed without much pressure on garbage collection or memory:

```
Observable
        .range(0, Integer.MAX_VALUE)
        .map(Picture::new)
        .window(1, TimeUnit.SECONDS)
        .flatMap(Observable::count)
        .subscribe(System.out::println);
```

So how do you avoid memory leaks related to distinct()?

- Avoid distinct() altogether. As simple as that, this operator is inherently dangerous when used incorrectly.

- Choose your key wisely. Ideally it should have finite and small value space. Enum and byte are OK, long or String probably not. If you cannot prove that a given type will only ever have very limited number of values (like enum) you are risking memory leak.

- Consider `distinctUntilChanged()` instead, which keeps track of only the last seen event, not all of them.

- Do you really need uniqueness from the very beginning or can you maybe relax this requirement? Maybe you somehow know that duplicates can ever appear only within 10 seconds of one another? Then consider running `distinct()` on a small window:

```
Observable
        .range(0, Integer.MAX_VALUE)
        .map(Picture::new)
        .window(10, TimeUnit.SECONDS)
        .flatMap(Observable::distinct)
```

Every 10 seconds we start a new window (see "Buffering Events to a List" on page 214) and ensure that there are no duplicates within that window. The `window()` operator emits an `Observable` of all events that occurred within each time window. Unique (with respect to `distinct()`) values in that window are immediately emitted. When the 10-second window is over, a new window starts, but more importantly, the cache associated with the old window is garbage-collected. Of course, within these 10 seconds we can still have a critical number of events causing `OutOfMemoryError`, so it is better to use a window of fixed length (e.g., `window(1000)`) rather than fixed time. Also, if nondistinct events appeared unfortunately right at the end of one window and at the beginning of the next window, we will not discover a duplicate. This is a trade-off of which you must be aware.

Buffering events with toList() and buffer()

The fact that `toList()` can consume an unlimited amount of memory is quite obvious. Moreover, using `toList()` for infinite streams makes no sense. `toList()` emits just one item on completion of upstream source—when the completion is not expected, `toList()` will never emit anything. But it will continue to aggregate all events in memory. Using `toList()` for very long streams is also questionable. You should find a way of consuming the events on the fly or at least limiting the number of upstream events using operators like `take()`.

`toList()` makes sense when you need to look at all events of finite `Observable` at the same time. This is rarely the case, you can apply predicates (like `allMatch()` and `any Match()`), count items (`count()`), or reduce them to single aggregate value (`reduce()`) without ever needing all events in memory at the same time. One use case could be transforming an `Observable<Observable<T>>` into `Observable<List<T>>` where the inner `Observable` has known fixed length:

```
.window(100)
.flatMap(Observable::toList)
```

This is equivalent to the following:

```
.buffer(100)
```

Which brings us to `buffer()`. Before using `buffer()`, think deeply if you really need to have a `List<T>` of all events within a time frame. Maybe an `Observable<T>` is enough, for example, suppose that you need to know whether there were more than five incidents of high priority in each second having an `Observable<Incident>`. You want to produce an `Observable<Boolean>` that every second either emits `true` if a large number of high priority incidents occurred within that second, or `false` otherwise. With `buffer()`, this is quite straightforward:

```
Observable<Incident> incidents = //...

Observable<Boolean> danger = incidents
        .buffer(1, TimeUnit.SECONDS)
        .map((List<Incident> oneSecond) -> oneSecond
                .stream()
                .filter(Incident::isHIghPriority)
                .count() > 5);
```

However, `window()` does not require buffering events into intermediate `List` but forwards them on the fly. `window()` is equally convenient for the same task but keeps constant memory usage.

```
Observable<Boolean> danger = incidents
        .window(1, TimeUnit.SECONDS)
        .flatMap((Observable<Incident> oneSecond) ->
                oneSecond
                        .filter(Incident::isHIghPriority)
                        .count()
                        .map(c -> (c > 5))
        );
```

`Observable` actually has much richer API compared to `Stream` from the JDK so you might find yourself converting a Java `Collection` to `Observable` just for the sake of better operators. For example, streams do not have support for a sliding window or zipping.

That being said, you should prefer `window()` over `buffer()` when possible, especially when the size of internal `List` accumulated in `bufer()` is impossible to predict and manage.

Caching with cache() and ReplaySubject

The `cache()` operator is another obvious memory consumer. Even worse than `distinct()`, `cache()` keeps a reference to every single event that it ever received from upstream. It makes sense to use `cache()` for `Observables` that are known to have fixed, short length. For example, when `Observable` is used to model an asynchronous response of some component, using cache() is safe and desirable. Otherwise, each Observer will trigger the request again, potentially leading to unanticipated side effects. Conversely, caching long, possibly infinite Observables, especially hot ones, makes very little sense. In the case of hot Observables, you are probably not interested in historic events anyway.

The same story goes for ReplaySubject (see "rx.subjects.Subject" on page 51). Everything you place in such a Subject must be stored so that subsequent Observers get all notifications, not only the future ones. The suggestions for both cache() and Replay Subject are pretty much the same. If you find yourself using them, it is up to you to guarantee that the source you are caching is finite and relatively short. Also if possible try not to keep a reference to a cached Observable for too long, so that it can be garbage-collected after a while.

Backpressure keeps memory usage low

Remember how we zipped together two sources of events that were producing events at a different pace in "When Streams Are Not Synchronized with One Another: combineLatest(), withLatestFrom(), and amb()" on page 83? If you try to zip two sources, one of which is even slightly slower than the other, zip()/zipWith() operators must temporarily buffer the faster stream while waiting for corresponding events from the slower one:

```
Observable<Picture> fast = Observable
        .interval(10, MICROSECONDS)
        .map(Picture::new);
Observable<Picture> slow = Observable
        .interval(11, MICROSECONDS)
        .map(Picture::new);

Observable
        .zip(fast, slow, (f, s) -> f + " : " + s)
```

You might expect this code to eventually crash with OutOfMemoryError because zip() supposedly[7] keeps its ever-growing buffer of events from fast, waiting for the slow stream. But this is not the case; in fact, we almost immediately get the dreadful Mis singBackpressureException. The zip() (and zipWith()) operator does not blindly receive events at whatever throughput the upstream dictates. Instead, these operators take advantage of backpressure (see "Backpressure" on page 226) and only request as little data as possible. Therefore, if upstream Observables are cold and implemented

---

7 Before backpressure was introduced in RxJava, that is how zip() was working. You could easily run into unsynchronized streams leading to slow memory leak. If you are curious how zip() was reimplemented, backpressure was first added to in version 0.20.0-RC2.

properly, `zip()` will simply slow down the faster `Observable` by requesting less data than it could technically produce.

In the case of `interval()`, though, the mechanism does not work this way. The `interval()` operator is cold because it starts the counter only when someone subscribes and each `Observer` gets its own independent stream. Yet, after we already subscribed to `interval()`, there is no way of slowing it down, by definition it must emit events at a certain frequency. Therefore, it must ignore backpressure requests and possibly lead to `MissingBackpressureException`. All we can do is drop the excess events (see "Producers and Missing Backpressure" on page 233):

```
Observable
        .zip(
                fast.onBackpressureDrop(),
                slow.onBackpressureDrop(),
                (f, s) -> f + " : " + s)
```

But in case of `MissingBackpressureException`, how is it better than `OutOfMemoryError`? Well, missing backpressure fails fast, whereas out of memory can build up slowly, consuming precious memory that could have been allocated elsewhere. But missing backpressure can also occur in the least expected moment—for example, when garbage collection happens. "Verifying emitted events" on page 263 discusses how to unit test backpressure behavior.

Summary

It is much easier to begin with RxJava when some source of `Observables` appears in our codebase. Implementing a new `Observable` from scratch is error-prone, so when various libraries (like Hystrix, Retrofit, database client drivers) have native RxJava support, it is much easier to begin. In "From Collections to Observables" on page 118 we slowly refactored existing application from imperative, collection-oriented style to stream-oriented, declarative approach. But after you introduce libraries that are sources of asynchronous `Observables`, the refactoring becomes much easier. The more streams you have in your application, the more reactive API propagates up. It begins at the data-acquisition level (database, web service and so on) and bubbles to service and web layer. Suddenly our entire stack is written reactively. At some point, when the usage of RxJava reaches a certain critical point in the project, there is no longer a need for `toBlocking()`, because everything is a stream, top to bottom.

CHAPTER 9

Future Directions

Ben Christensen

Because we took a long time in the 0.x phase before locking down the APIs in RxJava 1.0, it is a fairly mature and stable release. Also, as a result of our decision to support Experimental and Beta markers on APIs, ongoing experimentation can continue before promoting an API to Final. However, the 0.x/1.x phase still ended up with a few decisions that warrant a breaking release; hence, a version 2.0 (*http://bit.ly/2d5x8Fv*) is being worked on.

Fundamentally, it will be very similar to 1.x, so it won't require much change in your thinking nor will it be a significant change for usage. Even as 2.0 is released, this book will still apply in most regards. So why a version 2?

Reactive Streams

The first reason is to natively support the Reactive Streams API (*http://www.reactive-streams.org*). Despite the RxJava team being involved in the collaboration that led to Reactive Streams, RxJava v1 APIs were already locked in and couldn't change to adopt the interfaces in Reactive Streams. Thus, RxJava v1 requires an adaptor, even though it semantically behaves mostly like Reactive Streams. Version 2 will directly implement the Reactive Streams types and comply with the spec so as to better support interoperability across the Java community.

Observable and Flowable

Another reason is to split the `Observable` type into two types: `Observable` and `Flowable`. It was a mistake to make everything require backpressure because not all use cases warrant it. It has a slight performance overhead, but the primary reason why this was a mistake is that it adds significant mental complexity to using `Observable` and greatly increases the difficulty of creating custom operators.

Pure push use cases should be able to use `Observable` as originally designed by Erik Meijer without considering the `request(n)` semantics of Reactive Streams. These use cases are quite common. Basically, all user interface (UI) use cases, such as on Android, are pure push; the use of `request(n)` is confusing at best and unnecessarily complicates things. Yes, the `onBackpressureDrop` style operators can be quite useful in these cases, but those should be opt-in.

Thus, version 2 is going to return `Observable` back to being pure push without `request(n)` and it will not implement the Reactive Streams types or spec. A new type, `Flowable` will be added, which will be the "Observable with backpressure" that implements the Reactive Streams `Publisher` type and spec. The name "Flowable" was inspired by the Java 9 `java.util.concurrent.Flow`, which adopts the Reactive Streams interfaces.

Having `Observable` and `Flowable` will also better communicate in public APIs what the behavior of the data source is. If it is an `Observable`, it will push and the consumer must be ready. If it is a `Flowable`, it will do pull-push and only send as many items as requested by the consumer. Bridging between them will be possible, similar to how RxJava v1 does it, but it will be far more explicit, such as `observable.toFlowable(Strategy.DROP)` which converts an `Observable` into a `Flowable` with the appropriate backpressure strategy to apply if data is pushed faster than the consumer can handle.

Performance

The last major reason for version 2 is the ability to improve overall performance (reduce overhead) as it is no longer bound by the architectural limits of the version 1 design. This is partly achieved by reducing the allocation amount when building up chains of operators, subscribing to, and running them. By default, `Subscribers` are no longer wrapped into a `SafeSubscriber` (`Flowable.safeSubscribe()` is provided for that) and there is no longer a need to `cancel` (`unsubscribe` in version 2 terminology) the chain on a terminal event.

The second source of performance improvements is an internal optimization methodology called *operator-fusion* (which extends the Reactive-Streams protocol), greatly reducing the backpressure and queue-management overhead in many typical synchronous flow setups (and sometimes in asynchronous flows as well). In some benchmarks, throughput with backpressure-enabled flows are only 20–30% slower than Java 8's Stream (which is synchronous pull) implementation compared to the 100–200% slower throughput of version 1.

Migration

Because RxJava is heavily entrenched in applications, a breaking change would be very difficult to adopt. Thus, version 2 is going to have a different package name and Maven artifact IDs so that both version 1 and version 2 can coexist in an application.

v1 package	v2 package	v1 Maven	v2 Maven
rx.*	io.reactivex.*	io.reactivex:rxjava	io.reactivex.rxjava2:rxjava

Migrating from RxJava version 1 to version 2 will primarily come down to the following:

1. Changing package from `rx.` to `io.reactivex.`

2. If backpressure is wanted, changing from `Observable` to `Flowable`

RxJava v2 resides in the 2.x branch on GitHub, and the DESIGN.md (*http://bit.ly/2d5x8Fv*) document is an effort by the community to capture the design decisions for version 2. Further information on the differences between versions 1 and 2 can be found on GitHub (*http://bit.ly/2d42b29*).

More HTTP Server Examples

This appendix expands the contents of "Beating the C10k Problem" on page 165 by providing more examples of HTTP servers. These examples are not essential to understand Chapter 5, but you might find them interesting. Also, some of these examples are included in the benchmarks.

fork() Procedure in C Language

We will try to implement a concurrent HTTP server using C. If you are familiar with C, you will find the following program fairly straightforward. Otherwise, do not worry, you are not obligated to understand all of the details, just the overall idea. Invoking fork() makes a copy of the current process, so that suddenly two processes appear in the operating system: the original one (parent) and a child. This second process has the exact same variables and state, the only difference is the result value of fork():

```c
#include <signal.h>
#include <stdlib.h>
#include <string.h>
#include <netinet/in.h>
#include <unistd.h>
#include <stdio.h>

int main(int argc, char *argv[]) {
  signal(SIGCHLD, SIG_IGN);
  struct sockaddr_in serv_addr;
  bzero((char *) &serv_addr, sizeof(serv_addr));
  serv_addr.sin_family = AF_INET;
  serv_addr.sin_addr.s_addr = INADDR_ANY;
  serv_addr.sin_port = htons(8080);
  int server_socket = socket(AF_INET, SOCK_STREAM, 0);
  if(server_socket < 0) {
```

```
      perror("socket");
      exit(1);
  }
  if(bind(server_socket,
          (struct sockaddr *) &serv_addr,
          sizeof(serv_addr)) < 0) {
      perror("bind");
      exit(1);
  }
  listen(server_socket, 100);
  struct sockaddr_in cli_addr;
  socklen_t clilen = sizeof(cli_addr);
  while (1) {
      int client_socket = accept(
          server_socket, (struct sockaddr *) &cli_addr, &clilen);
      if(client_socket < 0) {
          perror("accept");
          exit(1);
      }
      int pid = fork();
      if (pid == 0) {
          close(server_socket);
          char buffer[1024];
          while(1) {
              if(read(client_socket,buffer,255) < 0) {
                  perror("read");
                  exit(1);
              }
              if(write(client_socket,
                "HTTP/1.1 200 OK\r\nContent-length: 2\r\n\r\nOK",
                40) < 0) {
                  perror("write");
                  exit(1);
              }
          }
      } else {
          if(pid < 0) {
              perror("fork");
              exit(1);
          }
      }
      close(client_socket);
  }
  return 0;
}
```

What really matters is the fork() invocation. In the parent (original process), it returns the PID (process ID) of the child process. In the child (copied process) it returns 0. In some sense, fork() is executed once (in the parent process) but returns twice. If we discovered that we are a child process (fork() == 0), we are supposed to handle the client connection. The server_socket is managed by the parent, so we can close it in the child. At the same time (concurrently!), the parent process closes the client_socket (the child process has it still open anyway) and can accept() another client connection. Of course, a parent can fork multiple child processes at the same time, achieving higher concurrency.

Thread per Connection

Knowing that one thread is not enough to scale a server properly (see "Single threaded server" on page 167), we are about to rewrite it using some threading techniques. Before we jump into implementation, let's rework the SingleThread class a little bit to avoid duplication in further examples:

```
abstract class HttpServer {

    void run(int port) throws IOException {
        final ServerSocket serverSocket = new ServerSocket(port, 100);
        while (!Thread.currentThread().isInterrupted()) {
            final Socket client = serverSocket.accept();
            handle(new ClientConnection(client));
        }
    }

    abstract void handle(ClientConnection clientConnection);
}
```

The ClientConnection class:

```
import org.apache.commons.io.IOUtils;

class ClientConnection implements Runnable {

    public static final byte[] RESPONSE = (
            "HTTP/1.1 200 OK\r\n" +
            "Content-length: 2\r\n" +
            "\r\n" +
            "OK").getBytes();

    public static final byte[] SERVICE_UNAVAILABLE = (
            "HTTP/1.1 503 Service unavailable\r\n").getBytes();

    private final Socket client;

    ClientConnection(Socket client) {
        this.client = client;
    }

    public void run() {
        try {
            while (!Thread.currentThread().isInterrupted()) {
                readFullRequest();
                client.getOutputStream().write(RESPONSE);
```

```
        }
    } catch (Exception e) {
        e.printStackTrace();
        IOUtils.closeQuietly(client);
    }
}

private void readFullRequest() throws IOException {
    BufferedReader reader = new BufferedReader(
            new InputStreamReader(client.getInputStream()));
    String line = reader.readLine();
    while (line != null && !line.isEmpty()) {
        line = reader.readLine();
    }
}

public void serviceUnavailable() {
    try {
        client.getOutputStream().write(SERVICE_UNAVAILABLE);
    } catch (IOException e) {
        throw new RuntimeException(e);
    }
}

}
```

This was just plain refactoring: we moved common boilerplate code like listening to client connections in a loop to base class. Also, handling of the client connection was factored out into a separate ClientConnection class. Extra serviceUnavailable() will be used a little bit later. The only responsibility of the actual implementation of the HttpServer is to somehow invoke run() of the ClientConnection—for example, directly in refactored SingleThread:

```
public class SingleThread extends HttpServer {

    public static void main(String[] args) throws Exception {
        new SingleThread().run(8080);
    }

    @Override
    void handle(ClientConnection clientConnection) {
        clientConnection.run();
    }
}
```

Having this basic *framework*, we can quickly build more scalable implementation that spawns new Thread per each ClientConnection:

```
public class ThreadPerConnection extends HttpServer {

    public static void main(String[] args) throws IOException {
        new ThreadPerConnection().run(8080);
```

```
    }

    @Override
    void handle(ClientConnection clientConnection) {
        new Thread(clientConnection).start();
    }
}
```

Taking advantage of the fact that `ClientConnection` is also `Runnable`, we simply start a `Thread` handling each new connection. Now the problem of the server being blocked by a slow client is mitigated: handling of the connection occurs in the background so that when data is read from and written to the client `Socket`, the main thread can keep accepting new connections. Of course, if two clients connect at the same time the main thread will start two background threads and continue operating.

Creating new threads without any limit has some drawbacks. On 64 bit JVM 1.8, each thread consumes 1,024 KB of RAM by default (see `-Xss` flag). A thousand concurrent connections, even idle, mean 1,000 threads and about 1 GB of stack space. Now, do not be confused, stack space is independent from heap space, so your application will consume far more than this a gigabyte.

Thread Pool of Connections

This time we will create a pool of idle threads at the outset, waiting for incoming connections. When a new `ClientConnection` wrapping client `Socket` appears, the first idle thread from a pool is taken. A thread pool has many advantages over simply creating threads on demand:

- `Thread` is already initialized and started, therefore you do not have to wait or warm up, reducing client latency.
- We put a sharp limit on the total number of threads running in our system so that we can safely reject connections under peak load rather than crashing.
- A thread pool has a configurable queue that can temporarily hold short peaks of load.
- If both the pool and queue are saturated, there is also a configurable rejection policy (error, running in client thread instead, etc.).

If we want to have a full control over threads being created, a thread pool is a much better approach compared to simply creating a new thread every time. But what is more important, we can put a strict limit on the total number of client threads and manage spikes:

```
class ThreadPool extends HttpServer {

    private final ThreadPoolExecutor executor;
```

```
public static void main(String[] args) throws IOException {
    new ThreadPool().run(8080);
}

public ThreadPool() {
    BlockingQueue<Runnable> workQueue = new ArrayBlockingQueue<>(1000);
    executor = new ThreadPoolExecutor(100, 100, 0L,
                        MILLISECONDS, workQueue,
            (r, ex) -> {
                ((ClientConnection) r).serviceUnavailable();
            });
}

@Override
void handle(ClientConnection clientConnection) {
    executor.execute(clientConnection);
}

}
```

When a `ClientConnection` needs to be handled, we off-load this task to a dedicated `ThreadPoolExecutor` internally managing 100 threads. There is a bounded queue in front of that pool (1,000 tasks) so in case of excessively large volumes of requests `RejectedExecutionHandler` kicks in. Our server simply calls `serviceUnavailable()` returning 503 immediately to the client (fail-fast behavior, see also "Managing Failures with Hystrix" on page 291) rather than making the client wait endlessly.

Servlet 3.0 specification made it possible to write scalable applications on top of asynchronous servlets. The idea is to decouple the processing request from the container thread. Whenever the application wants to send the response, it can do it from any thread at any point in time. The original container thread that picked up the request might be already gone or it might be handling some other request. This is a revolutionary idea; however, the rest of the application must be built this way. Otherwise, the application is more responsive (the container thread pool is almost never saturated), but if there is another user thread that must process that request, we just shifted the problem of thread explosion into a different place. When the number of threads reaches several hundred or a few thousand, the application begins to misbehave; for example, it begins responding slowly due to frequent garbage collection cycles and context switching.

A Decision Tree of Observable Operators

This appendix aims to help you find the appropriate operator from the RxJava universe. With more than a hundred possible options, it is getting increasingly complex to find a built-in operator that suits our needs best. The content of this appendix is entirely copied from the official RxJava documentation, A Decision Tree of Observable Operators (*http://bit.ly/2cOMRGL*), under Apache License Version 2.0. However, back references lead to proper chapters in the book rather than online documentation. Most often there is an entire chapter covering a given operator; sometimes there is just a brief mention or example.

- I want to create a new `Observable`...

  — that emits a particular item `just()`, see "Creating Observables" on page 34...

    — that was returned from a function called at subscribe-time: `start()`, see `rxjava-async` module (*http://bit.ly/2cONiAT*).

    — that was returned from an `Action`, `Callable`, `Runnable`, or something of that sort, called at subscribe-time: `from()`, `fromCallable()`,: `fromRunnable()`, see "Creating Observables" on page 34 and "Infinite Streams" on page 38.

    — after a specified delay: `timer()`, see "Timing: timer() and interval()" on page 43.

  — that pulls its emissions from a particular `Array`, `Iterable`, or something like that: `from()`, see "Creating Observables" on page 34.

  — by retrieving it from a future: `from()`, see "Creating Observables" on page 34 and "CompletableFuture and Streams" on page 193.

  — that obtains its sequence from a Future: `from()`, see "Creating Observables" on page 34.

— that emits a sequence of items repeatedly: repeat(), see "Reusing Operators Using compose()" on page 108.

— from scratch, with custom logic: create(), see "Mastering Observable.create()" on page 35.

— for each observer that subscribes: defer(), see "Embracing Laziness" on page 121.

— that emits a sequence of integers: range(), see "Creating Observables" on page 34…

    — at particular intervals of time: interval(), see "Timing: timer() and interval()" on page 43…

        — after a specified delay: timer(), see "Timing: timer() and interval()" on page 43.

— that completes without emitting items: empty(), see "Creating Observables" on page 34.

— that does nothing at all: never(), see "Creating Observables" on page 34

- I want to create an Observable by combining other Observables…

  — and emitting all of the items from all of the Observables in whatever order they are received: merge(), see "Treating Several Observables as One Using merge()" on page 78.

  — and emitting all of the items from all of the Observables, one Observable at a time: concat(), see "Ways of Combining Streams: concat(), merge(), and switchOnNext()" on page 97.

  — by combining the items from two or more Observables sequentially to come up with new items to emit…

      — whenever *each* of the Observables has emitted a new item: zip(), see "Pairwise Composing Using zip() and zipWith()" on page 79.

      — whenever *any* of the Observables has emitted a new item: combineLatest(), see "When Streams Are Not Synchronized with One Another: combineLatest(), withLatestFrom(), and amb()" on page 83.

      — by means of Pattern and Plan intermediaries And/Then/when(), see rxjava-joins module.

  — and emitting the items from only the most-recently emitted of those Observables: switch(), see "Ways of Combining Streams: concat(), merge(), and switchOnNext()" on page 97.

- I want emit the items from an Observable after transforming them…

— one at a time with a function: `map()`, see "Core Operators: Mapping and Filtering" on page 61.

— by emitting all of the items emitted by corresponding `Observables`: `flatMap()`, see "Wrapping Up Using flatMap()" on page 67...

  — one `Observable` at a time, in the order they are emitted: `concatMap()`, see "Preserving Order Using concatMap()" on page 75.

— based on all of the items that preceded them: `scan()`, see "Scanning Through the Sequence with Scan and Reduce" on page 88.

— by attaching a timestamp to them: `timestamp()`, see "When Streams Are Not Synchronized with One Another: combineLatest(), withLatestFrom(), and amb()" on page 83.

— into an indicator of the amount of time that lapsed before the emission of the item: `timeInterval()`, see "Timing Out When Events Do Not Occur" on page 251.

- I want to shift the items emitted by an `Observable` forward in time before reemitting them: `delay()`, see "Postponing Events Using the delay() Operator" on page 72.

- I want to transform items *and* notifications from an `Observable` into items and reemit them...

  — by wrapping them in `Notification` objects: `materialize()`, see "Verifying emitted events" on page 263...

  — which I can then unwrap again with: `dematerialize()`.

- I want to ignore all items emitted by an `Observable` and only pass along its completed/error notification: `ignoreElements()`, see "flatMap() as Asynchronous Chaining Operator" on page 131.

- I want to mirror an `Observable` but prefix items to its sequence: `startWith()`, see "withLatestFrom() operator" on page 85...

  — only if its sequence is empty: `defaultIfEmpty()`.

- I want to collect items from an `Observable` and reemit them as buffers of items: `buffer()`, see "Buffering events with toList() and buffer()" on page 318...

  — containing only the last items emitted: `takeLastBuffer()`.

- I want to split one `Observable` into multiple `Observables` (`window()`, see "Moving window" on page 220)...

  — so that similar items end up on the same `Observable`: `groupBy()`, see "Criteria-Based Splitting of Stream Using groupBy()" on page 104.

- I want to retrieve a particular item emitted by an `Observable`...

— the last item emitted before it completed: `last()`, see "Slicing and Dicing Using skip(), takeWhile(), and Others" on page 94.

— the sole item it emitted: `single()`, see "Asserting Observable Has Exactly One Item Using single()" on page 92.

— the first item it emitted: `first()`, see "Slicing and Dicing Using skip(), take-While(), and Others" on page 94.

- I want to reemit only certain items from an `Observable`...

  — by filtering out those that do not match some predicate: `filter()`, see "Core Operators: Mapping and Filtering" on page 61.

  — that is, only the first item: `first()`, see "Slicing and Dicing Using skip(), take-While(), and Others" on page 94.

  — that is, only the first item_s_: `take()`, see "Slicing and Dicing Using skip(), takeWhile(), and Others" on page 94.

  — that is, only the last item: `last()`, see "Slicing and Dicing Using skip(), take-While(), and Others" on page 94.

  — that is, only item n: `elementAt()`, see "Slicing and Dicing Using skip(), take-While(), and Others" on page 94.

  — that is, only those items after the first items...

    — that is, after the first n items: `skip()`, see "Slicing and Dicing Using skip(), takeWhile(), and Others" on page 94.

    — that is, until one of those items matches a predicate: `skipWhile()`, see "Timing Out When Events Do Not Occur" on page 251.

    — that is, after an initial period of time: `skip()`.

    — that is, after a second `Observable` emits an item: `skipUntil()`.

  — that is, those items except the last items...

    — that is, except the last n items: `skipLast()`, see "Slicing and Dicing Using skip(), takeWhile(), and Others" on page 94.

    — that is, until one of those items matches a predicate: `takeWhile()`, see "Slicing and Dicing Using skip(), takeWhile(), and Others" on page 94.

    — that is, except items emitted during a period of time before the source completes: `skipLast()`.

    — that is, except items emitted after a second `Observable` emits an item: `takeUntil()`.

  — by sampling the `Observable` periodically: `sample()`, see "Taking Periodic Samples and Throttling" on page 212.

— by only emitting items that are not followed by other items within some duration: debounce(), see "Skipping Stale Events by Using debounce()" on page
221.

— by suppressing items that are duplicates of already-emitted items: dis
tinct(), see "Dropping Duplicates Using distinct() and distinctUntil-
Changed()" on page 92...

   — if they immediately follow the item they are duplicates of: distinctUntil
   Changed(), see "Dropping Duplicates Using distinct() and distinctUntil-
   Changed()" on page 92.

— by delaying my subscription to it for some time after it begins emitting items:
delaySubscription().

Index

fork() invocation, 327-329
Functional Reactive Programming (FRP), 2

G

Gamma, Erich, 28, 292
Gatling, 177
Goetz, Brian, 3
Graphite, 273
Gregg, Brendan, 20

H

hot vs. cold streams, 43, 225
HTTP clients, 184-187, 280
HTTP servers
    blocking vs. reactive, 177-182
    fork() procedure in C language, 327-329
    nonblocking, 169-176
    scalability and, 183
    thread per connection, 329-331
    thread pool of connections, 331
    traditional thread-based, 167
Husain, Jafar, xvii
Hystrix
    batching and collapsing commands,
      297-302
    benefits of, 291
    bulkhead pattern and fail-fast, 295-297
    first steps with, 292-294
    monitoring with, 274, 303-305
    nonblocking commands with, 294

I

I/O (input/output)
    blocking vs. nonblocking, 20-25
    limitations imposed on scalability, 165
    with thread-based HTTP servers, 167
imperative, definition of term, 2
Implementing Domain-Driven Design (Vernon), 104
Iteratable<T>, 28

J

Jackson library, 280
Jacobs, Matt, xviii
Java 8 streams
    available abstractions, 310
    concurrency abstraction selection, 314
    selecting Observable, 315

usefulness of parallel streams, 312-314
Java Concurrency in Practice (Goetz), 3
Java Database Connectivity (JDBC), 187
Java Message Service (JMS), 136
java.util.stream, 311
JMeter, 177

K

Kafka, 227, 310
Kant, Nitesh, 20
Karnok, Dávid, xviii

L

lazy execution
    vs. eager, 12
    lazy paging and concatenation, 124
    making Observable lazy, 121
Lea, Doug, 3
LinkedBlockingQueue, 226
LISTEN (SQL statement), 189-192
lists, buffering events to, 214-220

M

mapping and filtering
    1-to-1 transformations, 64-67
    core operators, 61-64
    order of events, 73
    postponing events, 72
    preserving event order, 75-77
    simple example of, 62
    spawning asynchronous computation, 67-72
marble diagrams
    amb() operator, 87
    combineLatest() operator, 84
    concatWith() operator, 123
    distinctUntilChanged() operator, 139
    flatMap() operator, 67
    map() operator, 64
    merge() operator, 79
    structure of, 62
    toList() operator, 119
    zip() operator, 79
    zipWith() operator, 79
mechanical sympathy, 20-25
Mechanical Sympathy (forum), 3
Meijer, Erik, xviii
memory consumption and leaks
    in Android development, 278-280

About the Authors

Tomasz Nurkiewicz is a software engineer at Allegro. He has spent the last decade coding in Java and loves backend development. He is passionate about JVM languages and open source technologies. He is also a frequent blogger for DZone and speaks at leading Java conferences around the world. Tomasz can be reached on Twitter @tnurkiewicz and on his blog.

Ben Christensen is a software engineer focused on resilience, scale, and distributed systems. Open source projects created while addressing these requirements include Hystrix (*https://github.com/Netflix/Hystrix*) and RxJava (*https://github.com/ReactiveX/RxJava*).

Colophon

The animal on the cover of *Reactive Programming with RxJava* is a *grison*, or a South American wolverine (*Galictis cuja* and *Galictis vittata*).

Grisons grow up to 24 inches in length and weigh between 2–6 pounds. The main difference between the two extant species, the greater grison and the lesser grison, are their size. The grison resembles the skunk in coloring—with a sharp white stripe that extends from its forehead to the back of its neck; however, its body is more robust, with a wider neck, shorter legs, and a smaller tail.

Grisons often live in semi-open shrubbery and low-elevation woodlands or forests. They burrow and nest in holes in fallen trees or crevices in rocks. They mostly consume fruit and small animals.

Many of the animals on O'Reilly covers are endangered; all of them are important to the world. To learn more about how you can help, go to *animals.oreilly.com*.

The cover image is from a Hungarian Plate. The cover fonts are URW Typewriter and Guardian Sans. The text font is Adobe Minion Pro; the heading font is Adobe Myriad Condensed; and the code font is Dalton Maag's Ubuntu Mono.

Get even more for your money.

Join the O'Reilly Community, and register the O'Reilly books you own. It's free, and you'll get:

- $4.99 ebook upgrade offer
- 40% upgrade offer on O'Reilly print books
- Membership discounts on books and events
- Free lifetime updates to ebooks and videos
- Multiple ebook formats, DRM FREE
- Participation in the O'Reilly community
- Newsletters
- Account management
- 100% Satisfaction Guarantee

Signing up is easy:

1. Go to: oreilly.com/go/register
2. Create an O'Reilly login.
3. Provide your address.
4. Register your books.

Note: English-language books only

To order books online:
oreilly.com/store

For questions about products or an order:
orders@oreilly.com

To sign up to get topic-specific email announcements and/or news about upcoming books, conferences, special offers, and new technologies:
elists@oreilly.com

For technical questions about book content:
booktech@oreilly.com

To submit new book proposals to our editors:
proposals@oreilly.com

O'Reilly books are available in multiple DRM-free ebook formats. For more information:
oreilly.com/ebooks

O'REILLY®

Milton Keynes UK
Ingram Content Group UK Ltd.
UKHW032212111223
434185UK00004B/17